The Bosses' Union

THE WORKING CLASS IN AMERICAN HISTORY

Editorial Advisors
James R. Barrett, Thavolia Glymph, Julie Greene,
William P. Jones, and Nelson Lichtenstein

A list of books in the series appears at the end of this book.

THE BOSSES' UNION

How Employers Organized to
Fight Labor before the New Deal

VILJA HULDEN

UNIVERSITY OF
ILLINOIS PRESS
Urbana, Chicago, and Springfield

THE POLITICIAN
Words and Music by JACK BRUCE and PETE BROWN
© 1968 (Renewed) DRATLEAF MUSIC, LTD.
All Rights in the U.S. and Canada Administered by UNICHAPPELL MUSIC, INC.
All Rights Reserved
Used by Permission of ALFRED MUSIC

Library of Congress Cataloging-in-Publication Data
Names: Hulden, Vilja, 1977– author.
Title: The bosses' union: how employers organized to fight labor before the New Deal / Vilja Hulden.
Description: Urbana: University of Illinois Press, [2023] | Series: The working class in American history | Includes bibliographical references and index.
Identifiers: LCCN 2022027156 (print) | LCCN 2022027157 (ebook) | ISBN 9780252044830 (hardcover; alk. paper) | ISBN 9780252086922 (paperback; alk. paper) | ISBN 9780252053887 (ebook)
Subjects: LCSH: Labor unions—United States—History—20th century. | Labor unions—United States—History—19th century. | Open and closed shop—United States—History—20th century. | Open and closed shop—United States—History—19th century. | Industrial relations—United States—History—20th century. | Industrial relations—United States—History—19th century.
Classification: LCC HD6508 .H95 2023 (print) | LCC HD6508 (ebook) | DDC 331.880973—dc23/eng/20220707
LC record available at https://lccn.loc.gov/2022027156
LC ebook record available at https://lccn.loc.gov/2022027157

Open Access Version ISBN: 978-0-252-04497-7

Contents

Acknowledgments

This book has been longer in the making than it had any right to be, so the debts I have accumulated have grown correspondingly.

In its various stages, my work on this book has been financially supported by the Fulbright Council, the Hagley Museum and Library, the Thanks to Scandinavia Foundation, and the Otto A. Malm Foundation. Sustaining in a different kind of way have been the support and good company of my parents, Tapio and Terhi; siblings, Rauli, Tiia, and Ville; mother-in-law, Margetta; grandmother, Aili; and many other family and friends (among whom Niklas and Eva deserve special mention). They are all probably as surprised as I am to actually see this book in print. I am in their debt for regularly reminding me of The Things That Actually Matter.

The life of this book spans time spent at two universities. At the University of Arizona, I want to particularly acknowledge the help of David Gibbs, Karen Anderson, and Michael Schaller. David kept insisting that the text needed to be more argumentative; Karen pointed out that focusing on employers without corresponding attention to unions made for the sound of one hand clapping. Good advice.

At the University of Colorado Boulder, where I have worked for much of the time that this manuscript and its many tentacles have been cluttering my computer's hard drive, I have been excessively fortunate in my colleagues. At the history department, Susan Kent, Lil Fenn, Paul Sutter, and Marcia Yonemoto have all in their turn been supportive and encouraging chairs, while David Paradis, Nancy Vavra, and other colleagues have listened to me grumble about the manuscript and so much more with patience and good humor. The department staff, Kellie Matthews, Ted Lytle, and Abi Peters, have made my professional life easier in dozens of ways and responded to questions with unflappable good cheer, even when I have asked the same question for the umpteenth time. At the University Libraries, Thea Lindquist has been a great help, as well as a good friend, while Freddy Carey has helped me hunt down a variety of documents. Nickoal Eichmann-Kalwara and Phil White were always ready to help with all things digital. And of course, nobody could get anything done without the interlibrary loan staff. In general, CU Boulder is blessed with rock star librarians.

I would also like to thank acquisitions editors Laurie Matheson and James Engelhardt at the University of Illinois Press for having shepherded the manuscript along. James deserves special thanks for reading a full early draft and saying Many Encouraging Things at a stage when I was getting ready to find a suitable trash bin. When James moved on, Alison Syring Bassford took over with grace and enthusiasm, and I am obliged to her for her efforts and support. Thanks, too, to Dustin J. Hubbart for the beautiful cover, Sheila Hill for professional indexing, and Jennifer Argo for efficient project management. Along the way, archivists and librarians at the Hagley Museum and Library, the New York Public Library, the National Archives, the Walter P. Reuther Library, and the George Meany Memorial AFL-CIO Archive have provided valuable guidance.

For kind words, general encouragement, and valuable insights on things scholarly and otherwise, I am grateful to Julie Greene, Jim Gregory, Toby Higbie, Nate Holdren, Ben Irvin, Katrina Jagodinsky, Tom Klug, Martha Palmer, and Ahmed White. Special thanks are due to those long-suffering individuals who made their way through the whole manuscript, some more than once. Shel Stromquist was one of the official reviewers, and his extensive comments (two rounds of them!) not only saved me from many an embarrassing error but also prompted quite a bit of additional work and revision that has made this a much better book. One could not hope for a more knowledgeable, meticulous, or perceptive reviewer. Additional guidance was provided by Will Jones and an anonymous reviewer. (All remaining errors, of course, are mine.) Outside the official review process, CU Boulder history major Z MacLean read a full draft and provided many helpful suggestions for making it clearer and more readable. Chad Pearson's reading gave me the benefit of his encyclopedic knowledge and his no-nonsense take; I have learned tons from him. Joe McCartin generously volunteered to read a full draft, and his enthusiasm, confidence in the manuscript's value, and insightful suggestions have been crucial. Pam Laird has been a wonderful reader, critic, general cheerer-on, and chatting partner; our conversations have been a delight.

My husband, Mans Hulden, also read and commented on the full manuscript. But that is barely a drop in the ocean of everything I owe him.

The Bosses' Union

Introduction

Who Makes the Rules?

It's a big club. And you ain't in it.
—George Carlin, *Life Is Worth Losing*

"By the organization of labor, and by no other means, it is possible to introduce an element of democracy into the government of industry." So proclaimed the final report of the United States Industrial Commission in 1902. Having spent the previous three years investigating industrial conditions and labor relations at the behest of the United States Congress and President William McKinley, the commission was well aware that labor unions rarely received a warm welcome among employers. Nevertheless, it optimistically surmised that employers seemed to "view the organization of labor with increasing tolerance," perhaps because unions themselves were becoming better schooled in democratic ways. If employers only took a farsighted and broad-minded approach, "their guidance" of labor's organizational efforts could lead to a harmonious and more democratic industrial system. But if employers went down the path of repression, the commission warned, any success they met with would be temporary and might in the long run plunge the country into radicalism and socialism. This was because "so long as the tradition of freedom is strong in the minds of the working people," employers "can not destroy the aspiration for a measure of self-government in respect to the most important part of life."[1]

The historical moment when the Industrial Commission issued its report was one fraught with tension over the power of employers versus workers in the workplace and the society at large—so much so that contemporaries had a name for the controversy. They called it "the labor question."[2] Interest in and worry over the labor question peaked in the decades surrounding the twentieth century as sharp economic transformations convulsed the society. But self-government at work and consent of the governed in the economic sphere have been perennial goals in American history—the pedigree of demands for democracy is as long in the economic as it is in the political sphere. Even more than in the political sphere, though, when it comes to economic matters, self-government has been an elusive and contentious goal. It remains so today.

Think back to the last time you applied for a job. Who had a say over whether you were chosen for the job?

Then think about your current job. How much say do you have over what you do every day, when and how you do it, and what you get paid for it?

For most of us, the answer to the first question is "the manager" or some manager-like person. The answer to the second question, especially in blue-collar jobs, quite often is "not a whole lot."

To be sure, there are exceptions. You might be self-employed. Or you might be in management, in which case you probably have some control over what you do daily. The same is true if you are a professional such as a lawyer, or a freelancer, or a professor. In many of these positions, you might also have considerable leverage to ask for a raise. If you are a professor, even the answer to the first question changes—university faculty usually make departmental hiring choices, so your colleagues would have made the decision (or at least the initial decision; the administration does insist on having the final say).

Despite such exceptions, we generally take it for granted that the business and its appointed managers have the exclusive right to determine who is hired and fired and how they spend their days at work. The absolutism of employer control in the workplace has inspired the philosopher Elizabeth Anderson to call corporations "communist dictatorships in our midst," systems where the government (of the company) owns all the means of production, engages in a planned economy, and permits no democratic control by its subjects (the workers) over any of the decisions it makes. This is the case even though those decisions may involve highly personal aspects of the subjects' daily lives, extending beyond such issues as pay to intimate matters like what one must wear or how often one may go to the bathroom.[3]

As the Industrial Commission predicted in 1902, the desire for a "measure of self-government" with regard to work has persisted. People in all walks of life value autonomy—often, they value it above monetary reward. Researchers with lucrative job prospects in industry sometimes elect to work in academia at a lower salary, largely because they expect academia to allow them to pursue projects and collaborations of their own choosing.[4] Farmers often determine production not only based on pecuniary rewards but also with a view toward how a particular scale or type of production will shape their ability to make independent choices and pursue the parts of farm work they most enjoy.[5] Across occupational divides, national boundaries, and cultural backgrounds, significant numbers of people choose self-employment even when its material payoff is substantially lower than that of a regular job—and are happy with their choice, largely because of the value they place on "being their own boss."[6] Even at large corporate workplaces, it is not for lack of desiring self-government that workers are subjects rather than citizens at work. In the United States, a comprehensive 1990s study that has served as a model for studies carried out in several other industrialized countries found that one in three workers without union representation wanted it and that nearly two in three workers desired more participation in workplace decisions. The decisions where workers wanted a voice included benefits, training, goal-setting, safety, and the organization of work.[7] Not all these workers necessarily favored unions. Overwhelmingly, however, they favored some form of collective voice selected by themselves: over three-quarters of workers polled in 2001 said they would vote for "forming an employee association that was not a union to represent employee interests with management."[8] Those who had access to participation also wanted to keep and increase it. More than nine in ten union members wanted to keep their union, while participants in a management-designed employee-involvement plan valued their influence over workplace issues—and believed that the plan would function better if workers had more say in it.[9]

There is, of course, a crucial difference between a labor union and a management-designed employee-involvement plan: one is an organization created by workers to advance their interests, the other is a program created by management for its own purposes. Unions are not merely about participation; they are also about exercising power. In theory, if not always in practice, unions offer their members a real voice in making decisions and a means to implement them, not merely a suggestion box to relay ideas to the decision-makers in management. It is often precisely that exercise of power that makes unions controversial.

This book examines a moment at the turn of the twentieth century when the prospect of bottom-up influence at the workplace through union representation looked like it just might become a mainstream idea. The first decades of the new century were awash in projects and movements aiming to mitigate inequality and improve living standards, so much so that those years have earned the moniker "Progressive Era"—an ambiguous enough label for an ambiguous enough project, but one that nevertheless underlines the extent to which reforming the society was at the forefront of public consciousness. The era also witnessed intense scrutiny of the power of business to corrupt politics. As the report of the Industrial Commission suggests, there was widespread recognition that untrammeled power in the hands of corporations and men of wealth created power disparities and workplace conditions unacceptable in a democratic society and that proposing labor unions as a potential solution was becoming less controversial. Unions also had considerable momentum: membership growth and major agreements with employers seemed to indicate that unions could function as a counterbalancing power. However, employers were not about to simply roll over. On the contrary, employers resisted the growth of union power at virtually every turn.

Employer views have generally gotten short shrift in academic writing—perhaps because they do not, to academic eyes, always seem particularly sophisticated. As Howell Harris has noted, when we write about social policy and social problems, we often make "the implicit assumption that the ideas that *matter* are those of policy-oriented, reformist intellectuals."[10] In reality, though, employers' ideas often matter more because they have the resources to put them into action. It is a little like the old joke about who reads which American newspapers: according to the joke, the *Wall Street Journal* is the paper read by those who run the country, while the *Washington Post* is the paper perused by those who merely *think* they run the country.

To understand the role of employer resistance in countering union power and shaping societal perceptions about unions and about industrial relations more generally, the bulk of this book focuses on employers. It particularly zeroes in on the group of organized employers who mounted an intense campaign to discredit worker exercise of power. That campaign was aided by the considerable financial resources and the dense networks of influential people that employers could draw upon, as well as by the ambivalence that middle-class observers, even those sympathetic to workers, harbored about working-class power.

A key rhetorical tool in the employer campaign was a new term, "closed shop." The new term labeled a practice that had previously not really had a name: the requirement of many unions that any worker employed at a unionized workplace needed to be a union member either before or soon after being hired. As analyzed in chapter 1, that term refocused attention away from the discussions raging at the time about inequality, poverty, and dangerous working conditions and toward an entirely different question: how unions purportedly trampled on the individual rights of workers. Against this alleged violation, the employer campaign declared for the "open shop," a workplace that claimed to treat workers equally whether they belonged to unions or not.

The closed shop was a key term in the employer campaign, and it is a key term in this book. A note on terminology is thus perhaps in order here. First, although the closed shop as a term originated in employer propaganda, for practical reasons I use it throughout this book interchangeably with "union shop" and "membership requirement." I do not intend this to imply any particular judgment of union membership requirements. In any case, much of the rhetorical power lay not in the term as such but in employers' ability to make the practice itself a central focus of the debate about industrial relations (as discussed in chapters 1 and 2). Second, the meaning of "closed shop" has shifted somewhat over time. Around the time of World War II, the closed shop came to refer to a preentry membership requirement—that is, a requirement that a worker be a member of the union in order to be hired. By contrast, a union shop came to mean a workplace where hiring did not depend on union membership, but where a worker had to join the union within a set period of starting employment. In the early twentieth century, neither term was this specifically defined. Instead, employers and other critics of the practice called a workplace with any form of a membership requirement a closed shop, while unions tried to counter the negative associations by using the term "union shop."[11]

The membership requirement mattered to unions because unions relied on joint action by workers. If unions were going to compel the employer to pay better wages or change work rules, they needed to have as many workers as possible stand behind the demand. The greater the percentage of workers who ignored a union call for a strike or refused to contribute to union funds, the less power the union had. The closed shop enabled unions to make membership in the union mandatory and thus enforce both payment of union dues and adherence to union rules. If a worker refused to join or violated union rules, the union could demand that the employer dismiss that worker or risk all the unionized workers going out on strike.

The closed shop thus made the union as a whole more effective. It also boosted the members' sense that their efforts were worthwhile and reciprocated by their fellows—that nobody was unfairly benefiting without contributing. As the president of the British cotton spinners' union explained in 1903, "It is almost impossible for organized workers to have any sympathy with non union workmen, as the latter receive the full advantage of the good work which the trade unions perform in the interest of their members, and yet they are too mean in principle to subscribe anything towards the expenses incurred in making their labour lives far more agreeable than they otherwise would be."[12] The membership requirement was common among the "craft" unions—occupationally based unions mainly consisting of skilled workers. Skilled workers were harder to replace, so it was easier for them to get the employer to agree to demands like the closed shop: if the majority of the workers in a particular craft were unionized and insisted on working only with other union members, it was hardly worthwhile for the employer to hire a nonunionist and risk all the others walking out. The crafts also had long traditions of training new workers in the craft through apprenticeships, as well as of establishing rules and regulations for the craft, a topic discussed in chapter 2.

The craft unions were exactly the kinds of unions that the Industrial Commission had in mind when it praised the organization of labor and held it up as a bulwark against radicalism. To simplify a bit, craft unions generally advanced demands that focused on the workplace rather than, say, advocating for a complete reorganization of society or the nationalization of industry. By the turn of the twentieth century, they also generally entered into "trade agreements" (a new term at the time) with employers or groups of employers. These agreements spelled out what the workers expected of the employer; in exchange for the employer complying with those expectations, the union would not strike during the term of the contract. Such "business unionism," as it came to be known, became the hallmark of the era's premier umbrella organization of unions, the American Federation of Labor (AFL).[13] As explored in chapter 3, the AFL's longtime president Samuel Gompers, as well as other leading figures in the organization, insisted that abiding by contracts was the key to union success because it would show employers that unions were responsible organizations worth negotiating with. Quite a few employers, however, considered arguments about radicals and moderates beside the point. They saw the new business unions as a serious threat—such unions, after all, enrolled employers' most crucial resource: skilled workers. That the unions were willing to be "responsible" was little consolation to employers who viewed the unions' *power* as the fundamental problem. Anything that was likely to increase that power, such as the closed shop, was anathema to these employers.

Nearly across the board, employers resisted the unionization of their workers. Negotiating with unions in good faith and accepting the principle that unions had a legitimate governance role seemed a good idea only to employers in very particular circumstances, such as when unions seemed to be the only way to rein in cutthroat competition between businesses in a particular industry. However, employers were not a monolith. Although very few of them welcomed the presence of unions in their own companies, employers used different strategies to deal with the broader issue of labor relations and union growth. First of all, both the economic and the social position (and, to some extent, the idiosyncratic preferences) of an employer influenced how serious a problem that employer considered unions to be. Second, if the employer decided that the labor question merited action, such factors also shaped what kind of action to take. Some employers found open, outright, and organized resistance to the growth of unions an attractive strategy; others considered it more expedient to moderate their resistance or to strike a pose of benevolent cooperation.

The range of employer positions, examined in chapter 4, pulled employers into different types of activism and different organizations. The two main organizations discussed in this book are the National Association of Manufacturers (NAM) and the National Civic Federation (NCF). They adopted very different official positions, with the NAM loudly denouncing union "tyranny" and the NCF advancing a vision of a future rather like that depicted in the Industrial Commission's report: a world where moderate labor unions negotiated responsibly with employers, labor strife waned, and the threat of socialism and radicalism receded. The NAM and the NCF also clashed repeatedly in very public ways, which created the impression that employers fell into two diametrically opposed camps when it came to attitudes toward labor. Scholars have sometimes highlighted this division and roughly equated it with a division in size and structure, so that the large modern corporation, publicly traded and responsible to shareholders, has been associated with a more cooperative attitude toward unions, while middling firms, often owned by one man or one family (known as proprietary firms), have been linked to strident opposition to any union organizing. It is true that the list of businessmen affiliated with the conciliatory NCF was far more star-studded than the membership roll of the belligerent NAM. Thus, the NCF executive board boasted such names as Andrew Carnegie (the steel magnate who was the richest American at the time) and Franklin MacVeagh (the banker who became secretary of the treasury under President William Howard Taft). Meanwhile, many key NAM members represented sizable but not huge companies that were far less likely to be household names. But it is all too easy to read too much into these differences. The NAM-affiliated employers were generally vehemently antiunion, but they were hardly mom-and-pop shops; the NCF's corporations were usually large, but they were hardly beneficent toward labor. In their views on labor, NCF and NAM employers ultimately differed mostly in tone rather than in substance; indeed, some employers belonged to both organizations.

The NCF was not strictly a business organization; instead, it was self-consciously formed as a purported partnership between employers, labor, and members of "the public" (a vague entity consisting of academics and other intellectual types, as well as, somewhat redundantly, of representatives of business). Geographically, its core was in the Northeast; socially, the people associated with it tended toward the elite and the educated upper middle class. Founded in 1900, it was run by the energetic and determined Ralph Easley, a former newspaper editor who had made the problems arising from modern industry his life's work. Easley worked tirelessly to promote harmony between labor and capital: he wrote letters, organized fancy dinners that brought together labor leaders and industrial magnates, and maneuvered behind the scenes to resolve strikes and forge contracts between unions and employers. He was convinced that if labor and capital could not find a solution to the industrial problem, the future would belong to radicals and socialists—a thought he found repugnant and frightening.

Although Easley highlighted the benefits of unions as an antiradical barrier and a way to reduce strikes more than as a way to empower workers, he appreciated that to function as an effective negotiating partner, unions did need power. Thus, unlike many other middle-class reformers, he supported the unions' membership requirement. He believed that industrial peace could best be secured through a widespread use of the trade agreement, and he understood why the unions believed the closed shop to be essential to their ability to maintain such agreements. It would be a mistake, however, to confuse Easley's views with those of the businessmen who worked with or affiliated with the NCF and who financed its work. Those businessmen were drawn to the NCF's conciliatory tone out of a variety of motives, as discussed in chapter 4. But very few of them were willing to accept the closed shop, because very few of them were willing to support increasing or reinforcing actual union power.

Where the NCF positioned itself as a conciliator, the NAM spearheaded the open-shop campaign. As its name indicated, its membership consisted exclusively of manufacturers, though it sponsored or worked closely with other organizations (e.g., the Citizens' Industrial Association of America [CIAA]) that brought a wider swath of businessmen together around the open-shop cause. The majority of its member companies were in the industrial corridor running roughly from New York to St. Louis, but it also had active members in several western states, as well as among southern industrialists. From about 1903, when it elected the Indianapolis carriage manufacturer David M. Parry as its new president, opposition to the closed shop and to unions in general consumed much of the NAM's attention. Its publication, *American Industries*, brimmed with stories about the evils of the closed shop, the bravery of the employers who resisted it, and the righteousness of the judges who condemned it. Its circulars and newsletters exhorted the membership to stand up to demands for the closed shop. Its meetings and organizational initiatives gathered businessmen across the country to promote the open shop. Whereas the NCF invested significant resources in antisocialist publicity while promoting moderate unionism, the NAM primarily worried about the power of the AFL and the skilled workers affiliated with its member unions. In the NAM's view, to draw a contrast between business unionism and socialism was to make a distinction without a difference. Both unionism and socialism insisted on gaining more "control . . . over the men who own, operate, and employ"; both challenged the idea that "the world's progress and man's advancement" were rooted in a system that rewarded individual effort exclusively; both refused to see inequality as the result of "inborn differences between the weak and the strong, between the lazy and the industrious, between the thrifty and the improvident, between the genius and the fool." In the NAM's book, unionism was no bulwark against socialism. On the contrary, "it comes to pretty much the same thing."[14] Given that it was the business unionists whose power most immediately threatened the manufacturers' bottom line, the manufacturers mainly focused on them and attacked the closed shop that increased the efficacy of their organizations. The open-shop movement fundamentally objected to any worker power over management.

The open-shop employers, deciding that organizing to defend common interests was a tool too good to be left to the workers, exhorted employers to band together. They needed collective action because few of them were wealthy or powerful enough to deal with the union challenge on their own. As chapter 5 shows, employer collective action was facilitated by preexisting connections through shared commercial interests, as well as a shared social environment manifested in residential patterns and social club memberships. At the same time, as the chapter also highlights, engaging in campaigns that demanded solidarity could imperil the collective action project. Asking employers to take risks for the common cause could backfire, as the NAM and the Typothetae (the employers' organization in printing) found in the printers' strike of 1905–6, when many employers backed out of the fight and ditched their membership in the Typothetae.

Such costs of collective action probably played a role in pushing the NAM toward placing greater emphasis on its lobbying and publicity work, which promised higher rewards with fewer risks for members' balance sheets. Explored in chapters 6 and 7, these projects were helped along by members' financial resources and social networks. The advantages of money and particularly of social position afforded the NAM avenues of influence—personal friendships with important congressmen, funds used to purchase stories in newspapers, positions in party hierarchies—that were for the most part out of the reach of workers. Those advantages also kept employer influence out of the limelight. As Randall Bartlett notes in his 1973 classic *Economic Foundations of Political Power*, we do not expect to "see the combined Board chairmen of the Fortune Five Hundred marching on Washington."[15] That is not how elites exercise political power—which is why their exercise of power is less noticeable. Making one's case to a wide audience in order to mobilize large numbers of people, as labor unions and other grassroots organizations have to do, is by its nature a public process. Wielding influence on key pressure points behind the scenes is not. Employers made the most of this, loudly denouncing any labor influence in the press or in legislatures at the same time as employers themselves exerted a less visible form of power farther upstream. Yet the upstream was arguably the more important locus of power: as the NAM secretary put it early on, a politician might want to think twice about appealing to labor voters "when it might be another kind of people altogether who would have something to say about his nomination before such votes could be cast."[16]

The power exerted by the open-shop employers was all the more important for remaining somewhat hidden. It was also easier to discount because the men (and they were all men) who flocked to the NAM's new campaign did not stand at the zenith of wealth and power; they most certainly did not represent the pinnacle of eloquence or intellectual sophistication. The vernacular in which they expressed their disapproval of unions prized colorful expression and patriotic fervor over logical consistency, and their views were more likely to be propounded at the local chamber of commerce or in the pages of a trade publication than in a nationally prominent venue. They ran manufacturing establishments with a few hundred or a few thousand employees; they belonged to the important but usually not-quite-top-notch social clubs; and, though some called major metropoles such as Boston and Chicago home, they mostly lived in the nicer districts of the less prominent cities and towns. But that was enough. After all, public life was full of men just like them.

Although causalities are difficult to establish conclusively, the open-shop movement surely contributed to the stalling of labor's momentum. After significant growth around the turn of the twentieth century, in the years from roughly 1903 to 1910 union membership stagnated, judicial intervention hampered a greater number of strikes, and the legislative issues the AFL championed got stuck in congressional committees. These changes mattered on a practical level, but their symbolic significance may have been even

greater. The fewer members that unions managed to enroll, the less representative they could claim to be; the more times that strikers were reprimanded
by the courts or arrested by the police, the less their actions seemed within
the pale of the law; the greater the frequency with which labor bills failed
to pass in Congress, the more un-American such legislation came to seem.
The United States, after all, prides itself on being a democracy, where "the
people" take collective political action to change things. If they do not, or
if the effort fails, the implication is that the idea cannot have had sufficient
popular support.

In the first years of the century, the Industrial Commission had thought
it glimpsed ahead a road of labor-capital negotiation that would bring some
modicum of democracy to industry. The open-shop movement—through
the collective action it forged among employers, the publicity campaigns it
conducted, and the legislative efforts it managed to parry—dug large pot-
holes in that road. At the same time, the road was built on ground that was
always miry. Although some employers eschewed the vituperative rhetoric
cultivated by the NAM, few were willing to commit to good-faith bargaining with unions, and there was no real force capable of compelling them to
do so. By about 1908–9, as noted in chapter 8, disillusionment was gripping
even the union leaders who had closely cooperated with the NCF's project to
promote the trade agreement. Critique of the AFL's involvement in the NCF
and of its strategy in general was growing both within AFL unions and among
unskilled workers mostly left outside the AFL fold. Strikes, protests, and the
proliferation of radical ideas among workers convinced both middle-class
reformers and employers that the labor question remained very much on
the table; employers' very successes in tamping down unionization generated
a renewed wave of protest that crystallized in a demand for "industrial democracy."[17] Realizing that the fight was hardly over, in the years immediately
preceding World War I employers resolved to strengthen their organizations
and put the open-shop ideology on a firmer and more permanent basis. After
something of a hiatus during the war itself, they returned to this project in
the postwar years, the topic for chapter 9. The war years had not changed
open-shop employers' minds about unions, but they had made it clear that
employers needed to think long-term. The NAM therefore embarked on new
efforts to entrench the open-shop ideology in the society via experiments in
modern personnel management techniques, as well as via campaigns targeting clergy and educators.

Throughout the Progressive Era and beyond, employer input shaped discussion of the labor question in crucial ways, partly because it resonated
even with the era's reformers. Although the injustices of the industrial system

awakened the sympathy of many in the Progressive Era middle class, the specter of class sentiment and mob rule colored their thinking about labor unions and curtailed their vision of democracy in industry. To be sure, there was a wide range of opinion among middle-class thinkers. (Indeed, even the term "middle class" itself is fuzzy at best; in this book it refers mainly to the professionals whose main remunerative activity consisted of something other than the direct maximization of business profit.) Despite the range of opinion, however, many of these people found it difficult to deny that unions setting conditions on employment did indeed seem to run counter to individual liberty (though employers setting such conditions did not). Could one really trust workers to exercise power on their own account, untutored by their betters and unfiltered by the representative structures of the state? Many middle-class thinkers were not quite convinced that one could.[18] Even such staunch defenders of trade agreements as Ralph Easley rarely critiqued the NAM's claims about the closed shop in public; instead, Easley emphasized that labor leaders were more conservative than the rank and file and that unions served to keep volatile grassroots protest in check.

Unions themselves shared some blame in fostering doubts about worker power. Labor protest did sometimes involve violence, labor pickets parading outside a struck company did often intimidate and sometimes physically harass or attack strikebreakers, and the closed shop did imply a measure of coercion. Similarly, craft unions that were focused on protecting their skilled members sometimes resisted potentially beneficial technological change, raising the hackles of businessmen enamored of engineering feats, as well as of reformers keen to support progress and modern methods. Equally importantly, in their bid for status as responsible parties to negotiation, the unions that affiliated with the AFL traded on a language of respectability that potentially undercut their case. They painted the canonical American worker as white, skilled, Anglo-Saxon, and male—and, more specifically, as a white Anglo-Saxon family man with a strong work ethic and a healthy (but not frivolous!) taste for consumer goods.[19] They made those characteristics an important part of the argument for why unions should have more power, and they often rebuffed workers who did not possess them. Women workers, the unskilled, some European immigrants, and especially Asian immigrants and African Americans hoping for solidarity from unions often met a cool welcome at the very best and exclusion at worst. The emphasis on respectable Anglo-Saxon manhood could be efficacious in gaining a hearing with employers or legislators. It also, however, played into the hands of those who, whether from the left or the right, decried unions as selfish and unrepresentative. To be sure, employers, having themselves just found a measure of national unity after Civil War–era sectional divisions, had no intention of risking that unity by taking up the defense of racial minorities even if doing so would have bolstered their antiunion case. However, in implying—either by slighting them or by excluding them—that it would be a waste of effort to try to organize women, African Americans, Asian immigrants, or unskilled workers, the skilled white male leadership of unions inadvertently endorsed the idea that some workers were not fit to control their working lives. This was particularly deplorable in an era that witnessed significant growth in the number and importance of unskilled or semiskilled industrial workers, many of whom were immigrants or minorities. It also implicitly sanctioned viewing the capacity for self-government as a characteristic of a particular subset of people—a subset that might then exclude *any* worker.

As the Industrial Commission had noted back in 1902, introducing an "element of democracy" into industry required the organization of labor. Implied in that organization was the right to exercise some measure of power. Power in the hands of workers, however, made many reformers and most employers quite nervous; the same was true of many labor leaders when it came to power in the hands of the rank and file, or the unskilled, or women, or ethnic-racial minorities. This, ultimately, is why the story told in this book matters. Beyond the specific question of power in the workplace, it is a story about democracy: how and why working life has largely remained undemocratic, how easily supposedly democratic political structures can be circumvented by the power of money and social connections, and, in particular, who the society treats as capable of self-government. We profess to believe in democracy. The sometimes uncomfortable truth about democracy, though, is that democracy is like free speech in that it is meaningless unless we extend its promise to those who are not like us.

*   *   *

This book expands on existing scholarship in three key ways. First, it zeroes in on the concept of the closed shop, which is usually unexamined in the scholarly literature. That concept was not central to every fight between labor and capital in this period, but its framing of the issues underlay most of them. Second, it centers on the power that organized employers deployed to undermine unions in the public sphere. They did not always get what they wanted, but their influence was considerable. Third, it emphasizes both variation and continuity in employer resistance to unions. Employers have made specific choices in specific circumstances. At the same time, although employers are forever representing themselves as reacting to some new encroachment, the employer agenda has in fact been fairly consistent over time.

The closed shop matters, in part, simply because employers had the power to make criticism of it a central attack vector against unions. But it is also important because in exploring it, we see clearly that the contest between employers and workers was about who got to make the rules. It was about the government of the workplace. Employers took it for granted that their ownership of the business conferred on them more or less unlimited rights to dictate who got to be on the shop floor and what happened there. They decided on the work, and as long as a worker could be found who was willing to perform that work for X number of hours at pay Y under conditions Z, nobody had a right to interfere. Unions, by contrast, insisted that industry consisted of workers as well as employers and that organizations of workers had a crucial role in governing their craft. It was not only that a corporation had such an unfathomable power advantage over an individual worker that the worker's "consent" to the terms of work was little more than nominal. It was also that industry, in a sense, was too important to leave to industrialists. The traditions of the craft, the self-respect of its practitioners, the skills handed down from master craftsmen to apprentices—all these needed to be looked after by workers not solely concerned with profit. The aspiration of unions to function as the government of a workplace or even of an entire industry had deep roots in old practices and understandings about what work meant and how it should be organized; it harked back to a time when a "free man" was defined not as someone who had the right to choose which master to work for but as someone who worked for himself, who did not have a master. As such, demands for craft governance had grown in tandem with demands for political democracy in the eighteenth and nineteenth centuries, as historians like Howard Rock, Bruce Laurie, and Sean Wilentz have shown.[20]

The closed shop is also important because it reveals hierarchies beyond the central worker-employer divide. It highlighted divisions between different groups of workers, and it discomfited both middle-class observers and employers. In its efforts to institute workplace governance, it drew on nineteenth-century craft traditions, and that world sometimes sat rather uneasily with the twentieth-century workplace, as well as with ideas about liberalism and modernity. Besides manufacturing, the closed shop was common in what Andrew Wender Cohen has in *The Racketeer's Progress* termed the "craft economy" of locally based building, hauling, baking, butchering, and barbering. There, it undergirded semiformal contracts somewhat redolent of the tavern and the back alley and created an order enforced by social pressure and, sometimes, violence. The vision of order prevalent in the craft economy, Cohen argues, clashed with the emerging middle-class, corporate, national economy, which relied on the written contract enforceable at law (and on the state's official forces of order).[21] Similarly, for the middle-class reformers who put their faith in individuals and in good government, the closed shop's exclusionism and its association with solidarity enforced by physical coercion compounded its already worrying propensity to accord power to workers' organizations, that is, organizations that were class-based. The middle-class reformers of the Progressive Era faced the problems of inequality with heartfelt consternation. But they also worried about class and radicalism. They often supported vicious state attacks on radical labor organizations like the Industrial Workers of the World (IWW, also known as the Wobblies). More broadly, they strove to, in Shelton Stromquist's phrase, "reinvent 'the people'" in terms that sidestepped the problem of class.[22]

While the effort to introduce a measure of democracy into industry, then, was sometimes represented as part and parcel of modernizing labor relations, reconciling competing claims to what modernity might mean in the workplace was far from simple. The problem, though, was not in the main an intellectual one. Who won specific battles over unionization or legal treatment of unions and their demands influenced perceptions at least as much as learned discourses about unions' place in liberalism and modernity. The outcome of those concrete battles, in turn, was shaped by employer opposition to any reduction of managerial power. This book therefore pays close attention to employers' views and actions. Employer strategies with regard to unions varied depending on the employers' industry, size, societal position, and other factors. Variation matters, because it helps us understand when and why employers acquiesced in unionization. Analyzing variation shows that, apart from a few exceptional situations, employers virtually never *favored* the independent organization of workers—but given the right circumstances, most employers negotiated with unions. On the other hand, particular industrial conditions could also provide fuel for employer dislike of unions and make it flare up into effective organized resistance. This underlines that we need to pay attention both to employer attitudes and to the structures and material conditions that molded employer choices and refrain from assuming that a change in choices entailed a change in attitudes. Employer attitudes showed considerable consistency. Even when unionization was successful, employers generally remained on the lookout for ways to curtail or even undo union power; the struggle was never finished. On the other hand, specific concrete circumstances could create union victories without necessitating a change in employer attitudes. Indeed, if an a priori favorable employer attitude were necessary for labor to win concessions, any labor struggle would almost by definition be either futile or redundant.[23]

I am, of course, hardly the first person to write about organized employers. Works on local or industry-based employer associations, such as those by Howell Harris, Sidney Fine, and William Millikan, provide an important window onto the practical functioning of early twentieth-century employer organizations.[24] For comparative analyses, Jeffrey Haydu's voluminous scholarship offers much of value, and, as is clear in the pages that follow, I have drawn liberally on his insights.[25] For the postwar years, Elizabeth Fones-Wolf's *Selling Free Enterprise* is indispensable. (Indeed, I still think of this book in part as a prequel to her analysis of the contest over public opinion between employers and unions in that period.)[26] Many labor historians have also written about the NAM and similar organizations in the interstices of labor histories; the most influential of these for me has been Julie Greene's *Pure and Simple Politics*.[27] Most recently, and closest to my own work, Chad Pearson's *Reform or Repression* provides an abundance of analysis on how the local and national levels of employer organizing interlocked, how the open-shop movement transcended regional divides, and how, at key points, liberal reformers found themselves supporting the employers' open-shop claims.[28] Despite such fine examples, however, the volume of scholarship on employers remains decidedly limited; indeed, it was not until 2020 that we got a full-length monograph on the history of the NAM in Jennifer Delton's *The Industrialists*.[29]

The wealth of new scholarship on the post–World War II rise of the Right forms a partial, welcome exception to the overall dearth of scholarship on employer views. Works by Kim Phillips-Fein, Tami Friedman, Elizabeth Tandy Shermer, Nancy MacLean, and Lawrence Glickman, in particular, provide sharp insights regarding the connections between business antiunionism, the rise of American conservatism, and the dominance of a language equating business interests with the common good.[30] As they document, when, in response to the 1930s Great Depression, the state finally paid noticeable attention to the welfare of ordinary people in what became known as the New Deal, a coterie of employers, conservatives, and traditional elites was aroused into resistance. However, we need to remind ourselves to look back past this modern iteration of the business backlash. Otherwise, we run the risk of inadvertently endorsing businessmen's claims that the New Deal's use of collective mechanisms to secure basic rights was somehow aberrant or incompatible with American traditions—that employer campaigns against it were a reaction to "excesses" of state and collective power. This was not the case. Antiunion employers and the advocates of small government in the post–World War II era largely recycled rhetoric and arguments invented in the context of the first rise of modern trade unionism. In some cases, as analyses of nineteenth-century jurisprudence by legal scholars like Christopher Tomlins, William Forbath, and Victoria Hattam show, they redeployed arguments used in court cases against the very first trade unions.[31] These employers were not suddenly awakened to activism by unprecedented statist excess; they were reasserting beliefs they and their predecessors had held for a long time.

In the early twentieth century, employers, themselves arrayed into what amounted to bosses' unions, deployed a language of individual rights to discredit workers' organizations and reinforce government by the bosses. Their money and influence went a long way in helping their views spread, but they were also tilling a far from barren field: the "element of democracy in industry" that the Industrial Commission had thought might be developing was persistently undermined by the implicit assumptions of employers, reformers, and even some workers that only some people are capable of and entitled to self-government. At the heart of this book is the sheer strangeness—and fundamental antidemocratic tenor—of the claim of the open-shop movement and its modern heirs: that unions are bad for workers and that workers' rights are really better looked after by employers. It is quite an impressive feat, in a democratic society, to endow such a claim with credibility. This book tells the story of how it succeeded.

1 The Invention of the Closed Shop

The NAM Weighs In on the Labor Question

Car, n'oublions pas le vieil adage policier: "Cherche à qui le crime
profite."
—Les Dupont, quoted in Hergé, *Tintin au pays de l'or noir*

When David M. Parry took the podium at the 1903 annual convention of the
National Association of Manufacturers to submit his presidential report, the
delegates—some 250 businessmen—gave him a hero's welcome. The Tulane
Hall auditorium, festive with patriotic bunting and tropical ferns, rang with
their applause and cheers.[1] Their enthusiasm stemmed from their knowledge
that Parry was charting a new course for the organization. The NAM had been
founded in 1895, and in its first years it mainly focused on promoting foreign
trade. Parry, however, had other plans. Since being elected to the presidency
of the association in 1902, he had worked to turn it into the spearhead of a
fight that he and his allies saw as the main battle of the day: the effort to stop
the growth of labor unions.

At the time of the NAM's antilabor turn, workers' calls for a greater voice
at work rang out in loud tones. Whether they joined together in occupationally based craft or trade unions, formed radical organizations, or were active
in the central labor unions in towns and cities across America, workers at
the turn of the twentieth century were demanding more representation and
more rights in both the workplace and politics. The tools they made use of, as
well as the demands they advanced, signaled a potentially significant shift in
power. Sympathy strikes (strikes by one union in support of another union's
demands) could effectively shut down the critical services of a city. Labor-
organized boycotts of the goods produced by "unfair" employers (employers
in one way or another at loggerheads with unions) could withhold much of
the employer's customer base until the dispute was resolved to labor's satisfaction. Nor did labor merely demand more money. Workers raised fundamental
questions of governance: many strikes demanded recognition of the union

as the legitimate agent of the workers or union control over dismissals, work rules, and similar matters. Even the most moderate unionists were in some ways redefining the sources of legitimate power: for example, judicial attacks on union tactics prompted widespread labor sentiment in favor of disobeying court orders.[2]

The NAM, of course, did not invent employer resistance to unions; it stretched back deep into the nineteenth century. However, the NAM's 1903 New Orleans convention launched a new, focused, coordinated battle against the labor union challenge by organized employers, and it did so with great fanfare. Precirculated excerpts from Parry's presidential report had alerted newspapers that the convention would mark the entry of a new major player in the debate over labor relations.[3] The full report offered enough juicy quotes to attract press attention and ensure that the NAM's new line would be noticed by friend and foe alike. The report, copies of which had been distributed to the delegates in advance of the convention, laid out the main tenets of the NAM's new doctrine on the evils of labor unionism and the necessity of employer organization. In flowery language, it reminded the members that their association was the culmination of industrial progress and the defender of sound economic thought, both of which were under attack. The main threat was labor unionism, "a despotism springing into being in the midst of a liberty-loving people." Labor unions, the report alleged, forced workers to become members. Indeed, intimidation explained the growth of organized labor: "Thousands of its members are such to-day, not because they sympathize with its purposes, but because they fear the consequences of not yielding to its tyranny." It was the moral obligation of employers to counteract this "insidious growth." It was their duty to organize and help "thousands of men shake off the shackles of unionism."[4] Although unions claimed to represent workers and improve their lot, according to the NAM, unions were a force for neither democracy nor uplift. Instead, unions trampled individual rights, particularly the individual rights of workers.

To make the rather paradoxical case that workers' organizations were bad for workers, the NAM's attack on unionism centered on what it termed the "closed shop." By "closed shop," the NAM referred to the well-established union practice of requiring that all workers hired into a unionized workplace (or at least all whose jobs came within the purview of the union) needed to either be union members or join within a specified time of being hired.[5] If a worker failed to join, the employer was obligated to dismiss that worker or risk a strike. Unions found this an unexceptional device to ensure solidarity and the continued viability of the union. The NAM, though, latched on to the practice as a violation of individual rights—the employer's individual right to run his business, but also the worker's right to agree to work on whatever terms suited him (or her, though the canonical worker was represented as male by both unions and employers in this period). Employers who cared about their workers would therefore refuse to accept the membership requirement. Instead, they would insist on what the NAM termed the "open shop," where union membership supposedly was not inquired about and the employer negotiated with each worker as an individual. Apparently oblivious to the irony, the NAM called on employers to organize into a united front to secure the open shop by means of collective action.

This chapter focuses on the rise of the NAM as the driving force of the employer antiunion campaign. It first examines the collective action problems faced by the NAM in its efforts to get employers to join its project and the ways in which ideology and rhetoric served to alleviate those problems. It then turns to the dilemma of how to make employer collective action palatable to the general (middle-class) public in an era critical of business. Finally, it discusses how the concept of the closed shop undergirded both efforts, effecting a rhetorical coup that fundamentally shifted the conversation about the labor question.

Collective Action for Employers' Rights

Employers had good reason to work jointly against unions. Like workers who banded together to make demands of an employer, employers who joined forces to resist union demands could share resources and information (including strikebreakers and blacklists) and hold out longer against having to make concessions. Collective action, however, does not just "happen." As Mancur Olson points out in his classic work *The Logic of Collective Action*, that individuals act to further their individual interests does not lead to groups acting in the collective interest of the group. On the contrary, the first often precludes the second: whenever possible, it is in the interests of the individual to let others do the work and simply reap the benefits. This is known as the free rider problem.

Collective endeavors for the common good, almost by definition, result in benefits for everyone, regardless of whether they participate or not. Say a movement aims to obtain environmental regulation to ensure cleaner air and water. If the movement succeeds, the cleaner air and water will be there for everyone, not only for those who contributed to the movement. So why should anyone bother to contribute? People might, of course, work on behalf of an environmental cause out of altruism or out of concern for the planet. Individual motivation is not limited to narrowly self-interest-maximizing considerations; as Olson recognizes, people may also act out of ideological or sentimental reasons. Still, as he points out, since the efficacy of collective action arises out of uniting the actions of multiple people, participating will only be motivating for any individual if enough other people participate so the effort has a chance to succeed. Moreover, neither ideology nor sentiment is likely to form an effective defense against the free rider problem. After all, patriotism is a powerful ideology full of big emotions, but the state cannot expect to survive on voluntary contributions—it has to use its coercive power to tax.[6]

The free rider problem is a perennial issue in collective action. It was, indeed, a big part of why unions had created the membership requirement that open-shop employers decried as the tyrannical closed shop. Unions attempted to coordinate action between large numbers of people who had to be willing to risk a lot—at the very least their jobs and sometimes even their lives—for uncertain reward. Employers faced the same problem, if in a somewhat less acute form. Employers were a smaller group with greater resources, and they were already connected through ties of business, residence, and social circle (as discussed in chapter 5). Their interconnections made it easier for them to apply social pressure, while their resources and connections allowed them to achieve results more reliably and rapidly, thus making the rewards of collective action more palpable. Still, even simply becoming a dues-paying member of the NAM was not without cost: in 1903 the annual membership fee was $50, which is over $1,500 in 2020 dollars and which many manufacturers reportedly complained was "exorbitant."[7] Becoming an activist in the open-shop movement also involved expenditures of time, and it carried the risk that one's labor relations might sour.

Employers, then, needed some mechanism or incentive to ensure participation. Much as they excoriated labor's closed-shop rules, open-shop employers sometimes experimented with similar measures. For example, employers committed to the open-shop cause might refuse to do business with a manufacturer who accepted the closed shop. The Los Angeles Citizens' Alliance (an employer-led antiunion group), for instance, issued "union cards" to its members, who agreed that "any business house seeking favors from another must show one of these cards."[8] Similarly, during a building trades strike in 1911, the Citizens' Alliance of Minneapolis warned that its members would refuse to supply building materials to builders who signed agreements with the unions.[9] Employer organizations sometimes also created what are known as "selective" benefits—benefits available only to members. They might offer members-only legal, information, or translation services, as both the NAM and the American Anti-Boycott Association (AABA) did;

or, more directly related to labor issues, they might foot the bill for a semi-permanent crew of strikebreakers available only to members, as was done by the National Founders' Association (NFA), an organization of metal foundry operators.[10] The NAM, too, sometimes got involved in strikes. For instance, in 1909 the NAM sent its political worker and undercover operative, Martin M. Mulhall, to aid the shoe companies of Portsmouth, Ohio, in their struggle against a striking local of the Knights of Labor; Mulhall proceeded to bribe some strike leaders, convince others that the strike was doomed, and scout for replacement workers. Soon enough—whether due to Mulhall's efforts or other factors—the strike petered out.[11]

The NAM's broad ambition of reducing labor's influence, however, did not lend itself easily to the kinds of specific benefits or coercive measures that local or industry-based organizations could offer. On the contrary, it was a classic case of what is known as a "nonexcludable collective good": one could not limit it to only those who contributed. If some employers joined together and succeeded in demolishing unions, the noncontributing employer would reap the fruits of such efforts no less than those who had fought the good fight. In the meantime, the employer who stayed on the sidelines had saved time and money and perhaps avoided a retaliatory strike; maybe he had even managed to grab greater market share while his fellow employers were embroiled in their fight against unions.[12] Thus, although employers may already have believed that unions were a nuisance, the NAM had some work to do to convince them that unions were an *intolerable* and *vanquishable* nuisance that was in their interests to combat collectively.

Activist organizations invest considerable energy not only in promoting their members' interests but also in *defining* them, as William Roy and Rachel Parker-Gwin find in a study of business and labor publications.[13] For the NAM, too, making sure that manufacturers understood their interests in the same terms that the NAM did was key to the organization's growth and cohesiveness. The open-shop message did more than merely articulate what employers already believed. The NAM worked hard to get employers to see themselves as a part of a class of employers who shared an interest in working to defeat organized labor and to convince them that through organization they could be successful in this aim. To this end, the NAM's leading figures traveled around the country on speaking tours, visiting boards of trade, chambers of commerce, and businessmen's social clubs to preach the gospel of organization. During 1910, the association claimed, it had directly addressed some quarter of a million people at such "revival meetings."[14]

One part of the message the NAM delivered to businessmen was upbeat: organization worked and was fun besides. One prominent front-page story in *American Industries* explained that in Philadelphia, textile manufacturers had organized, which had enabled them to defeat the "unjust" and "arbitrary" wage and hour demands of their workers because, organized, the manufacturers were able to hold to the "firm and dignified position" of ignoring all arguments and claims made by the union and only talking to individual workers.[15] Another story (approvingly titled "How They Do It in South Bend") recounted that in South Bend, Indiana, a Citizens' Alliance was "growing in strength and enthusiasm" and working hard to convince employers to resist the closed shop.[16] Still another story noted that in San Francisco, the local Citizens' Alliance had brought an injunction suit against strikers and won the ruling that picketing is unlawful when "it becomes a nuisance."[17] And it did not all need to be serious and dour: lavish dinners, rowdy smokers, and cheerful outings accompanied employer association meetings, and though many speeches at meetings were filled with dire predictions and hortatory rhetoric, there was also plenty of self-congratulation as well as celebration of the accomplishments, virtue, and importance of businessmen.[18]

As the language of "revival meetings" indicates, however, appeals to self-interest and the pleasures of companionship were complemented by a more religiously tinged fervor. Much of the NAM's message highlighted the urgency and severity of the problem of unions. A constant refrain in the articles printed in the NAM's *American Industries* was that manufacturers were sorely behind in the organizational game: when the NAM was taking its first tentative steps in the 1890s, "labor was already united, labor was moving as one man; labor in splendid phalanx-like precision was moving like an army to the accomplishment of its great design."[19] Politicians and elected judges, the NAM claimed, were subservient to organized labor because they believed organized labor controlled votes. To receive fair treatment, employers needed to show legislators and judges that they were equally able to deliver votes. This, however, could only happen "if the manufacturing interests are organized."[20] The dangers facing employers if they failed to organize, the NAM claimed, could be directly observed in the British experience. The association laid the full blame for British economic problems on the success of British unions. Unions had pushed through a bill limiting the use of injunctions, and employers lost the control they needed to remain competitive—British unions had "driven English manufacturers out of the world's markets."[21] Such dire prospects admitted no compromise. Thus, at the 1903 convention that marked the start of the NAM's new antilabor line, any discussion of moderation in labor relations was nipped in the bud by the Parry faction, which had come prepared for a coup. For instance, when the progressive-minded small manufacturer and mayor of Toledo, Samuel M. Jones, rose to oppose a resolution condemning the "vicious element in unionism," which he considered inflammatory, the delegates tried to shout him down. Jones, in their opinion, was straying from the point: as one delegate put it, "If you will talk on the lawless and vicious, I wish you would do so." Jones gave up, and the convention adopted the resolution unanimously.[22]

In the NAM's own telling of its history, the 1903 convention in New Orleans became a seminal event, the moment when fearless leadership boldly charted a new course into a great future without heeding the doubts expressed by the association's less strident (or, in the Parry faction's view, less valiant) members. Retrospective reminiscences presented at the association's silver jubilee in 1920 hailed the wisdom of the open-shop campaign and paid tribute to Parry and his allies for "heroically" launching and enforcing the new line. It was the labor question that made the organization what it was, speakers at the jubilee argued.[23]

Such rhetoric of heroism, transcending humdrum daily concerns, was key in prompting employers to pay the NAM's membership fee and invest time and energy in the association's lobbying and publicity projects. They were joining a crusade as much as they were joining an organization. As Gerald Friedman has pointed out, a utopian, semispiritual awakening has been vital in getting workers to join unions. The heady crowd power of strikes, the reimagination of the world entailed in radical activism, the feeling of victory against great odds—these could overcome the incentives of free riding and the apprehensions and habits of disempowerment in ways that rational considerations of future benefit never could have. "Radical activists made collective action possible" for workers, Friedman argues.[24] The same was largely true for the NAM. Even though employers risked less than workers and could expect more—they had more resources and power to help in their collective endeavors—they, too, needed an emotional push. Language that painted the union threat as existential and the resistance of employers as heroic could help provide such a push. The fight, the NAM argued, would be hard—but necessary and just. Both "resources in men and money" and "an almost infinite amount of patience and loyalty" would be required to turn back the union threat, but employers could not shirk their duty to "protect . . . the property interests and the prosperity of the whole country."[25] Rather like a state devising an emotion-laden propaganda campaign to cajole its citizens to contribute to a war effort, the NAM heightened the ideological stakes in order to wring money and action from employers. The strategy seemed to work: the organization's membership, which had hovered around one thousand, shot up after the adoption of the new antiunion line, tripling in roughly the space of one year and continuing to expand more steadily for the following decade so that it reached just over four thousand by 1913.[26]

Justifying Employer Collective Action
in an Era Critical of Business

Employers were launching their movement in the context of acute societal awareness of how industrial change and business power had transformed the world, not always for the better. Decades of helter-skelter growth—of corporations, of factories, of cities, of the population, of the very size of buildings—had created a sense of chaos that grassroots critics, middle-class observers, and many businessmen themselves found rather unsettling. The power and wealth that the growth conferred on some had resulted in the fin de siècle years becoming known as the Gilded Age, a time when the monied classes seemed to vaunt their wealth and power without restraint. Even as growth signaled progress, it also produced industrial conditions that conferred misery on some, giving rise to increasing labor-capital conflict. In the decades after the Great Railroad Strike of 1877, which had brought out some one hundred thousand workers in cities from Baltimore to San Francisco, the language used to describe industrial conflict reverberated with metaphors of war.[27] Meanwhile, the rise of the "trust," a business conglomerate of a size that a few decades earlier would have seemed unimaginable, seemed to threaten small producers, workers, consumers, and the foundations of the political system. Popular opinion blamed the rising cost of living in good part on the monopoly power of big business, while the corrupting power of wealth was captured in the moniker attached to the US Senate: it was known as the Millionaires' Club. Industrial growth seemed equally likely to lead to perdition as to be the root of civilization.[28]

Taking stock of the situation seemed imperative, so academics delved into research on the work and home lives of workers and their families and developed new economic and social theories to explain the new order. Meanwhile, Congress instituted special commissions to investigate the causes and remedies of industrial conflict. Middle-class men and women, often from families with a tradition of reform activism, went beyond merely cerebrating on the question to acting on their ideas for solutions, and the landscape was soon dotted with new organizations to serve the poor, to lobby Congress, and to organize public activism.[29] The journalistically inclined among them became "muck-rakers," reporters scouring the not-so-sanitary sediment of American life to expose malfeasance by the rich and powerful. And the public clamored for such exposés. To take just one example, Ida Tarbell's series of articles in *McClure's Magazine* on Standard Oil, one of the largest of the trusts, garnered *McClure's* heaps of letters of praise and sold-out magazine issues while establishing Tarbell's fame as one of the foremost investigative journalists of the time.[30]

Investigation and activism so characterized the years between the turn of
the twentieth century and World War I that the period has become known
as the Progressive Era, a major period of reform and reexamination. In this
context, it was imperative for a movement of employers to dissociate itself
from the opprobrium directed at big business and try to represent itself as the
defender of ordinary people. This the NAM and its allied organizations did
by portraying the labor movement as a powerful, oppressive bully. Indeed,
far from being like the villainous trusts, the open-shop employers were the
victims of a trust. Despite all the focus on monopoly, the open-shop employers contended, the "public has seemingly failed to realize that there is one
trust that is piercing the very heart of American liberty, and striking at the
welfare and happiness of every man." That was, of course, the "Labor Trust."[31]

In the cartoon in figure 1, the open-shop employers implicitly associate
themselves with general public opinion and "the citizens." The cartoon was
produced by the Citizens' Industrial Association of America—an employer
creation, but one that billed itself as an organization of regular folks rather
than of employers or businessmen.[32] In it, the bloated "Labor Trust" with his
ruffians, including a striker carrying a baseball bat, is facing off against the
equally bloated "Oil Trust," "Beef Trust," and "Coal Trust" in their top hats.
On the lower right, an image shows how things would be if the labor trust
got its way—or perhaps it is supposed to represent the present or past state
of affairs. In any case, in that world "governed by the labor trust," cities are
burning while men with guns and sticks attack a streetcar—a reference to the
era's many streetcar strikes, during which strikers and prostrike community
members often tried to prevent streetcars staffed with replacement workers
from running.[33] Luckily for everyone, however, a benevolent, slim, clean-
shaven figure in a businesslike fedora is keeping the antagonists apart. This
figure is made up of a plethora of bodies flocking together; banding together
into "Organization," they gain the power to avert the bloodbath that would
ensue if the labor sluggers and the trusts were free to get at each other's
throats. Thus, "Industry Avenue" is clear to a peaceful future "protected by
the citizens" where both factories and streetcars run without interference.

Open-shop employers' rhetoric was careful to insist that it was not organization that they objected to; it was bullying. Countless speeches, pamphlets,
and articles produced by the open-shop activists repeated in various forms
the contention laid out in the NAM's 1903 "Declaration of Principles" on labor
that the association did not oppose labor unions "as such" but only objected
to the "illegal acts of interference with the personal liberty of employer or
employe."[34] As any reader of NAM material would have quickly realized,
though, in the NAM's view "illegal acts of interference" encompassed nearly

Figure 1: *Industry Avenue*. "The common people demand and can enforce protection for all industries and public utilities. No more interference by the labor or any other trust or organization with the affairs or means of livelihood of the citizens." *Source: Square Deal* 1, no. 5 (December 1905): cover page.

every conventional union activity, from boycotts to picketing to strikes to making rules about how much a worker could be expected to produce in a day (what employers termed "restriction of output").[35] Nor did the NAM's critique of unions really aim for intellectual consistency or rhetorical sophistication; it was happy to be eclectic, picking up any theme likely to discredit unions. The NAM's trade publication, *American Industries*, printed stories about violence on the picket line, union corruption, and unions' seemingly excessive or silly demands—a particular favorite was union men refusing to proceed with funeral processions because a nonunion coachman was part of the procession.[36] Besides complaints about violence or corruption, the NAM insisted that union practices destroyed initiative and thus stymied upward mobility, introducing "the foreign standard, where the workman is always a workman, where ambition is still-born and hope is dead."[37] The damage done by unions, the NAM contended, reverberated across multiple generations, since unions restricted apprenticeships and often opposed industrial schools sponsored by employers: in the NAM's view this impinged on "the freedom of every American boy to learn a trade."[38]

Aware that employers did not cut the most sympathetic of figures in the Progressive Era, the NAM did its best to ground its critique of unions in a selfless cause: protecting American workers and preserving American institutions.[39] In this cause, a new concept was of great help. This concept was the closed shop.

The Impact and Enduring Utility of Closed-Shop Rhetoric

For employers, the dichotomy of the open versus the closed shop had several virtues as a rhetorical device. First, it enabled employers to claim that they did not object to the idea of workers organizing, only to specific union practices. Second, the rhetoric of the closed shop allowed employers to portray unions as tyrannical toward *workers* and to pose as the protectors of workers unwilling to submit to union "dictation" in workplace or political matters.[40] Third, it allowed employers to portray themselves as abused victims at the hands of powerful labor bosses. Fourth, as labor leaders pointed out, it claimed openness and opportunity for the employer side, leaving labor to struggle with "the general antipathy which is ordinarily felt toward anything being closed."[41] Fifth, it focused attention not on the practices of employers but on the practices of unions.

The closed shop, the NAM claimed, proved that unions were fundamentally undemocratic. Mandatory membership made it clear that they had no faith in the workers' independent judgment, that they thought workers should "be placed under their guardianship"—a claim that "would do credit to the Russian autocracy."[42] If unions got their way, "independent" workers would be the losers, as the cartoon in figure 2 argues. Reversing the Left's traditional depictions of capitalist "fat cats," the cartoon shows double-chinned representatives of the "labor trust" feeding a gaunt employer with a variety of concoctions (restriction of output, shorter hours, higher wages). These concoctions make him weak; the knock-out dose is the closed shop.

The employer is at the center of this image, but the cartoon implies that those who really suffer from the employer's downfall are the workers. The

THE KNOCK OUT DOSE.

Figure 2: *The Knock Out Dose.* Labor Trust Doctor: "This dose will put you to sleep, my friend. It may produce nausea enough so you will throw it up. If not you will never come to; but don't worry, we will run the business for you." *Source: Square Deal* 1, no. 7 (February 1906): cover page.

employer, after all, having swallowed the forced medicine, will be blissfully oblivious, but his fate spells doom for the large crowd of nonunion, "independent" workers depicted in the top left corner of the image. With unions rather than employers in charge, they are left with "no right to any job," while selfish labor unionists scream at them from the factory windows to "get off the face of the Earth." The only hope for ordinary workers, as well as for employers, was that the closed-shop brew would "produce nausea enough" to cause the employer to vomit it out.

Organized employers, then, positioned themselves as the underdog fighting for principle. As the Redeemers (and other southern whites) demonstrated in the post–Civil War South, this could be an effective power play. The defeated Confederates portrayed every assertion of new rights by African Americans as a personal affront and every indication of Union presence as proof of the browbeating that long-suffering southerners had to endure. In an analogous manner, NAM members confronted with labor demands adopted a pose of injured pride. Here they were, the men whose ingenuity and enterprise had built the country, being harassed by reformers, pressured by labor unions, and harangued by politicians. Like the former Confederates in the South who parlayed their purported victimhood into a potent political language to successfully discredit Reconstruction policies that aimed at improving the standing of African Americans in the South, the NAM effectively deployed a woe-is-us pose to obscure employers' economic and social power and instead cast employers as the hapless victims of the labor boss.[43]

The employer antiunion buildup did not go unnoticed by the American Federation of Labor (AFL), the umbrella organization of the mostly occupationally based trade or craft unions that were the NAM's main target. Indeed, the new employer movement had already formed a topic of conversation at the AFL's 1902 convention. AFL president Samuel Gompers's first comments at the convention indirectly addressed the new employer push: he denounced an article praising strikebreakers as heroes that had just been penned by a close ally of the antiunion employers, Harvard president Charles Eliot. Newspaper reports on the eve of the convention were more explicit. As one put it, "Of the questions to be discussed, leaders of the labor movement who are already on the field deem most important those arising from the recent action of the National Association of Manufacturers," which was proposing a "counter movement" to labor.[44] Even though the AFL at first tried to downplay the significance of the employers' new initiative, by late 1903 it was becoming clear that the employer campaign, now prominently billing itself as the movement for the "open shop," was gaining momentum.[45] This prompted Gompers to pen a scathing critique of the new line of attack, insisting that the open-shop ideology created a double standard under which the employer was free to do as he pleased while denying workers' right to choose whom they would work with and under what conditions.[46]

As Gompers and others soon found out, however, the employer focus on the closed shop was hard to respond to effectively. According to contemporary observers, the open-shop campaign rapidly shifted public opinion. As early as the fall of 1904, the prominent social reformer William English Walling argued that until the open-shop crusade was launched, "public opinion, outside of the eastern money centers, was largely on the union side." Yet, "under the mistaken assumption that the open shop means nothing more than equal treatment for union and non-union men, public opinion has veered around and now stands almost solidly opposed to the organization of labor."[47] The new terminology established itself quickly. Before 1902 or so the phrase "closed shop" was almost never used to refer to union membership requirements. As a result of the NAM's new campaign, however, it became synonymous not just with required membership but also with all manner of union "tyranny." By 1911 both terms had become such household phrases that the author of a book on the closed shop opened his treatise by commenting that, after all the talk about the issue over the previous decade, "there are no terms in labor-union terminology more familiar to the average American citizen than 'closed shop' and 'open shop.'"[48]

Unions tried to deflect the negativity of the "closed" shop by referring to the "union" shop, but "closed shop" remained the dominant term, as figure 3 demonstrates.[49] More importantly, using a different label could not undo the change in the thrust of the conversation itself. Suddenly, discussion of "the labor question" had a key union demand rather than employer misbehavior in its crosshairs. While unions had faced generic accusations of "tyranny" before, such accusations could be turned around to point at the employers and their rather more obviously tyrannical practices: after all, in many industries at the turn of the twentieth century, workdays stretched to ten or more hours, child labor was widespread, and industrial accidents frequently left workers debilitated for life—or killed them outright.[50] The motif of the closed shop, though, centered the discussion on the logic of union practice. Defending that practice resulted in complex discourses on the procedural aspects of trade unionism, which few people could be bothered to follow. As the president of the Typographical Union, for example, contended, the reason for the popularity of the "cry against the closed shop" was that it served as an emotionally appealing attack on "a feature of trade union policy difficult for the inexperienced to grasp, analyze and understand."[51]

That was true. Why craft unionists saw the closed shop as so fundamental and nonnegotiable baffled many outsiders. Neither the roots nor the logic of requiring union membership as a condition of employment were transparent to the nonexpert, because both were intimately tied together with the long and complicated history of the development of craft unionism (a topic discussed in greater detail in chapter 2). This left the field open for employers to put their own spin on the matter and to frame the issue of the closed

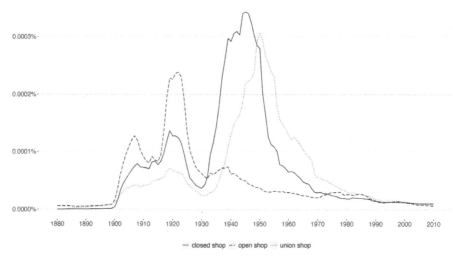

Figure 3: Google Ngram of the bigrams "closed shop," "open shop," and "union shop." The graph shows the frequency with which these bigrams (two-word phrases) have appeared in Google's corpus of American English (consisting of millions of books and magazines published in English in the United States). They are represented as a proportion of all bigrams in a given year. Note particularly how the terms "open shop" and "closed shop" suddenly appear in about 1900 and how the term "union shop" tracks these, though the former two phrases clearly dominate the discussion. Note also the persistence of this language: the highest peak of the usage of "closed shop" comes in the mid-1940s. For more comprehensive documentation of the creation of this chart and a sampling of related charts, including also the more modern phrase "right to work," see https://github.com/vhulden/bossesunion.

versus open shop in terms of right and wrong, with employers firmly on the moral high ground.

The closed shop was particularly useful to employers because the critique it entailed resonated with many reform-minded politicians and activists who otherwise might lean more toward concern for workers than for employers. As scholars have long pointed out, the relations between the working classes and middle-class reformers were fraught with multiple layers of complexity and tension. Genuine humane impulses to help others coexisted with patronizing efforts to "civilize" workers; honest endeavors to create more just structures vied with an inclination to boost those individuals most amenable to middle-class values. The closed shop was an exercise of power by workers' organizations into which the middle class had no input. Could one trust those workers to act responsibly? And besides, wasn't the principle of individual liberty a sacred one, and didn't the closed shop really trample on it?

The appeal to securing the rights of the individual from union coercion resonated at the highest levels: perhaps most famously, President Theodore Roosevelt endorsed the idea that unions had no right to coerce anyone to join or to require membership as a condition of employment. Although Roosevelt had shown a perhaps unprecedented courtesy to unions by inviting the United Mine Workers' leader to a White House conference, trying to solve a months-long massive strike in anthracite coal, he essentially endorsed the employers' open-shop views. When the Anthracite Coal Strike Commission (created at Roosevelt's instigation after months of deadlock between the union and mine operators) explicitly insisted on guaranteeing the "rights and privileges of non-union men," as well as of unionized workers, and when the agreement it produced explicitly rejected union recognition and the membership requirement, Roosevelt had nothing but praise for this outcome.[52] The same year, when a nonunion printer was dismissed from his position at the Government Printing Office on the grounds that he was not a member of the printers' union, Roosevelt intervened to have him reinstated. Roosevelt argued that the printer's dismissal was in violation of civil service law and that it contradicted the principle expressed in the Anthracite Coal Strike Commission's findings that there should be no discrimination in employment based on whether a worker belonged to a union—a principle that Roosevelt declared himself to "heartily approve."[53]

In his condemnation of union efforts to impose rules on nonunionists, Roosevelt was far from unique among politicians and journalists aligned with the Progressive movement. Indeed, one of the issues of *McClure's* that carried an installment of Ida Tarbell's Standard Oil exposé also carried an article criticizing union tactics by the prominent Progressive journalist Ray Stannard Baker. Although the article did not explicitly refer to closed-shop rules, it zeroed in on union coercion of nonunionists. Called "The Right to Work," the article recounted incidents of union violence and intimidation ranging from shootings to verbal harassment against workers who continued to work during the anthracite coal strike.[54]

The dilemma was real—early twentieth-century strikes were no picnics. Union members, even if they were often the targets rather than the instigators of violence, did regularly attack strikebreakers with fists and guns, as well as with verbal taunts. Yet the dilemma was not as easily solved as declaring that everyone had a sacred right to work as part of the heritage of American liberty and that unions should refrain from interfering with that right. Even as Baker's article appeared, the Anthracite Coal Strike Commission's hearings were demonstrating just how complex the struggle between the companies and the miners was.[55] It was not just that the companies had significantly more power than miners or that miners might not be paid sufficiently. It was that

the very nature of the work relationship was far more intricate than a sim-
plistic right-to-work framework could capture. A large percentage of miners
organized their own work; they were paid for the coal they mined rather than
by the hour or the day, and they saw themselves as basically selling "their"
coal to the company. These miners hired their own helpers, whom they paid
out of the money they received for the coal. If they struck a particularly rich
vein, they expected to reap the benefits from their discovery. The companies,
desiring more control and better profits, were trying to reduce the number
of such "certified" or "contract" miners and to undermine the freedom of
the ones who remained by reneging on purchase or payment agreements.
In other words, the contest in the anthracite strike was in large part about
workers' control of the work process.[56]

The NAM's rhetoric of the closed shop, as well as the language of right
to work in articles like Baker's, sidestepped the question of control. It also
naturalized the power of the employer. All attention focused on the power
of the union; the power of a business to determine who had a right to work,
how, and when disappeared entirely from the picture. Though the closed
shop was not always explicitly present in every antiunion argument, it was
the concept that allowed employers to portray workers' organizations as tantamount to monopolistic "trusts" menacing the rights of individual workers
and employers, while depicting employees as simply trying their best to be
fair to all, despite being hampered by the encroachments of unions.

That employers' invention of the closed shop had successfully set the terms
of debate is perhaps clearest in the fact that over four decades after the launch
of the first open-shop campaign, the AFL was still trying to dispel the same
haze of tyranny that the language of the closed shop wafted over unions in
1903. In a debate in 1946, with the postwar drive to make the membership
requirement illegal accelerating, the AFL's legislative representative noted
that the attempt to "pin this odious phrase, closed shop, on organized labor"
had been a favorite employer tactic for decades; "there is nothing new in
this present drive," he insisted.[57] He was right. But that was little comfort
when the strategy was as efficacious in 1946 as it had been in 1903. The next
year, the Labor Management Relations Act of 1947, better known as the Taft-
Hartley Act, prohibited a number of key union practices, made some versions
of the closed or union shop illegal, and in many other ways gutted labor's
momentum so that labor was, as Nelson Lichtenstein notes, "forced into an
increasingly defensive posture."[58]

The language surrounding the exclusionism of the closed shop was also
malleable and adapted itself easily to new opportunities. In the early twentieth
century—in what is perhaps a measure of the ordinariness of racism among

both employers and unionists—neither side had found the other's racially discriminatory practices worth remarking upon. But once the civil rights movement had made race-based discrimination a politically salient issue, employers began to attack unions on the racially exclusionary impact (and/or intent) of the closed shop. These 1950s campaigns had real examples of union racism and segregation to draw upon, but they conveniently omitted to mention that the National Association for the Advancement of Colored People (NAACP), the chief civil rights organization, adamantly opposed prohibiting the union shop. Nor, of course, did they rehash employers' record on race alongside that of unions.[59]

The early twentieth-century open-shop drive continues to impact how American public discourse frames labor unions; indeed, it is remarkable how similar it is to the antiunion language that can be heard today. "Right to work" has replaced the "open shop" as the favored term, but otherwise practically everything remains the same. Such organizations as the National Right to Work Committee promote laws ("right-to-work laws") that prohibit requiring union membership as a condition of continued employment on the grounds that "compulsory unionism" is a violation of individual rights. Like the early twentieth-century open-shop advocates, the modern-day movement claims that it is neither for nor against unions, only against "abuses" that violate "the fundamental human right that the [right-to-work] principle represents." Like the early twentieth-century employer movement, the modern version poses as the defender of individual workers' rights: the National Right to Work Legal Defense Foundation, for example, offers free legal aid to "[assist] employees who are victimized because of their assertion of [the right-to-work] principle."[60] Like the earlier open-shop movement, it claims—in none-too-subtle terms—to be a movement of the little guy against the tyrannical organization. As the foundation put it in 2019, "The battle against Big Labor's multi-billion dollar forced dues political machine is the ultimate David versus Goliath fight."[61]

2 The Deep History of the Closed or Union Shop

What's money? A man is a success if he gets up in the mornin' and
gets to bed at night and in between he does what he wants to.
—Bob Dylan, quoted in *New York Daily News*, May 8, 1967

In one of the first editorials he wrote about the closed shop, American Federation of Labor president Samuel Gompers in 1903 insisted that the "right to
refuse to work with non-union men" was "fundamental," so much so that to
relinquish that right would "make slaves of the most skilled and competent
of American workmen."[1] By contrast, the newly militant group of employers
that had emerged at the turn of the twentieth century insisted that demanding
a closed shop was "attacking a fundamental human right" and "opposed to
natural justice."[2] It sapped American productivity, "[barred] . . . the American
boy from learning the trade of his choice," and entailed "coercion, threats,
and intimidation" to force workers into unions.[3]

Why such strong language? Because the struggle over the closed shop—the
practice of requiring union membership as a condition of employment—encapsulated radically different views of the nature of labor unions and their
place in the broader society. Many employers, both those vehemently opposed to unions and those engaged in negotiation with them, represented the
choice to join a union as a purely private, individual decision akin to religious
affiliation or membership in a fraternal society. To require membership, they
argued, was a violation of the individual's civil liberties: if union membership
as a condition of employment was a fair demand, then "it is fair to say that
you can or cannot work, because you are a Democrat or a Republican, because
you are a Mason or a Hibernian, because you are a Catholic or a Protestant,
or an infidel."[4] To most unions, though, the parallel with religious, political,
or fraternal affiliation was completely misplaced. The appropriate analogy,
they argued, was not private conviction but public government: unions were
governing institutions, and one did not have a choice about whether to be

subject to government. As a British unionist pointed out, government applied to everyone within its purview: "Imagine a case of a few men becoming residents of Chicago, and refusing to pay rates [property taxes], whilst they were enjoying the sanitary arrangements & other privileges of the City, made at the cost of rate payers generally. I ask would such refusal be tolerated 5 minutes?"[5]

Like city government, the closed or union shop had (and continues to have today) a pragmatic aim: it prevented "free riding," that is, getting all the advantages while taking on none of the work or risk. Such solidarity mattered because it made the union stronger and because it was fair: all who benefited from the changes brought about by the union had an obligation to do their part, whether by paying union dues or participating in strikes or other actions aiming to secure such changes. To ensure this, workers could and should be required to join the union if they were to remain employed at a unionized workplace. Employer resistance to the membership requirement had (and has) an equally down-to-earth aim: to undermine union power. Employers also rather obviously used the closed shop as a cudgel against all labor organizing, and despite occasional protestations to the contrary, employers generally implicitly admitted that they did not much care to relinquish any power to unions. They did not approve of unions' efforts to exercise power on the shop floor, set rules about output, set wages, or have a say about hiring and firing.[6] Nevertheless, the chasm between employers' and unionists' views of the membership requirement went deeper than practical self-interest. The demand for mandatory membership asserted a union right to govern the work relationship, the shop floor, union members, or all three at the same time. It was rooted in a vision of governance very different from the laissez-faire view that employer organizations took for granted.

The membership requirement grew out of and in sync with the transition from the artisan system of production into the "modern" employment relationship. This transformation, which took place roughly over the course of the nineteenth century, was more than a shift from small-scale workshops to larger factories. It fundamentally changed how people thought about production and employment. In the older vision, employment relations were shaped as much by ritual, tradition, and multiple fields of governance and obligation as by the market, whereas the emerging vision was driven by the logic of labor as a commodity, a thing that could be bought and sold by individuals in accordance with the laws of supply and demand. That transformation was one aspect of the development of a classical liberal vision that was beginning to separate the market from governance and to imagine an unmediated relationship between the individual and the state. Labor's demand for an essentially parallel government sat uneasily with the developing liberal vision; indeed, in many of the nineteenth-century court cases where labor unions were indicted as conspiracies, the demand for a right of rulemaking was at the heart of the case.

Like any large-scale shift, the transition from an artisan-based and less market-driven society into the more transactional world of freedom of contract, commodities, and laissez-faire was ambiguous, uneven, and very much contested, and all these concepts shifted around, pushed by technological, economic, and cultural changes. Thus, competing strands of thought and conflicting interpretations of free labor or freedom of contract meandered through the nineteenth century like a great muddy river. Which meaning of a concept got fished out of the river in the service of a legal or political argument often depended as much on power relations as on intellectual traditions.

This chapter traces the way in which the evolution of the membership requirement fits into the larger puzzle of shifting ideas about the market, governance, and democracy in the century or so after the American Revolution. The chapter starts by examining the evolution of the membership requirement in the context of the nineteenth-century changes in the world of craft work. Because it is important to understand how demands over control of work related to traditional ideas about the meanings of markets, on the one hand, and to the new ideals of popular government elevated in the American Revolution, on the other, the chapter next turns to considering what the regulation of economic activity looked like in eighteenth- and nineteenth-century America. The final section considers how craft workers' claims to governance came into conflict both with a liberal interpretation of the exclusive powers of the state and with developing ideas about the liberty of workers and employers to enter into contracts in the untrammeled market, and examines how workers responded to the changing economic and political circumstances of the nineteenth century.

Craft Rulemaking and the Origins of the Closed Shop

The traditional system of artisan production as it had evolved in late medieval and early modern Europe had involved (at least ideally) a period of apprenticeship, followed by a period of honing one's skills as a journeyman, and capped by setting up one's own shop as a master artisan. To be sure, that system was never perfect or unambiguous. Many artisans had various side hustles; uncertainty and conflict characterized the working lives of many journeymen at various points in history; and the transition to wage work began earlier and was drawn out to a far greater degree than is stereotypically acknowledged—indeed, wage work is now estimated to have formed a significant contribution to the income of a third of rural English households by 1350.[7] Still, the craft system of production remained pervasive in the early nineteenth century; it also remained small-scale enough that the masters of many workshops were not that far removed from their workers. In 1820s New York City, for instance, the majority of workshops were tiny, with perhaps three or four journeymen and apprentices per workshop. While these craft firms were by no means indifferent or immune to economic forces, neither did they fully embrace a supply-and-demand view of proper wages. What journeymen were paid was at least in part dictated by established customs of a "just price," a somewhat vague but venerable principle that infused economic transactions with moral significance, aiming to curb greed and balance the reasonable needs of the payer and the payee.[8]

These older values persisted even as the intensifying market competition of the early nineteenth century propelled manufacturing toward larger workshops and pushed master artisans to become more employer-like and entrepreneurial (what Sean Wilentz terms "craft entrepreneurs"). In heavier trades like shipbuilding and leather tanning, in printing and construction, and in the production of clothing and shoes—where the new factories in New England set price standards far below traditional artisan workshop production—the opportunities and pressures of the market led masters to make more use of low-paid outwork and apprentice labor over skilled journeymen. To journeymen, this appeared as stagnation in the traditional progression from apprentice to master: journeymen found it harder and harder to set up shop on their own, and in response, journeymen's organizations emerged to protect the livelihoods of their members.[9]

In accordance with traditions of just price, protecting the members' livelihood took the form of defining a scale of wages dictated less by perceptions about the market value of one's labor than by ideas about the standard of living proper to a self-respecting, skilled artisan and about the exclusive rights of craftsmen to the practice of the craft. Journeymen's organizations, although a new development around the turn of the nineteenth century, drew on much older practices of craft regulation. Even in colonial America, following British tradition, craftsmen directed petitions to municipal and other authorities to keep newcomers, especially ones who had not completed traditional apprenticeships, from practicing a particular trade in their city.[10] In a way, the logic of the organizations of skilled artisans was the logic of the cartel: we have something that there is a demand for (our skill), and we agree among ourselves not to sell it for less than what we perceive to be a reasonable price. Yet the parallel of the cartel misrepresents the spirit of the organizations: rather than mere monetary calculations, these organizations were animated by a sense of the dignity of the craft and the kinship of those who mastered it. To refuse to work for less than the scale was an act of protecting the craft and its traditions as much as it was an act of economic calculation. How would the skill of the craft be preserved if the craft was cheapened by half-trained workers? Conversely, who would agree to be in training for years if even fully skilled men were working for a pittance? Without pride in the craft and knowledge of its various aspects, as well as the process of learning from one's elders that created both, what would be the basis of a shared work culture? Thus, while such measures as restricting apprenticeships and insisting on full training had the (intended) effect of limiting the labor supply, they also ensured the production of well-rounded workmen who were welded together by both socialization and skill.[11]

Early defenses of the wage scale often employed a fairly subtle form of collective action that relied on workers' semitacit mutual agreement about rules. Skilled craftsmen were relatively few in number, and if a large enough percentage of them joined together to uphold a scale of wages, an employer who refused to observe the scale would soon find himself in trouble. Without ever needing to make an explicit show of collective power, the craft society could enforce what it considered the proper wage because skilled workers were hard to come by. Instead of striking, the society offered its members unemployment benefits that were collectible if the member chose to quit work in a shop that did not pay the scale. Buoyed by that guarantee, the craftsmen could engage in what Sidney Webb and Beatrice Webb called the "strike in detail": one by one, workers would simply quit the employment of a master who did not observe the rates. If the craft was well organized, finding new permanent workers would prove impossible for the master; craftsmen would take up employment with him but quit within a week or two. Frustrated with the constant turnover, the employer would soon get the message and hasten to comply with union regulations. According to the Webbs, sometimes workers could make powerful use of this weapon to enforce the union scale and union rules nearly universally. Since it required no public collective action, it also shielded the union from public opprobrium.[12]

However, for the strike in detail to be feasible, the workers had to be unusually well positioned: the craft had to require significant skill, and the craft organization needed to be exceptionally wealthy and cohesive. Moreover, while a craft society offering an unemployment benefit to its members made it possible for them to refuse to work at less than scale, it could not ensure that the members would choose to do so. What if no "fair" work was available, and one's circumstances made work, even work at less than the scale, imperative? What if enough craftsmen for whatever reason thought it inadvisable to insist on the union scale? Unless the organization had the power to institute some real consequences for workers who undercut others, it would eventually become unable to enforce the scale.

To be sure, a member of the society who ignored the rules could be expelled. But what of it? What were the consequences of being expelled to be? One would, of course, lose access to the unemployment benefits offered by the organization, but in reasonably good times, at least, that might not be an overwhelming consideration. One might face the censure of one's peers, but perhaps that was an acceptable price to pay to get food on the table. To up the ante, as it were, the craft societies formalized the censure into a full-scale ostracism that attempted to ensure that undercutting the society would not be worth it in the long run. This ostracism could be very effective in prodding craftsmen to abide by a union rule or a strike demand. Among the Philadelphia cordwainers (makers of new shoes), for example, a craftsman who fell out of favor with the journeymen's organization might at best "hobble along for a while," and thus when the organization called a strike in 1805, even the large number of workers who had voted against the strike walked out and stayed out for weeks to avoid being "scabbed."[13] Such ostracism was the predecessor of the modern closed shop.

At first, union rules aimed at keeping the existing membership in line. In the early nineteenth century, they focused mainly on renegade members, that is, craftsmen who had been members of the union but had ignored or flouted its rules about the wage scale or some other aspect of practice. As punishment for having betrayed his fellows, a renegade member would be shunned: the members of the organization would refuse to work with him. If an employer hired such a "rat" or "scab," he might find that he had gained one employee but lost five others who quit in protest. Or, since the craft organizations were often the means of transmitting news about the need for craftsmen in a particular shop, the renegade member might never get as far as offering his services, since the news about an opening would simply never reach him.[14]

But what of workers who had never been members of the organization? Did the organization's jurisdiction extend to them, or could an employer freely hire skilled craftsmen and pay them below the scale as long as they had never been members of a craft organization? It seems that practices varied on this score: the cigarmakers, for instance, appear to have required their members to refuse employment at less than scale but not to have objected to working with nonmembers even if these were paid below scale. More common, though, was to only allow members to work at shops where everyone (member or not) was paid the union scale of wages; all other employers were "unfair" and therefore off-limits to society members. This was the practice of, for example, Buffalo tailors in the 1820s and New York tailors in the 1830s, as well as Baltimore printers in the 1830s.[15]

Requiring the employer to pay the union scale to all skilled craftsmen was all well and good when the union could set the scale. If, however, the number of nonmembers became too large, how would the union retain the power to enforce the scale? Eventually, this problem led to the demand that all skilled craftsmen be members of the union. Most organizations of journeymen printers, for example, switched sometime in the 1830s from simply requiring the payment of the scale and the nonemployment of "unfair" (renegade) workers to requiring that all printers accepting employment in a fair shop become members. By 1833 the rules of the New York Typographical Society dictated that its members "inform strangers who come into the office where they are employed, of the established wages, and also of the existence of the association and of the necessity of becoming members." Similarly, the 1842 constitution of the Baltimore Typographical Society required every printer working in the city to join the society within a month of beginning work; if he did not, the society members working at the shop where he was employed were required to refuse to work with him.[16] By the time of the Civil War, at least the printers, cordwainers, tailors, and cigarmakers had experimented with some form of a closed shop on at least a local level, though often customs varied from city to city or even from shop to shop. Usually, they were tied to specific circumstances rather than taking the form of categorical rules.[17]

It is impossible to ascertain exactly how widespread closed-shop practices were among early craft unionists and what precise form they took. This is partly because too few constitutions and minutes have survived and partly because the existing constitutions are sometimes vague. That vagueness signals both the degree to which these societies saw themselves as hewing to tradition and the precarity of their position in the broader society. Because the societies believed they were maintaining the traditional standards of the trade, even extant minutes might simply refer to maintaining the "customs of the trade" or a similar formulation; the customs were assumed to be clear to the members, so why state the obvious? In addition, secrecy itself was a time-honored element of craft culture. It was an essential component of the cementing of an exclusive craft identity into which apprentices were initiated and journeymen bound, and it enabled craft societies to present a united front even when internal dissension roiled.[18] In an often-hostile society, secrecy was also a practical safeguard. Employers and the broader society frequently frowned upon practices like restricting output and refusing to work with nonmembers, so it might be better to refer to them discreetly, if at all. Indeed, spelling them out might cost dearly: labor unions in the nineteenth century were regularly prosecuted as conspiracies in restraint of trade, and in these cases, the constitutions of journeymen's societies were sometimes used as evidence that they were, as one nineteenth-century prosecutor put it, "anti-republican, tyrannical, illegal, [and] despotic."[19]

The membership requirement was no panacea: changing markets and new technology put pressure on perceived traditional craft standards and on who exactly should be admitted to membership. Members of the craft organizations may have envisioned themselves as the legitimate representatives and upholders of craft traditions and the workers working below scale as intruders who were an aberration from the norm. Changing conditions, however, meant that the number of such "aberrant" workers sometimes grew large enough to influence organizing the craft. For example, when war orders during the Civil War increased demand at the same time that many men were called to the Union army, New Jersey hatters found themselves unable to supply all the labor required by employers. The employers therefore hired large numbers of workers who had not completed the hatters' strict apprenticeship requirements. Faced with being swamped by the new workers, the New Jersey local decided that the only remedy was to "whitewash" the workers already engaged by the employers, that is, accept them as members despite their lack of proper apprenticeships. That way, the shops would remain "fair" and the union would preserve its standing in the shop. Other locals, however, saw this as a betrayal of the trade, and the issue eventually caused the silk hatters to walk out of the recently created national union and establish a competing one, leading to decades of rivalry.[20]

The development of the closed shop, then, was a gradual process, one that took place against the backdrop of the rapidly changing economy of the nineteenth century. Its origins lay as much in pride in the craft and its traditions as they did in economic considerations, and in its early forms it was more akin to what modern professional organizations see as their ethos: the creation of rules and regulations to maintain professional standards among the members of the profession. From the earliest years, craft societies and unions incorporated practices well beyond the closed shop that indicated their image of themselves as a form of (self-)government. For example, Wilentz notes that craft societies administered mutual aid like sickness and burial funds, drafted meticulous rules about decorous behavior at union meetings, and might fine members whose workmanship was shoddy.[21] But pressures of craft dilution and market growth led the societies to focus more and more on the employer. Eventually, craft societies began to equate a fair employer with an employer who only employed union workers. The reason behind that was not an irrational prejudice against "independent" workers who did not wish to join a union, as employers often claimed. The practice had a clear logic of governance. Even if the shop only had one skilled craft worker who was not a union member, and even if that worker was paid the union scale, maintaining the principle of the craft workers' ability to set the wage scale and govern the craft's standards of skills required that union members force the employer to discharge the nonunion worker if the worker refused to join up. The logic of the closed shop was the logic of the slippery slope: if the principle was not maintained, the union scale and craft governance might quickly become unenforceable.

Markets, Morals, and Regulation

Craftsmen's efforts to regulate their craft reflected a traditional view of society that saw the profit motive not as a justification unto itself but as a disruptive force to be controlled. They, along with many mainstream thinkers, echoed a long-established understanding that unregulated pursuit of self-interest corroded the fundamental idea of society. As E. P. Thompson has famously argued, in the eighteenth century both folk and elite understandings of economic exchanges reflected a "moral economy" where the impact that wages and prices had on the society was at least as relevant a consideration as the abstract forces of supply and demand. It was assumed that wages and prices should be regulated and that people had a duty to abide by rather than skirt such regulations; they were part and parcel of civilized society. A British pamphlet from 1768 put the matter pointedly: to do as one pleased with one's property was not "the liberty of a citizen, or of one who lives under the protection of any community; it is rather the liberty of a savage; therefore he who avails himself thereof, deserves not that protection, the power of Society affords."[22]

The idea that civilization entailed regulation of economic activity for the common good and civic health of the nation was widespread both in Europe and in the American colonies on the eve of the American Revolution. It persisted well into the nineteenth century. In some ways, it got added force from the revolution, as critiques drawing on custom and tradition meshed with the fraying of hierarchy born out of colonial realities and the rhetoric of the revolution. Appealing to tradition did not preclude innovation; as Thompson points out, many eighteenth-century protests used the language of custom to claim entirely new rights, besides asserting traditional ones.[23] Such mixing of custom and new rights was common in the America of the revolutionary era as well, both in the elite discourses where the "rights of Englishmen" morphed into "natural rights" and in folk understandings where new ideas about liberty and popular government mixed with older English ideas about the right of the people to "regulate" their government through protest when necessary.[24]

During the lead-up to the American Revolution, arguments that economic inequality and profiteering undermined proper governance were advanced by colonists throughout the length of the Eastern Seaboard. After independence, ordinary people continued to draw on the revolution's language of liberty to make claims of self-governance that entailed curbing wealth and the power it could confer. Famous protests, such as Shays's Rebellion in 1780s Massachusetts and the Pennsylvania Regulation of the 1790s (better known as the Whiskey Rebellion), expressed a widespread sentiment that "moneyed men" possessed too much influence over legislatures and policy and used it to line their own pockets. Both the Massachusetts and the Pennsylvania protests, as well as many other protests and petitions in other states in the 1780s and 1790s, insisted that if allowed to continue, the power of the wealthy would lead to exacerbated economic inequality and threaten the very fabric of the republic. As a Connecticut assemblyman put it in 1787, "Continuing a popular government without a good degree of equality among the people as to their property" was simply not possible.[25]

The ideas and ferment of the revolution had percolated through the artisan community; for one, artisans often read and owned books. It is therefore perhaps unsurprising that artisans drew on both the revolution's republican ideals and "customary rights" to insist on craft governance.[26] However, the persistence of ideas that prioritized a moral economy over a liberal market-driven one reached beyond farmer or artisan ranks to those responsible for making and enforcing the laws of the new nation. As William Novak has shown, an insistence on society over markets characterized the United States well into the nineteenth century. Illustrating his point with long lists of state laws regulating inspection of foodstuffs, the duties and rights of servants, the obligations of debtors and creditors, weights and measures, offensive trades, nuisances, and many other aspects of ordinary life, Novak argues that the ideology that underpinned nineteenth-century American public governance was not laissez-faire but a "common law vision of a well-regulated society" in which the state's prerogative of curbing individual and property rights for the general welfare was taken as a given.[27]

Perhaps least surprisingly, states passed laws to protect public morals or public health, enacting rigorous regulations designed to guarantee the quality of products. For example, an 1817 Maryland statute governing pickled or salted fish, cited by Novak as typical, lavished over 150 words merely on defining what kind of a barrel is acceptable as a container for such fish. More broadly, though, legislators and courts did not see economic activity as divorced from the state's duty to use its power to bring about desirable social and public ends. Indeed, some states made it illegal to sell anything at all for profit unless one first obtained a "license to trade." Similarly, several American cities in the antebellum period allowed the sale of provisions only at the designated public marketplace, built and supervised by the city; persons caught selling provisions outside the market could be fined and have their goods confiscated. The purpose of such regulation was the same as it had been in early modern England: to ensure a fair price and prevent gouging or forestalling (in the older sense of this verb: to buy up goods before they reached the public market in order to make a profit, an offense under traditional English law because it was considered to result in excessive profits). Such regulations were occasionally challenged—with increasing frequency in the years just before the Civil War—but were usually upheld by lower-court judges and by state supreme courts as unremarkable and well within the tradition of local governance. Aware that other opinions on the matter existed, judges nevertheless frequently decided in favor of a version of a moral economy, as demonstrated in an 1841 ruling on the assize of bread (a law regulating the price, weight, and quality of loaves of bread) by the Alabama Supreme Court. "Whatever doubts have been thrown over the question by the theories of political economists," the court declared, "it would seem that experience has shown that this great end [urban bread supply] is better secured by licensing a sufficient number of bakers and by an assize of bread, than by leaving it to the voluntary acts of individuals."[28] Nineteenth-century America, then, was shot through with ideas that placed society over markets and regulation over "voluntary acts of individuals." The reach of such ideas extended beyond the plebeian strata into the middling and upper ranks of society.

Placing the needs of the society over those of individuals could, of course, be quite coercive. Kate Masur has cogently pointed out that although local governments regulating the nineteenth-century market might commend themselves to modern progressives' eyes, their use of police powers to maintain a "well-regulated society" also took forms that are hard to stomach these days. Their regulatory practices rested on an ideology that emphasized good public order over individual rights. That ideology might indeed rein in the excesses of the marketplace. It was, however, the same ideology that regulated "outsiders" to the community: it asked vagrants or prostitutes or jugglers to post bonds guaranteeing good behavior, and it required free African Americans to register with county clerks. It was also the same ideology that accepted slavery. As Masur notes, "The great moral evil of slavery found ample justification within the 'well-regulated society,'" and it is by no means clear whether it could have been dislodged without the growth of a different vision of individual rights.[29]

The potential for liberty (and equality) through collective regulation vied with visions of liberty through individual rights and the liberty to use one's property "free from the restraints of collective regulation."[30] Some of this tension existed within workers' movements themselves, as Christopher Tomlins argues. For example, some activists in the Working Men's Party in the 1830s expressed doubts about the wisdom of advocating state-sponsored and state-controlled education because such advocacy clashed with the critique of monopoly. Other worker activists, though, argued that one needed to pay attention to who benefited from reform, not to abstract principles. Monopolies of the wealthy were evil because they by definition benefited a small minority of people. Workers' combinations, however, were a different matter altogether. Indeed, it was preposterous to claim that they could threaten the public good— to all practical intents and purposes, they *were* the public good. As Ely Moore, the president of the General Trades' Union of New York (and soon to be a congressman), put it in 1833, it was silly to claim that "it is setting a dangerous precedent for journeymen to combine for the purpose of coercing a compliance with their terms." After all, these were organizations that represented the people—the workingmen were the majority. Dangers lurked in "an alliance of the crafty, designing and intriguing few," not in "a general effort on the part of the people to improve and exalt their condition."[31]

Moore had a point. Yet his own attitudes also underline Masur's contention that the vision of a well-regulated society, with its emphasis on tradition and the collective public good, implicitly drew a boundary that left many on the outside. Again, the issue of slavery is the most revealing. Though antislavery sentiment was widespread in the General Trades' Union and the labor movement in general, it had limits: if allowing slavery was the price for the "public good" of maintaining the Union without disruption, then so be it. Many, including Moore, also worried that abolishing slavery would flood the labor market and undermine the standing of white workers. Like many other Democratic politicians of his era, he thought that the concerns of white workingmen unequivocally took precedence over the plight of nonwhite slaves. Not for the first or the last time, "the people" did not encompass quite *all* of the people.[32]

The quandaries of what liberty meant and whose liberty was of concern is particularly clear in the different and contradictory interpretations of "free labor." One meaning of free labor derived from classical political economy, where the concept portrayed the laborer as a free agent in the marketplace and labor as comparable to coal, wheat, or any other commodity. In the nineteenth-century American context, the presence and prominence of slavery strengthened the freedom that such a vision of labor seemed to embody: the liberty of the free worker to sell his labor to the highest bidder seemed an obvious antithesis of the slave's very person being sold.[33] Abolitionist rhetoric enshrined the liberty to make contracts in the marketplace; that, after all, was something the slave conspicuously lacked. Against the unfreedom of being owned by another person, the abolitionists set the freedom to choose how and with whom to contract for the sale of one's labor, regulated not by personal bondage but by the supply and demand of the market. The abolitionist William Jay explained that when the slave became free, "labor is no longer the badge of his servitude . . . for it is *voluntary*. For the first time in his life he is party to a contract. . . . [T]he value of negro labor, like all other vendible commodities, will be regulated by supply and demand."[34]

The fact of slavery also highlighted that curbing the risks involved in trying to survive by one's labor amounted to limiting one's freedom. Who, after all, would argue that enslaved men and women were better off with the (at least theoretically) assured sustenance and basic care under slavery than with the freedom of the marketplace, even as the latter provided no guarantees whatsoever?[35] That freedom of the marketplace, many abolitionists argued, required cooperation rather than conflict between capital and labor. Thus, for the abolitionist Wendell Phillips, labor and capital formed "a pair of scissors," indispensable to each other.[36] Labor unions, many antislavery advocates argued, only disrupted this liberty and harmony and were coercive in their claim to regulate the right of a worker to dispose of his labor as he saw fit. The orator and abolitionist Anna Dickinson, for instance, censured unions for requiring membership and objecting to the employer paying a nonmember more than a unionist; that was exercising "absolute power . . . more tyranical [*sic*] than a European despotism."[37]

Where middle-class abolitionists emphasized the freedom of the marketplace, however, another meaning of free labor explicitly rejected the idea that seeing labor as a commodity could confer freedom. This meaning, derived from the republican tradition and developed further in the post–Civil War years, saw employment in the service of another as "wage slavery" that cut into a worker's independence as a citizen. As a "vendible commodity," labor was of a special sort: it could not be separated from the laborer. Because the commodity that a laborer was actually selling was time, it was also eminently perishable. To support themselves, workers had to sell labor day after day for the duration of their lives. According to worker intellectuals like George

McNeill, the labor reformer and Knights of Labor leader, this amounted to a significant degree of unfreedom. One might have the choice to change masters, as it were, but if one were forced to continue to sell one's labor to survive, one could not choose to *not have* a master. Thus, since labor could not be separated from one's person, permanent wage work essentially meant selling oneself for the duration of one's life.[38] Real freedom and independence, in the view of many workers and small proprietors, resided in property ownership and self-employment, not in the liberty to contract for wage work. These ideas persisted beyond the Civil War. Analyzing testimony at the congressional hearings on the causes of the 1870s economic depression, Rosanne Currarino shows that "the Jeffersonian ideal of the small property owner as the moral center of the republic" resonated deeply among the craftsmen and small businessmen whom the depression had hit hard. They used that ideal to argue that the government should facilitate the path to property ownership by grants of money, distributions of land, or other means.[39]

Neither market regulation nor the idea of free labor offered any straightforward message regarding how to best secure a society in which all could have a dignified existence. The economic visions of the nineteenth century were not cleanly separated and opposing positions; rather, they were entangled in each other. Thus, for example, as the ideology of the Republican Party developed in the 1850s, it drew on ideas about the liberty of contract *and* on ideas about collective regulation to ensure the continued viability of independent producers. It emphasized class harmony and individual responsibility for upward mobility even as it critiqued the excesses of wealth and the power of corporations. It presented the North as economically and socially superior to the South because it was founded on free labor—efficient, intelligent, and productive men making good use of their faculties to develop the country. But it also reacted to the dislocation of economic depressions, such as the one following the Panic of 1857, by reproaching individual excesses and counseling those affected to frugality and hard work. In some ways, the contradictions in these ideas stemmed from the constant and rapid change of the economy. If upward mobility through small entrepreneurship indeed was within everyone's reach, then it was no hypocrisy to ask that people attempt to reach for it or even to argue that regulation would only hamper their ability to do so. But if economic change was fast making a whole class of workers into permanent wage laborers with no hope of independent proprietorship, matters were rather different. Collective action by workers seemed to imply that the latter was closer to the reality than the former; often, the reaction of middle-class Republicans was to attack the collective action rather than revise their ideas about what the realities were.[40]

Whose Rules, Whose Power?

Workers navigated the marshy terrain of ideas about markets, free labor, and governance as best they could. Their specific position in the society and the labor force shaped their interpretations of these ideas. Thus, the craftsmen whose skills continued to be in demand even as the ground under them shifted tended to continue to emphasize control of the craft. Meanwhile, workers whose industrial or labor market position gave them less skill-based leverage with employers might gravitate toward broader solidarities or more far-reaching demands for social change. All, however, repeatedly butted against a skepticism in the nonworker ranks of society about workers' right to claims of independent decision-making, let alone collective governance.

One institutional setting where this suspicion against working people's claims to independent rulemaking was prominently on display in the nineteenth century was the judicial system. Labor unions were frequently prosecuted as "conspiracies in restraint of trade," and these conspiracy cases repeatedly took issue with precisely the thing that craft societies considered their main function: regulating the craft. The very first of these cases (*Commonwealth v. Pullis*, 1806), in which the first known organization of workers in America, the Federal Society of Journeymen Cordwainers of Philadelphia, was indicted for conspiracy, explicitly condemned the attempts of the journeymen to govern their trade. This the court viewed as encroaching upon the privileges of the state: there could not be, "besides our state legislature, a new legislature consisting of journeymen shoemakers."[41]

A crucial part of the case was that the journeymen had joined together not merely to set a price on their *own* labor (though that was bad enough); they also meant to make rules binding other shoemakers. They had presumed to "regulate the whole trade," causing hardship for those who were forced out of work unless they joined the organization and abided by its wage demands. This, the prosecution contended, was "the chief charge in the indictment." It showed that the aim of the case was "to secure the rights of each individual to obtain and enjoy the price he fixes upon his own labour," that is, not to be bound by the wages set by the journeymen's association but to be allowed to work for whatever he could get for his labor. The prosecution, in other words, set itself up to defend the rights of workers unaffiliated with the journeymen's association, expressing its horror of the "fetters" that the association put on independent journeymen by demanding that they abide by its rules.[42]

The defense of independent journeymen was a constant refrain in the conspiracy cases; indeed, the case that is famous for overturning previous court interpretations of all craft organizations as conspiracies, *Commonwealth v. Hunt* (brought first in the Municipal Court of the City of Boston in 1840) was brought not by employers but by a journeyman. The journeyman, Jeremiah Horne, alleged that his employer, Isaac Wait, had discharged him at the instigation of the Boston Journeymen Bootmakers' Society.[43] Horne had been a member of the Bootmakers' Society, but the society claimed that he had broken its rules and slandered it, and it imposed fines on him for these offenses. Horne refused to pay the fines and therefore was no longer a member of the society in good standing. The constitution of the Bootmakers' Society (adopted in 1835) stated that all journeymen in the city were expected to join if invited. If a shop where a majority belonged to the society employed a journeyman who was not a member of the society, the members of the society employed at that shop would be expected to quit. Wait, who knew the society's rules, therefore discharged Horne rather than risk other workers walking out.[44]

The society had not threatened a strike against Wait; as its constitution stated, its rules applied in the main to its members. Nor is it clear that Horne suffered economically: on Wait's advice, he had sought work at another shop (although he was later let go for lack of available work).[45] The prosecution, however, insisted that "to prevent a man from working lawfully, as he pleases, and for whom he pleases, is an invasion of the liberty of the subject" and that the society's actions were "tyrannical" because they required all journeymen in the trade to submit to the society's "dictation and rules" or risk being shut out of employment.[46]

On appeal to the Massachusetts Supreme Court, *Commonwealth v. Hunt* was decided in favor of the Bootmakers' Society on the grounds that the society did not force anyone to become a member. However, several cases in the latter half of the nineteenth century repeatedly condemned any agreements between employer and employees that limited the individual rights of workmen by requiring them to join a union, as well as agreements that limited the rights of the employer to hire whom he pleased.[47] Throughout the nineteenth century, the courts' supposed defense of workers and employers from union dictation was echoed by the commercial classes. For example, in the 1830s the editor of the *New York Journal of Commerce*, David Hale, argued that British employer combinations' success in breaking up unions had been "a blessing most devoutly to be desired, chiefly for sake of the workmen themselves," because unions forced otherwise contented workers to leave their positions and thus attempted to subvert the laws of supply and demand.[48]

The claims of unions to governance were, then, in constant tension with the state's claims to the exclusive power of formal coercion, the development of ideas about liberty of contract, an expanding faith in the impartial laws of supply and demand, and a growing emphasis on personal rather than communal assumption of risk. Collective protections increasingly became interpreted as collective shackles, and true freedom was construed to reside in individual decision-making in the impersonal marketplace. These ideas extended to aspects of the workplace beyond the specific question of union rules. For example, in the 1842 *Farwell v. Boston and Worcester R.R. Corp.* decision, the Massachusetts Supreme Court decided against Nicholas Farwell, an engineman who had sued his employer for compensation for his right hand, destroyed in a workplace accident. The decision rested on the definition of risk: according to the court, Farwell had personally assumed a risk in accepting employment, and that risk was already factored into his wage. Like Farwell's labor itself, the risk was his personal "property," as it were—a commodity for which the railroad corporation compensated him in the premium it paid for his work.

The court's rewriting of the rules in *Farwell* echoed the development of the ideology of free labor as the sale of a commodity through a contract entered into in a free marketplace. Farwell's suit had rested on an older legal construction of the employment relationship, that between a master and a servant. The difference in power relations meant that a servant was expected to submit to a master's will, but a master assumed some responsibility for the actions and well-being of his servant. Farwell's accident was caused by a fellow worker, and so he appealed to a common-law principle of respondeat superior (let the master answer), which extended the master's responsibility to damage caused by his underlings. The court, however, very explicitly rejected this older construction and affirmed the interpretation of employment as a commodity exchange by free individuals, neither of whom was responsible for the other. In fact, in finding legal precedent, the court drew on the law of maritime insurance and equated Farwell's labor with a ship's cargo—a physical, tangible commodity. Just as a cargo could be destroyed, the "commodity" of Farwell's productive labor had been destroyed or damaged in the accident, and thus Farwell would suffer a monetary loss—the wages he could no longer expect. But that was not his employer's problem.[49]

In the decades after the Civil War, court decisions affirming the primacy of the liberty of contract became ever more dominant, and liberty of contract was frequently used to strike down attempts at legislative regulation of work or wages. For example, courts ruled against laws prohibiting cigar manufacturing in tenement houses. They also ruled against requiring that workers be paid in cash rather than in scrip (vouchers redeemable in company-owned stores that generally charged well above market prices). In both of these, the courts' logic was that such laws violated the employer's and the employee's right to contract on such terms as they saw fit.[50]

Yet the development of ideas about labor as a commodity or workers as free individuals entering into a contract between equals was hardly straightforward or unambiguous, let alone philosophically consistent. Decisions emphasizing the liberty of contract were amply counterbalanced by decisions reaffirming the older doctrines of master and servant. Even as courts refused, as in *Farwell*, to apply the master-servant doctrine to hold the master (employer) to account, they did not balk at affirming the servant's (worker's) subordination and obligations. Thus, even in the post–Civil War era, courts routinely convicted union organizers on the grounds that it was "a familiar and well established doctrine of the law upon the relation of master and servant, that one who entices away a servant . . . may be held liable in damages therefor" if doing so broke the "servant's" contract.[51] In other words, which principles applied and how could depend on who was in the dock as much as on legal precedent. While legal discourse mattered, so did power; as David Montgomery has pointed out, "Employers' awesome power [in the nineteenth century] would have existed whatever the discourse with which it was sanctioned."[52]

Workers trying to gain power over their working lives reacted in a variety of ways to the constraints of legal doctrine and the shifting industrial and economic landscape. Rank-and-file workers and labor leaders drew different and sometimes conflicting conclusions about how one should go about demanding a worker voice in the new context. Should one emphasize the need to maintain economic independence and craft governance? Or should one devise a new strategy to respond to the changing realities of industrial scale, of unskilled labor, of state expansion? Some hewed to the older interpretation of free labor as the opposite of not just slavery but also wage labor: they argued that a worker who was free was an independent producer, not an employee, and that the system of wage labor supported a consolidation of power and wealth that represented a fundamental threat to popular government. Therefore, worker strategy should defend workers' political and economic position as an inseparable whole. Others accepted, more or less, that wage labor had come to stay. Therefore, workers should focus on raising the level of wages, securing control on the shop floor, and building power through organizing the craft or trade.

The manifesto of the Knights of Labor (KOL)—the era's premier labor organization, founded in 1869, reaching a membership of nearly fifty thousand by 1883, and soon to explode (if briefly) to more than three-quarters of a million—insisted that there was "an irresistible conflict between the wage-system of labor and republican system of government."[53] As Leon Fink has argued, the organization drew on a set of deeply held cultural values that emphasized "productive work, civic responsibility, education, a wholesome family life, temperance, and self-improvement" but insisted that both the marketplace and the rather placid-sounding cultural values needed to serve the needs of human beings embedded in a community, not empower impersonal market forces or grasping individualism.[54] To pursue the goal of a "cooperative commonwealth" of producers, the Knights aimed for a broad-based strategy that incorporated politics, education, cooperatives, and workplace organizing of different kinds. The organization welcomed into membership a wide range of people—craft workers as well as unskilled workers, shopkeepers, and other small entrepreneurs who were supportive of its goals. It excluded only those it deemed to engage in no useful, productive labor (such as bankers and lawyers). Unlike the craft unions, the KOL was also open to organizing both on an occupational basis and along some other continuum such as industry or an even broader identity such as "producers." Thus, local KOL assemblies were of two types: trade assemblies organized around a craft or occupation, and mixed assemblies, with boundaries defined by the local itself and open to a mix of occupations and skill levels.[55]

The American Federation of Labor, which was formed in 1886 as an umbrella organization of mainly craft unions, often clashed with the Knights over strategy and emphasis. An important point of disagreement was the issue of "dual unionism," that is, whether it was permissible for workers to belong to multiple labor unions at the same time and whether multiple organizations representing the same group of workers should be allowed to exist. The AFL insisted that dual unionism hurt labor's organizational basis because unions representing the same occupational group might compete with each other for members and otherwise come into conflicts that employers could then exploit. An especially contentious point was that workers expelled from an AFL-affiliated craft union for violating the union's rules might be able to enroll in a competing KOL assembly, which undermined the AFL union's governance of the trade; the ability to sanction renegade members was, after all, a key feature of the idea of craft governance. The AFL's leadership also tended to consider the KOL too undefined in its goals and insufficiently cognizant of the necessity for tight and carefully thought out institutional forms, while the Knights viewed the AFL's craft-based trade unionism as too narrow.[56]

If philosophical and practical conflicts formed a rift between the leaders of the KOL and those of the AFL, those differences were often less prominent among the rank and file. Individual unions and locals that formed under the umbrella of each organization, as well as the workers who joined them, often had their own ideas about what constituted legitimate strategy or goals for organized labor. Even if they joined an AFL-affiliated craft union or one of the occupationally based railroad brotherhoods, workers did not necessarily align themselves with the leadership's doubts about broad-based labor politics or opposition to dual unionism. Similarly, even if they joined a KOL assembly, they did not necessarily share the leadership's official aversion to strikes. Moreover, the leadership's differences were neither immutable nor all-encompassing. For all its "business unionism"—an emphasis on effective and reasonably well-funded union structures, a focus on the workplace rather than politics, and a rejection of "theorizing"—the AFL drew heavily on the older craft ideals that had animated artisan republicanism and that echoed in the philosophy of the Knights of Labor as well. Similarly, despite the Knights' emphasis on a more capacious solidarity and a broader philosophy than that of the AFL, the local and district assemblies affiliated with it could engage in hard-nosed and pragmatic trade union–style organizing and bargaining; they also sometimes made use of the closed-shop requirement.[57]

Unity on the best strategy to advance labor's cause remained elusive, even within the AFL's own ranks. By the early 1890s the AFL had largely eclipsed the Knights of Labor. That did not, however, mean that key questions had been resolved. Even within the AFL fold, unionists continued to vehemently argue about such matters as the advisability of independent labor politics, the extent to which the goals of capital and labor were fundamentally incompatible, or the proper role of the state in the quest to improve the position of the working class. Even AFL president (and quintessential business unionism proponent) Samuel Gompers deployed in those years language that was, in Shelton Stromquist's felicitous phrase, "resolutely ambiguous" regarding producerist hopes of the eventual demise of the wages system.[58]

The early 1890s offered some heady prospects for broadening the base and strategy of working-class activism. On the railroads, a new industrially based union, the American Railway Union (ARU), had won an important victory in 1893 and was growing rapidly, largely because it had seemingly finally found a formula to build solidarity among a large swath of railroad workers, whose organizing had long been complicated by divisions between skilled and unskilled workers. This mattered, since railroads were massive businesses that together employed hundreds of thousands of workers.[59] On the political front, the rise of the Farmers' Alliance in the South and West had created what Lawrence Goodwyn called the "largest democratic mass movement in American history."[60] By the early 1890s the movement was busily building a third party intended to bring together farmers and urban workers in a "People's Party" (also known as the Populists).[61] Politics was also debated among the trade unions: the American Federation of Labor's 1894 convention considered an extensive "Political Programme" that originally included an affirmation of independent labor politics, as well as a plank calling for "collective ownership by the people of all the means of production and distribution."[62]

Much of the momentum of these developments, however, collapsed quickly. The "Political Programme," despite its apparently significant popularity among the AFL's membership, was defeated, and while the AFL in the coming years continued to push for specific legislative goals, it did not embrace a labor party or a broad labor politics.[63] The People's Party failed to build a strong alliance of farmers and workers, and in the election of 1896 it endorsed the Democrat William Jennings Bryan rather than fielding a third-party presidential candidate. Bryan's campaign hardly lived up to the Populists' broad democratic agenda, though it was enough of a threat to elite businessmen to drive many of them from the Democratic to the Republican Party and to galvanize them to mount a massive campaign that secured the victory to the Republican William McKinley.[64] Meanwhile, successes that People's Party candidates (some elected by biracial coalitions) had garnered in the South were met with harsh repression from the lily-white Democratic establishment.[65] The new American Railway Union was undone in a failed strike and boycott. In the summer of 1894 workers making Pullman sleeping cars went on strike, and in a sympathy boycott, much of the railroad traffic in the western half of the country was brought to a standstill by workers refusing to handle Pullman cars. They were soon greeted by a federal court injunction and federal troops, and the ARU was left in shambles. The fate of the boycott strengthened the conviction of the business unionists within the AFL that prudently steering clear of mass politics, as well as mass worker action, was the better part of valor. In the subsequent years the AFL leadership leaned ever more heavily on a program of trade union organization and lobbying on specific issues. In other words, Gompers and his allies agreed that politics mattered. However, they contended that instead of focusing on parties and broad agendas, political action needed to target specific goals—such as lobbying against the use of court injunctions against unions, which had been crucial in defeating the Pullman boycott.[66]

In some ways, these developments signaled the passing of a more broad-based vision of labor unionism, a shift from a political activism to the workplace, and from coalitions across skill levels and even across racial and gender lines to a narrow focus on the interests of workers who were white, male, and skilled. The repression of unions like the ARU diminished the voice of labor activists advocating a more politically oriented and inclusive strategy in the society at large, as well as within the labor movement. This did not necessarily mean that workers as such became less drawn to broad solidarities, but it did shift the calculus for the unions left standing. As Gerald Friedman points out, "Union strategy, or *the strategy followed by unions that survive*, reflects not only the workers' wishes but what they do to establish and maintain unions against opposition from employers and state officials."[67]

By the turn of the twentieth century, the chief "strategy followed by unions that survive[d]" emphasized clearly defined, limited goals that were to be achieved through well-funded and carefully planned actions by workers well placed to succeed. The closed shop became an integral part of that strategy. It allowed unions to enforce agreements made with employers, and it undergirded the maintenance of union membership in workplaces where the unions got a foothold. Although it had deep roots, the centrality of the closed shop to modern union strategy was not inevitable; rather, it grew out of specific circumstances. Had the political challenges of the nineteenth century succeeded, labor might have adopted a different direction; indeed, many European unions, especially on the Continent, eschewed membership requirements in favor of broad-based political alliances or other alternative strategies.[68] Even in the United States, the landscape of opinion within the labor movement was never reduced to the views represented at the AFL executive council. Miners in the Rocky Mountain West, Jewish garment workers in New York, and even rank-and-file rebels within the AFL fold continued to find a range of radical ideas and tactics appealing—and sometimes the moderate business union leaders partly accommodated them.[69]

Crucially, whatever critique the Left leveled at business unionists and the closed shop, in the view of employers neither looked tame. Employers found the American Federation of Labor a serious threat to their power. For one, the AFL insisted on workers' right to organize and strike. This was a considerable challenge to ideas about who should hold power in the employment relationship and flew in the face of the ideology of worker obedience and master authority embedded in the master-servant doctrine, which the courts continued to uphold.[70] The AFL unions also continued to assert the governance rights of workers' organizations. As the membership requirement became a standard feature of union contracts, it underlined workers' claim to governance and secured the position of the national union through more reliable membership dues and union authority over workers. The power in this vision, though very different from either the old artisan republicanism or the cooperative commonwealth of the Knights of Labor, was hardly negligible. Its potential was evident, if in nothing else, then in the vehemence with which a large segment of employers attacked it and in the unease with which even prolabor middle-class reformers greeted it.

3 The Potential and Limitations of the Trade Agreement

I support the left
though I'm leaning, leaning to the right
—Cream, "The Politician"

"It seems to me that I hear nothing but strikes now," Gertrude Beeks wrote in May 1901 to Ralph Easley, the secretary and driving force of the newly founded National Civic Federation, an organization whose goal was to bring the leading lights of business, labor, and the general public together to solve industrial conflict. With a palpable sense of urgency, Beeks reported how workers in several cities prepared protests, "threaten[ing] catastrophes."[1]

Beeks was not wrong that strikes seemed to be everywhere. From 1897 to 1902 union membership had more than tripled, and the last two years of that period witnessed nearly three times as many strikes as the first two.[2] If the late nineteenth century had seen the pragmatic, occupationally focused business unionism of the American Federation of Labor eclipse the more idealistic rhetoric and broader base of the Knights of Labor, the turn of the twentieth century was nevertheless a time of vigorous labor mobilization. That mobilization made use of new language and new interpretations of old concepts. This did not necessarily mean that workers endorsed the new order of things. Many workers may have continued to prefer the vision that construed "free labor" as economic independence to the turn-of-the-century interpretation that portrayed it as selling a commodity in the free marketplace. They may have scoffed at the idea that "liberty of contract" put workers and employers on an equal footing. But that did not prevent workers from taking these new orthodoxies and making use of them to demand a better deal for workers.

After all, if labor was a commodity and the market was free, surely workers could not be castigated for deciding when, where, and how to contract for the sale of their labor. If they wished to contract collectively rather than individually, was it not within their liberty to do so? Since the 1880s, an increasing number of political economists had begun to find such arguments compelling. The general consensus by the turn of the twentieth century was that wage work, mass production, and long-distance trade had irredeemably eclipsed the world of the small independent producer; there was no return to the artisan republic. Given this new reality, unless workers had a right to act collectively, they would hardly be in a position to bargain with the employer on equal terms.[3] Such assessments became common among the young economists who founded the American Economic Association in 1885 and focused their attention on historical and empirical economics. As these economists tried to reconcile the idea of democracy with the now seemingly permanent industrial society, one practical answer that many of them came to support was the organization of labor.[4]

In some ways, this vision fit well into the turn-of-the-century moment. It was the "age of organization," after all. The economic upheavals of the post–Civil War decades—the massive growth in manufacturing output and the size of factories, the shock of the 1870s and 1890s economic depressions, the competition that pushed down profits and caused business failures, the new extremes of wealth and poverty, the violent labor conflicts—had generated a sense of malaise in which laissez-faire ideas about the economy appeared entirely inadequate to address new realities. It increasingly seemed that the modern thing to do was to replace unfettered market competition with orderly and coordinated transactions. The depth of the desire for a well-governed modern society was revealed in everything from corporate mergers to demands for municipal ownership to government-run projects. Businessmen sought ways to rein in cutthroat competition and to make production more efficient. Critics of corruption in the cities called for more efficient city government. Both socialists and reformers drew up schemes for municipal ownership or at least regulation of public utilities.[5]

The apprehensions of the era's reformers were tempered with a generous dose of optimism and an industrious sense of purpose. Like Gertrude Beeks, they may have feared catastrophe, but they remained hopeful: Beeks concluded her letter by telling Ralph Easley, "Well, when one hears of these threatened catastrophes now, it is with a feeling of relief that one remembers that you are in the field actively at work."[6] And Easley was—so much so that by 1909 Easley's doctor ordered him to take a two-week vacation in Europe to alleviate his serious fatigue.[7] Such incessant, energetic activity characterized many of the middle-class reformers of the Progressive Era, who tended to possess a heartfelt if amorphous desire to remedy society's many ills. Especially female reformers, whose experiences had perhaps made them more sensitive to the habitual exclusions of public discourse, sometimes came to question received wisdom about not only gender relations but also relations between the classes. These reformers created settlement houses as hubs of reform in immigrant and working-class neighborhoods, pursued litigation and legislation in behalf of workers, investigated the conditions of work and life around the country, and formed alliances with each other and, sometimes, with workers.[8]

The era's emphasis on efficiency, coordination, and reform provided a potential opening for labor organizing. Besides dousing the raging fires of class conflict, labor unions and collective bargaining might ameliorate the era's persistent economic malaise, which economists increasingly began to diagnose as a problem of overproduction and underconsumption. If the health of the economy depended as much on consumption as it did on production, perhaps it made sense to improve the ability of workers to bargain for higher wages, as that would allow them to buy more goods and services. Some labor leaders, especially AFL president Samuel Gompers, latched on to such arguments, perceiving in it not just an economic logic but also a way to defend workers' dignity: workers were entitled to bargain for wages that could sustain a level of consumption and comfort worthy of a citizen in a democracy.[9]

For a time, the trade agreement—a formal accord over wages, working conditions, and other parameters of the employment relationship, generally between a union and an employer or employers' organization—became the favored solution to the problem of labor conflict among many reformers and even some businessmen. It seemed to offer hope of an orderly and rational solution that provided real benefits without requiring too much upheaval. Yet if the idea that workers could collectively set the price of their labor was becoming more respectable, it nevertheless remained in constant conflict with ideas about the rights of employers to dispose of their property freely. How was one to square the property right of the employer in his business with the mechanisms workers found necessary to enforce the price of labor that they had collectively set? Could workers picket a factory or demand that all employees join the union? And what about the employer's property rights in the labor he had bought—didn't the logic of labor as a commodity sold by the laborer and purchased by the employer confer to the employer a right to dispose of it as he saw fit? If it did, where did that leave workers' claims to control on the job?

The enthusiasm for agreements had at its heart something of a paradox. To be meaningful, agreements clearly needed both parties to have access to some power to enforce them, but workers' means of enforcement worried many of the same people who found the idea of agreements attractive.

When workers insisted on mechanisms that would enable them to enforce agreements—strikes, picketing, boycotts, shop-floor control, required union membership—many economic and legal authorities found their cautious acceptance of collective bargaining wavering.[10] Without such mechanisms, though, the collective voice of workers would be a reedy one indeed. The unwillingness of middle-class economists, lawyers, and reformers to face this fact signaled their deep wariness about worker power. It also meant that unions found such people fickle allies at best.

This chapter focuses on what the trade agreement meant to the different parties interested in it and what they saw it as requiring. The chapter starts with a section examining the rise of the trade agreement as the solution to intractable labor strife. The next section analyzes where the membership requirement (closed shop), whose development was discussed in the preceding chapter, fit into the trade agreement idea, while the subsequent section considers who was left outside the fold. The final section examines both left-wing critique and middle-class apprehensions about the trade agreement system.

Averting Industrial War

The late nineteenth and early twentieth centuries witnessed many governmental investigations that attempted to get a handle on the labor question and to find a way to alleviate industrial strife. Drawing on experiences abroad, these investigations began to portray moderate unions—unions asking for limited practical improvements rather than an overhaul of economic and political relations—as both a bulwark against radicalism and a legitimate form of worker organizing. For example, the governmental investigation into the Pullman strike and boycott, a major labor dispute that pitted the American Railway Union against the intransigent Pullman Palace Car Company, praised moderate trade unionism not only as a counterpoint to the radicalism of the ARU but also as a corrective to the unequal power relations in corporate workplaces. The investigation noted particularly that collective bargaining had a "record of success both here and abroad."[11] Similarly, the US Industrial Commission, tasked in 1898 by Congress with investigating industrial conditions in the country, claimed in its final report in 1902 that "there is a general consensus of opinion that the voluntary extension and perfection of systems of collective bargaining, conciliation, and arbitration within the various trades themselves would prove highly advantageous, both to employers and working men, and to the general public." Drawing on the British experience as the standard to which it compared American labor relations, the commission noted that although collective bargaining and conferences between organized workers and employers were not a universal guarantee of industrial peace, "experience both in England and in our own country shows that where these practices have once become fairly well established they greatly reduce the number of strikes and lockouts."[12]

As the Industrial Commission was aware, collective bargaining could take many forms and result in many different types of arrangements. A union local could bargain with a single employer for a local contract. Employers and workers could haggle over work rules or wages without the talks resulting in a formal contract. Or, in the most comprehensive manifestation of collective bargaining, a national union could negotiate a national trade agreement that set the terms for all or most employers (represented by an employers' association) and all (unionized) workers in that industry. By the same token, some form of agreement between labor and management could result from mechanisms other than actual collective bargaining between organized parties. For example, reflecting older craft governance practices, a union might offer a wage scale for the employer to simply approve, with little negotiation. Alternatively, some third party or a more informal group of workers and employers could mediate between workers and employers to either "conciliate" their interests or "arbitrate" between them (the latter usually implying that the third party had some authority to decide between competing claims). All these practices remained in flux, as did the language about them: the commission observed that the phrase "collective bargaining" was not widely used in the United States, and "no little confusion" reigned about the practices themselves, while "the terms used in describing these practices are often misapplied."[13]

At the time of the Industrial Commission's investigations at the turn of the twentieth century, formal collective bargaining enjoyed the sheen of an exciting new idea, and wide-reaching trade agreements were often represented as the (at least temporary) pinnacle of evolution in the relations between employers and workers. This was the view of the British socialist reformers and scholars Sidney Webb and Beatrice Webb, who were influential with economists closely associated with the Industrial Commission. The Webbs saw bargaining between workers and employers progressing from more or less ad hoc local arrangements toward organized, bureaucratized contracts between parties increasingly well versed in the machinery of the trade agreement. The "most highly developed form," the Webbs contended, clearly distinguished between *bargaining over* the terms of the agreement, which should take place rarely and where the "representative element" was needed, and *applying* the terms, which should be the job of a well-trained "professional expert" (who, to be sure, could be a specially trained worker).[14] The commission followed the Webbs' emphasis on distinguishing contract negotiation from contract interpretation: conciliation and arbitration, the commission argued, were appropriate for settling minor matters of interpretation of contracts, whereas collective bargaining entailed direct negotiations between organized workers and employers and thus was more likely to produce lasting agreements between them.[15]

Collective bargaining became, in some ways, unions' ticket to respectability. Instead of challenging the basic contours of the economic system, men like Samuel Gompers insisted on labor receiving its full share within that system. Reframing the workers' quest in terms of greater freedom *from* work rather than greater freedom *at* work, Gompers posed labor's demand as "more." As Rosanne Currarino has argued, this was not merely a narrow economic demand; instead, it made a powerful claim to full participation. "More" encapsulated a vision of freedom in a society in which wage work was permanent. It was the freedom to enjoy the fruits of one's labor and to spend one's wages on what one pleased, but it was also the freedom to shape one's life. It meant "better homes, better surroundings," and other material things, but it also included, Gompers insisted, "higher education, higher aspirations, nobler thoughts, more human feelings, all the human instincts that go to make up a manhood that shall be free and independent and loving and noble and true and sympathetic."[16]

Unions explicitly connected their project to a modern movement toward organization, arguing that as industry had become larger and more concentrated, so had unions. There was no turning back the clock to the era of small workshops. Given that reality, labor had every right to organize to get its due in the new industrial regime: unions were, in Gompers's words, "the legitimate outgrowth of modern societary and industrial conditions."[17] The emphasis on efficiency and modernity was also reflected in the changing practice and language of the major US unions on symbolic and tangible levels: the railroad brotherhoods, for instance, shifted from the trappings of fraternalism, with its "lodges" and "grand masters," to the presidents, secretaries, and associations of twentieth-century business unionism. They built hierarchical, bureaucratic, and well-resourced structures and self-consciously positioned themselves as legitimate on account of their good business organization.[18] Such responsible, efficient unions, the implication was, were respectable partners in collective bargaining with employers.

The trade agreement was the practical expression of this businesslike approach to labor conflict. In exchange for the employer agreeing to certain wages, hours, and working conditions, the union would undertake to police its members and see to it that during the life of the agreement they would not strike. In industry-wide agreements, the union would also act as a rule-setter for the industry: the union would use its power in numbers to ensure that all employers paid the same or similar rate of wages and observed certain rules of production. The result would be better living standards for the workers and relief from cutthroat competition for the employers. At least as importantly, the trade agreement would eliminate the chaos of pitched battles between strikers and private or public security forces and minimize disruptions to orderly production and distribution. The trade agreement was, as the labor editor and statistician Ethelbert Stewart put it in 1910, "the embodiment of the exhortation 'Come, and let us reason together.'"[19]

Although the trade agreement was still relatively new, various forms of it had taken root in a number of industries in the United States. Results were mixed, but—especially at the turn-of-the-century moment before the employer counteroffensive took off—there were enough successes to bolster the optimism of those inclined to see agreements as the wave of the future. Besides a variety of local and limited agreements, national-level agreements had been forged in several industries in the late nineteenth century. Most branches of the glass industry instituted national agreements in the 1890s; the pottery industry transformed its local agreements to national ones in 1900; the longshoremen on the Great Lakes forged agreements with lumber shippers and ore and coal docks; an agreement in bituminous coal in the late 1890s equalized wages (and, importantly, costs of production) throughout much of the industry; the stove founders had by 1900 almost a decade of comprehensive collective bargaining experience with the Iron Molders' Union (IMU, after 1907 called the International Molders' Union).[20] The printers, with a decades-long union tradition, had moved toward written agreements and increasingly centralized control of bargaining; by the turn of the century the International Typographical Union had become a central clearinghouse for approving local contracts, as well as arbitrating (together with representatives of national employer associations) disputes arising from them.[21]

To be sure, some industries, such as steel, had tried but failed to institute wide-reaching agreements, while others that the Industrial Commission was optimistic about were about to be disrupted by technological change or the growth of organized employer resistance.[22] But for the time being, there seemed to be hope, and in any case the turbulence of the preceding years made orderly industrial relations imperative. The Industrial Commission's approval of the emerging practice of trade agreements and collective bargaining was echoed in the views of the National Civic Federation, with which it shared some personnel (e.g., the economists E. Dana Durand, John

R. Commons, and Jeremiah W. Jenks). In the words of the NCF's publication, the *NCF Review*, the trade agreement was "by no means perfect" but nevertheless constituted "the only practical present-day method for averting industrial wars."[23]

Neither the NCF nor the Industrial Commission ignored the challenges the trade agreement faced. They seemed to hope, though, that moral exhortation would suffice to overcome the disparate interests of the parties: the Industrial Commission warned that collective bargaining could only be effective if the organizations on each side represented "fair minded," "intelligent," and "conservative" workers and employers, while the NCF emphasized the need for the "sane and patriotic leaders" of both labor and capital to overcome the impulses of the hotheads. If they only acted reasonably, the commission and the NCF insisted, workers and capitalists could lead the country to a bright future where the "cumulative" benefit of collective bargaining produced mutual understanding between employers and workers, improved knowledge of industrial conditions on each side, and led to the general democratic and civic development of workers.[24]

The trade agreement as the foundation of a more peaceful and civilized future was a key project for Ralph Easley and therefore the NCF, which he headed. Founded in 1900 as an explicitly tripartite organization with members from the top echelons of labor, business, and "the public," the NCF centered much of its early work on promoting the trade agreement conceptually and in practice. Actively looking for sites of industrial conflict that it considered "ripe for rational treatment" through negotiation and agreements, the NCF formed a strong alliance with labor's top leadership, particularly AFL president Samuel Gompers and United Mine Workers of America (UMWA) president John Mitchell.[25] It also claimed rapid successes: in 1903 alone, according to Easley, the NCF had successfully conciliated nearly one hundred disputes, while by 1906 its services had been enlisted in over five hundred cases.[26] Though it developed a clear understanding of the trade agreement and of union priorities, it nevertheless continued to emphasize harmony over strengthening unions; indeed, Easley often continued to use terminology of "conciliation" even as he promoted concrete agreements. He also often praised the fact that a conflict had been resolved over the content of the resolution. For example, Easley hailed the settlement in the famous anthracite strike of 1902 as demonstrating "the great value of the conference method of settling differences between capital and labor." He did so because it ended the strike and resulted in a commission that eventually issued an award including a raise, shorter hours, and a board of conciliation—even though the settlement explicitly did not result in recognition of the UMWA by the coal operators.[27] Such vacillation between an emphasis on harmony and an emphasis on orderly, formal relations continued to plague both the NCF's work on trade agreements and the development of formalized bargaining and agreements more generally.

The Trade Agreement and the Logic of the Closed Shop

If the trade agreement—or, indeed, any form of effective collective bargaining—was to be the vehicle for creating a reasonably peaceable and smoothly functioning regime of industrial relations, unions needed some real power. A powerless party to a negotiation, after all, would have a hard time keeping up its end of the bargain. The membership requirement—the closed or union shop—undergirded union power. Therefore, in the view of unions, it was part of the bedrock on which agreements rested. Without it, unions could neither function nor survive.

Some employers, as well as some reformers, argued that unions should instead make themselves into legal persons—to incorporate so as to have standing to enter into agreements enforceable in a court of law. This idea, as well as state-administered arbitration of labor disputes, had in fact received some support among unions in the nineteenth century. In the 1880s the predecessor of the AFL had supported a national law on union incorporation, and unions had backed arbitration laws that had passed in several states. The attraction of state adjudication of labor matters, however, quickly faded. The attempts to punish unions under the Sherman Antitrust Act of 1890, which outlawed combinations in restraint of trade, convinced unionists that incorporation posed too much risk; it would only make union finances vulnerable to court-ordered damages. Similarly, arbitration could easily be made to favor employers, some of whom embraced it as a means to prevent strikes. Merely involving the state did not solve the problem of whose interests would be protected; whether they were to be enforced through the state or through union contracts, workers' demands only had weight if their voice could not be ignored.[28]

Required membership is not, of course, the only way of ensuring that workers have a voice and that unions have some power. Indeed, the closed or union shop has traditionally been rare everywhere except in the English-speaking world. It rarely made an appearance in continental Europe, perhaps in part because the union movement on the Continent generally had a much clearer and stronger political thrust. This meant both that it was more focused on gaining sufficient influence with the state to ensure the state's backing for union activity and that it self-consciously wanted to portray the unions as the representatives of the whole working class, not of an exclusive group. In cases where continental unions' bids for a hold on state power succeeded and they managed to establish, for example, state-sponsored tripartite bargaining systems, they also had less need for a mechanism like required membership to boost their stability.[29]

In the United States, though, the membership requirement—the closed shop—was the chief instrument unions employed to ensure their persistence and power. The logic of the closed shop had several components.

First, a trade agreement without the membership requirement left the employer free to rid himself of the union simply by hiring nonmembers. The union, having done the hard work of recruiting members and using the strength of its membership to wrest concessions from an employer, would be constantly faced with the employer's attempts to weaken the union by hiring nonunion workers. Eventually the shop might revert to nonunion conditions entirely. The leeway that the open-shop policy gave employers to do this, unionists argued, was precisely why employers favored it: they knew that "freedom to employ non-unionists is, in present conditions, sufficiently destructive of unionism," and so they could hide their antiunionism behind the claim that they respected workers' right to organize and only opposed the demand for a closed shop.[30]

Second, not requiring workers to join the union would weaken the union through free riding and through the union's inability to exercise shop-floor control. If workers knew that they could get benefits without paying union dues, why should they join the union? By the same token, how would it be possible to keep up the morale of union members who felt they were exposing themselves to retaliation and risks while others benefited? According to its proponents, the membership requirement was no infringement on rights but a guarantee of them: it guaranteed rights collectively. Employers might "quote the one man who is trespassed," but against this the unionists "quote the fifty men whom the one man trespasses."[31]

Finally, and crucially, without the membership requirement, the union would not be able to guarantee the workers' adherence to their contracts. After all, how was a union supposed to "sign a trade agreement for workers who are nons [nonmembers]"?[32] What power would the national union have to "compel the local members to toe the mark" if they could simply leave the union without suffering any consequences? Only under union shop conditions could a national union keep its members from striking in violation of a contract, as the UMWA had done with regard to the bituminous field during the massive anthracite strike of 1902.[33] Thus, to be against the union membership requirement—against the closed shop—was tantamount to being against unions and trade agreements entirely.

The union shop lent worker power to the vision of the trade agreement. It rooted collective bargaining in the mechanisms of craft rule and union governance. It made an explicit claim to the union being the collective government of the workers, negotiating with the employer as an equal. In this vision of union governance, workers were not individual atomized actors in a marketplace where the employer set the rules. Instead, they operated within a governing structure of their own making—one that had jurisdiction over the price of labor, as well as over many aspects of working conditions, and that asserted the power to enforce its decisions over the whole body of workers under its purview (whether this was defined as a whole industry or a particular craft). It was, in essence, the same claim as that excoriated by the court in the *Commonwealth v. Pullis* case back in 1806, that the workers were raising "besides our state legislature, a new legislature" consisting of themselves.[34]

Part of the difficulty in the fights about the closed or union shop lay in how difficult it was for those outside the union fold to understand the depth of the unions' claim to governance. As David Montgomery has argued in his classic work on nineteenth-century iron puddlers and other craftsmen, craftsmen possessed a "functional autonomy" derived from their exclusive familiarity with the work process and its requirements. This autonomy eventually morphed into formal written union rules. These rules governed everything from the number of apprentices and the rate of wages to when particular work tasks could be performed, how much could be produced in a set amount of time, and how promotions should function. In the highly skilled crafts, such workers' control measures made sense, as the employer's role was mainly to offer the conditions for completing the product (equipment, raw materials) and to take it to market when it was done. In such a work process, there was little to negotiate with the employer about.[35] Many craft unionists took it as a given that they had the right to refuse to work with someone who flouted the union-enforced rules of the craft. Indeed, they reacted rather like a modern-day academic might if someone from outside one's discipline presumed to have input on who should be hired on a departmental faculty or what should be taught in the introductory course in one's field.[36] Retaining the traditions and dignity of the craft required certain standards—of apprenticeship, of income, of skill. The craft society created those standards and held its members to them. The role of the employer was somewhat incidental to this process: if the employer came up to the standards (paid sufficiently, did not abuse the apprenticeship system, etc.), then members were allowed to work for him; if he did not, they were not. Therefore, despite employer cries of union "tyranny" in collective bargaining, in the view of many unionists the very idea of negotiating with an employer was already something of a concession.

Even as industrial conditions changed and negotiation with employers became a more central part of labor union activity, the claim to governance remained an important part of union ideology. The employer, after all, asserted the right to govern his side of the business; to have anything like equal weight, unions needed to counter this right with jurisdiction of their own. In a way, retaining the right to legislate for the craft made unions "schools of democracy and independence," as Clayton Sinyai has argued. The features of craft unions that are most often criticized as overly conservative can, Sinyai points out, also be seen in the light of creating enduring institutions that proved the civic virtue of workers and undergirded workers' claims with real and enduring power. High membership dues can have the effect of excluding less well-off workers, but they also helped ensure the financial stability and thus the longevity of the organization. An aversion to sympathy strikes can be seen as indicating a lack of solidarity, but it can also signal a disciplined husbandry of the organization's resources and future. Resisting state legislation on social welfare can be cast as reactionary antistatism, but it might also spring from a commitment to building workers' institutions, such as fraternal insurance, instead of looking to a paternalistic state. Perhaps most starkly, the insistence on disallowing dual unionism that can look like cantankerous power-grabbing can equally well represent a logical corollary of the claim that unions are really government-like institutions: one can hardly be subject to multiple competing governments with conflicting rules.[37]

The assertion that unions had the right to demand membership was part and parcel of this conceptualization of unions as government. The vision of governance that the union shop entailed, however, could also widen the gap between the rank and file and the union leadership. Part of the explicit logic of the union shop, after all, was the enforcement of union rules *on the members*, including enforcing the contract the national union had signed, sometimes over the objections of rank-and-file members. Indeed, this was a big part of how the unions sold themselves as responsible negotiating partners and how allies like the NCF promoted them. Easley regularly cited as proof of "what organized labor has learned" instances when the leaders of national unions went against their members. For example, Easley approvingly noted that when Buffalo longshoremen had struck despite being under a current trade agreement, Daniel O'Keefe, the president of the International Longshoremen's Association, had told them to get back to work and had brought in nonunion workers to break the strike when they refused.[38]

Unlike many other Progressive Era reformers, Easley understood and accepted the central role that the unions accorded the membership requirement in the trade agreement system. Because he realized its centrality to the unions' ability to enforce contracts, he was also willing to defend it to those of the NCF's employer members who were less than enthusiastic about it. For example, Easley explained to the clothing manufacturer Marcus M. Marks that Marks's insistence on unions operating without the closed shop made no sense to unionists: "From Mr. Gompers' standpoint it is folly for you to say in one breath that you believe in organized labor . . . and then in the next breath demand that he shall surrender to a policy which he knows by experience means the utter disintegration of the union."[39]

Such flank support held significant value for labor leaders like Gompers and Mitchell. Their goal, after all, was not to eliminate capitalism or employers but to establish unions' control over specific aspects of the work relationship. Having allies who understood and accepted the need for that control and were willing to explain it to employers was nothing to be sneezed at. However, because it was tied to a vision where the key role of labor leaders was to be enforcers of collective bargaining contracts vis-à-vis rank-and-file demands, it reinforced the hierarchical aspects of the union shop instead of its democratic potential. As Craig Phelan notes in his biography of Mitchell, for example, the "success of the trade agreement depended on the existence of a highly centralized and bureaucratic union." It also kept Mitchell talking to coal operators rather than to miners, and over time he came to identify more with the "attitudes and values" of the operators than with those of the miners. The end result was "a union in which rank-and-file sentiment would exercise limited influence."[40] For Easley, this was a key attraction of the trade agreement. A great believer in "conservative" leadership, he saw labor's functionaries as men he could level with, men who were "much broader and more intelligent than the members of the rank and file."[41] Similarly, for such leaders as Gompers and Mitchell, strengthening union hierarchy dovetailed with an emphasis on responsible and pragmatic action over pipe dreams about far-reaching social change; it also caressed their egos and amplified their power. For the union rank and file and for those left outside the union fold, though, the vision of unionism peddled by the NCF presented a less happy reality in which the union shop controlled them as much as it liberated them—or, at worst, actively excluded them from the ranks of organized labor.

Craft Unionism and the Nonunionist

The employers, especially the activists of the open-shop movement, accused unions of coercion and violence to maintain their closed-shop rules. Such accusations were calculated to rob unions of legitimacy as the voice of workers and were no doubt advanced far more often than the evidence warranted. The employers did not, however, manufacture them out of thin air. Even when craft unionism fulfilled its democratic potential for union members, it did not always treat kindly nonunion workers who refused to join in protests, crossed picket lines, or otherwise ignored union rules.

Employers emphasized violence against nonunionists; unionists denied the accusations. But violence did sometimes occur. Sometimes violence was directed against a lone individualist willfully defying the union and (at least in unionists' perception) currying favor with the employer. Montgomery recounts a case of a worker in a machine shop who consistently sided with the boss and strove to be a model of efficiency, readying his tools before work officially began, for instance. He also showed up for work when everyone else turned out to demand the eight-hour day in 1886, with the result that "when he sauntered out at noontime for his can of beer, he was viciously beaten by his mates."[42] More often, violence—or coercion that slid into violence—formed part of a concerted effort to prevent strikebreakers from doing the work the strikers were refusing to do. Usually such violence was limited to punches, but sometimes workers greeted strikebreakers with guns and even dynamite. This happened in some of the most famous strikes of the era, such as the strike at Andrew Carnegie's steelworks in Homestead, Pennsylvania, in 1892 and the strike at the Pressed Steel Car Company in McKees Rocks, Pennsylvania, in 1909.[43] In the mining industry, too, where strikebreaking was frequently accompanied by armed guards (themselves often guilty of excessive violence), strikebreakers might be the target of unionists' bullets.[44] In some cases, violence was directed at the employer's person or his property; for example, in 1860s Manchester, England, employers trying to wrest control of hiring, firing, and the work process from unionized brickmakers sometimes gave up the attempt for fear of their lives.[45] Usually, though, violence was less extreme: most commonly, a worker crossing a picket line might be roughhoused either at that moment or outside of working hours, or in cases where the workplace itself was exposed (as in, say, a streetcar strike) the strikebreaker might be attacked on the job.

Noting that strikers sometimes engaged in violence against strikebreakers should not be confused with claiming that strikebreakers bore the brunt of strike-related violence. Data on historical strike violence is severely lacking, but all indications are that strikers themselves, as well as their supporters, suffered the most from violent attacks, the vast majority of which were committed not by strikers but by state actors, company-hired guards, or even vigilante businessmen themselves. In a recent effort to create a more reliable data set of strike fatalities, for instance, Paul Lipold and Larry Isaac found that between 1877 and 1947, in cases where the "affiliation" of the victim could be identified, 64 percent were strikers or allies; strikebreakers accounted for less than 12 percent of victims.[46] However, one might plausibly speculate that the disparity could well be far less extreme with regard to less severe violence, that is, the kind intended to convince strikebreakers to leave their positions. No real statistics exist on the matter, but certainly nonunion workers willing to take up strikers' jobs often did so at some risk if not to life, then at least to limb. This was perhaps particularly the case when the strikebreakers were African American: the Chicago packinghouse strikes of 1894 and 1904, as well as the Chicago teamsters' strike of 1905, for instance, involved multiple severe attacks on African American strikebreakers by strikers and strike sympathizers.[47]

Some violence committed by unionists against strikebreakers came about when frustration and animosity boiled over in unplanned mob attacks on replacement workers. But violence could also be a calculated and deliberate tactic. In the Manchester brickmakers' case cited above, for instance, the decision to apply violence against employers was taken democratically in a general union meeting.[48] Similarly, in the Chicago teamsters' strike, president Cornelius Shea of the International Brotherhood of Teamsters reportedly informed the employers' association, "You have the Negroes in here to fight us, and we answer that we have the right to attack them wherever found."[49]

Even when violence was not involved, the craft unions' insistence on government and jurisdiction placed limits on the freedom of workers who did not fulfill the requirements of the craft. Craft unionists tried to deflect the accusations of the closed shop's exclusiveness by arguing that unions were open to membership—as Gompers put it and other craft union leaders echoed, "Any qualified non-union wage worker can enter any union shop through the union door."[50] The catch, though, lay in the word "qualified"—almost every declaration of the openness of unions was accompanied by a more or less inconspicuous proviso that the applicant for membership had to be "qualified" and otherwise acceptable.[51]

There were several ways in which a worker might not be eligible for craft union membership. Most simply, a worker might not possess the specific training or skill that the union demanded. Given the AFL's well-known lack of interest in organizing unskilled workers on the basis of industry, this excluded significant numbers of workers from its ranks. More nefariously, some workers were not welcome because of immutable characteristics: women workers found themselves slighted by male unionists, while African Americans often found themselves categorically shut out. Though the AFL promoted immigration restriction, European immigrants might become full-blown union members; the same was not, however, true of Asian immigrants, whom the AFL treated as unassimilable and inferior. Employers rarely expressed concern about bigotry, but they did call attention to how skill or training prerequisites set by the craft unions excluded workers. Together, all these exclusions caused union claims of openness to ring hollow and seriously undermined the unions' claim to be the representative voice of workers. If workers outside unions declined membership out of selfishness, as unions regularly claimed, then the claim that the union shop simply prevented unfair free riding had a basis. But if those workers were excluded from membership to begin with, matters were rather different.

The exclusionism of craft unions was the flip side of their self-regard as upstanding citizens. Their embrace of a posture of respectability helped them gain acceptance with entities like the NCF and the Industrial Commission, which viewed these unions as providing desirable and moderate leadership. But the politics of respectability could also constrain the strategies available to unionists and spill over into contempt for those whose social status was lesser than their own.

The railroad brotherhoods, for example, quite explicitly positioned themselves as a "conservative" worker organization. Especially early on, strikes were very low on the list of union activity, which instead concentrated on mutual aid, such as cooperative insurance and traveling systems. In the aftermath of the 1877 Great Railroad Strike, which witnessed massive worker unrest throughout the country, Paul Taillon argues, such conservatism became a key element in the brotherhoods' attempts to convince employers that it would be better to deal with them than with a mass of unruly workers. In the two decades following the strike, the brotherhoods concluded written agreements that "provided favorable wages and working conditions while protecting railwaymen against the vagaries of railroad work and arbitrary management."[52] When relations became more contentious, the brotherhoods considered federating their respective trades but worried that managers would see such efforts as embodying a more radical class spirit: "We have been favored by the great majority of railroad managers for our conservatism. . . . Are we going to cast it aside?"[53]

The brotherhoods' concern to appear respectable and conservative reflected a more general tacit skepticism among labor leaders about ordinary workers' capacities that perhaps underlay the AFL's lackluster interest in industrial unions. Despite occasional nods toward the necessity of creating industrial unions, the leadership of the AFL never followed through on such ideas with much conviction. It also often attacked actual industrial organizing projects as dualistic, that is, as splitting the loyalties of the workers between two unions and leading to recrimination and disputes between workers who should be under a single jurisdiction (in the AFL leadership's view, the jurisdiction of the AFL). After being practically forced to organize a Building Trades Department in 1907 by the intensive industry-wide organization in the building trades, the AFL did charter a number of industrial departments. However, as one scholar points out, these "might be said to have presented a cover for inaction" more than a new departure.[54]

Concerns about respectability and a rather limited view of solidarity also showed in the AFL's attitudes toward immigrants, African Americans, and women. The AFL favored restricting all immigration but particularly that of Asians. In arguing for restriction, the AFL did not limit itself to straightforward economic arguments about the impact of supply and demand of workers on wages but also appealed explicitly and implicitly to race-based thinking. The labor movement's opposition to Chinese immigration had always depicted the Chinese as constitutionally different from white Americans. In the early twentieth century, although the immigration of Chinese workers had been banned since the Chinese Exclusion Act of 1882, Chinese workers remained on the AFL's radar because of their role in the construction of the Panama Canal and because of their presence in Hawaii and the Philippines. Some of the objections to Chinese workers at the canal focused on contract labor—that the Chinese, having signed exploitative multiyear contracts, were basically being used as slave labor in Panama and that this "set a pernicious example to some of our states where the demand for peon and contract labor is steadily increasing."[55] It was clear, however, that such objections were not distinct from objections on racial grounds. Indeed, the racial difference (and inferiority) of the Chinese seemed so blindingly obvious to many labor leaders that they could forswear prejudice in one sentence and invoke racist arguments in the next. Thus, UMWA president John Mitchell wrote in 1909 that "the American workman, be he native or immigrant, entertains no prejudice against his fellow from other lands." In the next sentence, Mitchell explained that "the demand for the exclusion of Asiatics, especially the Chinese and the Hindus, is based solely on the fact that, as a race[,] their standard of living is extremely low and their assimilation by Americans impossible."[56]

Other Asians were equally explicitly racialized and seemed perhaps even more of a threat, because some continued to be able to immigrate until the completion of Asian exclusion in the Immigration Act of 1924.[57] For example, the October 1907 issue of the *American Federationist* contained an article by one Albert S. Ashmead, identified as the "former medical director of Tokio Hospital," titled "Japanese Atavism." The article was packed with language that seemed to aim more at impressing the nonexpert with its scientific ring than at helping a general reader understand complex biological theory. For example, Ashmead wrote of "the increased or diminished torsion of the Japanese humerus" and "the incurvation of the ulna, below the sigmoid cavity," noting that these were "distinctly simian." Armed with this scientific sheen, most of the article then devoted itself to recounting various disagreements among ethnologists about the origins and traits of the Japanese "race," but the main point was clear in the first paragraph: in considering immigration policy, it was a mistake to assume that the "Japanese are a superior race" compared to "Chinese and Hindus." They were not. "To one who has studied the Japanese closely," Ashmead assured his readers, "there are many racial traits which betray an origin and development that are not a good basis upon which to hope to make American citizens."[58]

The language that the AFL used of European immigrants was generally more sympathetic, emphasizing that employers took advantage of their desperate circumstances. For example, an editorial by Samuel Gompers in the *American Federationist* approvingly quoted the "conservative and dignified newspaper" the *Boston Transcript*, which argued that garment industry sweatshops were the result of allowing manufacturers to "take advantage of unrestricted immigration, and . . . the cheap labor of distressed European refugees." Gompers argued that it was the closed shop that abolished the sweatshop and "secured for the garment workers . . . decent conditions."[59] However, in other writings in the *Federationist*, the immigrants' plight appeared less susceptible to the salutary influence of unionism. For example, in an article against child labor, Eva McDonald Valesh argued not only that the constant supply of immigrants made the employing class less concerned to protect the future supply of workers by trying to ensure that American children got to grow up healthy but also that the nature of the immigrants contributed to the prevalence of harsh treatment. "These immigrants," Valesh wrote, "come from generations of hardy peasants who have toiled in the fields, and they really bring with them a sturdy health and vigor that takes more than one generation of factory life to bleach into impotence." Moreover, being peasants, they failed to "understand the dangers of factory and mine work for children."[60] A few months later, Valesh mused about the differences between union families and nonunion ones. Imagining an exhibit of the makers of the goods and not just of the goods themselves, she wrote, "Contrast pictures of the southern cotton mill children or the women slaves of New York sweatshops or newly arrived immigrant mine workers, with union men, their children going to school, their wives well dressed and in comfortable homes. Contrast the homes as well as the places of employment."[61] In a similar vein, a partial defense of the closed shop in the *National Civic Federation Review* by the economist Edwin R. A. Seligman argued that the closed shop had the virtue of protecting wage rates against "the cheap labor of ignorant and indigent immigrants."[62] In all these, the emphasis was clearly on how unions had improved the lives of workers, but the repeated references to the immigrants' "ignorance" and to the proper home life of the union men as contrasted with that of immigrants and nonunion workers still left the latter looking faintly disreputable. Such condescension was surely not lost on nonunion or immigrant workers.[63]

Perhaps most explicitly, union chauvinism excluded African Americans. Black workers frequently found their entry to skilled trades or desirable jobs barred not by employers but by unionized workers. As documented extensively by W. E. B. Du Bois in 1902, the majority of American unions had few or no African American members due to either explicit clauses excluding them or an unwritten practice of not accepting African American apprentices (thus resulting in no applications from African American skilled workers).[64] Indeed, the AFL's policy on allowing racial exclusion actually worsened as the organization grew. In the 1880s and 1890s Samuel Gompers had repeatedly insisted on the necessity of organizing African American workers, and in the 1890s the AFL had refused to charter unions that excluded them from membership. The AFL accepted separate locals for African Americans but viewed them as temporary and exceptional rather than as desirable and permanent. However, by 1895 the policy was fraying. That year, the International Association of Machinists (IAM) was allowed to affiliate with the AFL by simply removing from its constitution the explicit clause barring African Americans from membership, with the tacit understanding that each of its locals would be free to exclude them. Other unions were soon welcomed using the same subterfuge, and by the turn of the century even the implicit requirement of keeping discrimination discreet was dropped.[65] Meanwhile, some strikes that were ostensibly prompted by hiring nonunion workers were in fact specifically directed at the hiring of African American workers who were not union members, often because they were explicitly or implicitly excluded from membership.[66] Even unions with a relatively large African American membership and a reputation for fair treatment, such as the International Longshoremen's Association, were less than egalitarian, favoring white workers in employment both when union strength made strikebreaking less of a concern and when hard economic times made work scarce.[67] Unsurprisingly, some African Americans believed that unions' exclusionary policies and white workers' racism fully justified taking up jobs that became available due to strikes, which in turn solidified white unionists' conviction that African Americans were a "scab race."[68]

Women workers, too, found it challenging to gain respect or representation in unions. Despite the crucial role that wives' and daughters' earnings played in family budgets, the growing proportion of women in the paid workforce, and repeated proof of women's capacity for militant unionism, union hierarchies and (male) union leadership found it hard not to treat women's work roles as secondary or to see working women as temporary (and unwelcome) sojourners into the world of paid work. Of course, it was true that women's labor force participation was often temporary and that the idea of insisting on a male breadwinner's "family wage" that allowed his wife and children to stay at home had appeal for both women and men.[69] Nor were women workers immune to the broader gender divisions of society in thinking about their roles as potential unionists. Some women saw public activism not as liberating but as unfeminine and onerous and were not eager for leadership roles. For example, Dorothy Sue Cobble points out that unions of wait staff succeeded best in attracting active women unionists and women leaders when they were segregated into waitresses' and waiters' locals, which both kept male unionists from grabbing all the leadership positions and prevented "the girls" from "leav[ing] the work to the boys."[70]

Women's low unionization rates (much lower than working men's) were cited as evidence—by some women, as well as by men—that women's interest in unionizing was fickle at best.[71] Others, though, insisted that the problem was unions' refusal to take women seriously. The legendary garment worker and labor organizer Rose Schneiderman, for example, kept trying to tell male unionists that women would join if the unions bothered to listen to the women's concerns. At the very least, unions might stop refusing to sign women up as union members when they actually struck for better conditions, as the International Ladies' Garment Workers' Union (ILGWU) had done with the young female underwear makers who successfully wrested concessions from their employer. To be sure, women also had allies among male unionists, more of whom were induced to revise their skepticism as women engaged in multiple massive strikes in the second decade of the twentieth century and as women's unionization rate in the garment industry, for instance, began to push 50 percent.[72] Still, convincing male unionists that women could and should be organized remained an uphill battle.

In addition to lackluster interest in organizing the unskilled and frequent explicit exclusionism on the basis of race and sex, the craft unionists wore their unionism as a badge that in their view set them above other workers. The language they used in talking about nonunionized workers often showed a palpable measure of contempt. Sometimes unionists merely took a somewhat patronizing attitude: if "the nonunionist . . . does not know how to protect himself, then we will have to protect him, even if it is against his will."[73] At other times, they were nonchalantly insulting: in a routine defense of the union shop, for example, Gompers explained that agreements between employers and unions "should not be made subject to the irresponsibility or lack of intelligence of the non-unionist."[74] And sometimes they explicitly asserted their own greater worth: the *Shoeworkers' Journal*, for example, argued that unionists were drawn from the "socalled [sic] better classes," while "the slums represent the miscalled free workman or non-unionist."[75] Thus, the craft unions, ironically enough, both confirmed employer accusations that they viewed nonunion workers as needing union "guardianship" and replicated the employers' disdainful attitude toward workers.

The vision of the union shop as governance and the emphasis on collective bargaining as providing labor an equal seat at the table held considerable potential. At the same time, they rested on a claim to respectability at the expense of other workers that ate away at the solidarity the unions claimed to foster. Such claims to respectability were also inherent in Gompers's construction of "more" as a means for workers to pursue the finer things in life, including such classically bourgeois accoutrements as a piano in one's parlor.[76] While Gompers was of course right to insist that workers were as entitled to material comforts as anyone else, when combined with the patronizing or contemptuous attitudes craft unionists frequently displayed toward immigrant, African American, female, and unskilled workers, respectability traced the contours of an acceptance of hierarchical divisions that undermined the whole union project.

Too Conservative or Too Radical?

The prominent British industrial relations scholar Richard Hyman once noted,

> Collective organisation is the means whereby workers create social power far greater than the sum of that which they possess as individuals, for unity and coordination replace competition and division. This power is a weapon which can be used to win real improvements in their situation: the organisation of conflict gives their discontents direction, and is thus the precondition of any significant remedy. Yet the organisation of conflict also makes their disaffection *manageable* by employers and by governments: for grievances are brought into the open, channelled to appropriate authorities, expressed in a form which makes compromise possible, and articulated by a bargaining "partner" with whom an agreement can be reached which employees will feel some commitment to observe.[77]

In making labor conflict manageable, unions could gain respectability, a place at the table, and even real power. But they might have to sacrifice for it: a regime of collective bargaining and trade agreements could strain relations between the rank and file and labor leaders, and it could fray solidarity between different groups of workers (e.g., through prioritizing not breaking contracts over supporting other workers through a sympathy strike). Manageability also undermined the disruptive potential of worker assertiveness; its chief promise to employers was, after all, the maintenance of labor peace.

Radical unions, such as the Industrial Workers of the World, sharply criticized the AFL and other "moderate" unions both for their exclusiveness and for their willingness to constrain labor militancy. For such unions, organizing needed to be inclusive. It should not be restricted by craft: as the president of the Western Federation of Miners, by far the strongest component of the IWW, had put it in 1897, "Open our portals to every workingman, whether engineer, blacksmith, smelterman, or millman. . . . The mantle of fraternity is sufficient for all."[78] Nor should organizing be impeded by lines of race or ethnicity: as an IWW organizer in Canada declared, "When the factory whistle blows it does not call us to work as Irishmen, Germans, Americans, Russians, Greeks, Poles, Negroes or Mexicans. It calls us to work as wage-workers, regardless of the country in which we were born or color of our skins. Why not get together, then . . . as wage-workers."[79]

For the Wobblies, as the IWW was also known, the goal of organizing was working-class power, not industrial peace. Trade agreements in themselves were anathema to this philosophy: all they did was hamstring workers' freedom of action during the contract, while employers in practice remained at liberty to break the agreements. The IWW believed that it was crucial to be able to strike while the iron was hot, so to speak. Unions needed to respond to employers as the unions deemed fit, not wait for the contract to be up for renegotiation. Nor should union responses to employer actions be limited to the strike, even to the mass strike extending beyond a specific group of workers to the broader community. Union responses should instead encompass all forms of day-to-day resistance, ranging from sabotage to slowdowns. To focus on collective bargaining, that is, haggling within a capitalist, employer-dominated framework, such critics argued, distracted workers from the more important project of building a truly democratic and just society. If the union was to focus on a wage scale, it had better be one that represented the "full product of workers' work" and one that the union could enforce, not negotiate with the employer. The Wobbly theorists insisted that collective bargaining between workers and capitalists could never be a negotiation between equals. Thus the whole foundation of the trade agreement as equalizing power relations between workers and employers was, in their view, misleading.[80]

Although the IWW is better known for its revolutionary politics and dramatic tactics—and the repression directed at it—than for securing pragmatic gains for its members, the Wobblies' emphasis on broad-based working-class power over trade-based negotiation did not necessarily mean that they forswore practical improvements in favor of dreamy-eyed revolutionary goals. Like other strikes, those backed by the IWW aimed at securing essential bread-and-butter improvements for the workers—wage raises, decent working conditions, relief from employer coercion—even if limited resources or poor strategy caused many a strike to fail.[81] Nor was rebuffing trade agreements necessarily tantamount to eschewing durable and effective organization-building. For example, Peter Cole has demonstrated that in the 1910s Local 8 of the IWW successfully maintained an extraordinary interracial organization among Philadelphia longshoremen. Local 8 did not sign contracts, but it asserted power by other means. To be hired on an IWW dock, a worker had to be a paid-up member—a union official would frequently be present when workers were hired to ensure this, and this demand could also be enforced by a strike threat. And since solidarity among the IWW longshoremen was high, the workers could make use of strategic work stoppages to enforce demands or rectify deteriorations in work conditions.[82]

The Wobblies did not have a monopoly on either organization on the basis of industry, or militant tactics, or a radical political outlook. Industrial unionism, as well as socialism, held broad appeal across the union rank and file. As John Laslett has pointed out, even some craft unionists were drawn to industrial unionism, as well as socialist ideas, because they seemed like appropriate responses to the economic and industrial changes taking place. Many machinists and boot and shoe workers, for example, began to suspect that maintaining control on the basis of skill would simply become unfeasible as the craft became more and more mechanized and deskilled. This was true even in unions with a conservative leader and conservative origins, such as the International Association of Machinists: the union's president remained adamantly opposed to socialism, but "by the turn of the century most of the union's leading officials were socialists."[83] Socialism also appealed to workers who found trade unionism to be too much of an uphill struggle, too slow and too ineffective against employer intransigence. Only state action seemed to hold realistic promise in solving the problems they faced.[84]

Besides complaining that the AFL's focus on craft unionism and on the trade agreement was too narrow, socialist and other left-wing critics of the AFL's leadership also zeroed in on the affiliation of Samuel Gompers and other AFL leaders with the NCF and, through it, with some of the largest businessmen in the country. At the American Federation of Labor's 1911 annual convention, multiple resolutions called on the convention to condemn the NCF and demanded that AFL officers rescind their association with it. Although the resolutions were defeated, the brisk debate that accompanied them—and that took up more than one full day—aired the sense of many of the delegates that the NCF corrupted labor's leaders by inducing them to hobnob with men who expressly attacked unions in their companies while offering paeans to conciliation at NCF dinners.[85] A few years later, a similar scene played out at the hearings of the US Commission on Industrial Relations (USCIR) as Morris Hillquit, a labor lawyer and prominent socialist, and Samuel Gompers clashed over the goals and strategy that would best advance labor's cause. To Gompers's growing irritation, in his cross-examination Hillquit—accompanied by much clamor among the audience—lobbed question after question about the NCF at Gompers. Did Gompers really believe he could change employer minds through the NCF? Did trade unionists in other countries consider participating in such cross-class organizations? Was it even "proper," Hillquit wanted to know, "for an official representative of the American Federation of Labor to cooperate with well-known capitalists for common ends?"[86]

Gompers responded to Hillquit with the same line that he and others had taken at the AFL's 1911 convention to defeat the resolutions calling for labor officials to resign from the NCF. The NCF, he insisted, was merely a forum—it in no way dictated his views or action, and neither he nor other labor leaders were children easily bedazzled by capitalists' wiles. Nor did speaking to capitalists compromise his convictions or get his "skirts besmirched." Much of the point of the labor movement, after all, was to speak to capitalists—to make demands of them. Who cared if capitalists were hostile? That was to be expected; but then, friendship was no prerequisite for discussion.[87] Indeed, as Gompers said in a much-quoted quip, he would "appeal to the devil and his mother-in-law to help labor if labor can be aided in that way."[88] All this was an integral part of the AFL's pragmatism, Gompers argued—of securing improvements by sticking to the "terra firma" of what was actually happening rather than "build[ing] castles in the air."[89]

The AFL leadership's defense of associating with the NCF implicitly leaned on the conviction that craft unionism and trade agreements were no less militant or powerful than socialism or industrial unionism. They drew, after all, on the tradition of craft rulemaking. The trade agreement, in this view, legislated standards that the union then imposed on the employer. That was what the closed shop accomplished: union control of at least parts of the work relationship. The potential power inherent in this approach was considerable. In fact, in the view of many of labor's middle-class allies, it was excessive.

Far more palatable in their view was the aspect that men like Ralph Easley emphasized: imposing order on industrial relations by imposing order on the rank and file.

For Easley, the attraction of working with labor's leaders was not only that trade agreements had the potential to result in "rational" labor relations and orderly conduct in accordance with signed contracts. It was also that those leaders could be talked to as individual people, not as members of the abstract entity of "workers." Although he understood that unionism derived its power from organization, Easley valued informal understandings between individuals above procedures and structures. Individuals were hampered by structures—even if those structures were meant to guarantee a fair voice and democratic representation. In this sense, the Left's critique of union officers' association with the NCF hit the mark: the NCF did not intend to involve union leaders as the legitimate representatives of their organizations or even of the labor movement more broadly construed. It aimed to involve them as "individuals." As Easley explained to one of the business members involved in organizing a new branch of the NCF: "We get the labor side . . . by picking out the most conservative and best members [of unions] and inviting them as individuals, not as officials. The committee selected by a central [labor] body would simply be a nuisance, as it would not feel that it was acting for itself, but for another body, and would have to go back to the central body every time before acting. You get all the strength of a labor situation when you get their best men to come into a movement as citizens."[90] It does not seem to have occurred to Easley that to function, the trade agreement system that the NCF was so fond of as a means of averting industrial war required rank-and-file involvement; without collective structures and accountability, labor leaders would be unable to lead. For Easley as for many other middle-class reformers, the attraction of the trade agreement as a system of coordinated and rational conflict management in industry constantly clashed with a liberal vision of individuals as the measure of all things. In this vision, problems would be solved not by developing appropriate collective governance structures but by individuals reaching understanding and harmony through rational discussion. Whether employers were willing to reach any sort of an understanding with unionists, however, was very much open to question.

4 The Range and Roots of Employer Positions on Labor

> It is difficult to get a man to understand something when his salary depends upon his not understanding it.
> —Upton Sinclair, *I, Candidate for Governor: And How I Got Licked*

In 1903 the president of the St. Louis Metal Trades Association wrote National Civic Federation secretary Ralph Easley inquiring "what is being done . . . to apply in practice the beautiful sentiments contained in the various speeches made" at the NCF's recent Industrial Conference in New York. Probably pushed by the approach of the Louisiana Purchase Exposition (more commonly known as the St. Louis World's Fair), the letter writer asked for Easley's help in creating a local Civic Federation in St. Louis, there being "no better place to show the progressiveness in the question of [the] labor problem, than the City of the Worlds' [*sic*] Fair."[1] After several exchanges with Easley, the letter writer concluded that St. Louis needed both a local Civic Federation and an employers' organization that could coordinate discussions with unions. Once these were established, "an attempt must then be made to get the employers' organization and the unions in the control of level headed, liberal minded men who will consider and use the local branch of the Civic Federation as a means of understanding each other."[2]

The inaugural meeting of the St. Louis Civic Federation was held on May 1, 1903. In attendance, besides local actors, were NCF president, US senator, and industrialist M. A. Hanna; American Federation of Labor president Samuel Gompers; Ralph Easley; and former US president Grover Cleveland, a member of the NCF executive committee.[3] Throughout the summer of 1903, the St. Louis Civic Federation continued to correspond with Easley and to promote negotiations between employers and organized labor in St. Louis. By early 1904, however, St. Louis employers had adopted a different tune. Perhaps convinced that they no longer needed labor's cooperation to accomplish the goals of the fair or irritated at what they thought excessive concessions extracted by labor using the fair as a bargaining chip, they began to abandon the St. Louis Civic Federation for a newly organized belligerent organization, the Citizens' Industrial Association (CIA).[4]

Easley's correspondent and the organizer of the St. Louis Civic Federation, Ferdinand C. Schwedtman, now became the secretary of the CIA and quickly developed into a key open-shop activist.[5] St. Louis workers noted the employers' new mood with resentment, complaining that they could detect in it "the hand of Mr. Ferdinand Schwedtman," whom they suspected of aiming to "force all other employers to be as unfair to their employees as he is to his."[6] When fellow St. Louisan James W. Van Cleave became president of the National Association of Manufacturers (NAM) in 1906, Schwedtman became his secretary and continued to play a major role in the NAM open-shop campaign.

Schwedtman's evolution and the fate of the St. Louis Civic Federation underline that employers accommodated unions when they had no choice or when doing so conferred some specific advantage. Such accommodation emphatically did not mean that the employer had become a prounion convert. Edwin Freegard of the employing printers' organization United Typothetae made that point explicitly in 1904, as the Typothetae was in the process of moving away from negotiating with unions. "Some employers," Freegard admitted, "have asserted a positive preference for the employment of those allied with labor unions" because unions helped them get workers, and union workers were a "better class of workmen." But, he pointed out, "under present conditions both these positions might be true, and yet . . . if all things were equal and he could as easily obtain the needed service outside as inside the union, he would prefer to do so."[7]

Schwedtman and Freegard illustrate a number of key themes for understanding the range of American employer opinion. First, employers, like anyone else, formed their ideas constrained by context: which courses of action appeared *feasible* shaped perceptions about which ideas seemed *attractive*, and both could change over time. Second, it was perfectly possible for employers to adopt a particular course of action that served a pragmatic purpose without changing their fundamental outlook, as well as to try to associate themselves with ideas they did not actually wish to put into practice. Third, there was no uniform "American" position on how to deal with the rise of organized labor; American employers ran the full gamut from accommodation with unions to stiff-necked resistance, and where a particular employer fell on that scale was a fairly complex matter.

In a comprehensive 1922 study of American employer associations, Clarence Bonnett classified associations into two basic types: "belligerent" associations, which fought unions, and "negotiatory" ones, which entered into trade agreements with them.[8] In subsequent historiography, the belligerent/negotiatory divide has generally been linked to company size and type, with large corporations on the negotiatory side and moderately sized industrial firms on the belligerent one. The "magnates," as Robert Wiebe put it in 1962, "devised policies to protect profits and security values and, if possible, to win public approval as well," while the "smaller employers, whose pride and habits depended upon full control over their companies, thought first of protecting a way of life."[9] James Weinstein elaborated on this theme in his 1968 book *The Corporate Ideal in the Liberal State, 1900–1918*, which argued that the top businessmen of the nation crucially shaped Progressive Era reform and thus the shape of the "liberal corporate social order" that emerged then and developed in the New Deal of the 1930s and later.[10] According to this view (which usually goes by the name of "corporate liberalism"), the heads of large corporations had become, as Weinstein puts it, "fully class conscious," as opposed to the belligerent employers, who were "narrowly interest conscious."[11] This greater "flexibility and sophistication" allowed the corporate liberals to think long-term and to use organizations like the NCF to forge alliances with such moderate labor leaders as Samuel Gompers and John Mitchell, whom they saw as allies against an unruly rank and file, as well as against socialism and radicalism. Large businessmen, in other words, were willing to accept concessions to unions as the price for maintaining the capitalist system—a stitch in time saves nine, so to speak.[12]

It is true that the NAM and the NCF were rivals and were perceived by the public as representing opposite employer viewpoints regarding labor. To use Bonnett's terminology, the NAM was the organization of the belligerents, while the NCF represented the negotiatory employers. The NAM's message vilified any type of union; the NCF drew a clear distinction between moderate unions, which it supported, and radicals and socialists, whom it attacked at every turn.[13] It is also true that the businesses linked to the NCF were on average clearly larger than those that affiliated with the NAM (or the open-shop movement generally). However, a simple large/small, conciliatory/belligerent division quickly runs into problems. First, the NCF companies were rarely prolabor in any fundamental sense. Second, though the NAM companies were smaller than the NCF ones, they were hardly "small"—and in any case, small size in itself did not an antiunionist make. As Andrew Wender Cohen has shown for Chicago, for instance, the actual small businesses of what Cohen terms "the craft economy" were a stronghold of unionism, while corporations tended to resist unions using all means at their disposal.[14]

Positing a division of employers into those who accommodated unions and those who refused to deal with them, as well as equating this division with company size and type, tends to flatten the complexity of the business landscape. This flattening is not necessarily inherent in the works that have crafted such divisions; as often happens, the interpretations get simplified in what might be termed "historiographical memory," and the division seems starker in the realm of what "everybody knows" than it perhaps ever was in the scholarship. Clarence Bonnett, Robert Wiebe, and James Weinstein all recognized multiple fault lines, evolving positions, and the possibility that what employers said might not match how they acted. Assessing the range and roots of employer positions on labor is thus more complicated than drawing one simple dividing line, whether between negotiatory and belligerent or large and small(er).

This chapter examines the range of employer views and strategies. It argues that employer strategies reflected industrial position and other structural factors more than they did individual employers' views of unions; most employers wished to minimize the influence of unions, but different social and industrial positions lent themselves to different styles of rhetoric and different practical approaches. The chapter starts by examining the complex appeal of the NCF to a particular type of employer; this section argues that the NCF's assistance on negotiating trade agreements was at best a minor draw for employers. The next section shifts the focus to the NAM companies, showing how the economic realities of their industrial type and position made banding together to fight unions an attractive option. The final section provides a comparative look that juxtaposes different national, regional, and industrial realities to underline that American employers were not that different from their European counterparts—employer choices everywhere were generally shaped more by pragmatic considerations than overarching ideologies.

The Uses of Conciliation: Employers and the NCF

The men who formed the core of the NCF's business supporters were drawn from the upper echelons of business achievement. This was a deliberate strategy on the NCF's part: having prestigious members helped the NCF argue that the trade agreement (and the NCF's other projects) represented the best economic and political thought in the country, not the views of radicals. Thus, for the NCF's purposes, the key characteristic of these men was their elite status. Ever on the lookout for prominent men to enlist in its projects, the NCF collected a roster of household names: mentioning Andrew Carnegie (the steel tycoon known for his philanthropy and his rise from modest beginnings), Franklin MacVeagh (President Taft's secretary of the treasury), Frederick P. Fish (president of American Bell Telephone), Frank A. Vanderlip (head of the National City Bank), or Marvin Hughitt (president of the Chicago and Northwestern Railroad) carried significant clout. Indeed, the NCF was well aware that having the use of their names was at least as important as their actual contributions—if not more so.[15] The NCF, though, was not the only one more focused on image than on reality: many of its business members themselves were more interested in gaining the cooperative glow that an NCF affiliation could lend to them than they were in actually abiding by the trade agreements promoted by the NCF.

Some employers who were involved in the NCF's conciliation work, to be sure, did believe in and practice negotiation and trade agreements. One such example was Francis Le Baron Robbins (Jr.)., son of a merchant turned coal baron. Educated at the Penn Yan Academy, a private preparatory school, he took over from his father at the Midway Block Coal Company and went on to extend the business until it consolidated as the Pittsburg Coal Company in 1899 at a capital of $64 million (over $2 billion in 2020 dollars).[16] Active in Republican politics, Robbins also took a keen interest in the NCF's efforts at promoting industrial conciliation and, together with United Mine Workers president John Mitchell, cochaired the NCF's Trade Agreement Department.[17] Robbins praised the coal operators' agreement with the mine workers as "a signal example of benefit to the general social welfare." Besides improving conditions for the workers, trade agreements were also vastly better for the employer: "It is far more advantageous, far more profitable to deal with the leaders of organized labor than with the rank and file. Leadership tends to conservatism."[18]

Robbins portrayed the trade agreement as simply one of the many ways in which modern society was governed by agreements. In Robbins's view, an employer who blustered about the trade agreement limiting his rights was at best misguided and at worst insincere: "Such an employer forgets that he is continually making contracts, other than with labor, and entering combinations, that restrain and modify his conduct of his business." Robbins went on to describe the trade agreements achieved in bituminous coal and to argue that the stability they provided benefited the operators, the miners and transport workers, and the general public.[19]

It is little wonder that Francis Robbins thought the trade agreement a commendable idea. Bituminous coal, his home industry, had a dire need to mitigate intense and chaotic competition, and unions provided the means to do that. Labor costs made up some three-quarters of the costs of producing coal, and though that could make unions a severe threat, it also meant that controlling those costs uniformly could reduce the stresses of cutthroat competition, a point that unions sometimes explicitly emphasized.[20] Achieving such cost control required unionization across regions. Once the union held enough sway in some regions, the operators in those regions had a vested interest in helping the union capture nonunion producers lest they outcompete unionized producers.[21] This was precisely what happened: in 1897 coal operators in the central competitive field from Pennsylvania to Illinois struck an agreement with the United Mine Workers of America that required the UMWA to both enforce the agreement among its own members and try to bring the West Virginia coal fields into its orbit.[22]

Besides Robbins, the coal industry contributed another key NCF member, Samuel Mather of Pickands, Mather & Company, which in addition to producing iron ore was the owner of several important bituminous coal fields. Indeed, even Henry G. Davis, a US senator and probably the most important mine operator from the notoriously antiunion West Virginia mine fields, joined the NCF executive committee, though his association only lasted a year.[23] In other industries where unions possessed sufficient strength to seriously challenge employers and to effectively police competition in the industry, employer organizations behaved similarly to coal even when they ideologically chafed at having to do so.

In the stove industry, employers who had at first united to oppose union demands soon found themselves in a long-term relationship built on negotiations and trade agreements. In 1887, soon after the founding of the Stove Founders' National Defense Association (SFNDA) to coordinate employer strategy, a strike that began with the Iron Molders' Union demanding higher wages at one plant in St. Louis quickly spread throughout the industry. The employers mostly had to give in, and the IMU entered a period of rapid growth. At the same time, the stove industry was suffering from cutthroat competition and a declining rate of profit. Unable to defeat their skilled workers and powerless to control competition among themselves, the stove founders made a virtue out of necessity and negotiated a trade agreement with the molders. This served both the stove founders and the workers: "The union was able to provide something of inestimable value for members of the defense association—namely, a successful strategy to reduce inter-capitalist rivalry through the equalization of molding labor costs among competing firms."[24] The SFNDA president, Chauncey N. Castle, was a member of the NCF's Trade Agreement Department, headed by Francis Robbins, and generally praised the functionality of the system of agreements. In his annual report in 1905, he noted that he was "pleased to be able to say that in all cases the letter and spirit of the agreements have been carried out, so that peace and harmony have prevailed."[25]

In the building trades, employers similarly acquiesced to a union presence even as they groused about it. The construction industry was highly vulnerable to strikes. A building job obviously could not be moved elsewhere. Moreover, agreeing to workers' demands usually cost the contractor less than resisting them. A contract for a building usually included a substantial fine for delays, while on the other hand, contracts were commonly cost-plus; that is, the contractor would be paid what erecting the building had cost plus a percentage or fee on top of that. Accordingly, higher costs resulting from the contractor agreeing to wage demands would be passed on to the owner of the building, whereas risking labor-related delays could result in fines for the contractor. Unions in construction had, therefore, gained considerable power.[26]

As in the stove industry, employers organized—but given the substantive union power, they made no attempt to defeat the union. Instead, they concentrated on using organization to help them negotiate far-reaching trade agreements. This was true although the union they were faced with had all the hallmarks of the worst kind of corruption the NAM loved to highlight: the building trades union was well known for the practices of the (in)famous union leader Sam Parks, whose "entertainment committee" of thugs kept workers in line, while his power to call strikes unless bribed kept employer money flowing into his pockets. Employers found a remedy in centralized bargaining. The Building Trades Employer Association (BTEA) of New York, founded in 1903, proposed an arbitration board that sidestepped the union walking delegate (the union agent charged with overseeing that job sites adhered to union agreements) and denied him the power to call strikes. Once this system was in place, the NCF declared it an "unprecedented opportunity" for the expansion of the trade agreement, as it had secured peace and granted workers the union shop, as well as high wages and short hours.[27]

Building employers, then, granted unions significant concessions because employers had few other options, not because they liked unions. Despite negotiating with unions, for example, the BTEA of New York cultivated language very reminiscent of the open-shop activists, referring to the "unreasonable" demands of labor and its "arbitrary tyrannical demagogue[s]," "vicious system," and "brutality" and insisting that employers needed to band together to fight union corruption.[28] The brothers Charles and Otto Eidlitz, active members of the NCF and key actors in the formation of the BTEA, similarly both endorsed the need for arbitration and negotiation in the building trades and chafed at them. They recognized its necessity; indeed, Otto Eidlitz insisted that the only way to arrange the "relations between the employer and employee" was "to have both sides thoroughly organized" and constantly on guard against any violation by the other side of their "absolutely contractual relation."[29] But that did not mean the Eidlitzes had any liking for unions or agreements. Charles, especially, was dissatisfied—on one occasion, he disrupted the harmony at a conciliatory NCF dinner that the *New York Times* described as "designed to be a love feast between the representatives of capital and labor" by blurting out that "the entire structure on which these [trade] agreements is founded is wrong" because the closed shop was not "an American proposition."[30] The Eidlitzes maintained contacts with the open-shop movement, but given the strength of unions in the building industry, they continued to engage in negotiation and remained in the NCF through the First World War.[31]

Negotiation, then, required no fondness for unions, nor did it necessarily mean that an employer had stopped looking for a different solution or thinking of ways to challenge unions' interpretation of what trade agreements required. Some employers arguably played both sides at once. One such employer was William Pfahler, officer and treasurer of the Abram Cox Stove Company of Philadelphia. Pfahler had been a leader in the SFNDA, which maintained a consistent negotiating relationship with unions, and one of the founding members of the National Founders' Association, which initially negotiated with the molders and achieved an agreement with them in 1899. He sat on the executive committee of the NCF, as well as on its trade agreements committee, and he spoke in favor of trade agreements at NCF events. Yet Pfahler and the NFA also coordinated strikebreaking, and over time Pfahler became increasingly active in the open-shop drive.[32]

Some employers also found it useful to participate in the NCF's activities and gain its approving nod while keeping all options open. Participation without any commitment to conciliation was available because the NCF wanted very much to attract new employer members—partly because it was good for donations (on which the NCF's work depended) and partly out of hope that the discussions and human connections at NCF events would beget a more conciliatory attitude in the employers. In 1904 the NCF organized the employers-only Welfare Department, whose purpose was to promote and assist in employers' welfare work (i.e., voluntarily providing their workers with nonwage benefits ranging from nicer lunchrooms to pension plans), with no particular mention of unions or more influence for worker voices.[33]

Employers could use the NCF's Welfare Department to gain positive publicity with few or no concessions to worker or union power—which was often the purpose of welfare work more generally as well. For example, the National Cash Register Company (NCR), presided over by the idiosyncratic John Patterson, had in the early 1890s faced serious worker resistance in the form of shoddiness and outright sabotage. In response, Patterson made the company an early leader in welfare or industrial betterment work, instituting a library, a clubhouse, a kindergarten, low-cost lunches, and scenic gardens designed by the famous landscape architect Frederick Law Olmsted.[34] When workers at NCR around 1900 began to unionize despite these placatory efforts, Patterson at first claimed to welcome the development and soon had concluded contracts with over twenty unions. Not averse to hardnosed negotiation, Patterson constantly held the threat of going entirely open shop over the unions, using it as a bargaining chip in a 1901 strike precipitated by the molders' dissatisfaction with a particularly autocratic foreman. At the same time, Patterson pursued other possible solutions: with the NCF's help, he instituted the first modern personnel department, the Labor Department, headed by the (antiunion) Charles U. Carpenter. Once the personnel department was in place, the NCR no longer signed contracts with unions, with the rationale that the new department served the needs of employee representation. In subsequent years, union presence at NCR faded.[35] Despite the NCR's decision to stop signing union contracts, its programs earned it positive publicity from the NCF: the NCF's Conference on Welfare Work in 1904 featured Patterson as a speaker, and he was specifically asked to explain how the NCR had used the Labor Department to solve its personnel problem, "which presented itself in their trouble with the unions."[36]

When employers kept one foot in the open-shop movement while working with the NCF, the result (and possibly the intent) of their NCF involvement could be to subdue union leaders' militancy. That might buy the companies time to institute other means of dealing with their labor problems. For example, U.S. Steel, which had a representative on the NCF executive committee, gradually introduced more and more mechanized work processes yet enjoyed some success in maintaining cordial relations with the union even in the wake of a serious 1901 strike (mediated by the NCF). As David Brody notes, relieved that the newly formed steel giant did not immediately launch an all-out attack on unions, union leaders "kept silent and hoped for the best." Within a few years, however, the steel corporation threw cordiality by the wayside and declared itself an open-shop concern. Labor leaders were shocked at the harshly worded announcement, especially given the lack of any precipitating conflict.[37] It was clear that U.S. Steel had simply decided to go nonunion; as the labor economist John Rogers Commons, who worked closely with the NCF, pointed out, later congressional investigations revealed that the company had from the beginning been "bent on destroying ultimately all labor organization," despite the conciliatory pose it adopted for publicity reasons.[38] The NCF, it seems, had provided a convenient forum for avoiding conflict while building up strength.[39]

The size and resources of the employers that joined the NCF provided them with multiple options for dealing with their labor forces, ranging from mechanizing production (as at U.S. Steel) to instituting complex welfare programs to pacify their workers and reduce turnover (as at NCR). Yet their size and prominence could also make them in some ways more vulnerable, and some of these vulnerabilities help explain their association with the NCF and their need to project a conciliatory image.

A large percentage of the employers involved in the NCF were publicly held corporations, which, while it testified to their size and importance, could constrain their options to fight unions. A corporate manager could be held responsible by the shareholders if his actions hurt the bottom line. Indeed, unions sometimes explicitly played on the power of shareholders. As one British unionist wrote Ralph Easley,

> For a time . . . strikes often appear to have gone against us, the employers having secured a sufficiency of "scabs" to carry on their shop without us, coupled with the fact that they have made up their minds to make any sacrifice rather than have it said that they have been defeated by a trade union. But by & by the shareholders['] meeting takes place, the usual dividend has largely diminished or disappeared altogether, ti [sic] may be that the balance is on the wrong side of the ledger, which may be tolerated for a time, but the end must come, you cannot convince shareholders better than by reducing the dividend. The management are asked to give a reason for this falling of divi[dend], [and then] the truth has to be admitted: "the molders' strike." It frequently happens [that] after . . . we have considered the shop as lost to us, the employers have caved in.[40]

Less concretely but nevertheless importantly, public relations mattered far more to a large corporation than to a midsized manufacturing firm. The kind of "public be damned" attitude epitomized (fairly or not) by the railroad magnate William Henry Vanderbilt in the 1880s would put a large corporation into all too bright a spotlight.[41] Men who breathed the rarefied air of the nation's top economic strata—men of the ilk of Andrew Carnegie, Henry Frick, and George B. Cortelyou—and whom the NCF explicitly courted were of course the very men whose status as "robber barons" or "captains of industry" the nation debated. They headed corporations that resembled empires, and the power of such corporations was very much a cause of concern in the Progressive Era.[42] Indeed, the legitimacy of the corporation was by no means an established fact: the Supreme Court had granted corporations legal personhood only a couple of decades earlier, and the "soullessness" of corporations—in the sense of both lacking a conscience and being too impersonal—was a constant theme of critique.[43] The favorable publicity provided by participation in the NCF helped dispel criticism and humanize the men at the helm of these corporations. The NCF encouraged industrial leaders to arrange social events that allowed them to display their largesse and their lack of class prejudice; thus, the reformer Florence Jaffray Harriman, wife of financier J. Borden Harriman, wined and dined a hundred labor delegates and some of their wives at her summer home to highlight "her attitude toward labor and the doctrine of good fellowship," while Mr. and Mrs. Andrew Carnegie held an "Industrial Peace Evening" at their home, entertaining three hundred labor, business, and public members of the NCF.[44]

Favorable publicity had great value to massive corporations in an era when proposals for public ownership of some or all industries had significant traction. Socialists, of course, called for full collective ownership, demanding that "the land and . . . all the means of production, transportation and distribution" should be owned by "the people as a collective body."[45] A similar declaration had been supported by many member unions of the American Federation of Labor at its 1894 convention. That declaration (which did not pass) called for the "collective ownership by the people of all the means of production and distribution."[46] In a somewhat more limited manner, the People's Party (the Populists) had in its Omaha Platform in 1892 demanded that "the government should own and operate" railroads, as well as the telegraph, telephone, and postal systems, "in the interests of the people" due to their public significance.[47] Moreover, public ownership appealed to Americans well beyond the left edge of working-class politics. The economist Richard Ely, for example, argued in an 1894 article that the importance of transportation, communication, and utilities to the national infrastructure meant that the country could not afford to leave them in private hands. They were "natural monopolies": structural reasons made it impossible for several companies to operate profitably, while at the same time their services were indispensable to other businesses and to individuals. To avoid waste and graft, such "non-competitive businesses should be owned and managed by the government, either national, State, or local."[48] At the municipal level, public ownership enjoyed some popularity. Members of the Socialist Party sometimes gained public office, and even many non-Socialists supported the public ownership of utilities.[49] As Gail Radford has noted, "It is often forgotten how much public support once existed for the urban vision that the reformer Frederic C. Howe articulated as cities 'that owned things and did things for people.'"[50]

The industries that were at the center of the public ownership discussion, such as railroads, banking, insurance, and utilities, were all prominently represented in the NCF. These industries were also frequently hit by scandals. Railroads were accused of "fleecing farmers" and buying legislators, while the

life insurance industry was investigated by Congress for all kinds of malfeasance, from nepotism to bribery. Utility companies were another target of
suspicion: to take just one example, in 1905 Consolidated Gas, headed by key
NCF member George B. Cortelyou, found itself among a number of utility
companies "investigated and roundly condemned" for stock-watering by a
committee of the New York state legislature.[51]

The positive publicity that a corporation could gain from an association
with the NCF had great value in such a context; occasionally, the NCF's investigative projects also provided more direct opportunities to launder corporate
views. In the fall of 1905, for instance, the NCF created the Commission on
Public Ownership, which was to study the topic both in the United States and
abroad—in the NCF's own words, with an "impartial attitude" that would
result in a "purely scientific inquiry."[52] The NCF's business members had
clearly hoped to use the investigation to condemn public ownership while
appearing scientific and were disappointed when the report of the commission (published in 1908 and taking up over twenty-five hundred pages) did
not take an explicit position on public ownership. In an indication of what
they had hoped the "impartial" report would say, three business members
of the investigative committee submitted dissenting reports that explicitly
emphasized the dangers of municipal ownership.[53]

Given the enthusiasm for public ownership schemes and the ascendancy of
Socialists at local levels, one may understand why massive corporations might
appreciate Ralph Easley's vehement antisocialism. Easley was constantly on
the lookout for socialist influences and sometimes talked as if he possessed
something like a socialist radar, claiming that he had stopped "accepting a
man's own statement" denying being a socialist, as "I have had in my office too
frequently men who were Socialists and everybody knew it but themselves."[54]
Occasionally, the popularity of Progressive or even socialist-leaning ideas
struck close to home for the industrial magnates involved in the NCF: both
their sons and their wives were sometimes drawn to such ideas. It is not clear
how much the magnates themselves worried about such leanings, but Easley
became increasingly concerned with the issue. The wives and daughters of
wealthy men were susceptible to socialist influences, Easley thought, because
of their interest in Progressive social causes and in woman suffrage (which
the Socialist Party supported but the NCF did not). Meanwhile, "most of our
large men" had sons of college age.[55] Elite colleges, Easley felt, were "reeking
with Socialism," and even the few antisocialist professors' "arguments are so
namby-pamby that the Socialist party welcomes an opportunity . . . to debate
with them."[56] As a result, Easley feared, "the young men who are to be our
future captains of industry are getting some queer notions in their heads."[57]

The NCF attacked this issue on multiple fronts. In 1908 it organized the Woman's Department, which counted among its founding members the wives and daughters of the NCF's key men of wealth: Miss Anne Morgan (daughter of banker J. P. Morgan), Mrs. John Hays Hammond (wife of the mining baron), and Mrs. Joseph Medill McCormick (wife of one of the grand-nephews of Cyrus McCormick and daughter of Senator Mark Hanna). The aim of the department was to bring a feminine touch to the organization's work on industrial questions and to offer conservative women "a fine op-portunity . . . to do important work among the women of this country" who "for a long time . . . have needed a leader to take them away from the Jane Addams–Mary McDowell–Florence Kelly [*sic*] type."[58] Part of the rationale for the Woman's Department was that it would be a safe outlet for NCF members' wives' activism; for example, an NCF officer mused that "it might be a fine piece of missionary work to get" the suffragist Katherine Mackay, wife of NCF-affiliated financier Clarence Mackay, "interested in our work and turned away from the radicals who have been running after her the last two or three years."[59]

If woman suffrage or Progressive causes drew upper-class women too far left, upper-class young men, Easley believed, were susceptible to socialist arguments because of their family traditions of philanthropy, their interest in reform, and perhaps even their admiration for efficiently administered systems. For instance, H. H. Vreeland Jr., the son of the street railway expert and director of several railway companies, had reportedly been impressed by the Socialist John Spargo's argument that the philanthropic work carried out by a mix of private organizations could be much better performed by the government. Similarly, Sam Lewisohn—son of the copper magnate Adolph Lewisohn, who was generously philanthropic with his massive wealth—had become "practically a Socialist, having imbibed the principles at Princeton."[60] Easley therefore worked to create a program to inoculate the "sons of rich men" against socialism. He recruited key scions of prominent families, in-cluding Vincent Astor (son of the fabulously rich John Jacob Astor IV) and Ogden L. Mills (son of the prominent financier Ogden Mills). They then did their best to recruit their friends, while Easley wrote to the fathers recom-mending that they suggest to their sons the benefits of NCF work. Soon the NCF had organized the Young Men's Branch of the Industrial Economics Department.[61]

There were, then, multiple reasons for businessmen to affiliate with the NCF, among which the trade agreement held at best a minor place. Even in the publicity materials put out by the NCF, the number of businessmen on record as fully supporting trade agreements and strong unions capable of enforcing them is exceedingly small. There was Francis Robbins, noted above; there was also department store owner Edward A. Filene, who argued that strong unions would bring about labor stability and uniformity of wages, and therefore it was in the employers' interest to encourage the growth in union coverage and power.[62] But there were far more employers who paid mere lip service to some vague form of conciliation, or who entered into trade agreements but only as a temporary measure, all the while keeping their options as open as possible. Employers could be involved in the NCF's work out of motives that bore little relation to their actual views about unions or the trade agreement, let alone to their concrete labor practices.

The Attractions of Belligerence: Open-Shop Employers

A typical example of a vehemently open-shop employer is John Kirby Jr., a manufacturer of railway brass and supplies in Dayton, Ohio, and president of the NAM from 1909 through 1913. Born in Troy, New York, Kirby had worked since his early teens—at a stove works, at a photography shop, in his brother's jewelry repair and manufacturing shop, and finally in the Illinois Manufacturing Company, which made railway brass and bronze supplies. There he acquired the experience to set up on his own, and in 1883 he founded the Dayton Manufacturing Company and became its general manager. Having settled in Dayton, he also became deeply involved in the city's civic and economic life, serving on various boards of directors, becoming the president of the local board of trade, and promoting the construction of a new, well-appointed building for the Dayton YMCA. Kirby had no use for unions; on the contrary, as someone who saw himself "a friend to workingmen," he considered it his duty to combat them. In 1900 he founded the Dayton Employers' Association, one of the first (if not the first) citywide, multi-industry employers' organizations of the open-shop era specifically created to resist unions.[63] At the NAM convention in 1903 that inaugurated the association's new open-shop movement, he gave a fiery speech that forswore any negotiation. "Whatever may be the provisions of any agreement you may make with labor unions," he warned his fellow manufacturers, "it carries with it the surrender of your manhood and your American citizenship, and makes you a party to a conspiracy to rob others of those God-given rights."[64]

Like Kirby, many of the NAM's members saw themselves as self-made men or, at the very least, as men whose own pluck and effort had been essential in making them successful and whose entrepreneurship had contributed to the development of engineering and the progress of American industry. In their minds, this meant both that they were justified in demanding to run their businesses as they pleased and that anyone else could do what they had done.[65] In reality, most of the NAM activists had enjoyed advantages not available to everyone. They were largely native-born and Protestant (though there were some Catholics and Jews and some Scandinavian and German immigrants among them).[66] A significant percentage had college degrees, an indication of privileged status in an era when only 2 or 3 percent of the eighteen-to-twenty-one age group attended college.[67] Many continued businesses (large and small) that their fathers handed down to them or drew on their families' multigenerational roots in regional business and politics.[68]

The NAM prided itself on its pugnacity as much as the NCF emphasized conciliation. Similarly, where the employers in the NCF tended to praise the broad-mindedness of labor leaders, the NAM extolled the virtues of ordinary workers, who, open-shop employers claimed, were "willing to assist [their employers] in times of necessity" because they understood the mutual dependence of labor and capital.[69] In general, the ordinary worker was good at heart, even "a gentleman," whereas union leaders were "unreasonable," and unions themselves were really just violent "strike societies" that pushed down wages for everyone but their members.[70] As we saw above in the discussion of the NCF, however, employers' views about unions did not really determine how those employers decided to act. What, then, explains the choice of the open-shop employers to resist rather than conciliate? What made organized belligerence attractive for these employers?

In some cases, resisting union demands might have been a straightforward question of business survival, especially for an individual business that had built its competitive edge by producing more cheaply than the industry standard.[71] Indeed, the experience of the firm that brought what became one of the iconic labor cases of the era, *Loewe v. Lawlor* (1908), is an illustration of that. D. W. Loewe made his hat manufacturing business competitive by saving money through employing more apprentices than union rules permitted. When the hatters' union struck his firm in order to bring its wages and hiring practices into line with other firms in the industry, Loewe refused to negotiate because he was convinced that adhering to union rules would destroy his business. His retailers told him as much. One wrote to Loewe estimating that unionization would require Loewe to raise his prices to the same level as those of his competitors. This would eliminate the retailer's interest in his products, since the competitors had a broader selection of goods than Loewe, who only offered a basic line. So Loewe decided to fight the union in court. In the resulting case, the Supreme Court eventually found that the union had violated the Sherman Antitrust Act when it called a boycott of Loewe's hats. Employers considered this a major victory both because it conclusively established the applicability of the Sherman Antitrust Act to labor organizations and because it declared illegal the practice of secondary boycotts—boycotts that targeted not the employer involved in the dispute but a third party, such as a shop that sold goods from a factory the union considered "unfair." Loewe's personal victory was less clear: while he eventually collected significant damages from union members, the process was costly, and during the litigation his company went into receivership.[72]

Loewe may genuinely have been between a rock and a hard place, since his competitive strategy was based on low prices and low wages. That is, even had he wanted to, he perhaps could not have paid the union scale and remained competitive, at least not without transforming and diversifying his business. While that raises some interesting questions about businessmen's willingness to apply to themselves the basic precepts of free markets—that efficient and innovative businesses outcompete others, while those that cannot flexibly adjust will be eliminated—it does explain why Loewe would have found the union such a threat. Meanwhile, one can perhaps also understand why Loewe felt so wronged by the union: he was neither born to wealth nor at loggerheads with his employees. A German immigrant who arrived in the United States with very little money, Loewe had trained and worked as a journeyman hatter himself before managing to set up his own business. Moreover, the local hatters' union did not mind Loewe's hiring of a large number of apprentices because it gave work to the adult hatters' children. Loewe's low-cost production, however, jeopardized the national union's ability to maintain standards for the trade as a whole. If Loewe's production methods were allowed to stand, the union argued, they would undercut wages for hatters across the country.[73]

Loewe was thus a type example of a complaint that the NAM repeatedly advanced: that unions "interfered" in relations between an employer and "his men." Sometimes, this was of course true—that was the logic of the control of the craft or trade. To safeguard the position of *all* workers in a craft, a union could not allow a particular employer to pay substandard wages, even if his employees agreed to the lower pay.

The open-shop employers, however, hardly limited their objections to cases where the union was an external force in the sense it was in Loewe's business. Indeed, sometimes the very thing that inspired employers to break their relations with unions was union weakness rather than union power. This is part of what explains the deep roots of the NAM in the metal and foundry industries. In most branches of those industries, unions were too weak to enforce national, industry-wide agreements controlling both employers and workers. Nor were most employers as direly in need of some means for policing competition among themselves as was the case in, for example, coal. Thus, agreements easily broke down in mutual recriminations. Meanwhile, that so much of the work was skilled made labor costs high and replacing workers difficult, giving employers a strong incentive to find some way to reduce the power of their workers. The foundry and metal manufacturing industries, in fact, became the backbone of the employer open-shop movement.

The famous Murray Hill Agreement of 1900–1901 is a case in point. The National Metal Trades Association (NMTA) and the International Association of Machinists had arrived at a national agreement over the nine-hour day, primarily promoted by Chicago employers faced with union power in their own city and aiming to ensure that any concessions they made would apply to other metal trades employers as well. However, the much-vaunted agreement (mediated by the NCF) broke down in less than a year. Pressured by his increasingly radical-leaning membership, who were dissatisfied with the implementation of the agreement, the quite moderate IAM president, James O'Connell, was eventually convinced to call a national strike and include in the strike even those shops that were under national contract with the NMTA. This, of course, was a red flag for the employers: if the union was willing to strike even when there was a contract in force, what use was the agreement in maintaining labor peace? Moreover, many NMTA members complained that at the local level, the agreement had failed to prevent disputes about wages or spontaneous walkouts over work practices. It had, though, succeeded in convincing workers to join the union in droves. The agreement, then, threatened to present employers with the worst of both worlds: large numbers of unionized workers fired up to defend their interests and a national union unable or unwilling to control them.[74]

The agreement between the National Founders' Association and the Iron (later International) Molders' Union, first negotiated in 1899, lasted longer, but by 1904 that too was in shambles.[75] Unlike one-product foundries, such as those in the stove industry, which used unions to police competition, many foundries that produced on the basis of individual orders had at least as many cooperative as competitive relations with neighboring foundry shops.[76] Using unions to stabilize labor costs and prevent firms from undercutting each other held few attractions for them. Collaborative relations among foundries, of course, also fostered impulses toward employer-directed rather than union-led coordination on labor matters.

The character of the manufacturing process in the metal trades made that industry particularly reluctant to yield to unions, even as it made it particularly vulnerable to the demands of workers. As Philip Scranton has pointed out, historians and economists may have been enthralled by the assembly line and the giant firm, but a substantial portion of industrial production in the early twentieth century continued to be characterized by custom and batch rather than bulk or mass processes. Production that was made-to-order or that was based on the creation of a sample that would bring in a limited number of orders so a batch of a particular item could be produced had little use for standardized machines and little ability to thoroughly mechanize labor processes. Instead, custom-and-batch producers relied on all-purpose machinery that could be adapted for several different tasks. They also relied on skilled workers who understood the principles of the production methods, could perform a variety of difficult tasks, and could perhaps even contribute to the firm's reputation or product offerings by their mechanical ingenuity.[77] Indicative of the industry's appetite for skilled workers is that of all skilled workers in 1910, some 23 percent were trained in the metal and machining trades.[78] For the employer, skilled workers meant high labor costs. Even if less-skilled occupational categories are included, foundry and machine shop workers commanded clearly higher average hourly wages than most manufacturing workers.[79] More importantly from the company's perspective, wages made up 30 percent of total costs in the foundry and machine shop industry, the second-highest figure for leading US industries (see table 1).[80]

While foundry and machine shop proprietors actively sought ways to reduce labor costs, their options were limited. Many other industries had in the post–Civil War decades successfully implemented a strategy that has become known in the literature as "deskilling," that is, developing a labor process that had a clear set of constituent tasks and then hiring cheaper unskilled laborers for all but the few tasks for which skill was a necessity. This strategy was generally accompanied by the development of machinery that could be operated with limited training and that would produce many more units for the same input of labor, but this mechanization was not, strictly speaking, a requirement.[81] As early as the 1840s, Charles Babbage famously explained how significant cost savings could be achieved through the division of labor. Adapting the pin factory example that opens Adam Smith's *Wealth of Nations*, Babbage pointed out that the cost savings did not merely arise from efficiencies or mechanization possibilities generated by dividing up the labor process. Even if producing a pound of pins took exactly the same amount of time as when the process was completed by a single worker, it would be much cheaper if some of the tasks involved could be completed by women, children, or unskilled men—these, after all, could be paid far less than the worker who had the strength and skill to perform every task.[82] This deskilling strategy, however, was simply not available to

Table 1. Wages as a percentage of aggregate costs in the fifteen US industries with the highest value of product.

	Wage earners (thousands)	Value of product (millions of $)	Aggregate expenses (millions of $)	Wages (millions of $)	Value added by manufacturing (millions of $)	Wages as % of aggregate expenses
Cars and general shop construction by steam RR	282	405	405	181	206	45
Lumber and timber products	695	1,156	996	319	648	32
Foundry and machine shop products	531	1,228	1,078	322	688	30
Printing and publishing	258	738	619	165	536	27
Cotton goods	378	628	554	133	257	24
Clothing women's	153	385	341	79	176	23
Clothing men's	239	568	514	106	271	21
Boots and shoes (not rubber)	198	513	478	98	180	21
Woolen, worsted, and felt goods	168	435	388	72	153	19
Tobacco manufacture	166	417	366	69	240	19
Iron and steel, steel works, and rolling mills	240	986	890	163	328	18
Bread and other bakery products	100	396	340	59	159	17
Iron and steel, blast furnaces	38	391	363	25	71	7
Slaughtering and meat packing	89	1,371	1,317	51	168	4
Flour-mill and grist-mill products	39	884	828	21	116	3

Note: Industries marked in bold were fairly prominent among active NAM members. Calculated on the basis of data in US Department of Commerce, Bureau of the Census, *Thirteenth Census of the United States, 1910*, vol. 8, *Manufactures* (Washington, DC: GPO, 1913), 40-45, 518-63. For further discussion, see note 77.

foundry and machine shop proprietors because most foundries' profits relied on their capacity for quick-response custom production for a competitive and demanding local market. In foundry work, therefore, the contribution of skilled molders proved indispensable halfway into the twentieth-century heyday of mass production. As late as the mid-1920s, machine operators were a distinct minority of the foundry workforce, and shovel-and-wheelbarrow methods persisted into the 1940s. This afforded considerable power to the molders: the IMU was one of the strongest unions in the early twentieth-century United States.[83]

Craft workers in the foundry and metal manufacturing industry had more than just a specific manual skill: they understood the work process from beginning to end and were often responsible for planning it, as well as for adjusting and adapting the process as necessary. Much of the "manager's brain" remained "under the workman's cap," as David Montgomery has put it.[84] Foundry and machine shop proprietors were therefore highly vulnerable to union demands. If a particular group of skilled workers struck, the employer could rarely afford to dismiss them en masse. Even when replacement workers were available, which was rare, the quality of the work would inevitably suffer, and the business with it. Union density in the foundry and machine shop industry, therefore, was fairly high for the time, reaching about a quarter of all workers by 1909 and being far higher for some crafts, notably molders, as many as half of whom were at times represented by the International Molders' Union.[85]

Looking for a way to manage their costs and wrest control of the work from their skilled workers, many NAM members were attracted by the ideas of Frederick Taylor and his "scientific management." Taylor's method promised to replace knowledgeable but recalcitrant skilled workers with a cadre of "functional foremen," each with a specific area of responsibility. These foremen would then supervise the work of machine operators. Unlike craftsmen with all-around craft skill and considerable autonomy, the machine operators would be trained to perform specific tasks. Their training would be guided by careful time-motion studies, where a worker performing a particular task repeatedly would be observed by a researcher with a stopwatch, timing the worker's every move. The time-motion research would indicate what the most efficient series of movements was, how the process might be made more efficient, and what was an acceptable amount of time for a worker to spend on that particular process. Behind the scenes, engineers using the best scientific methods would design the products, as well as the machines that made all this possible. Even if most manufacturers balked at the vision of a whole new group of nonproductive workers (the functional foremen) cluttering their balance sheets, the basic idea was tantalizing. The work would be fully in the control of management. Workers performing manual labor would be assigned specific, well-defined tasks, while brain work would be reserved for the engineers, and the organization of work would be handled by the foremen. The autonomous skilled worker would essentially disappear. Workers would thus be much easier to replace, and the work would run more smoothly.[86]

Accordingly, some NAM members experimented with scientific management. Henry R. Towne, a prominent NAM member, was one of the earliest advocates of scientific management. Montgomery points out that as president of the American Society of Mechanical Engineers in 1886 Towne called upon engineers to turn their attention toward "the executive management of works," resulting in "a flood of papers concerning incentive pay," with Taylor's paper being one of the most noted ones.[87] Another NAM member, the H. H. Franklin Manufacturing Company (makers of the Franklin car), adopted scientific management methods in 1908, following a long strike by the IAM—not coincidentally, one suspects.[88] Reporting on the process some years later, the production manager praised the system for increasing production, reducing labor turnover, and generally promoting both more efficient methods of production and greater accord between workers and management.[89] Similarly, officials at the Ferracute Machine Company, whose secretary and treasurer, Enos M. Paullin, was a longtime NAM director, were so pleased with the system that the scientific management expert Frederic Parkhurst had installed for the company in 1907 that several of them wrote testimonials to accompany the second edition of Parkhurst's *Applied Methods of Scientific Management*.[90]

The promise of scientific management, however, was limited. Although the Ferracute Machine Company claimed that, far from being inapplicable to specialty work, scientific management was particularly useful in a company producing a great variety of different items, this does not seem to have been the experience of most companies.[91] The key element in scientific management—the clear division of labor between semiskilled operatives and "white shirts"—was simply impossible to implement at most companies engaged in custom-and-batch production. Skilled workers, troublesome as they were, were essential to foundry and machine work.

Like the foundry and metal shop proprietors, employers in other industries facing the same problem of high wage costs and substantial union presence gravitated toward the open-shop movement; examples include printing and publishing and boots and shoes (see tables 1 and 2).[92] Such industries provided many of the NAM's most active members, such as George Selby of the Selby Shoe Company in Ohio and F. C. Nunemacher of the Nunemacher Press in Kentucky. This is not to say, however, that one can simply read open-shop activism from the wage bill and union density figure. For example, the lumber industry was fairly well represented despite a low union density—partly, perhaps, because unions may have posed a threat to lumbermen in other ways.[93] Given the significant portion of costs represented by wages and the competitiveness of the industry, even logging and sawmill employers may have considered open-shop activism a kind of preventative measure. Moreover, lumbermen were worried about the prospects of an eight-hour day on government contract work, a major AFL legislative proposal.[94] Finally, the NAM invested particular effort in recruiting lumber manufacturers because of the vast resources represented by the industry.[95]

Just like employers in whose industry unions did not have a strong presence sometimes nevertheless got involved in open-shop work, employers who faced high labor costs and union densities sometimes stayed away. In addition to industrial structure, employer decisions were mediated by specific circumstances and cultural patterns. As noted in the previous section,

Table 2. Union density in selected industries.

Industry	Union members	Total workers	Union density (%)
Printing and publishing	77,200	258,000	30
Iron and steel, highly elaborated[1]	171,500	692,000	25
Clothing (men's and women's)	71,300	393,000	18
Boots and shoes	34,500	198,000	17
Paper and wood pulp	6,000	76,000	8
Leather, excluding boots and shoes	5,300	111,000	5
Lumber and timber products	19,000	695,000	3
Iron and steel, crude	6,300	279,000	2
Textiles	14,400	908,000	2

Sources: Leo Wolman, *The Growth of American Trade Unions, 1880-1923* (National Bureau of Economic Research, 1924), 110-19; US Department of Commerce, Bureau of the Census, *Thirteenth Census of the United States, 1910*, vol. 8, *Manufactures* (Washington, DC: GPO, 1913), chapter 15.

1. This category includes the foundry and machine shop industry, as well as products such as cash registers, safes, typewriters, and so on. For further discussion of the table, see note 92.

in some industries specific circumstances either made unions attractive partners in policing the industry (e.g., coal) or simply too powerful to defeat (e.g., the building trades). In other industries, such as garment and tobacco (cigar) manufacturing, specific structural features and cultural influences discouraged the open hostility exhibited by the open-shop employers.[96] Thus, neither the garment industry nor the cigar industry figured prominently in the open-shop movement, despite high labor costs. In the garment industry, the prevalence of small (sub)contractors made unionization difficult and wage negotiations indirect.[97] Equally importantly, the trade was dominated by Jewish entrepreneurs as well as Jewish workers, whose attitudes toward class, work, and entrepreneurship were complicated by their experience of downward mobility in Europe, migration, and a complex cultural attitude in which socialist ideas about the value of work vied with middle-class respectability and high-brow culture. Together with the already structurally complex contractual and employment relations, these ambiguities created a situation in which "not only did many workers aspire to become capitalists, but more than a few employers retained ties to the labor movement and radical politics."[98] In cigarmaking, on the other hand, the industry's many small shops probably found it excessively expensive to become active members in the organizations that promoted the open shop, while the largest shops could solve their labor problems through changes in both the labor process and the labor force.[99] Although it was skilled work, cigarmaking required facility with a specific task rather than time-consuming and complex all-around training. Parts of the labor process could also be simplified with the aid of machinery; this was especially the case for the cheaper class of five-cent cigars. Cigarmaking was also reasonably clean, stationary, indoor work—in other words, work culturally suitable for women. Women were not members of the union, and—for all the complex reasons explored by historians of labor and gender—they could be paid even less than nonunion men.[100] By the 1890s the larger cigar manufacturers were busily training and employing young women, so that by 1919 women came to dominate the five-cent cigar workforce. Although the women eventually proved less docile than the manufacturers had hoped, this gender-based, mechanization-aided solution replaced the need for employer collective action in the cigar industry.[101]

Despite these exceptions, high labor costs, a significant but not pervasive union presence, and the need for skilled workers primed particular manufacturers to gravitate toward the NAM's collective antiunion project. In addition to the constraints placed on them by specific production processes like custom-and-batch production, the moderate size of many of these manufacturers also shaped their choices. To be sure, the membership of the NAM hardly consisted of actual "small" businesses. Of the more politically active NAM members, about half employed more than 250 workers, which made them far larger than the average manufacturing business: according to the 1910 census, 95 percent of manufacturing establishments employed under 100 workers.[102] But their size was still a far cry from the multiplant conglomerates like those headed by most of the NCF business members.

In some respects, moderate size was a constraint: it meant that the kinds of complex strategies based on welfare programs or investment in mechanization employed by the National Cash Register Company or U.S. Steel were difficult or impossible to implement. In other ways, moderate size was a boon: a manufacturer of wooden boxes in Evansville, Indiana, with a few dozen employees was unlikely to be perceived by the general public as a tycoon whose business dealings were a matter of public concern.[103] This meant that the typical NAM business was less inhibited by considerations of publicity. Such moderate-sized manufacturers could also more plausibly portray themselves as the little guy harassed by the union bosses (as they did in, e.g., figure 2 in chapter 1).

Most of the open-shop activists also ran proprietorships rather than publicly traded corporations.[104] In a proprietary firm, the owner had full managerial control; he did not need to answer to a board of directors representing the shareholders. Thus, he could, if he so wished, truly fight the union to the finish. NAM president James Van Cleave, for example, seriously endangered his company, Buck's Stove and Range, over a labor dispute that started out as fairly insignificant, apparently chiefly out of bloody-mindedness and a desire to needle both the leaders of the molders' union and those of the AFL.[105] The dispute put the company in dire financial straits, and after Van Cleave's death, Buck's Stove and Range quickly reverted to being a union shop.[106]

The attractions of belligerence for the employers who decided to join the NAM were thus partly negative: there were few forces compelling them to negotiate with unions or even to portray themselves in a conciliatory light. They could, in other words, give free rein to the fairly universal employer feeling of disgruntlement with unions and with workers' demands more generally. Partly, though, they were also positive. Employers faced with high labor costs, dependence on hard-to-replace skilled workers, and financial or skill constraints to mechanization often found that there is power in a union, as the saying goes. Indeed, as Howell Harris has pointed out, organizing could give midsized employers "the same freedom to . . . do an end run around a union whose strength was patchy and concentrated, as was possessed by multiplant industrial giants like U.S. Steel."[107] The open-shop organizations offered their members a slew of practical assistance measures, ranging from information about how other employers had dealt with tricky situations with their workers to a lobbying presence at state and national legislatures to "loans" of workers to replace one's own striking workforce. The organizations also provided camaraderie and a cause to join, both of which must have pleased men who often were "joiners" active in local chambers of commerce, social clubs, and civic organizations.[108] Finally, they provided an ideological project, wrapping their members' concern for their pocketbooks in the warm glow of righteousness.

Nation, Region, Industry

Despite many efforts over the years to lay it to rest, "American exceptionalism" still looms in the background of discussions about labor's fate in the United States. Whether in its older guises that emphasized American labor's apolitical stance and lack of radicalism or in somewhat newer versions that highlight American employers' unique intransigence toward unions, the idea that the United States is an exception to a common pattern continues to have some purchase.[109] Yet the evidence for it is limited. Even if American managers held an unusually "deep belief in the virtues of individualism and personal achievement" that "made them less willing to accept collective bargaining," as Sanford Jacoby has suggested might be the case, they did, in fact, often engage in collective bargaining.[110] Meanwhile, their European counterparts usually very much preferred to avoid unions if they could. Many of them resisted with all the means at their disposal and only accepted negotiation with unions when circumstances forced them to do so. Just like their American counterparts, they then usually continued to keep an eye out for any opportunity to reassert managerial power.

Several comparative and country-specific studies emphasize the role of specific, contingent conditions rather than national patterns (let alone national character) in shaping employer courses of action. For example, Jeffrey Haydu has found that the essential difference between the British and American scenarios of labor relations in the early twentieth century stemmed not from the classic ingredients of American exceptionalism (such as a penchant for individualism or a lack of feudalistic traditions) but from the timing of technological change versus union growth. If technological change happened before union growth and consolidation, that tended to weaken unions enough to make antiunionism attractive for employers, regardless of whether the employers and unions in question were British or American.[111] Focusing particularly on the machine trades, Haydu points out that the key technological changes were already in place before the IAM achieved an established position; this made the IAM (which represented only about 11 percent of skilled machinists in 1900) both less effective in policing its members and less of a threat to employers. By contrast, the IAM's British counterpart, the Amalgamated Society of Engineers (ASE), had existed for nearly half a century and achieved a well-established pattern of collective bargaining; by 1900 it and allied organizations represented about half of skilled craftsmen in the machine trades. Haydu argues that the more established position of the ASE and the long-standing tradition of collective bargaining led British engineering employers to aim at concessions from unions rather than elimination of unionism.[112]

It was not that British employers took a more benign attitude toward unions or eschewed militant methods; indeed, in the 1890s some British employers instituted highly coordinated strikebreaking practices.[113] Even the British engineering employers, tired of frequent and unpredictable strikes and union work rules, precipitated a confrontation that in 1897 culminated in seven hundred firms nationwide locking out nearly fifty thousand of their workers.[114] The language cultivated by the engineering employers as they rallied their peers to "fight it out to the last" could just as easily have flowed from the pens of their American colleagues. Their strategies to fight the union also matched those of American metal manufacturers, complete with paid travel and lodging for strikebreakers (even when they were at first useless at the job), a private police force, and effective cooperation with the local police.[115] Yet the significant presence of the ASE made the union hard to crush. Thus, British engineering employers, having won their lockout, imposed not a complete antiunion environment but rather very management-favorable

"Terms of Settlement" that rejected any closed-shop-like arrangement and provided a dispute resolution procedure that employers used aggressively and effectively to their advantage.[116]

A rather similar pattern underlay the creation of the 1899 Danish "September Compromise." That agreement—famous as the first comprehensive central agreement between employer and worker umbrella organizations—set the pattern for twentieth-century Danish labor relations. Danish employers were no more philosophically inclined to cooperate with unions than American or British ones; they, too, complained that they suffered "under the strain of no longer possessing the authority to run their own enterprises," as workers controlled everything from wages to "the division of labor" to "the number of workers employed."[117] Denmark in the 1880s and 1890s witnessed widespread employer intransigence in the face of growing union challenge, including a protracted lockout in the metal trades, again the most vehemently antiunion sector. But like their British counterparts, the Danish metal trades employers were unable to entirely crush the union. In the booming economy of the late 1890s, unions were growing rapidly and picking off small employers with few resources to resist by making effective use of leapfrogging (also known as the serial strike—striking first one employer and, when that employer conceded, moving to the next). Given these circumstances, Danish employers saw centralized collective bargaining as a *boost* to management prerogatives: only by negotiating centrally would they be able to enforce their demands for managerial rather than worker control of the shop floor. Instituting a lockout that eventually covered nearly the whole unionized labor force, the Danish employers' organization successfully concluded an agreement that accorded final responsibility for collective agreements to the central bodies of employers and workers. Crucially, the agreement decreed that the workers' central federation was to recognize management's prerogatives in directing work and employing what labor they deemed necessary.[118]

Stiff-necked resistance to unions was, then, no monopoly of American employers. Neither was repression. In imperial Germany, as in the United States, the chief employer response to the rise of unions and the Social Democratic Party (SPD) in the late nineteenth century was to coordinate repressive action through existing sectoral or regional industrial organizations and to exhort all member firms to resist union demands. In the opening years of the twentieth century, as the union movement spread and intensified, these organizations expanded and consolidated their efforts through the creation of new centralized employer associations, which aimed to better coordinate support for individual employers through providing strike insurance and lockout funds and sharing information about workers (as well as forbidding members to hire locked-out workers). These repressive strategies were only traded for collaboration in the press of wartime, as the government, fearing serious damage to the war effort from strikes, insisted that employers recognize unions. This wartime exigency continued into the early years of the Weimar Republic. Prodded by the extraordinary explosion of socialist and radical activity in the last days of World War I, industrialists thought discretion the better part of valor and formed an agreement with moderate labor leaders (who themselves were less than excited about the prospects of socialist revolution). The result was the famed Stinnes-Legien Agreement of 1918, in which unions pledged their support for the capitalist system in exchange for an acknowledged bargaining role for unions, along with such basic guarantees as the eight-hour day. Yet as conditions changed again, employers quickly backpedaled, and the institutional framework for collective bargaining collapsed.[119]

The more one examines specific cases, the less important the explanatory power of national traditions seems when it comes to employer decision-making. Specific conditions seemed to matter much more. As Haydu notes, when British employers experienced "American-style" conditions or vice versa, neither conformed to the expected national pattern. Rather, British employers in the city of Coventry, where the local economy relied on "modern" items like bicycles and automobiles and where craft traditions were not well established, used "American" antiunion strategies with particular vehemence. At the same time, American employing printers, faced with the strong International Typographical Union, which had been well established before the introduction of the Linotype machine in the late nineteenth century, negotiated trade agreements with the union that kept Linotype work within union control.[120]

Geography and labor market structures mattered in the United States as well. The classic case of this is San Francisco. Geographically isolated, San Francisco employers put a premium on their skilled workers and had difficulty recruiting strikebreakers even when they wished to do so. Manufacturing remained small-scale, locally based, and not particularly profitable. This made it difficult and unattractive to invest in mechanization and gave craft workers greater control of the labor market. Combined with other circumstances—such as the ethnic homogeneity and shared anti-Chinese racism of the white population and easier worker entrance into politics in the absence of an established elite—these labor market factors made San Francisco a fertile ground for unionism. In the first decade of the twentieth century, at least one-third of San Francisco wage earners were union members, enrolled in what Michael Kazin notes were "durable organizations that wielded significant power over working conditions and elected officials."[121] Indeed, an attempt by the open-shop wing of San Francisco employers to organize an employers' association and defeat strikes in several industries, from restaurants to the waterfront, besides being rebuffed by unions, was also reprimanded by other employers, whose businesses suffered as a result of what they perceived as the association's intransigence. In response to union strength, most San Francisco employers resorted not to belligerent antiunionism but to a "practical corporatism" that emphasized the common values of the middling folks, from craftsmen to small manufacturers, and their role as a bulwark against both the encroaching power of great corporations and the Chinese underclass.[122]

Whether compared in international perspective, by industry, or by size, then, employer approaches to labor unionism were always formed in an interplay of union power, industrial exigencies, political considerations, and, yes, employers' own ideas and ideologies. Words, however, were not always a reliable guide to ideas, nor ideas to actions. Regardless of what they said about unions, most employers tended to react to the union challenge by closing ranks—usually first to crush unions and, failing that, to exercise maximum power within an industrial relations regime that included, contained, and perhaps even utilized unions.

5 Employers, Unite?

The Bases and Challenges of Employer Collective Action

Don't mourn, organize.
—Joe Hill, telegram to William "Big Bill" Haywood

The concluding dinner of the 1897 reunion of the commercial clubs of Boston, Chicago, St. Louis, and Cincinnati was a grand affair. Held at the palatial mansion of the oil tycoon Alexander MacDonald, the six-course dinner had begun with *lucines orangées* (hard clams) accompanied by Clos Blanc de Vougeot, proceeded through *chapon toulousaine* (capon, i.e., castrated rooster) paired with an 1864 Château Lescours, and concluded with *sorbet Moscatel*, Camembert cheese, and glasses of Veuve Cliquot Brut and liqueurs. The nearly 150 guests at the dinner included such well-known names as the railroad magnate Melville Ingalls; the president of the Pullman Palace Car Company, George M. Pullman; and the department store innovator Marshall Field. Not everyone was a businessman: there were also other men of rising importance, such as the lawyer Charles Nagel (later to become President William Taft's secretary of commerce) and the head of the newly organized Associated Press, Melville E. Stone. The assembled guests had enjoyed two days of outings, luncheons, and entertainments ranging from viewing military parades to running humorous races (the potato race was won by St. Louis, while victory in the sack race went to Boston).[1]

As speakers throughout the reunion made clear, however, the reunion had a larger purpose than to entertain. It was a manifestation of the conviction among the nation's businessmen that their similarities surpassed their differences and that their guiding hand would keep the country on the right track. As Jerome Jones, the president of the Commercial Club of Boston, told the dinner guests, "We are all alike in seeking to solve, intelligently, the commercial problems of the day; and there is nothing in any of these that should divide businessmen." His sentiments were echoed by the next speaker, the president of the Commercial Club of Chicago, John J. Glessner, who reminded the listeners that "the delightful social contact is but a means to an end," namely, "the cultivation of civic pride, the advancement of civic interest and prosperity, not along narrow lines, but over a field wide as commerce itself." Men of commerce were particularly needed in such a task, Glessner told his audience, because "commercial life tends to high morality, a keen sense of honor, a detestation of fraud; and when associated in bodies like this, it makes a potent force for truth and justice and right throughout the world."[2]

As reunions like the one in Cincinnati indicated, by the turn of the twentieth century, the salience of many nineteenth-century divisions (manufacturer vs. merchant, North vs. South, East vs. West) was receding, and businessmen were finding common ground socially and to some extent also politically. Meanwhile, class divisions were gaining in significance: developments like the growth of factory size and the rise of railroad suburbs produced a wider gulf between employers and their workers. Yet such broad shifts in cultural and economic patterns did not in and of themselves produce a commonality of interest that was actionable. Even when businessmen agreed that as employers they had shared interests, for example, that agreement did not always suffice to sustain collective action over individual self-interest. Just as workers' common interests as workers did not automatically translate into solidarity or successful united action, employers, too, needed to both articulate their common interests and to develop strategies to maintain collective action.

This chapter starts with an overview of how broad economic and social developments in the late nineteenth century had created a firmer common ground for employers to stand on. It then offers two case studies. The first one, on St. Louis, draws on social network analysis to explore the local landscape of upper-middle-class society and to demonstrate the multiple connections between businessmen. The second, on the printers' strike of 1905–6, examines a case where open-shop employers attempted to build a united multiemployer front against a strong union and suggests that the failure of that effort underlines the limits of employer solidarity.

What Employers Shared

Over the course of the late nineteenth century, many of the older divisions between industrialists, financiers, and merchants lost force. Regional fault lines remained but were less and less salient, markets stretched over ever longer distances, economic interests became increasingly intertwined, and challenges from below alerted industrial and financial elites to what they shared rather than what set them apart. Interest conflicts hardly disappeared, but many strands connected businessmen to each other in ways that facilitated joint action and a common purpose—especially when it came to labor.

Most obviously, the end of Reconstruction had set white businessmen from different sides of the Mason-Dixon Line well on the way to reconciliation. Indeed, businessmen had lobbied for achieving the Compromise of 1877, which ended Reconstruction, and implicitly accepted the displacement of elected Reconstruction governments that white southern "redeemers" had achieved through violence. Sacrificing the basic rights of African American citizens and sidestepping the centrality of slavery and emancipation to the war, these businessmen promoted soothing narratives of the honorable pursuit of reconciliation, the romanticism of the Old South, and the valor of soldiers on both sides (with African American veterans largely written out of the story).[3] Soon, southern boosters envisioning a New South, economically thriving and industrially modernized, could remain unrepentant and still receive a favorable reception from their northern brethren. For instance, an 1886 speech at the New England Society of New York by the Atlanta businessman Henry W. Grady was received with enthusiastic cheers, despite Grady's insistence that "the South has nothing for which to apologize."[4]

Other regional lines (West and East, but also to some extent city and country) that had divided businessmen were also fading. The incredible postbellum growth of railroads meant faster and easier transportation of goods and people, expanding markets, and improving interregional connections. What the railroad was accomplishing for physical goods, the telegraph and faster mail service were doing for information about goods' availability and prices.[5] Railroads had another effect as well: as an investment opportunity, they fused together the capital and the interests of merchants, bankers, and manufacturers. Meanwhile, manufacturing grew rapidly and boosted the economic and social position of industrialists, partly fueled by the enormous profits of the Civil War years, which had made manufacturers less dependent on merchant capital. Perhaps most significantly, the turn-of-the-century merger movement intertwined financiers and manufacturers as never before: in just a few years, consolidations swallowed over eighteen hundred firms. The growth in size of industrial corporations made them a more attractive investment, while profits from manufacturing involved industrialists in increasingly diversified portfolios.[6] Economic convergence promoted social convergence. By the 1880s manufacturers were increasingly accepted in institutions previously reserved for merchants, such as the New York Chamber of Commerce and prestigious social clubs. At the same time, the sheer number of commercial associations—trade associations, boards of trade, chambers of commerce—mushroomed in the 1880s and 1890s.[7]

As the worlds of different kinds of businessmen drew closer together, their social distance from their employees grew. In the antebellum working world, while conflict was certainly not absent, ideas about a republican community of producers and faith in social mobility had encouraged the containment of conflict in expected and even ritualized channels of at least some give-and-take. In specific trades, especially engineering, identities based on skill and craftsmanship had given proprietors and craftsmen common ground in, for example, mechanics' institutes. By contrast, in the last decades of the nineteenth century, these conflict-mitigating identities fractured. One can read that fracturing directly in, for example, a set of obituaries commissioned by Cincinnati's chamber of commerce. As Jeffrey Haydu demonstrates, whereas those obituaries in the 1870s often praised their subjects' civic uprightness as a "mechanic and manufacturer," by the 1890s they described the deceased's civic contributions as related to his role as a businessman, "a category that excluded even skilled manual labor while encompassing proprietors and managers, employers from different industries, and capitalists from both manufacturing and commerce."[8] One can also see it in organizational shifts: mechanics' institutes declined, while the new-style "engineer-entrepreneurs," as David Montgomery has termed them, formed a clique knit together locally by polytechnic institutes and nationally by the American Society of Mechanical Engineers.[9] Instead of craft traditions, these proprietors extolled progress and efficiency; more and more explicitly, they came to see their workers' customary rules about the content of a "fair day's work" as impeding both their business profits and the nation's progress.[10]

Residential patterns mirrored the workplace: there, too, the distance between employer and worker lengthened as the middle and upper classes drew away from city centers to the proverbial leafy suburbs. The decades surrounding the Civil War witnessed the rise of a number of residential developments designed to highlight their contrast to the city, with parklike, quiet surroundings from which work was conspicuously absent. At first, only the upper crust could achieve such physical and experiential separation from the city while maintaining access to it for business purposes; these early developments included such iconic neighborhoods as Llewellyn Park in New Jersey (about fifteen miles from Manhattan), Riverside outside Chicago, and Chestnut Hill outside Boston. With the rise of the railroad suburb in the latter third of the century, however, the suburban haven became accessible to the next level of commuter, the reasonably affluent businessman and his family. Demographics between railroad suburbs varied, but generally some 30–50 percent of households fit this characterization. Another third or so of the households in these suburbs consisted of the people required to provide the services required by these families aspiring to healthy country living—the gardeners, the maids, the cooks.[11] Work and workers could not, then, be entirely banished from upper-middle-class lives. Still, a new physical distance had grown between those who produced manufactured goods and those who designed them or planned their marketing or financing.

Further widening the gap between manufacturers and workers was the fact that the working classes were becoming quite literally more foreign. The growth in immigration and the shift in sources of immigration to southern and eastern Europe brought in great numbers of new arrivals from Italy, Poland, and Bohemia; soon, major cities seemed to teem with a medley of tongues, cultures, and religions. Many of these immigrants were Catholic or Jewish, and native-born Americans viewed them with at least as much wariness as had greeted upon the Irish immigrants arriving in the 1840s and 1850s. The America these new arrivals entered was also different. It was an America of factories and cities, a place where the middle class had at least in part replaced the antebellum religious hopes about the perfectibility of the world with new, darker ideas about evolution and the dangers of biological degeneration. By the 1890s representatives of the old Anglo-Saxon Protestant elite had begun to portray the new immigrants as imperiling the racial fabric of the nation. Citing studies demonstrating declines in the native birth rate, these elites argued that native-stock Americans were committing "race suicide": they did not reproduce because their children would have to compete "with those they did not recognize as their own grade and station."[12] Even some of those who did not attribute the declining native-stock birth rate to immigration worried that the end result would be a shift in the genetic quality of the nation.[13]

At the turn of the twentieth century, however, worries about the economy and class conflict were much more acute than the brewing fears of racial degeneration through immigration. For employers, in any case, immigration was a double-edged sword. Many employers, while they worried about immigrant radicals, also welcomed immigrants as an important addition to the labor pool, one whose presence employers believed helped them keep wages down and unions at arm's length.[14] Employers feared workers bent on challenging upper-class rule more than they feared immigrants. And such grassroots challenges abounded in the post–Civil War decades. In 1877, just as the end of Reconstruction was promising new sectional unity, a massive railroad strike witnessed tens of thousands of workers in dozens of cities walking off the job and proceeding to burn thousands of railroad cars, profoundly unsettling the elites in whose eyes the masses of citizens impoverished by the severe 1870s depression already looked very much like a threatening "dangerous class." The 1880s saw the rise of the Knights of Labor and widespread agitation for the eight-hour day, as well as the Haymarket Affair, in which a bomb exploded at a Chicago labor rally, killing several and resulting in the trial of eight anarchists. The 1890s witnessed another severe depression, spectacular clashes between workers and private as well as public security forces, and the rise of a potential political challenge to established elites from the People's Party, a serious third-party challenger that built a broad political movement across especially the South and the West.[15]

The elites' response to these challenges was to involve themselves more and more intensely in civic associations. These associations reflected businessmen's desire for a well-run society with more efficiency and less corruption, as well as their growing conviction that they were specially equipped for decision-making not only in the field of commerce but also in the civic and political fields.[16] Such a "search for order," as Robert Wiebe termed it in his classic work, formed a conspicuous theme in turn-of-the-twentieth-century American society. As Wiebe recognized and as others have elaborated upon, for the well-heeled this search for order was closely related to a fear that democratic politics might shift the balance of power toward ordinary people, and much of their response was directed toward insulating institutions of local governance against popular influence.[17]

In these business-led local organizations, the line between the classes burned much brighter than the divisions between businessmen. For example, the Committee for Public Safety, which crushed the 1877 general strike in St. Louis with mass arrests and threats of violence, united businessmen across industrial, ethnic, and sectional lines while also reflecting a worry about the lower classes potentially uniting across the divide of race. The committee included merchants, financiers, manufacturers, professionals, and smaller businessmen, many of them of German or Irish origin. Its leadership explicitly transcended the sectional rift: it included men born in both southern and northern states and even two ex–Civil War generals, one from each side. Meanwhile, the press zeroed in on the presence of "brutal" and "dangerous-looking" African Americans among the strike marchers.[18] In other cities, the threat from below elicited similar responses. The elites of New York reacted to demands of economic redistribution in the 1870s by supporting an amendment to the state constitution that would have transferred questions of municipal taxation, expenditures, and debt to a board of finance elected only by citizens of considerable means. The 1877 upheaval prompted them to call for military force to be applied against the strikers.[19] In Chicago, where the crush of the 1870s depression was exacerbated by a fire that destroyed a sizable portion of the city, the city's leading businessmen formed the Citizens' Association (CA) to promote efficient government and order. The CA hoped to concentrate power in the hands of the mayor, his appointees, and newly created positions within the executive while diminishing the influence of ward-elected aldermen and the elected police board. The CA also funded a businessmen's militia and worked to strengthen the police. The Chicago police department succeeded in suppressing the 1877 protests with considerable efficiency (not to mention brutality), which the CA took as evidence of the benefits of its efforts. Accordingly, the CA reaffirmed its support for the police, purchased more weaponry (including a Gatling gun, a forerunner of the modern machine gun), and, in the words of historian Sam Mitrani, "expanded to virtually shadow the elected government."[20]

The civic and political unity of businessmen got an additional boost from the nomination of William Jennings Bryan as the Democratic Party's presidential candidate. Bryan, whose rhetorical gestures toward labor and farmers secured him the endorsement of the People's Party, scared the nation's leading businessmen. His call for an end to the gold standard alarmed financial elites who perceived the gold standard as the key to economic stability, growth, and the integration of US and British financial markets, and it dismayed industrial elites whose investments spanned an increasingly broad scope. As a result, many former Democrats transferred their allegiance to the Republican Party; as one scholar has put it, "Money flowed like water" into the Republican campaign coffers to elect William McKinley and defeat Bryan.[21]

To be sure, businessmen in the early twentieth century continued to be divided over a variety of issues, and open-shop activists sometimes warned each other to make clear to potential members that cooperation was expected on "labor matters, *and labor matters alone*."[22] Especially the question of the tariff caused friction. There was general agreement that while tariffs were a good thing (the NAM declared itself "unalterably opposed to free trade"), reform was also necessary. Yet any concrete proposals for reform risked conflict. Purchasers of raw materials (such as small manufacturers) resented raw material tariffs that benefited steel and other raw material trusts, while producers with older plant and equipment feared competition from the modern facilities that new competitors might be induced to set up if tariffs kept prices high, but all of them also had their pet tariffs.[23]

Yet if conflicts remained, the developments of the late nineteenth century had nevertheless done much to smooth cooperation between businessmen. Collective action on specific issues was further facilitated by the many tangible interconnections among businessmen through residential patterns, business activity, and leisure pursuits.

St. Louis as a Case Study

The National Association of Manufacturers and trade-based employer organizations aspired to shape labor relations and state policy on labor on a
national scale. However, their power largely derived from the organizations
and networks they built on the local level, and they invested considerable
energy in exhorting employers to build local associations and in converting
those local-level connections into the foundation of their national influence.[24]
It is therefore informative to inquire into the local connections that formed
the basis of employer collective action at the grassroots level.

There were multiple ways in which local ties facilitated employer collective
action. For one, local ties meant that much of the groundwork of establishing trust and credibility had already been performed. One was much more
likely to listen to a proposal for, say, political action if it came from someone
whom one already knew as a neighbor, a fellow member of a social club, or
a colleague on a philanthropic association board. Second, local ties formed
a ready-made network for dissemination of information about things like a
proposed organized response to a labor problem or a planned lobbying effort
against a state or national labor law. Third, the existence of local networks
inspired confidence in employers that their actions would be efficacious:
social clubs, bank directorates, fancy neighborhoods, and philanthropic organizations enrolled a variety of social notables whose support would likely
significantly help any project.[25] These links afforded employers significant pull
in the community, which could then be translated into political influence on
regional and national scales. The significance of this last point for the NAM's
lobbying efforts is taken up in the next chapter. For now, the focus is on the
web of connections that institutional, residential, and social affiliations spun
around the business and political community at the local level.

To explore that web of connections, this section delves into the social
and political scene of St. Louis, a useful case study for a number of reasons.
First, it was a central locale for the National Association of Manufacturers: the NAM had over one hundred member companies in St. Louis, and
its president from 1906 through 1908 was the St. Louis stove manufacturer
James W. Van Cleave.[26] The NAM also got involved in local strikes: in connection with a shoeworkers' strike in 1907, the NAM covertly investigated
strikers and unionists and paid workers to gather information on strikers
and to try to persuade strikers to return to work. It also sponsored a branch
of an "astroturf," or fake grassroots, workers' organization in St. Louis (the
Workingmen's Protective Association) and worked hard to create the St. Louis
Citizens' Industrial Association, a multi-industry league against unions.[27]

St. Louis was also the site of major confrontations between employers and unions—confrontations that were sometimes quite literal and physical, such as during a 1900 streetcar strike, when businessmen joined an armed sheriff's posse that, among other things, fired into a crowd of strikers, leaving three strikers dead and fourteen wounded.[28] Finally, St. Louis was firmly in the Northeast–Midwest industrial corridor, which supplied a large portion of the NAM's members, but at the same time it was a city with strong inter-regional ties, mirroring the presence of southern and western businessmen in the NAM's ranks.

St. Louis also has the added benefit of being the subject of two digitized editions of a biographical compendium (*The Book of St. Louisans [BSTL]*, first edition 1906, second edition 1912) and a digitized directory of social clubs with their membership lists (*Gould's Blue Book for the City of St. Louis*, 1913).[29] These provide a glimpse of the landscape of the city's notable and seminotable residents, their connections, and their residential patterns and allow a number of computational analyses of their characteristics and inter-connections.[30]

The City of St. Louis

Founded by French fur traders in the years immediately following the Seven Years' War when nobody really knew who governed the massive swath of land termed Louisiana, St. Louis remained a settlement of a few hundred Europeans and a shifting number of Missouri and Peoria Indians for most of the eighteenth century. Its European American population had barely surpassed one thousand when the Louisiana Purchase transferred it from Spanish to American ownership in 1803. The town's population growth and prominence, though, began a steady upward climb with Missouri's statehood in 1820—and, perhaps more importantly, with the coming of the steamboat in the 1820s, a development that firmly linked St. Louis into a transporta-tion network stretching east to the great seaboard cities and south to New Orleans. Because the upper Mississippi and the Missouri could not accom-modate vessels as heavy as those that plowed the lower Mississippi, St. Louis became a significant unloading and reloading point, and the low cost of steam transport made the city an important transfer point for shipping agricultural products from the surrounding areas to eastern cities. St. Louis also became a hub for the increasingly lively Santa Fe trade, which brought significant quantities of Mexican silver to St. Louis in exchange for manufactured goods. Stimulated by such developments, as well as by the growth of the US Army's projects in the West—especially the Mexican War in 1846–48—and the wave of Irish and German immigration beginning in the late 1830s, the population of St. Louis had by 1840 passed sixteen thousand. It had soared to more than seventy-five thousand by 1850, of which nearly half had been born in Germany or Ireland. The population also included a few thousand enslaved and free African Americans, though these numbers belied the significance of slavery for St. Louis: in the 1850s, the city became a major slave trading post, with agents for more than two dozen slave dealers.[31]

These antebellum developments prefigured the post–Civil War nature of St. Louis in many ways: though increasingly eclipsed by its main rival, Chicago, the city remained a nexus between East and West, as well as between North and South. Its population, culture, and economy reflected the manufacturing and immigration patterns of the Northeast, the raw materials focus and admiration of ruggedness of the West, and a sympathy for southern viewpoints. Southern sympathies had established a strong foothold in the 1850s as a consequence of growing commercial ties with the South; despite Missouri's decision to remain in the Union, these ties intensified during the war due to a blockade of the Mississippi that made those ties practically the only ones available.[32] The early, sizable, and sustained German immigration also left its mark on the city's elite, as well as its working class, even if the crème de la crème continued to bar the door of the highest levels of high society to the immigrant or second-generation men of wealth, "no matter how many German princes they knew."[33]

The post–Civil War era brought a slew of efforts to reform city government and services, which the decades of semichaotic growth had left in a rather haphazard state. It also brought further growth in both population and especially manufacturing. As the downtown businesses expanded, the city's elite began to withdraw from the hustle and bustle. The central Washington Avenue, the fashionable address of the 1860s, shifted from elite residences to garment manufacturing. The luster of Vandeventer Place, the exclusive West End address of the 1880s, began in the 1890s to give way to the even more westerly new private streets, or "places"—prime among them Westmoreland Place and Portland Place—on the edge of Forest Park. Many, such as Westminster Place and Kingsbury Place, were designed by notable architects and came complete with sculptures and arched entrances. The leafy surroundings were complemented by services catering to persons of means, such as exclusive decorators, doctor's offices, and clubs.[34] Though some of the older neighborhoods remained desirable, in the early twentieth century power and prestige "were concentrated within a half-dozen blocks of Lindell and Kingshighway." This area plus Vandeventer Place represented "the city's economic power, wealth, and social elite"—as is clear in that more than 90 percent of the members of the city's most exclusive social club, the St. Louis Country Club, had their residences there. Meanwhile, some of the great names of St. Louis preferred country estates both as summer homes and as permanent residences, facilitated by the laying of narrow-gauge railways from the 1870s onward.[35]

Like the fancy neighborhoods, the social clubs of the city reflect an elite that was closely interconnected if somewhat divided by ethnicity.[36] Thanks to directories like the *Gould's Blue Book* and an early twentieth-century enthusiasm for local biographical compendia, one can extract enough information to computationally construct a social network of St. Louis clubs. The network is based on shared membership between clubs: many individuals belonged to three or more clubs both because clubs had different domains (country clubs for recreation, business clubs for work) and because more memberships offered more networking opportunities. Figures 4 and 5 show two versions of the network, with figure 4 providing an overview and figure 5 highlighting the particularly closely interconnected clubs. Both networks indicate the links, divisions, and hierarchies in the city's elite: who associated with whom, as well as, to an extent, who was climbing their way up. Everyone in the clubs was firmly in the middle or upper middle class: occupationally, the club men were presidents, vice presidents, managers, and secretaries of a variety of financial and manufacturing establishments; manufacturers and merchants; and lawyers, physicians, and architects (and some simply listed their position as "capitalist"). But some, of course, were a little more elite than others.

The city's top dogs hobnobbed in ten clubs that form a closely interlinked cluster (these clubs are depicted with a darker border in figure 4 and in gray in figure 5). Especially the central quintet formed by the St. Louis Club, St. Louis Country Club, Racquet Club, Noonday Club, and Commercial Club demonstrates the many overlapping connections between the city's political and commercial elites. About 50–60 percent of the members of the exclusive Commercial Club, with a membership limited to some one hundred, also belonged to the other prestigious clubs of St. Louis, such as the St. Louis Club, the Noonday Club, and the St. Louis Country Club. Similarly, nearly half of the top-echelon members of the St. Louis Country Club also belonged to the Noonday Club, a club aiming to educate and entertain its members while advancing their commercial and business interests and offering them a well-appointed locale with the requisite billiards, dining, and library spaces at the top of the downtown Security Building.[37]

In addition, a number of the members of the core clubs also belonged to one or both of the two clubs that were so exclusive they only had a handful of members: the Log Cabin Club and the Cuivre Club, with a partially

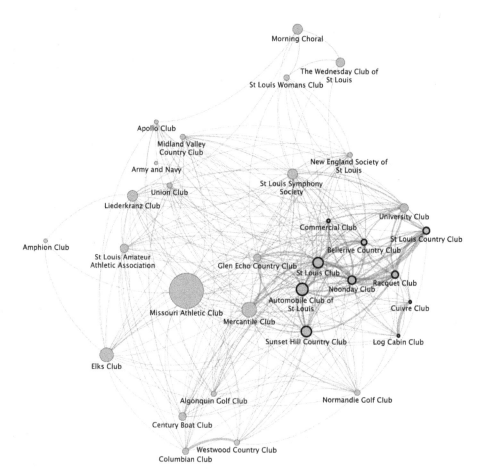

Figure 4: St. Louis social clubs. Connections are based on shared membership. Edge weight (the thickness of the connecting line) represents the percentage of shared membership between two clubs, calculated as

$$\frac{\text{(number of shared members)}}{\text{(Club A members + Club B Members - shared members)}}$$

This varies from just over 27 percent for the edge between St. Louis Club and Noonday Club to 0.03 percent for the Missouri Athletic and Cuivre Clubs. Size of node (circle marking club) indicates total membership of the club, ranging from a high of 2,718 for the Missouri Athletic club to a low of 20 members for the Log Cabin Club. The triad at the upper edge of the image (Morning Choral, Wednesday Club, and St. Louis Woman's Club) shows women's clubs. Central clubs that enrolled much of the city's elite are marked with a darker border. Network drawn in Cytoscape using the default Prefuse Force Directed Layout.

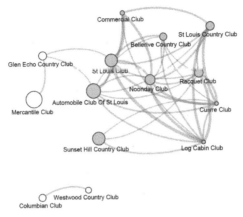

Figure 5: St. Louis social clubs with particularly heavily overlapping membership. Calculated as a percentage represented by the shared membership of the membership of the smaller club. Only clubs connected by edges representing shared membership of 25 percent or more of the smaller club's membership are displayed. Thickness of edge (connecting line) reflects how large a percentage of the membership of the smaller club is shared with the larger (max is 80 percent, represented by the edge between the Log Cabin Club and the St. Louis Club); size of node (circle marking club) reflects total number of members (max is 989, represented by the Mercantile Club). Network drawn in Cytoscape using the default Prefuse Force Directed Layout.

overlapping membership between them. The Cuivre Club was a hunting club for "wealthy amateur sportsmen of ample leisure and means" with a membership limited to twenty, an initiation fee of $500, and an annual membership fee "not to exceed" $200 (some $15,700 and $6,300, respectively, in 2020 dollars).[38] The Log Cabin Club likewise limited the number of its members to twenty-five and provided them with a nine-hole golf course.

Membership in these core clubs was usually accessible only by nomination, often required a long waiting period, and came with a price tag that ensured one's financial, as well as one's social, standing.[39] However, the club scene also accommodated the lesser rungs of the elite and shifted in response to new power centers. Some clubs, such as the Missouri Athletic Club, were open to a large swath of the middle-class population of St. Louis. As one can see in figure 4, it had a large membership that was not strongly connected to the core clubs that enrolled the elite. Others provided avenues of social mobility, reflected the rise of new elites, or delineated ethnic-religious divisions within the upper rungs. The Glen Echo Country Club, on the somewhat less fashionable but up-and-coming north side of town, apparently provided something of a route for the city's upwardly mobile businessmen into the more established elite. As one can see in figure 5, it formed a link between the Mercantile Club, an exclusive but not-quite-so-exclusive club with a business-oriented membership and a penchant for civic involvement, and two central clubs, the St. Louis Club and the Automobile Club.[40] The Sunset Hill Country Club, on the other hand, had its roots in "new money" economically as well as ethnically. It was founded in 1909 by August A. Busch, the son of the German-born brewing magnate Adolphus Busch; the story goes that August was galled by years of being refused membership in the St. Louis Country Club, whose elite members looked down their noses at the fantastically wealthy but in their view crude and flashy Busch family.[41] In the club network, one can see how it remained slightly off-center from the older elite clubs, though it shared significant membership with the Racquet Club and the two small exclusive clubs, Log Cabin and Cuivre.[42] Yet it was much better connected than the city's two major Jewish social institutions, the Westwood Country Club and the Columbian Club. These were linked to each other by a significant shared membership, and though they were not entirely isolated, they stood somewhat apart, as many of the city's clubs either explicitly or implicitly refused Jewish members.[43]

Membership in the lower-tier clubs was not insignificant—club life could provide important networking opportunities, especially if one could afford multiple memberships. Membership in the top-tier clubs, meanwhile, was exclusive enough that they potentially offered a real means of forging connections with (other) influential people. The Noonday Club, for example, had a membership of a few hundred and numbered among its members many of the top businessmen and top politicians of the city (although there was a strict prohibition, a contemporary history noted, against discussions of "any political or religious questions").[44] And the smaller clubs especially vividly illustrate the links between the business, political, and opinion-making elites of St. Louis: the Log Cabin Club, for instance, enrolled a prominent St. Louis newspaper editor and publisher, a former Republican candidate to the US Senate, and the mayor of St. Louis, besides a variety of bankers, stockbrokers, and top-echelon businessmen.[45]

Manufacturers and Organized Businessmen in the St. Louis Social Map

By 1900 the population of St. Louis had reached nearly six hundred thousand, and manufacturing employed nearly 40 percent of the city's workers.[46] Where, then, did organized employers fit in the city's socially, economically, and culturally interconnected landscape? And did such employers demonstrate the kinds of multiple connections to each other that characterized much of the city's top echelon? In other words, what connections and social resources could employers draw on when crafting a collective response to labor?

The Book of St. Louisans lists 472 men who represented a company belonging to the NAM and/or belonged to one or more of the local business organizations: the Businessmen's League, the Manufacturers' Association, and the Citizens' Industrial Association. Many of these men had a strong foothold in the St. Louis elite: 149 of them belonged to one of the city's core clubs, displayed in figure 5. A further 71 belonged to the Mercantile Club or to one or more of the significant second-tier country clubs: Glen Echo, Algonquin, and Normandie Golf. Nearly half, then, held membership in one or more of the top-rung or near-top-rung clubs.[47] They also lived in the "right" areas of town. Figure 6 shows the residences of the men who represented NAM's St. Louis member companies and who appear in the *BSTL*. They, like

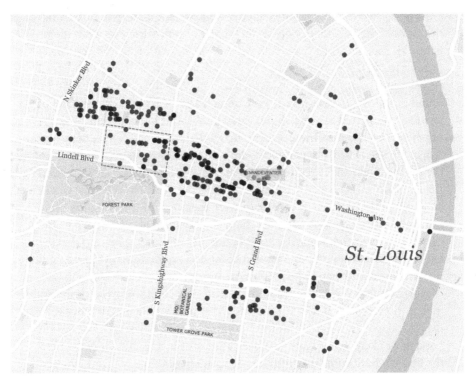

Figure 6: St. Louis NAM members' residences, *n* = 87. Westmoreland, Portland, Westminster, and Kingsbury Places were all within the dashed-line square. Addresses were extracted from *The Book of St. Louisans* and geolocated with the US census geocoder. Map created with MapBox. For data and discussion, see https://github.com/vhulden/bossesunion/.

the city's other middle-class residents, mainly kept to the area west of South Grand Boulevard, which divided the industrial parts of the city from its more comfortable residences. Most NAM members lived in two particularly nice areas: a corridor extending from South Grand Boulevard to North Skinker Boulevard, concentrating in Central West End, east of Forest Park; and the square mile or so flanked by Tower Grove Park to the south and Missouri Botanical Gardens to the west. Both areas consisted of large, fine, single-family residences and private "places," many of them newly built in the late nineteenth century.[48] In the hierarchy of St. Louis society, then, organized employers in St. Louis placed mainly in the tier just below the top, though with a solid foothold in the most exclusive circles.

Equally importantly, organized businessmen were also well connected to each other, even regardless of the organizations they built for themselves. The network in figure 7 shows that of the 472 organized businessmen in the *BSTL*, more than half (242) also either lived near or belonged to the same clubs as another member of these business organizations.

As always with networks, it is of course important to keep in mind what the network actually represents. In this case, the network shows those members of the businessmen's associations active in St. Louis (the Business Men's League [BML], the Manufacturers' Association, the Citizens' Industrial Association, and the National Association of Manufacturers) who can be found in the *BSTL* and who can be connected to each other on the basis of residence or shared membership in social clubs (*not* including the business organizations listed).[49] There are 242 such individuals. The connections—or "edges," in social network parlance—are based on two types of links between the businessmen: close residence and membership in the same clubs. So if Benny Businessman and Ernie Employer lived close to each other, that would be a link between them. If they both were members of the St. Louis Club, that would also be a link between them. If they both also belonged to the Mercantile Club, that would be another link. If both further belonged to the Glen Echo, that would be one more link (and so on for as many shared club memberships as they possess).[50]

Note that these types of links mean that an edge connecting two businessmen in the network is not direct evidence of personal interaction between the two people connected; it is merely something that makes such interaction possible or likely. To mitigate the uncertainty inherent in this, the network in the figure is built with fairly restrictive requirements. First, an edge between Benny and Ernie based on shared club membership is drawn only if they belonged to at least three of the same clubs—so above, they would be connected if both belonged to St. Louis *and* Mercantile *and* Glen Echo. Second, an edge based on residential proximity is only drawn if Benny and Ernie lived

Figure 7: Network of members of BML, CIA, MFA, and NAM in St. Louis, n = 242. Each node represents an individual. Network based on shared membership (edge drawn if the linked nodes are members in three or more of the same clubs) and on geographic proximity of residence (edge drawn if the distance between the nodes' residences <0.1 mile). Dashed edges are on the basis of residential proximity, solid edges are on the basis of shared club membership, and vertical slash edges are on the basis of both. Diamond-shaped nodes are NAM members, and round nodes are members of BML, CIA, or MFA (but not NAM). Size of node indicates number of connections (degree), varying between one and seventy-three. Network drawn in Cytoscape using the Allegro Fruchterman-Reingold layout. Note the size of the interconnected network (n = 187) and how its center is tied together by multiple connections.

within 0.1 mile of each other as the crow flies, that is, about the distance of one or two blocks.[51] These restrictions would seem to make it fairly likely that they would have at least a passing acquaintance with each other. Moreover, the network implies the availability of secondary connections: residence or three shared club memberships connect 187 of these men into a single network (the rest are represented in the triads and dyads at the bottom of the image).[52] Indeed, 117 of these men (more than one in four) shared a club or residential connection with at least 5 other organized businessmen and often many more. That indicates that even if Benny Businessman had not personally met Ernie Employer, they might well have had one or more mutual acquaintances and therefore be at least semiknown quantities to each other. And at the very least, residential and social club ties would have served as a basis of recognition of shared membership in the "better classes."

Beyond residential patterns and club memberships, the manufacturers of St. Louis were also of course often welded together by business connections, industry, and common work histories. Business connections could come in many forms: buying from and selling to each other, subcontracting, being hired by one firm and then leaving to set up one's own business, and so on. These are more difficult to extract computationally from the data and have therefore not been analyzed. However, skimming *The Book of St. Louisans* gives one the impression that these interactions were quite numerous and thus further bolstered the interconnectedness of St. Louis businessmen.[53]

Connections through social clubs, residential patterns, and business ties were further cemented by social and family ties, often not isolated from the ties of business. The marriage ties of the Busch family, makers of Budweiser, illustrate such multiple links. The storied wedding of Anna Busch and Edward Faust raised Faust from a well-to-do restaurateur to the very top of the wealth (if not social) pyramid: as the son-in-law of Adolphus Busch, he became the second vice president of the massive Anheuser-Busch Brewing Association. In doing so, he joined a firm that had itself been solidified by marriage, as Adolphus Busch had married Lilly Anheuser, the daughter of his partner, Eberhard Anheuser (in a double wedding in which Adolphus's brother Ulrich also married Lilly's sister Anna). A few years after Anna's wedding to Edward, Lilly Anheuser Busch's nephew married Stella Nicolaus, the eldest daughter of Henry Nicolaus, formerly associated with E. Anheuser & Company but by then president of the St. Louis Brewing Association, a local brewery "trust" of sorts. Industrial ties, then, intermingled with ethnic ones (all these families were of German origin), which in turn were cemented by marriages.[54]

All these ties mattered: building an organization out of strangers would have been a far more challenging proposition than building a movement and pursuing organizational goals within a network of people who, besides being like-minded, also occupied a similar social rung, met each other in a variety of contexts, and already knew many of the same people.

Clubmen as Street Fighters

There were, then, multiple ties that bound the businessmen of St. Louis together. The city's labor movement, though, was also a force to be reckoned with. Indeed, joint action to blunt the impact of workers' movements had repeatedly brought St. Louis businessmen together not only in social clubs but also in sheriff's posses. The upheaval of the great strike year of 1877, to the surprise of the city's elites, was felt strongly in St. Louis: although the protests remained admirably nonviolent, they were that much more comprehensive. Beginning with railroad and transit workers on July 22, the strike spread rapidly to practically all industries, so that within two days, nearly all shops, saloons, and manufacturing plants were closed, and within three, the strikers had taken over a number of factories and the railroad depot and had de facto control of the city. Despite press reports that painted the strikers as "rabble" and as "tramps," with particularly harsh words reserved for African Americans among the protesters, the strike was led by local skilled workers, who also represented a significant portion of the overall strike movement.[55] The "better elements" of the city, though, were determined to retake command: by the fifth day of the strike, the police force and a posse comitatus composed of six hundred merchants, manufacturers, financiers, professional men, and others with ties to business moved on the strikers. With orders to shoot to kill, this posse arrested more than 150 strike leaders. The strikers surrendered more peaceably than anyone had expected, but the episode had demonstrated what the working classes were capable of, and the city's elites shuddered at the thought of what might have been.[56]

The suppression of the 1877 strike did not bring an end to labor agitation. In the 1880s dozens of Knights of Labor locals formed in St. Louis, and the city witnessed significant strike activity throughout the decade among a wide variety of the city's industries, from brewing to street railways to railroads to construction.[57] When another citywide labor disturbance arrived in the form of a streetcar strike in 1900, then, St. Louis businessmen were determined to take a more active stance from the start, even if the strike itself developed out of business rather than union intransigence.

The roots of the streetcar strike were in the city's lackluster streetcar service, made no less lackluster by a politically aided consolidation in 1899 of the city's various lines into a near monopoly in the St. Louis Transit Company, headed by the banker and broker Edwards Whitaker (residence: Westmoreland Place, clubs: St. Louis, Cuivre, Noonday, etc.).[58] After the consolidation, the new company made it clear that workers would be expected to fall into line: workdays were further increased from an already hefty twelve hours, and the company hired a notorious foe of unions, George W. Baumhoff, as the general manager.[59] The union, after failed attempts at negotiation, finally called a strike on May 7, 1900. The company rapidly brought in replacements and provided them with basic accommodations and meals at no charge.[60] The streetcar company was widely unpopular, and strike supporters engaged in a number of provocations, ranging from blockading the tracks with massive boulders to physically dragging both passengers and replacement workers off the cars and manhandling them, sometimes quite severely. In an effort to maintain a respectable image, the union condemned violence and destruction of property, assigned strike committees to maintain order, and attempted to dissociate itself from any destructive acts that did occur, instead focusing on a show of mass support in the form of a parade of ten thousand unionists on May 20. Meanwhile, the president of the Board of Police Commissioners, Harry B. Hawes (member BML; clubs: St. Louis, Jefferson, etc.), though a good friend of Whitaker's, was constrained in devising a police response by the popularity of the strike. Instead, he devolved the responsibility for peacekeeping to the city's Republican sheriff, John A. Pohlman, who on May 30 was charged with calling up a posse of a thousand men (quickly increased to twenty-five hundred).[61]

By June 4 over six hundred men were armed and drilling; two days later, recruits had reached over twelve hundred. The leadership of the posse quickly decided not to accept union members into the posse, ostensibly because they hampered mobilization by refusing to ride on the streetcars (which the strike sympathizers boycotted, first informally and later by union decree).[62] Instead, companies were formed from the city's lawyers (Company 23), its businessmen (Companies B and F) and generally its "very best element."[63] Some volunteered for duty; one businessman even refused to take a leave offered for the completion of out-of-town business. Many were drafted, too; according to the *St. Louis Republic*, there was some genuine anxiety about having to serve on the posse but also plenty of "good-natured joshing," and the paper's tone generally implied that at least the younger men of the business elite treated the whole thing as a bit of a lark, even if not an entirely welcome one. For example, August "Gussie" Busch (residence: Busch Place; clubs: St. Louis, Mercantile, Noonday, Racquet, Liederkrantz, etc.), the son of the beer magnate, Adolphus Busch, was handed a conscription notice on a Sunday morning visit to his brother-in-law Edward A. "Eddie" Faust (residence: Portland Place; clubs: St. Louis, Glen Echo, Mercantile, Union, Noonday, Liederkrantz, etc.), one of the first to be drafted. The same fate befell a number of other young gentlemen that day, causing the *Republic* to chuckle that "Sheriff Pohlman caught the flower of the flock for his posse comitatus" as a result of the young gents' ignorance of the fact that "warrants could be made out on a Sunday."[64]

The "flower of the flock" was in for some real enough confrontations—which, it seems, many were quite eager for. In its Sunday, June 10, issue, the *St. Louis Republic* praised the "amazing cheerfulness with which men summoned to the posse have performed their duties." It continued: "Men of affairs and prominent in the community have left their business interests without complaint to assist in restoring order, leaving comfortable homes and accepting the hardships of sleeping on narrow cots, eating at haphazard and walking four and five hours a day with shotguns on their shoulder without protest. Some even have persisted in serving, although incapacitated by sickness, after the first two days' experience."[65] The very same day as this story ran, these "cheerful" servants of the public good were rewarded with "thrilling encounter[s]" with protesters. One group of possemen ordered protesters yelling insults at replacement workers to keep quiet and stop their vehicle; when the protesters ignored those orders, the possemen pursued them for several blocks, firing shotguns at their buggy and receiving fire in return. In the end, the possemen killed the horse drawing the buggy, but the men riding in it escaped.[66]

More serious incidents the same day resulted in a higher human toll. In one case, the posse, pursuing men who had tried to stop a streetcar from running, shot and killed an old man who was a bystander to the action. In another incident, which became known as the Washington Avenue Massacre, three strikers lost their lives, and many more were wounded. While some confusion surrounds the sequence of events, apparently a procession of strikers was ordered to disperse but refused and instead tried to take over a streetcar. They were fired upon by members of the posse who had been stationed deliberately to await the strikers' return from a picnic demonstration in East St. Louis. According to a posse captain, on their way to East St. Louis that morning the strikers had "jeered at the possemen as they passed," and thus, fearing "there would be trouble when they returned," the posse captain "ordered all the deputies to load their guns and be ready for any emergency on a moment's notice." The *St. Louis Republic* called the confrontation a "riot" by the strikers, but it seems clear from the captain's statements that the possemen were expecting a confrontation, and while shots fired by the strikers were also reported, strikers themselves denied any "rioting." The only ones left dead or wounded were strikers.[67]

The strikers and their sympathizers were by no means innocent of violent actions: rowdy jeering and physical attacks on the replacement workers driving the streetcars occurred throughout the strike. It was clear, though, that one standard applied to strikers and another to posse members: for example, the same issue of *St. Louis Republic* that reported the killing of strikers by possemen also reported that forty-three posse deputies were discharged. However, these were not the possemen who had engaged in excessive violence; rather, these men were let go for being union members and refusing to ride on the streetcars.[68]

In the wake of the violence, the union set up its own horse-drawn bus line, and the effective boycott of the streetcars temporarily succeeded in bringing about an agreement with the transit company. The truce only lasted a week before the union, charging that the company had violated the agreement, reinstituted the strike. Backed by the city's political establishment, though, the transit company had little incentive to conciliate, and by the fall the strike had fizzled out.[69]

For the city's business elite, the lessons of the strike were somewhat contradictory. On the one hand, serving on the posse comitatus had provided businessmen an opportunity to demonstrate their masculine prowess in addition to their public-spiritedness. On the other, the violence inflicted on the strikers was widely condemned.[70] In the wake of the strike, and hoping to avoid disruptions during the Louisiana Purchase Exposition (better known as the St. Louis World's Fair), St. Louis moved in a more conciliatory direction: as noted in chapter 4, the city's leading lights established a local Civic Federation to smooth things over with the unions. The conciliatory mood, however, passed with the end of the world's fair, after which St. Louis businessmen returned to a more confrontational stance.

The case of St. Louis illustrates both the multiple local connections between businessmen and the willingness of such businessmen (and other elites) to put those connections into action when confronted with a challenge from below. Through building multiple organizations with a variety of civic and social aspirations and through direct confrontation—even violent confrontation on city streets—they positioned themselves as the guardians of law, order, and civic virtue while securing each other's economic interests. Such local connectedness and common purpose formed a basis on which to build national cooperation.

Antiunion Unity? Employers and the Printers' Strike of 1905–1907

When the International Typographical Union (ITU) called a strike in 1905, the NAM saw an opportunity to cement ties with an important ally, the employing printers. Besides being major employers in an important industry, the employing printers had the means—their print shops—to produce and

distribute material designed to sway public opinion.[71] The employing printers, the NAM contended, "are apt to be well acquainted and influential men;
many have publications or are interested in them; and all feel the same way
about the excesses of labor unions." This was a slight exaggeration for effect
(not all employing printers were particularly antiunion), but it highlights
the NAM's hopes that printers could become strong partners in the NAM's
efforts to build a coalition against labor on both workplace and political
questions.[72] If the employer side emerged victorious in the printers' strike, the
conflict would showcase the ability of interindustry employer unity to defeat
a powerful union and thus bolster the NAM's prominence and reinforce its
message that if employers only stood together, they would prevail.

The printing industry was roughly divided into two branches: newspapers
and book and job (or commercial) printing. Each had its own employer association: the master printers in book and job printing were organized in the
United Typothetae of America (UTA), while the newspapers were represented
by the American Newspaper Publishers Association (ANPA). Both employer
associations had a history of negotiating with the ITU, which was not divided
by branch but enrolled printers in both newspaper and book and job printing.
The printers' strike that began in the fall of 1905 and dragged on into late 1907
concerned the book and job printing industry and thus involved only the
UTA. Formed in an attempt to strengthen employers in the face of the ITU's
demand for the nine-hour day in 1887, prior to 1905 the UTA had maintained
a pragmatic attitude rather than repudiating relations with the union entirely.
It continued the practice of the local Typothetae of negotiating with the union
while keeping up a search for ways to undermine union power. Indicative
of this double-pronged strategy, the same year (1898) that it concluded its
first national agreement with the ITU, the UTA also initiated a campaign
against the union label, which was a potentially highly significant device in
cementing a union's position, especially in printing. Most unions using the
union label produced consumer goods popular especially among workers
(hence allowing a worker to show solidarity by buying goods that could be
identified as union-made), and this was of course also true of newspapers.
But printers had an additional lever of power: in the last few years of the
nineteenth century, the ITU had succeeded in getting several municipalities
and some states to adopt a requirement that all public printing (abundant in
this era) had to display the union label.[73]

Despite its original negotiatory stance, then, the UTA continued to look
for ways to strengthen its position against the union. By 1905 a growing
number of local Typothetae, many of which were becoming involved in the
open-shop movement, had begun to promote combative policies. This was

particularly true of the Typothetae in the midwestern states, where employer organizations were growing rapidly; for example, the St. Louis Typothetae in 1903 instructed its members to cooperate with the NAM to lobby Congress against an eight-hour workday bill promoted by the American Federation of Labor.[74] The open-shop advocates within the UTA had been preparing the organization for a confrontation with the union over the course of several years. The printing trade journal, *American Printer*, had begun to exhort employing printers to organize and to stand firm against unions, running stories that purported to show how this would pay off for one and all.[75] More tangibly, the UTA had created both a substantial emergency fund built from mandatory member contributions and a strict centralized policy requiring member adherence to the stated positions of the organization.[76]

The concrete spark for the strike came from the ITU call for an eight-hour day. The ITU had announced that any employer that did not grant the eight-hour day by January 1, 1906, would be struck. In September 1905 employing printers in Detroit, San Antonio, and Chicago decided to precipitate the conflict by hiring nonunion men and posting notices stating that in the future they would run on an open-shop basis. In response, ITU members in the affected shops walked out and initiated the fight for the eight-hour day. Since it suspected that employers were trying to choose the weakest cities as the first battleground, the ITU decided to lend support to the workers already on strike by calling out all locals except those whose contracts with the Typothetae or individual employers were still in force.[77] On the original D-Day of January 1, 1906, the strike spread further; most importantly, that was the date when the contract of the New York Typographical No. 6 expired, thus allowing it to join its considerable force to the ranks of the strikers without breaking its contract with the employers.[78]

The NAM swung into action as soon as the strike began. It promised to "stiffen up manufacturers and employers generally" against the ITU in the cities affected by the strike. It encouraged its members to purchase printing from the open shops and refrain from enforcing contract clauses providing that print jobs were to be delivered on time even in strike conditions. It also told them to use their influence as advertisers to get publishers on the side of the employing printers (something that carried weight in an era when much of book printing consisted of catalogs and directories that contained quite a lot of advertisements for local businesses). It reminded employers in other industries that they might well be the next target if the ITU was successful. And it gave the employing printers prominent support in articles and editorials in the NAM trade journal, *American Industries*.[79] The NAM secretary also wrote to the daily papers in the name of the manufacturers ("many of them advertisers and friends of yours") with a letter asking for their "considerate interest" in the cause of the employing printers; he also contacted advertisers with pleas to aid the printers by, for instance, running their largest advertisements without changes (changes, of course, would cause problems when compositors were on strike).[80]

Throughout the fall and winter of 1905–6, the NAM worked hard in the employing printers' cause. When the UTA set up a trade school to secure its future access to skilled printers without having to rely on union-controlled apprenticeships, the NAM gave the school its patronage by having *American Industries* printed there. To further help the print shops continue operations, the NAM attempted to help struck printers find replacement workers.[81] It also hoped to help the UTA spread its antiunion convictions to the newspaper publishing business: the NAM and the UTA drafted plans (which, in the end, failed) to create a new organization to replace the ANPA, which continued to negotiate with the ITU and had not joined the open-shop crusade (although the ANPA did contain some open-shop advocates, whom the NAM had supported from the beginning).[82] If newspapers were to join the struggle, this could result in a potential publicity coup: newspapers embroiled in active disputes with unions tended to take an antiunion stance in their reporting as well.[83] So, for instance, the *Philadelphia Inquirer*, which had been the target of an ITU organizing drive, strike, and boycott since the summer of 1904, consistently gave ample space to the views of the Philadelphia Typothetae in the eight-hour fight and headlined its stories in ways that favored the employing printers.[84]

The NAM also got involved in the UTA's fight at the grassroots level, sending its operative Martin M. Mulhall into the field almost as soon as the printers' strike started. Mulhall, who had once been a labor union member himself and who regularly conducted political campaign work of various degrees of covertness for the NAM, apparently worked in several cities, but his main field of activity was in Philadelphia in the spring and summer of 1906. Philadelphia was probably chosen partly because of Mulhall's labor contacts in that city and partly because Philadelphia's numerous nonunion printers weakened the strike there.[85]

Mulhall's work in Philadelphia involved both open persuasion and stealthy methods. Openly, Mulhall was appointed one of a committee of three manufacturer representatives, which met with three representatives of the Philadelphia Central Labor Union to discuss the situation. This committee also took a number of union members on a tour of struck Philadelphia plants in an effort to show them that the strike would certainly fail, as the plants were operating regardless of it, and to get them to report this unhappy state of affairs to the ITU. The following June, Philadelphia ITU members were taken on a similar tour of New York shops to convince them that despite the greater power of the New York local, the strike was failing there as well. Neither effort appears to have achieved its aim, as the unionists insisted that what they had seen had merely convinced them that the strike was indeed succeeding.[86]

An undercover operation supported these aboveboard efforts. Mulhall later claimed that he had worked in Philadelphia on and off for over a year and spent an average of $300 a week on undermining the strike while there, money that he got in part from the Philadelphia Typothetae and in part from the NAM. Mulhall had a propensity to exaggerate the finances he had control of, so his claims have to be taken with caution, but even a fraction of such a sum would have been serious money. In the course of a year, $300 a week adds up to $15,600; the equivalent in 2020 dollars would be over $470,000. Another point of comparison is that in 1910 the average wage in the printing and publishing industry was around $12 a week, so $300 a week would have amounted to the weekly salary of twenty-five printers.[87] With the aid of this budget, Mulhall said he bribed striking workers to return to work and paid weekly salaries to a number of members of Philadelphia unions so that they would act as spies in their unions. As documents beyond Mulhall's own statements corroborate, these spies reported to Mulhall what happened at union meetings, what the general atmosphere was among the membership, and what strategies the union was planning to use; Mulhall then relayed this information to the Typothetae. In addition, the men on Mulhall's payroll worked to put a damper on initiatives among the Philadelphia unions to collect funds for the striking printers or to start sympathetic strikes in support of the ITU.[88]

There was, then, nothing half-hearted about the effort mounted by the NAM and the UTA. They meant business, and they meant to win. Repeatedly, the UTA expressed confidence in its impending victory, stressing its members' determination and preparation, citing the number of strikebreakers those members had managed to recruit and the number of union men they had convinced to return to work, and claiming that all orders were proceeding on time as usual.[89] But it seemed that the ITU had more grounds for its equally insistent optimism: soon, newspapers began reporting defections from UTA ranks and running stories of strikebreakers who were lured away from the shops by the union or decided to join the strike because conditions failed to match the claims made by the employers.[90]

Company after company decided to abandon the struggle and negotiate with the union. By late 1907 the ITU had succeeded in getting several smaller cities completely on the eight-hour basis, and nationally over 80 percent of union members had achieved the eight-hour day.[91] By contrast, the ranks of the UTA were depleted. The UTA's strict requirement that members should abide by the association's official policies meant that as soon as a member felt obliged to give in to the union in order to get his men back to work, that member had to resign from the UTA. As a result, the UTA lost nearly half its members. In 1908, in acknowledgment of its inability to keep most employing printers in the antiunion camp, it removed the objection to the eight-hour day from its declaration of policy, decided against excluding union-shop employers, and explicitly affirmed that its members and local Typothetae "shall be at liberty to make contracts with local unions."[92]

To be sure, many large book and job printers in major cities became non-union even if they conceded the eight-hour day, partly supporting the UTA's claim that on the crucial point of ending the practice of closed-shop union-ism the Typothetae had prevailed. Nor did the ITU come out of the fight unscathed: according to one source, the union lost over two thousand of its roughly forty-five thousand members between 1905 and 1907.[93] In Philadel-phia it seems that Mulhall's efforts paid off: no sympathetic strikes emerged, nor did the union have much success in convincing Philadelphia employers to negotiate.[94] But the employing printers themselves admitted that gauging the success of Mulhall's tactics was difficult. Philadelphia had been known to be a weak point for the union, and in most cities the ITU fared much better: for instance, by late 1907 nearly all major New York shops, including the shop owned by the secretary of the New York Typothetae, had acceded to union demands.[95]

The striking printers enjoyed a number of advantages in their struggle. First, they were mostly native-born and white, and printing was a respect-able craft. Even many employers had sympathy for their men: employers and workers often shared an ethnic as well as a trade background, and many master printers could still remember their journeyman days. At least as im-portantly, public opinion was fairly well-disposed toward a strike of upstand-ing native-born craftsmen, especially as the printers were careful to avoid any semblance of violence. The *New York Times* even contended that the men gathered at strike headquarters seemed so courteous that "the outsider would have never taken them for strikers in the accepted sense."[96] Second, printers were exceptionally well-organized and cohesive: the roots of the ITU stretched back to the 1850s, and there was a strong tradition of cooperation among the different printing crafts even as they remained organized in dif-ferent unions.[97] Third, there was no division by branch of industry. Thus, while the employing printers were divided into book and job printers (the

Typothetae) and the newspaper division (the ANPA), the ITU represented all typographers. This was a distinct advantage in the eight-hour workday strike: the ITU's strike assessments covered its whole membership, but the strike itself only concerned the book and job industry. In other words, the securely employed newspaper compositors could help fund the struggle of the book and job compositors.[98]

The printers' strike, then, was perhaps an unusually well-organized, well-funded strike under unusually favorable conditions for the union. In less propitious circumstances, the employers' unity strategy might well have succeeded. Nevertheless, the outcome of the fight demonstrated to organized employers that nationwide employer solidarity in a strike situation could not be counted upon. As a consequence, the UTA turned away from labor issues, ensuring its survival by focusing on topics less controversial among its members.[99] The NAM kept its focus firmly on labor, but it is hard to imagine that its faith in employer solidarity remained unshaken. It had sunk considerable effort—not to mention money—into creating a united front against the ITU, and even if some individual employing printers successfully instituted open shops, losing the national fight was embarrassing.

The printers' strike was the only time that the NAM publicly and prominently engaged in a fight that was premised on employers' ability to hold the line against unions. This did not mean that in the wake of the strike the NAM softened its line. It did not back down from its intransigent position, nor did it let up on its efforts to facilitate and lead a cross-industry antiunion movement. On the contrary, it continued to devise ways to make use of the networks of camaraderie and economic interconnection that the St. Louis case study illustrates and to transform those local networks into national webs of influence. But it steered clear of strategies that required individual members or allies to withstand union pressure at a potential cost to themselves. Instead, in the years after the printers' strike, the NAM redoubled its efforts in politics and publicity, which offered wider views—while putting less pressure on individual members' pocketbooks. Solidarity, it turned out, could be too risky.

6   The Battle over the State

All animals are equal, but some animals are more equal
than others.
—George Orwell, *Animal Farm*

In its favorable December 1902 report on a bill that would have made eight
hours the maximum length of the workday on government contract work,
the Senate Committee on Education and Labor emphasized that it was "the
settled policy of Congress" stretching back decades to expand the reach of
the eight-hour day. It also approvingly quoted the words of Commissioner
of Labor Carroll D. Wright that "it has always been expected" that laws limiting working hours would help a worker "in the acquisition of knowledge,
thus tending to make him a better and more contented citizen," and pointed
out that "Congress and the Federal courts have advanced and approved the
moral effect of an eight-hour law." In other words, the committee tried to
make clear that the bill advanced a policy that was incontrovertibly positive
and generally accepted; as Wright had put it, "This policy must be admitted
by all to be a good one."[1] Had it been enacted, the eight-hour bill would have
constituted a major government endorsement of an important labor union
goal. Employers, however, mounted an effective opposition that blocked the
bill's passage in that Congress and several subsequent ones.

The power of the state was considerable, and neither labor nor business
scorned it. Both well understood that the state's judicial and legislative powers
set the parameters within which each side could maneuver, while the state's
coercive power could tilt the playing field in favor of one side or the other.
They also understood the legitimizing power of the state. In a democracy,
the unstated assumption is that a law the legislature passes and the courts
enforce has the implicit support of the majority of the people; certainly, this
is part of the narrative of American democracy. False as that assumption may
be in specific cases, its ability to legitimize—and, perhaps even more starkly,
delegitimize—particular claims and positions is considerable.

To be sure, both organized labor and organized employers had reservations about the state. The American Federation of Labor tended to favor solutions that prioritized union power; for example, it generally opposed maximum hours or minimum wages legislation, arguing that the only way workers could be sure of good wages and decent hours was to enforce them through union contracts. The AFL also resisted proposals that would have given the state power over unions or labor-management negotiations, such as calls for unions to incorporate (and thus become entities with a legal existence that could, e.g., be sued) or schemes for compulsory or binding arbitration of labor disputes.[2] Similarly, the National Association of Manufacturers and most other business and employer groups wanted to be left alone on matters that they believed they could sort out themselves, and they frowned upon any proposals that would have limited managerial autonomy. As David Vogel has argued, corporate executives and other businessmen tend to consistently be against regulations that diminish their managerial freedom but often support programs that provide them with useful services, which they simply do not perceive as "government intervention." This was true for the NAM as well.[3]

Despite their reservations, both organized labor and organized employers appealed to the power of the state to promote their interests and to confer a stamp of legitimacy on their views. Because they were fundamentally different kinds of organizations, though, they went about this in different ways and found allies within different branches of government. To simplify somewhat, labor preferred the elected parts of government and tried to use them to rein in the state's coercive and judicial powers, while employers took precisely the opposite view, praising courts and the police while frowning upon elected officials. Some of these battles took place at the local and state levels.[4] But the federal government and the national level were growing in importance; indeed, it was precisely because of the increasing importance of the national level that there was by the turn of the twentieth century a strong *National* Association of Manufacturers, a *National* Civic Federation, and a nationally oriented *American* Federation of Labor. Thus, much of the battle took place in the national legislature. The NAM had from the start focused on influencing national legislation.[5] The AFL had in 1895 moved its headquarters from Indianapolis to Washington, DC, to facilitate lobbying.[6]

This chapter examines how the state influenced the struggle between labor and employers both in terms of practical assistance or hindrance and in terms of how its actions (or its inaction) influenced public perception of the legitimacy of each side. The first section delves into the world of local conflicts, exploring the power that workers could wield at the level of the city and the ways in which employers tried to counter that power. The second section examines the judicial branch, which frequently intervened in labor disputes; indeed, it intervened to such an extent that its actions spurred labor to national-level legislative lobbying to curb its powers. The next section turns to that national level, focusing on what the AFL tried to accomplish in Congress and what strategies the NAM employed to torpedo those efforts. The final section uses some examples of the NAM's electoral campaigns to explore the limits of employer power while also emphasizing how the NAM's lobbying successes denied labor important victories that might have brought with them concrete benefits as well as a shift in public perception.

Control of the City

Even as both employers and workers took their efforts to influence the state to the national level, the city continued to be an important site of contestation. Significant economic activity—baking, brewing, printing, building— happened at the level of the city. In many of these pursuits, working people played an important role as producers, service providers, and consumers. Moreover, even the manufacturing establishments of a city were heavily dependent on urban services, especially the urban transportation network and hauling services. The workers running those services thus had a crucial role. Without streetcar lines to shuttle workers between the factory and their homes or horse-drawn wagons to bring in basic supplies, few manufacturing establishments could keep up business as usual. Working people thus had potential power in the context of a city, and they exercised this power as both workers and consumers.

As workers, they might adjust their workaday routines to lend support to fellow workers on strike. In providing such flank support for a strike, the Teamsters—the union of the workers who drove the wagons that were drawn by teams of horses and that hauled most goods in urban environments—were especially strategically placed. Teamsters might, for example, use their teaming wagons to block streetcar routes run with replacement workers during a streetcar strike. Similarly, they might refuse to make deliveries to employers embroiled in labor conflicts with their workers. Given the dependence of almost any establishment on regular hauling service to either get supplies or get its finished goods delivered, such support could make or break a strike. In San Francisco, for instance, the Teamsters' refusal to haul non-union-made goods shifted the power balance in a 1901 dispute between workers in carriage-making and their employers, forcing the employers back to the negotiating table.[7] On the flip side, in a 1902 Chicago freight handlers' strike, the decision of the Teamsters to honor their own contract with the team owners and order their members to cross picket lines caused the freight handlers' strike to collapse.[8]

As consumers, working people could wield power by withholding their patronage from an "unfair" employer. This was particularly effective at the local level and in industries where workers made up a large percentage of customers, such as food, tobacco, newspapers, clothing, and stoves. Boycotts, which became popular in the early 1880s and enjoyed notable successes for the subsequent decade, could bring a recalcitrant employer into line within weeks or even days. Often, boycotts reinforced union control in a double sense: a large percentage of boycotts accompanied conflicts over the employment of nonunion workers, so that union victory in the conflict secured an acknowledgment of the union's right to a say in hiring, as well as the union's more permanent status at the workplace. Boycotts were an especially common tool in food production: in New York State, for instance, producers of bread experienced three times the number of boycotts wielded against any other product, and bread boycotts also enjoyed the greatest degree of success. An establishment that was locally based and rooted in a working-class clientele would find it difficult to resist a determined boycott, and the overall success rate of boycotts could be impressive. In New York between 1885 and 1893, over two-thirds of boycotts whose outcome was recorded were successful, and even with unresolved boycotts included, the success rate was nearly one in four. An 1885 report based on national data cited similar figures.[9] Boycotts often succeeded by convincing other businesses to abide by a boycott of a particular unfair employer and his goods. For instance, hotels, railroads, and anyone else needing printing services might be asked to join a boycott of a printer, or advertisers could be persuaded to withdraw their ads from a boycotted newspaper on pain of being themselves boycotted.[10]

As both workers and consumers, then, urban working people asserted considerable claims to control over the functioning of the urban economy. Courts, as they had with labor unions' claims to craft governance, found such assertions disturbing. In the words of legal scholar William Forbath, courts saw in boycotts a threat to the legal order because they envisioned "a world of exchange relations under the rules and norms of working-class organizations . . . rather than under the norms of the marketplace and the rules of the courts."[11] As was the case with craft governance, boycotts challenged the exclusive right of the state to lawmaking and instead posited a collective system of governance rooted in working-class solidarity and grassroots views of acceptable business norms. As Andrew Wender Cohen has argued, such views of alternative governance permeated what he calls the "craft economy" of urban life—the small-business world of bartending, barbering, butchering, construction, and other urban trades. These, of course, were largely the same sectors in which boycotts were particularly popular and effective. And it was not just the workers, Cohen notes, who considered craft rule unremarkable in these trades; so did the associations of employers, which often enlisted the unions' assistance in enforcing rules about prices and requirements of association membership. Entrepreneurs attempting to buck the rules found themselves short on supplies and devoid of labor. Seeing their arrangements as legitimate forms of government, craftsmen (whether employers or workers) did not shy away from enforcing them by force if necessary, and both employers and workers could find themselves the targets of the hard punches of the professional "slugger." In early twentieth-century Chicago, "violence," Cohen contends, "derived from order rather than disorder."[12]

By the opening years of the twentieth century, employers' organizations on a local scale were formulating explicit responses to working-class power in the city. In 1901–3 they began to organize what became known as Citizens' Alliances or Citizens' and Businessmen's Alliances, whose main purpose was to band local employers together in opposition to labor. These organizations usually arose during strikes, but they generally aimed for a more sustained opposition to labor. The nomenclature varied somewhat between "alliance," "committee," "league," and the like, but the theme was the same: combating labor. In particular, these alliances focused on undoing the effectiveness of community tactics employed by labor, such as the boycott. Thus, an early alliance formed in Pennsylvania during the anthracite strike of 1902 offered substantial cash rewards for "the arrest and conviction of all persons engaged in boycotting, hanging effigies, and other criminal acts of intimidation prejudicial to the rights of American freedom."[13] In a pattern that would hold in future local alliances, the Citizens' Alliance of Wilkesbarre claimed that it was "not an adjunct to or organized by the [mine] operators"; instead, it was born out of ordinary people's "desperation" in the face of labor union intimidation.[14] In conjunction with the same strike, a report in the *New York Times* noted the organization of a statewide "semisecret" organization of Citizens' Alliances in Pennsylvania, claiming a (probably highly exaggerated) membership in the thousands.[15] By the spring of 1903 there were Citizens' Alliances in a large number of states, and some, like the ones in Minneapolis and Denver, began to play quite prominent roles in local labor relations.[16] Plans for a national association were also in the works by early 1903. In October of that year, the Citizens' Industrial Association of America (CIAA) was formed, with NAM president David Parry and other activists of the employers' open-shop campaign in the lead.[17]

The law-and-order rhetoric of the CIAA and the local alliances reflected employers' concerns over local power—specifically, power over law enforcement. Working-class ideas about what kind of order should be enforced in a city could sometimes also be found among the state's forces of order—the police largely drew on the working classes in its recruitment, after all. For example, in the late 1880s Chicago police officers' previous occupations included "machinists and other skilled factory operatives, teamsters, construction workers, railroad men, and craftsmen of various sorts"; twenty years later, the force was still dominated by former "street car motormen, press feeders, teamsters, city firemen, clerks and patrol wagon drivers."[18] The class background of the police could form a serious drawback to employers hoping to get the police to control strikers: as one Denver open-shop activist complained, "The police was not in sympathy with anybody opposed to the unions, no matter how radical or lawless the unions might be, because most of the policemen came from the ranks of labor in the beginning, and their positions as policemen are more or less temporary, and when they go out by change of administration they have to seek employment in their old-time vocations, and have to conform, I suppose, to union regulations and so forth."[19] Police reform was a major concern of business-directed civic associations. In Chicago, for instance, as early as the mid-1870s, the Citizens' Association, composed of the city's most important businessmen, made a more professional police force with a stable hierarchy one of its key governmental aims. Forming a "Committee on Police," the association began systematically advocating increases in the police force; it also directly donated weapons to the department. Over the course of the next decade or so, Chicago hired more policemen, instituted more complicated tests of admission for officers, provided incentives (such as higher pay for senior rank) for officers to stay with the police, and installed a police telegraph system.[20]

A professionalized police force offered multiple benefits from a business point of view. Public order and protection of property were obviously good for business, and a more professional police force would maintain those more efficiently. From a labor relations point of view, though, the most important function of the police was its role in strikes. In most strikes, the strikers aimed to halt production as completely as possible. Thus, they would form picket lines to persuade, or shame, or intimidate replacement workers or those who had not joined the strike so as to convince them to not go to work. They might also directly attack the strikebreakers (replacement workers). Employers wanted to be able to rely on police to protect the strikebreakers and possibly also to forcibly disperse the strikers' picket lines. If the police had working-class roots and sympathized with the strikers, it might not carry out these duties with satisfactory vigor. Although instances of police rank and file spontaneously acting in sympathy with strikers are not numerous, this was nevertheless a potential concern. Professionalization could provide a partial remedy: the more professionalized a police department was, the more there was hope for advancement through loyal service and thus the greater the individual officer's incentive not to challenge his superiors; insubordination was swiftly punished. Such incentive structures could undermine potential police sympathy with striking workers.[21]

Still, why go to all this trouble to mold police departments? Why not simply bring in security guards? In fact, employers in the late nineteenth and early twentieth centuries regularly hired armed guards and private forces, of which the Pinkerton Detective Agency was the most famous. But these forces had severe drawbacks. First, they often failed in their task, and second, employers' use of paramilitary forces invited public opprobrium, especially when the workers were respectable, white, and native-born. The steel strike at Andrew Carnegie's Homestead Works in Homestead, Pennsylvania, in 1892 illustrates both problems. The strike is famous for the pitched battle that ensued when workers clashed with the Pinkertons, leading to the deaths of three Pinkertons and ten strikers. The company—which refused to negotiate—had engaged the Pinkerton Detective Agency partly because it was convinced that the town's proworker officials would not help it break the strike. The Pinkertons, arriving by river, found themselves faced with gunfire, volleys from a Civil War–era cannon, and burning barrels of oil floating toward their barges. When word reached them that more workers were on the way, the Pinkertons decided to surrender. They were then paraded through the town and further abused.[22] To the company's dismay, the Pinkertons were thoroughly routed. Moreover, the publicity costs were significant. In subsequent days, the steel company's decision to engage a paramilitary force elicited outrage. Locally, a broad sector of the public from clergymen to newspaper editors supported the strikers and condemned the use of Pinkertons; nationally, both the House and the Senate opened investigations into the incident and the use of Pinkertons in general. Homestead also illustrates that state forces could succeed where private ones had failed. At Homestead, it was the state militia, sent by the Pennsylvania governor, that successfully opened the plant to replacement workers and thus broke the strike.[23] Finally, besides problems of publicity and efficacy, price was an issue: not all employers had the resources to hire a private army.[24]

On the whole, then, although strikebreaking services continued to thrive, a police force with some professional standards and a degree of legitimacy could offer benefits these services could not. Such a police force mattered particularly to employers whose workforce consisted of a skilled (and largely native-born) workforce and whose resources were limited—in other words, to the kinds of employers who were drawn to the open-shop movement. Moreover, even a drawn-out strike of skilled workers that did serious damage to a business was rarely accompanied by the level of disruption in the community at large that could have justified a governor calling in the militia. It was therefore important to have routine access to a security force that could ensure the ability of a few dozen strikebreakers to get in and out of the factory and to disperse a picket line. Employers, then, generally supported expansion and professionalization of the police force. They also greeted with horror and indignation any developments that would have reduced the police's insulation from the working class at large. When the AFL announced that it intended to start a unionization drive among government employees, including the police, the NAM labeled the campaign a part of an effort "designed to emasculate the law-enforcing powers of the nation."[25]

Most scholars agree that as an institution, the police tended to be on the side of the employers, and the lamentations about the union sympathies of policemen reflected less actual employer experience than employer desire to deflect worker complaints about the proemployer bias of policing. Although police came from working-class origins, their loyalties with strikers were always tenuous. Often strikers represented the lower rungs of the working class, while police came from the skilled sectors or at least were paid at the skilled level. This could mean double the wages of a laborer, enabling police to live in the city's middle-class rather than working-class neighborhoods. In many cities, there was also an ethnic division between police and other workers, with the police frequently being of Irish or German ancestry, while protesting workers increasingly came from eastern European roots. And strikes, for policemen, meant long hours with little or no extra pay, hardly endearing strikers to police.[26]

Professionalization was important in reinforcing such divisions by cementing the rewards for loyal service and the penalties for insubordination within the police. Professionalization also had another benefit from an employer point of view: to a degree, it insulated the police from control by the mayor or the municipal government and thus raised a barrier between the police and democratic pressure by the city's workers. As muckraker journalist Ray Stannard Baker had put it in 1904, "A Union Mayor can be of little service to unionism, except in the case of a strike, when he can refuse to call out the police to protect non-union labor. Both potentially and actually, this is a very great power."[27] A neutral or labor-friendly mayor or governor might resist calling out a stronger police presence to protect strikebreakers even when urged to act by police leadership themselves—at least for a time.[28] The police were generally at least partly under the control of municipal authorities and might act very differently under a labor-friendly administration than without such restraint; thus, the Toledo police force remained aloof in a 1906 Toledo labor dispute because the mayor refused to use it to protect strikebreakers, but in a 1911 strike in nearby Cleveland the police intervened violently to protect strikebreakers and harass strikers.[29] Professionalization could make the police more independent of mayoral sympathies. Moreover, the more the police could appeal to a professional codex, the more legitimate police use of force appeared, and the more effectively that force could then be applied not just to attack strikers but also to undermine a strike's legitimacy.

The Courts

Growing professionalization notwithstanding, the police continued to be under the authority of elected municipal officials, and this could put obstacles in the way of employers hoping to draw on the state's coercive resources. "It is a well-known fact that when politics come into play . . . the Police Departments are not inclined to carry out their sworn duty," the Cincinnati Metal Trades Association complained in a letter to the chairman of the Senate Judiciary Committee. To remedy such problems, the next instance of state power employers turned to was the judiciary. As the Metal Trades Association's letter continued, in cases of lackluster police response, "employers are compelled to seek refuge in Courts of Equity."[30]

Using its equity powers—powers to determine what is fair and equal rather than simply what the law on the books says—a court could forbid particular union practices that it considered to violate the employer's property rights. In specific terms, the court could issue an injunction prohibiting an action if it deemed that such action would result in "irreparable injury" to property or property rights. The injunction was usually a temporary order that applied until such a time as the issue could be fully heard and resolved in court; the purpose of the injunction was to prevent damage in the meantime.[31] A typical example of the basic procedure in labor injunction cases went roughly as follows. An employer or a group of employers filed a bill of complaint with a trial court. The complaint described the property involved, the defendants, and the actions of the defendants against which the complaint was directed. It alleged that irreparable harm would result from the defendants' actions and went on to request an injunction that ordered the defendants to stop engaging in these actions so that they could not cause further harm in the period preceding the court's hearing of the case. If the court issued the injunction, the defendants had to cease the prohibited activities immediately; should they persist, they would be in contempt of court and could be fined or jailed without a jury trial. In a strike situation, of course, the issuing of such a restraining order, no matter its temporary nature, was often enough. Even if a subsequent hearing found the order unjustified, the employer had gained an edge, as strikers had been forced to, for instance, abandon the picket line or stop publicizing their boycott.[32]

The frequency with which injunctions directly addressed local officials underlines that one important function of injunctions was to serve as a remedy for a recalcitrant local administration: among other things, injunctions told justices of the peace not to issue warrants against strikebreakers and mayors not to enforce city ordinances that complicated employers' hiring of strikebreakers.[33] A comparison between San Francisco and Los Angeles further underlines this role of the courts as circumventing municipal authority. San Francisco was densely unionized, and unions had substantial weight in municipal governance; Los Angeles was largely an open-shop city. Indeed, in the view of the president of the San Francisco Citizens' Alliance, San Francisco was "one of the worst union-ridden cities on earth" where everyone "from mayor on down to dog pelter" supposedly had a union card. This, the Citizens' Alliance claimed, had caused the police to do its job in an entirely topsy-turvy manner. Influenced by union sympathies, "the police commission direct the chief of police to send policemen to protect pickets" rather than using the police to break up the picket line or shield replacement workers. If it weren't for the courts and their injunctions, the alliance claimed, "San Francisco would be helpless in the hands of the unions."[34] San Francisco employers sought court protection frequently—and often successfully. Between 1897 and 1907 judges in San Francisco issued injunctions on at least thirty occasions, whereas their colleagues in open-shop, antiunion Los Angeles only issued two—and even of these two, one was requested "by an employer who only wanted his name removed from the Labor Council's 'fair' list, so as not to be known as a pro-union employer in open-shop Los Angeles."[35] To be sure, San Francisco had more strikes to issue injunctions in. Within that ten-year period, however, San Francisco only saw twice as many strikes as Los Angeles, yet the courts issued fifteen times as many injunctions. The simple explanation for this discrepancy is that in Los Angeles, employers had little need of injunctions: unions were much less powerful than in San Francisco, and if necessary, local authorities would aid a struck employer. In such circumstances, there was little point in filing for an injunction, which cost money in lawyers' fees and required the posting of bonds of $500 to $1,000 (some $15,000 to $30,000 in 2020 dollars).[36]

Courts proved an amenable ally for employers: the number of injunctions issued in labor disputes quadrupled from the 1880s to the 1890s and doubled again from the 1890s to the 1900s. Overall, there were at least two thousand injunctions issued in labor disputes between 1890 and 1920. To be sure, strikes in which an injunction was issued probably did not exceed 5 percent of all strikes before 1920. However, because of their breadth and vagueness, injunctions had an important chilling effect. Injunctions were by no means limited to violent or destructive behavior: according to Forbath, they could cover almost anything, such as "shouting 'scab', marching with cowbells and tin cans, publishing unfair lists [lists of employers to be boycotted] in local newspapers, [or] holding meetings." Nor were injunctions clearly targeted; instead, they might "address ten thousand workers and 'whomsoever' would aid and abet them."[37] Thus, they instilled doubts about the legality of standard union techniques in ways that affected all strikes.

In a typical case, H. N. Strait Manufacturing Company of Kansas City, Kansas, requested an injunction in 1906 in a strike by the Iron Molders' Union local 162; the court obliged, decreeing that the several named union officials, as well as "all parties acting in combination and conspiracy with" them, were commanded "to refrain from injuring, molesting, or interferring [*sic*] with the property or business or the employees of the complainant . . . by coercion or intimidation of any character whatever either directly or indirectly."[38] Such decrees in practice meant that the legality of almost any action that could be construed as "intimidating"—a vague standard indeed—was in doubt, and seemingly mundane efforts to uphold a strike could result in charges for contempt of court. As injunctions usually directly named union officials, their activities became particularly difficult, complicating the leadership of strikes. For example, in another molders' strike, this one at the Niles-Bement-Pond Company of Philadelphia, a number of the most active union members, along with the vice presidents of the molders' union, found themselves charged with contempt of court and therefore embroiled in preparations for their case instead of engaged in keeping the strike alive. Finally tiring of the courts' restrictions of their actions, the vice presidents left Philadelphia, leaving the local strikers to muddle on as best they could. As a result, Niles-Bement-Pond managed both to bring in replacement workers and to have some of its work performed at other companies.[39]

Like all state actions in labor cases, injunctions mattered beyond their tangible restraining of union actions. For one, the proliferation of injunctions shaped the behavior of local authorities toward unions, even when no injunction was issued in a particular case. Police officials as well as company guards frequently made reference to injunctions in other, similar cases that

they considered to justify their actions.[40] Injunctions probably also strengthened employers' perception that they, rather than unions, were in the right.
The bill of complaint elaborately set out the illegality of union actions and
highlighted union forays into violent or threatening behavior. For example,
the H. N. Strait Manufacturing Company's bill of complaint contained eight
affidavits from workers, each of whom accused union members of having
insulted and/or assaulted them; an affidavit from a "special policeman" at-
testing that he knew pickets behaved badly; and a similar affidavit from a
foreman in the shop. The complaint itself explained that the molders' union
"pretended" that it merely wished to achieve "fair" and "reasonable" hours
and wages for its members and to contribute "to their moral and material
advancement," but its "real object and purpose . . . is to have all of its members
act in concert upon every question" between workers and the employer, implying that the union had no legitimate aims and was a sheer grab for power.
The union, the complaint continued, "wrongfully conceives that it has the
right to demand from employers of those members such sums for wages as
it may fix, such hours . . . as it may wish to fix, and to compel the employers
of such members to recognize its organization and . . . employ none other
than members of its order."[41] When the court granted the injunction without
further discussion or delimitation, it also implicitly endorsed the employers'
reading of the union's demands as fundamentally "wrongful," quite apart
from the claims regarding violence.

Courts were not entirely the exclusive domain of employers. Labor unions
sometimes managed to secure injunctions as well. In a Denver strike in 1903,
several labor unions in the city got together to lodge a complaint with the
district court against the Denver Citizens' Alliance. The unions alleged that
alliance members had bullied their fellow employers to join the alliance,
prompted landlords to evict unions as well as tenants who were union members, and pressured workers to desert unions. The depositions attached to
the complaint bore witness to several such instances of intimidation. They
claimed, for instance, that alliance officials had cut off or threatened to cut off
supplies of goods to employers of union members, hampering those employers' ability to run their business. Similarly, they claimed that alliance members
had told their workers that if they refused to come back to work they would
be blacklisted all over the country. The Citizens' Alliance of course denied
the charges, but Judge John I. Mullins issued the injunction, which followed
nearly to the letter the complaint lodged by the unions. It prohibited the leaders of the Citizens' Alliance from engaging in a long list of actions, including
intimidating someone to get them to join, imposing fines for employing
union labor, refusing supplies to employers of union labor, importing workers

with the goal of destroying labor unions, influencing landlords to evict union tenants, and bringing injunctions whose aim was to break up unions. Though the injunction did little to help the unions win the strike (which concluded with a fizzle rather than a bang, as unions agreed to a peace settlement that employers then did not follow), it did receive a fair amount of publicity.[42]

The vast majority of injunctions, though, were secured by employers. In one of the few studies of injunctions requested by labor, Edwin Witte in 1930 succeeded in locating a little over seventy injunctions requested by labor between 1892 and 1929 (excluding those requested against rival unions or unionists), of which fewer than half were granted, and even of those, several were later dissolved. Though Witte's report is old and his data set (according to himself) is undoubtedly incomplete, this contrasts starkly with the thousands of injunctions actually issued against labor unions.[43] Moreover, a clear majority of the labor-requested injunctions (forty-four out of seventy) dated from the 1920s, when some unions briefly advocated a more concerted effort to give employers a dose of their own medicine.[44]

Courts, then, shaped local labor struggles; in the vast majority of cases, they did so in ways that undercut unions. In concrete terms, judges' willingness to forbid basic labor protest strategies disrupted countless strikes and, perhaps more importantly, forced the abandonment of broad community-based tactics such as the boycott. On a more symbolic plane, as Forbath has pointed out, the enforcement of antipicketing injunctions made a reasonably "peaceful, if vociferous," scene of protest into "the scene of arrests and more or less violent frays," eroding public sympathy for unions. Nor was it unusual for injunctions to directly address local officials, ranging from justices of the peace to mayors, often prohibiting them from acting against strikebreakers or private police, while the pep talks that police chiefs gave to their troops repeated the language of rights of property and the right to work often employed in injunctions.[45]

Beyond their usefulness to employers in strike situations, courts also represented, in David Brian Robertson's phrase, the "veto point of last resort" for employers when it came to legislation on hours, wages, or working conditions. In the decades following the Civil War, especially between the mid-1880s and mid-1890s, state legislatures responded to union requests by passing dozens and dozens of labor laws, ranging from maximum hours statutes to factory inspection laws to the creation of public employment offices. Courts, however, struck down many of these laws as unconstitutional, diminishing the attractiveness of campaigning for legislative changes.[46] In other cases, courts stretched the language of laws to circumvent their intent. This was particularly true in the conspiracy trials that were the preferred antiunion legal strategy before the popularity of the injunction. While counts are unreliable because many conspiracy cases went unreported, numerous workers' associations were convicted for conspiracy and disbanded in the postbellum decades. In response, labor organizations initiated intensive campaigns to remove labor unions from the sphere of conspiracy doctrine through legislative action. Between 1869 and 1891 New York and Pennsylvania enacted no fewer than four anticonspiracy statutes each, usually containing some variant of a declaration that peaceful collective action by workers was not to be considered a conspiracy or punished as such. The courts' response was simple: expand the definition of what made something not peaceful. Courts repeatedly argued that picketing, attempts to persuade others to follow a boycott, and exhortations to join a union were nonviolent only in a technical sense. In fact, the tactics of the unions were merely disguised as "moral suasion" while really being intimidating and therefore not peaceful. What, then, might cause "moral suasion" to tip over into intimidation? This was a fairly subjective standard, it turned out. One New York judge instructed the jury that it might look for an "attitude of real menace" on the part of strikers and prompted them to consider the number of workers involved as potentially contributing to intimidation. In a Pennsylvania case, the court charged the defendants with intimidation because they had planned to bring a brass band to the scene of a strike.[47]

As is often true with activist legal strategy, the open-shop employers saw a double benefit in favorable court decisions: they provided pragmatic relief, and they wrapped the employer viewpoint in the warm cloak of official sanction. Thus, the NAM sought publicity for court decisions that supported its case. *American Industries* regularly published antilabor judicial decisions, noting that judges had declared pickets illegal, considered the closed shop an illegal objective, prohibited boycotts, and handed out damages to employers hit by union boycotts.[48] It was particularly fond of judicial decisions that took an extreme view, such as that picketing was illegal even if the picket consisted of only one striker with a placard or that it was "unlawful to induce another to break his contract."[49]

These stories had a pragmatic component: they educated the membership of the options available to them in strike situations. For instance, an extended survey of court decisions concluded that "the federal courts can give ample relief in almost any kind of labor trouble when organized labor uses coercion, intimidation and threats" and encouraged readers to forward the article "to their attorneys for the purpose of future reference."[50] The effect of court decisions was also cumulative, partly because of the logic of legal precedent and partly because previous legal decisions offered conceptual resources to draw upon. In issuing an injunction in a printers' strike in the fall of 1905, for example, Judge Jesse Holdom made implicit reference to the famous *Lochner v. New York* case, decided by the US Supreme Court that spring. In that case, the Supreme Court had declared unconstitutional a New York statute limiting the hours of bakery workers. Holdom argued that the printers' effort to bring about the eight-hour day by force must therefore be an illegal objective, since "what the sovereign power of a state cannot do cannot be done by any other power."[51] But court decisions also had symbolic value. As *American Industries* noted, "A few cases in the courts vigorously pushed would soon put in jail" unionists favoring the closed shop, "and in time the public conscience would become thoroughly aroused over the menace to liberty that lurks in the trades union movement of today."[52]

The weight that open-shop employers put on court decisions is highlighted in the substantial resources, even at the local level, that they invested in legal argumentation, the investigation and prosecution of potentially criminal union actions, and the publicizing of injunctions and other court decisions favoring employers. The San Francisco Citizens' Alliance, for instance, had "a legal department of its own, keeping five to seven lawyers busy." The alliance secured injunctions and made sure the police enforced injunctions once they were granted, provided defense lawyers in cases where unions could be discredited, investigated cases of "assault and picketing disturbances," and brought suits testing the legality of closed-shop agreements.[53] At the national level, open-shop employers supported organizations like the American Anti-Boycott Association (AABA), whose main purpose was to use the courts to invalidate union tactics and, if possible, union aims: a clear court decision declaring the closed shop illegal would have crowned the judicial achievements of the open-shop movement. The movement never quite reached that goal; despite many other victories, in the end the legal status of the closed shop remained ambiguous.[54]

While court decisions had publicity uses, too many employer victories might deflate their value. An injunction that was perceived as extremist and unjust to labor, for example, might turn public opinion against the court rather than against the strikers. This was in fact what happened with Judge Jesse Holdom's injunction, mentioned above. Holdom was already well-known for his hostility to labor, and the terms of the injunction seemed to prohibit labor activity well beyond what was reasonable. Also, the printers were well-paid, skilled, native-born workers who generally enjoyed community respect, and they were careful to avoid any semblance of violence. Instead of casting a pall on the strike, the injunction instead prompted resolutions of censure of Judge Holdom from the Methodist ministers' association, which considered the restrictions excessive and "un-American."[55] Indeed, Forbath has argued that reform of the injunction powers, when it finally came in the form of the Norris-LaGuardia Act of 1932, was spurred by the worries of lawyers and middle-class observers alike that if the excessive use of injunctions continued, the legitimacy of both the courts and the industrial order would crumble.[56]

Thus, although the ornate language of legal argumentation, the complicated references to precedent, the presumption of impartiality, and the societal prestige of judges themselves all made court decisions an important legitimating tool, there were limits to how often this tool could be used. Some semblance of judicial independence and impartiality was required to preserve the courts as adjudicators of legitimate legal claims. In E. P. Thompson's phrase, people are not so stupid as to "be mystified by the first man who puts on a wig"—the law must "apply logical criteria with reference to standards of universality and equity," and exceptions from these cannot be too numerous or too flagrant. Otherwise, the law "will mask nothing, legitimize nothing, contribute nothing to any ruling class's hegemony."[57]

The Congress

The most problematic sector of the state for antiunion employers was the legislative arm—in other words, the part of the state where popular input could be felt most directly. Open-shop employers repeatedly berated legislatures as too susceptible to labor union influence, though they vacillated on whether to frame the problem as legislators catering to "irresponsible" constituents or as a takeover of the democratic process by a unionized minority pretending to speak for all workers.

At the time that the first open-shop campaign was launched, the American Federation of Labor was pursuing two significant pieces of legislation of interest to employers in the US Congress: legislative limitation of the courts' injunction powers in labor cases and an eight-hour day both in positions where the federal government was the direct employer and also on government contract work.[58] A few years later, after the decision in the case *Loewe v. Lawlor* had made prosecution of labor unions for violations of the Sherman Antitrust Act a much more immediate threat than before, exempting labor unions from the antitrust law became an additional priority.[59] The open-shop employers viewed the possible passage of any of these legislative initiatives as little short of unmitigated disaster, although they were well aware that the initiatives had substantial congressional support. The NAM's secretary admitted that the eight-hour bill "*would undoubtedly pass the House without a roll call if it came up*," while a congressional opponent of the anti-injunction bill noted that had the Judiciary Committee reported this and similar bills, they would have passed the House by a wide margin; indeed, the anti-injunction bill had passed the House nearly unanimously more than once.[60]

The legislative program of the AFL reflected a clear understanding of the legitimating power of law. Securing passage of the eight-hour and anti-injunction bills, beyond having important practical effects, would fundamentally have shifted the light in which labor union actions appeared to the public. Prohibiting the use of injunctions in labor cases would have clearly signaled that the state viewed labor's basic protest tools as legitimate or at least unremarkable. Similarly, making the eight-hour day the standard on work done for the government would have indicated that the government believed a shorter workday to be in the public interest. Explicitly exempting labor from the operation of the antitrust act would also have lifted the taint of being a "trust" from unions. The antitrust act, after all, had been passed in 1890 in response to the massive growth of "trusts," large business conglomerations that had been perceived to pursue monopoly power by underhanded means. Applying it to unions not only potentially placed significant roadblocks in the unions' efforts to organize but also smeared them with an accusation of unfair dealing.[61]

Since one of the priorities of the National Civic Federation was to boost the respectability of moderate unions, such as those belonging to the AFL, and to promote them as responsible partners in putting labor relations on a contract-oriented, well-regulated basis, one might imagine that the NCF would have lent significant support to the AFL's legislative agenda. The NCF had excellent connections at the highest levels of government, as even a few examples illustrate. At least three US presidents were closely associated with the NCF or Ralph Easley: Grover Cleveland sat on the NCF's executive committee, while Theodore Roosevelt and William Howard Taft were more or less close acquaintances of Easley's. Several members of presidential cabinets also served on the NCF executive board or its other bodies, including Franklin MacVeagh (secretary of the treasury under Taft) and Oscar Straus and Charles J. Bonaparte (secretary of labor and secretary of the navy, respectively, under Roosevelt).[62] Support on legislative initiatives from the NCF could, in other words, have been highly efficacious. Such support was quite limited, however.

The problem, as with most NCF initiatives with regard to labor, was the organization's dependence on its business members. Even when they were more willing to contemplate some forms of legislative regulation, the NCF-affiliated businessmen viewed legislation strengthening labor's position with practically as much suspicion as the NAM did. Thus, when the AFL wanted the NCF to support it on the problem of the injunction, all that happened was that the NCF decided to set up a commission that never took any action.[63] On the Sherman Antitrust Act, cooperation seemed more promising. Several NCF businessmen viewed reform of the antitrust laws as necessary, since their sprawling businesses might easily run the risk of falling afoul of the act, and to gain a broad-based consensus in favor of reform, they apparently were willing to contemplate concessions to labor. In 1908 the NCF was closely involved in the drafting of the Hepburn bill, the proposal to amend the antitrust act named after its House sponsor, William P. Hepburn, and strongly backed by President Roosevelt. Some drafts of the bill provided significant relief from antitrust prosecution to labor organizations. However, the final bill offered labor much less. In any case, in the end, the effort to amend the antitrust act failed, and the labor provisions in that reform effort stood practically as the lone example of the NCF's legislative backing of labor's demands.[64]

If the NCF mainly stepped aside in the fights over the eight-hour and anti-injunction bills, the NAM took the leading role in opposing them. In the view of the NAM and other open-shop employers, the approval rate of the AFL's bills in Congress did not represent the democratic result of the preferences of the people. Rather, it revealed congressmen's subservience to the labor union lobby. NAM officials were always keen to remind the public that organized labor represented only a small percentage of the US population. Therefore, when congressmen supported labor bills, they were not responding to democratic wishes but bowing to pressure and shirking their duty to look after the interests of the country as a whole.[65] Listening to labor voices earned a politician the NAM's scorn for being "scared out of their boots when a labor union passes a resolution"; introducing a labor-supported anti-injunction bill was something a congressional representative would surely "have resisted . . . if he had any backbone."[66] Yet the NAM lobbyists did not see anything wrong with expecting congressmen to dance to the manufacturers' tune: in the same breath as lamenting the lack of backbone of the representative who had introduced an anti-injunction bill, the NAM's secretary wondered "how such a man can expect to be renominated" after angering businessmen so blatantly and suggested that perhaps pressure should be applied so "he will be frightened enough" to listen to people who mattered.[67]

Overall, the NAM's attitude toward the legislative arm of the state was one of derision laced with suspicion. Often, NAM members expressed frustration with the fact that legislatures persisted in considering labor or regulatory legislation. One manufacturer, for instance, grumbled to the NAM secretary that "our State Legislature adjourns today, and it would be a boon to our State if it did not meet again for ten years." Luckily for employers, as the same manufacturer noted in another letter, if "the power of the legislature to injure the manufacturers" was considerable, "the influence of the Governor upon the legislature" could form a barrier against the legislature's influence.[68]

Even as they worried about legislatures, the orchestrators of manufacturer lobbying also delighted in their role as marionette masters of sorts. When the NAM failed to convince a senator to take an explicit stance against the eight-hour bill but managed to convince him to remain absent from a crucial committee vote on it, the NAM secretary philosophically commented that "perhaps for the first attempt he has been doing pretty well."[69] Similarly, when a congressman (Republican Richard Bartholdt of Missouri) had been "effectively prodded" to vote the NAM's way (and probably against his constituents' wishes), the NAM counsel mused, "I don't think he relished it but he stood there and voted like a little man."[70]

Keen to deny labor the publicity benefit of implicit government endorsement of its key demands, open-shop employers worked hard to stop the eight-hour and anti-injunction bills from becoming law. They also hoped to reframe the debate over them. In the employers' depiction, the contest over these bills did not pit working people's rights against those of well-heeled employers; rather, it set labor union demands for special privileges against the interests of the country at large. The eight-hour day, open-shop employers insisted, was a case in point. It might destroy American prosperity. Most certainly, because it raised the cost of producing for the government, it would mean that the government had to pay more for the goods it purchased, and thus taxpayers would be forced to support the wages of a special class of workers.[71] The anti-injunction bill, meanwhile, merely showed that labor wanted "free conspiracy" and "free riot" and flouted the rule of law.[72]

Employers supplemented such public-interest arguments with references to tangible consequences for their businesses—and one suspects that these tangible consequences were foremost in their minds. The passage of anti-injunction legislation would have robbed employers of a tool they often turned to (and found of great use, as discussed in the previous section). The eight-hour issue, meanwhile, agitated so many employers in good part because their businesses would be directly impacted by the bill. The growth of the federal government in the decades after the Civil War meant that many of the open-shop employers derived an important portion of their business from government contracts. For example, the Baltimore firm of James S. Gary & Son produced cotton duck for the War, Navy, and Interior Departments; the Long-Arm System Company of Cleveland performed contract work on ship fittings and power doors of battleships and cruisers; the E. W. Bliss

Company of Brooklyn held government contracts of about a million dollars annually for mines, air compressors, punching presses, and other supplies for the torpedoes of the navy. All these companies were active members in the NAM's open-shop crusade and testified in Congress against the eight-hour bill.[73] Others with lesser contracts argued that it would be impossible for them to set an eight-hour day on government work while maintaining the ten-hour day on other production. The bill would therefore work a hardship on small manufacturers in favor of big producers, as smaller players would be forced to stop bidding on government orders.[74] Still other manufacturers worried that the eight-hour law would work (as the AFL intended it to) as an entering wedge that would bring about the eight-hour day among all workers.[75]

How, then, did the open-shop employers try to stop these bills becoming law? A key tool in this project was delay. The employers did not aim to get the bills defeated in Congress; instead, they worked to keep the bills from being voted on. The first line of defense was to ensure that crucial committees contained as many NAM-friendly congressmen as possible and preferably had no members really interested in passing one of the bills the AFL favored. In that way, the bills could stay safely in committee: hearings could be ordered and extended, the committee might not meet for weeks, the bill could be referred for further study to some other entity or to a subcommittee, or other bills might be considered in its stead. If the bill had to be reported out of committee for one reason or another, the second line of defense was to keep it from actually making it onto the calendar for consideration on the floor. In the House, this could be accomplished through close contact with the representatives who sat on the Committee on Rules; in the Senate, the procedure was more complicated and informal, but a decisive element was friendly relations with the Steering Committee, as well as with other influential senators who might be willing to use delaying tactics.[76] If the bill could be kept off the floor, the circus would have to begin all over again in the next Congress. If this procedure could be repeated Congress after Congress, the bill would, of course, never become law. The NAM thus defined delay as success and repeatedly aimed explicitly to defeat a bill not by getting it voted down but by preventing its full consideration.[77]

The beauty of the delaying strategy was that it was tailor-made for influential people. It depended not on democratic politicking or issue-oriented argumentation but on personal influence brought to bear on key congressmen. While the NAM headquarters did spur manufacturers to send letters (preferably personalized) to their congressmen and to testify against the bills at congressional hearings, the main part of its strategy was to create and deploy a network of influential open-shop manufacturers ready to act on legislative matters.[78] The NAM wished to ensure that, for each important member of Congress, it could call on a substantial number of manufacturers from his state or district to convey to him business's displeasure at prospective labor legislation. In particular, the NAM was looking for individuals who knew a key congressman personally or had some direct influence over him. Sometimes, this strategy succeeded dramatically. For example, as Julie Greene notes, in late 1903 the NAM learned that Representative Richard Bartholdt of St. Louis "dances like a jumping jack whenever Mr. [Adolphus] Busch pulls the string," in the words of future NAM president James Van Cleave.[79] Adolphus Busch was the head of the massive Anheuser-Busch Brewing Association, and by early 1904 the NAM had established a sufficiently strong line to Bartholdt through Busch that it could simply request Busch for an extension of the eight-hour hearings, which Bartholdt obligingly arranged.[80] This was a particularly impressive display of raw power, since Representative Bartholdt had somewhat successfully cultivated a reputation as a moderate on the "labor question" and in his autobiography underlined the need for the state to protect "the welfare of the masses" and to ameliorate the inevitable conflicts between capital and labor.[81]

In a similar vein, about the same time that it enlisted Busch to influence Bartholdt, the NAM was looking for a route to influence another Missouri politician, Senator William J. Stone. Stone had just been appointed a member of the Senate Committee on Education and Labor. Given that Stone was a Democrat and might therefore be expected to favor the AFL's legislative aims, the first priority was to prevent him from giving a definite statement saying he would support the eight-hour bill. The NAM's secretary therefore sent out a circular to the association's Missouri members, urging them to write Stone and explain to him that "it would not be wise for him, taking a political view of the situation, to commit himself."[82] The next step was to map his social and political contacts: to find out his "closest friends" and "to get as much information as possible as to the springs of action which usually affect him."[83] Stone had formerly been governor of Missouri, as well as a US representative, so information on his political contacts and inclinations was not difficult to come by. Having discovered that Judge O. M. Spencer and manufacturer Roderick Abercrombie were both influential with Stone, the NAM bombarded the former to put pressure on Stone and recruited the latter to testify at the eight-hour hearings.[84] The NAM's strategy, then, relied particularly on highlighting to congressmen that people who were highly influential either at the national level or in the congressman's local circle agreed with the NAM's position.[85] In both cases, the personal-influence strategy worked, at least up to a point: Bartholdt did arrange for the extension of hearings, and Stone did not obstruct the NAM's plan to postpone consideration of the eight-hour bill by having it referred to the Department of Commerce and Labor.

Congressmen were not remote-controlled robots, of course, and the NAM was often dissatisfied with its level of influence. For example, the NAM secretary complained that Stone "has been very difficult to influence," and any sway the NAM had managed to gain with him had only come about "through the greatest effort."[86] Nor was it necessarily the case that the NAM convinced senators or representatives to oppose something they might otherwise have favored. However, it made all the difference that the NAM had a direct line to members of Congress via personal connections (see figures 8 and 9). Those connections allowed the NAM to quickly call congressional representatives' attention to the eight-hour bill and make it clear that letting the bill die was of great importance.[87] This was particularly crucial at the start of the NAM's antilabor lobbying campaign in late 1902 and early 1903, when the momentum still to some extent lay with the AFL. The eight-hour bill had been favorably reported by the House Labor Committee, had passed the House, had been favorably reported by the Senate Committee on Education and Labor, and was waiting for the Senate Steering Committee to allow it to go on the floor. The NAM feared that though the Senate had blocked the passage of the bill before, this time the senators might vote it through. Therefore, it decided that its best hope was to convince the Steering Committee to keep it back. The NAM secretary reported that several senators on the committee "received hundreds of letters from our people"—letters that probably counted, as the senators often knew their authors personally.[88] The eight-hour bill died—and that was only the start of the NAM's successes in hamstringing the AFL's legislative program. After the NAM got its lobbying network running, Greene notes, the AFL "achieve[d] no more lobbying victories until the Republicans lost control of Congress in 1910."[89]

To be sure, in the same way that court decisions lost some of their weight if they were perceived to be overly biased, legislator allies, too, could be compromised if they were viewed as employer marionettes. The NAM well understood this and considered it imperative to keep its influence discreet; secrecy had been a key facet of its strategy from the beginning.[90] As one NAM official explained to a newly hired publicity man, the NAM had learned early on that requiring public pledges of allegiance from congressmen was in neither the NAM's nor the congressmen's best interests. The congressmen, after all, needed to get elected:

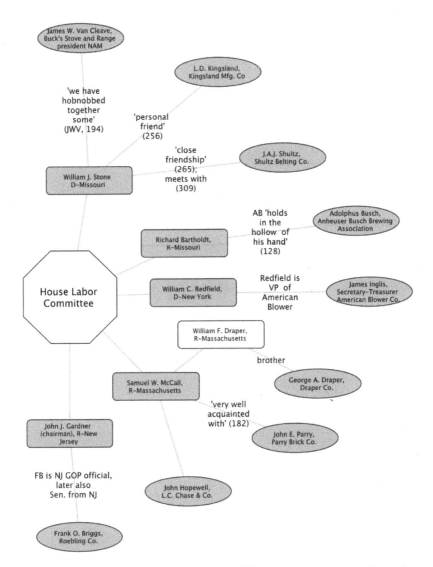

Figure 8: Selected relationships between members of the House Committee on Labor and members of the NAM, 1903–4.

Legend: ellipse = NAM member, filled box = congressional representative, outline box = other. Page references are to US Congress, Senate, Subcommittee of the Committee on the Judiciary, *Maintenance of a Lobby to Influence Legislation: Appendix: Exhibits Introduced during the Hearings*, 63rd Cong., 1st sess., 1913.

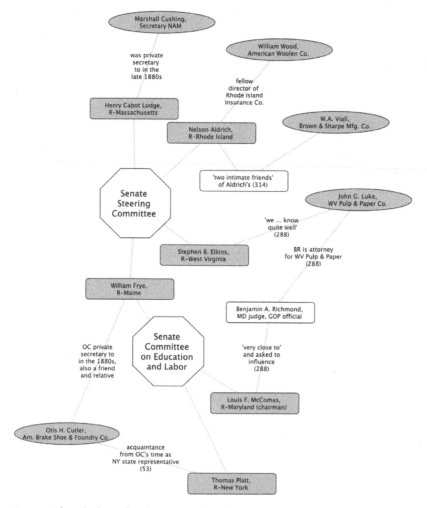

Figure 9: Selected relationships between influential members of the Senate and members of the NAM, 1903–4.

Legend: ellipse = NAM member, filled box = senator, outline box = other. Page references are to US Congress, Senate, Subcommittee of the Committee on the Judiciary, *Maintenance of a Lobby to Influence Legislation: Appendix: Exhibits Introduced during the Hearings*, 63rd Cong., 1st sess., 1913.

Some of the best friends we have in Congress on labor questions, anti-injunction or eight-hour had pledged themselves originally to labor people, but they found it possible to make a complete somersault and when the questions came up for consideration not only voted but effectively worked for our side, again reversing themselves at election time and giving reassurances to labor. . . . [T]o give much publicity [to these politicians in NAM publications] beforehand may hurt us, and it may place the very politicians after whose interests we must look in the limelight for an attack of labor leaders.[91]

It could therefore be prudent to find cover under which legislators willing to assist the NAM could do so without publicly appearing to repudiate labor. One way of doing this was to request more investigation, perhaps via the referral of a bill to the appropriate government bureau or department. For example, in 1904 the NAM suggested that it might be wisest to refer the eight-hour bill to the Department of Commerce and Labor for further study. For congressmen who were on the record as favoring the bill, such referral would be "a good way out of" the dilemma of how to do what the NAM wished without looking like a turncoat.[92] Given that the NAM's main legislative goal was to ensure that the AFL's projects made no progress, it considered the delay such further study would cause a success. And indeed, the strategy succeeded marvelously: it took nearly a year for the secretary of commerce and labor to issue a report. The report itself, moreover, was pleasing enough to the NAM that the association wished to distribute it by the thousands and advertise it as "sustain[ing] our contention at every point."[93]

Over time, the NAM's lobbying became more sophisticated and less exclusively reliant on party hierarchies and personal influence. During 1906 and 1907, the NAM worked hard to create a new lobbying-focused umbrella organization of antiunion employers' associations, the National Council for Industrial Defense. This project had been initiated by James W. Van Cleave, who had ascended to the NAM's presidency in 1906, and its goal was to make the NAM's lobbying work more respectable and effective as well as better funded. Van Cleave had also come into conflict with Marshall Cushing, the NAM's secretary since 1902 and the man mainly in charge of the association's lobbying work. Though Cushing had many enthusiastic supporters in the NAM, Van Cleave was dissatisfied with what he saw as Cushing's self-importance and inability or unwillingness to cooperate.[94] Accordingly, Van Cleave and his close associates pushed Cushing to resign. To handle the NAM's future lobbying campaigns, many of which were to be conducted under the guise of the new National Council for Industrial Defense, Van Cleave selected James A. Emery. Emery, a lawyer who for several years had been the secretary of the Citizens' Industrial Association of America, was just as much a pragmatist as Cushing and just as much committed to the open shop, but his style was much more sophisticated. Formally, Emery became the counsel for the new multiorganization council, but he had all the NAM's resources at his disposal and his role in the NAM soon became central, adding some ballast of erudition to the association's strident opposition to unions. Emery was also better than Cushing at cooperating and at presenting matters in a diplomatic light; among other things, he struck up a fruitful friendship with Daniel A. Davenport of the AABA, the organization working in the legal front against the closed shop and other union demands.[95]

Although the change in personnel and the new emphasis on cooperation among open-shop organizations via the new council thus led to some useful collaborations and a somewhat more upscale tone in lobbying, getting other organizations to actually contribute funds proved difficult.[96] However, the council did serve well as a sleight of hand: it created the impression that a growing number of business organizations were becoming concerned about labor legislation while keeping the NAM in control behind the scenes. As one NAM official noted a couple of years into the council's existence, the NAM "must always control" the council, but not publicly: "It would in a measure nullify the good work of the Council to advertise widely that it is nothing but an annex of the National Association of Manufacturers."[97] Although not explicitly stated, part of the council's objective was probably also to establish a level of deniability, that is, to be able to shift blame onto other organizations should lobbying activities come under embarrassing public scrutiny. This was in fact precisely what happened when the NAM became the target of a congressional lobbying investigation in 1913: NAM witnesses constantly drew distinctions between the actions of the council, the NAM, and the Citizens' Industrial Association (another umbrella group whose leadership also closely overlapped with that of the NAM), effectively resisting the increasingly desperate efforts of the questioning senators to pin down who exactly had done what when.[98]

The Vagaries of Electoral Politics

The NAM's legislative strategy mainly built on finding the pressure point for each important congressman and then leaning on it. However, this strategy relied on two things: first, the NAM members had to have some leverage over the congressman, and second, the congressman had to get put up for candidacy and to get elected. Beginning in 1906, the AFL launched an intensive electoral program to "reward our friends and punish our enemies"—in other words, to evaluate the records of members of Congress on labor matters and exhort workers to vote accordingly. The AFL invested considerable resources in this explicitly nonpartisan electoral program, including shifting much of the energy of fifty salaried and thirteen hundred volunteer organizers to political work.[99] The NAM was determined to counter the AFL's impact. More broadly, the NAM's electoral program reflected its awareness that help with campaign financing and its members' support in the candidate-selection stage were key ways in which it gained influence over congressmen.

For all their contempt of legislatures, active NAM members were steeped in party politics, mainly those of the Republican Party. Many active NAM members had held positions of power in state legislatures, Republican National Convention meetings, and even presidential cabinets. Thus, John Hopewell of the blanket and plush seller L. C. Chase & Company had been a representative to the Massachusetts General Court (the Massachusetts state legislature) and a delegate to the Republican National Convention; according to his obituary, he had been "a welcome friend of President McKinley." Leather manufacturer Charles Schieren had been mayor of Brooklyn. Brick manufacturer Anthony Ittner had in the 1860s and 1870s served in the Missouri General Assembly and the Missouri State Senate, as well as in the US Congress. James Gary had been "prominent in every [Republican] National Convention," besides having served as postmaster general under Grover Cleveland.[100]

Given the active roles many of its members held in the party organization, the NAM was well placed to influence who got to run for office. It was also well aware of this fact and far from shy about making use of it. As Cushing, the NAM's secretary, noted in a circular letter, it might not help a politician much to be popular among labor voters "when it might be another kind of people altogether who would have something to say about his nomination before such votes could be cast."[101]

The NAM also made clear to political officeholders that it stood ready to help—or hinder—their campaigns. It created detailed tables of how many NAM members there were in key congressional committee members' districts, along with what other commercial associations existed in the district. Apparently, it provided these tables to selected "business man's candidate[s]" and their campaign managers with a memorandum explaining how an attitude critical of unions would appeal to these individuals and how these associations might be able to help. NAM members, the memo noted, would probably always listen to anyone who "is prepared to resist the demands of Gompers and his crew of labor mercenaries," and most businessmen certainly wanted to "support their friends and defeat their enemies."[102]

This wasn't merely talk: the NAM did get involved in several electoral campaigns, and presumably the financial contributions that it encouraged its members to make were welcome to the candidates receiving them. Yet maneuvering actual elections and voters was a complex proposition, and not one ideally suited for top-down influence. That, of course, was why the NAM was so distrustful of legislatures in the first place. Even as the NAM got involved in campaigns, it understood that it probably should keep its influence hidden and ideally try to mask it as coming from workers rather than employers. As the memo to campaign managers noted, campaigns should make sure that any business organizations that helped them "do this privately . . . or otherwise it is a boomerang."[103]

The NAM's first documented foray into electoral politics aimed to defeat or undermine Louis E. McComas, a Republican senator from Maryland and the chairman of the Senate Committee on Labor and Education since 1901. As chairman, McComas had presided over the hearings on the eight-hour bill and apparently worked in its favor too energetically for the NAM's liking.[104] It was in this campaign that the NAM established its connection with Martin M. Mulhall, the political operative who later became famous for denouncing the NAM and turning over documents in his possession to the *New York Sun*, precipitating a congressional investigation of lobbying. Mulhall's role in the campaign was to try to convince McComas that there was little grassroots support for the eight-hour bill among workers and, failing that, to foment the existing factional rifts in the Maryland Republican Party and to weaken the prolabor wing that McComas represented.

Toward this end, the NAM first had Mulhall reactivate the Workingmen's Protective Association (WPA), a Baltimore-based Republican political club he had been instrumental in creating a few years earlier. The WPA was one of the organizations, common at the time, that provided candidates and parties with political workers in exchange for governmental jobs; it had worked for the McComas faction in 1900 and 1901 but was growing dissatisfied with the rewards. The organization mounted an effort to convince McComas that ordinary workers opposed the eight-hour bill because it angered employers and caused reductions in wages.[105] When neither this nor letters and personal visits from Maryland businessmen (again prodded by the NAM) swayed McComas perceptibly, the NAM called on James A. Gary, postmaster general under president William McKinley and an important power broker in the Maryland Republican scene, and his son E. Stanley Gary, poised to become a political force of similar stature. With their help, the NAM tried to block McComas's reelection to the Republican National Committee.[106]

The campaign was not a success—McComas continued his advocacy of the eight-hour bill and was reelected to the RNC. (He did not return to the Senate, but only because the Democrats won the state elections and thereby the right to choose Maryland's senator.)[107] Voters, after all, had a say in the matter, and it was not easy to convince them that the NAM's candidate represented their interests. Indeed, trying to do so sometimes backfired badly, as when the NAM tried to elect Republican James Watson into the governor's seat in Indiana in 1908 but only succeeded in providing the Democrats with delicious opportunities to smear Watson as being in cahoots with antiunion forces and in uniting union labor against Watson.[108]

Not all of the NAM's campaigns fell as flat. Sometimes its rather unsavory strategies did in fact apparently help elect its favorite candidate. For instance, the campaign to reelect Representative Charles Littlefield of Maine—one of the NAM's staunch allies and one of the AFL's main targets for electoral defeat—ended in Littlefield's victory. The NAM had invested considerably in the campaign. To start with, it raised significant money among New England manufacturers. Next, it again sent Mulhall to run the grassroots campaign. Mulhall built a political club, fomented suspicion against the AFL among workers, and distributed money among anti-Littlefield workers. As a final push, Mulhall got enough Democratically inclined workingmen so drunk on election day that they could not make it to the polls (or at least that apparently was the hope). Littlefield's reelection margin was thin enough that keeping a few dozen voters away from the polls by the force of whiskey may indeed have been of some use.[109]

The NAM's electoral efforts never achieved the successes it witnessed in its lobbying. When the Democrats gained control of the House in the 1910 elections, and especially after 1912, when they increased their majority in the House and also gained control of the Senate for the first time since 1893, the NAM's lobbying prospects suffered a blow. Suddenly, the NAM was hard put to get friendly congressmen appointed on committees. Although the NAM had for a long time paid special attention to its southern membership so as to have a line to both the Democrats and the Republicans, and although it now tried to get those members to put pressure on the Democratic majority in Congress, its influence had decidedly diminished. For example, when the new Congress was seated, the chairmanship of the House Committee on Labor went to William B. Wilson, a former miner and union member for whom the NAM had little but contempt.[110] Electoral politics, unsurprisingly, had made the NAM enemies as well as friends: as one NAM officer rather ruefully pointed out, if a Democratic congressman was feeling unfriendly toward the NAM, "we cannot altogether blame him . . . in view of the position the 'American Industries' took during the election."[111] By the end of 1911 the NAM's James Emery was forced to concede that "with the labor committee we have had" it had been impossible to keep the eight-hour bill in committee as "during the old regime." Having been reported, the bill passed the House in December 1911.[112] By early 1912, with bills for limiting injunctions, enacting the eight-hour day, and creating a Department of Labor floating about the House and the Senate, Emery was fuming that "the time is almost at hand when the 16th amendment will provide for the possession of a union card by the President."[113]

The victory of the Democrats in the 1912 election was soon followed by Mulhall's decision to spill the beans on his former employers, and for most of 1913 the NAM was embroiled in a massive congressional investigation into its activities. After the investigation, the NAM had little power to prevent the AFL from finally achieving many of the legislative aims it had been pursuing for years: the eight-hour bill passed in 1912; the Department of Labor was created in 1913; the Clayton Antitrust Act, which limited court injunctions, was enacted in 1914; and a slew of other labor bills also made it through Congress and were signed into law.[114]

So did all the NAM's political work represent a brief anomaly, a mere wrinkle in the successful onslaught of popular reform? In part, yes: the NAM was unable to prevent the electoral defeat of its allies, and it was certainly deeply displeased with the result. There were definite limits to the NAM's political clout in other respects as well: few if any of the NAM's proposals for cabinet positions or other important federal-level appointments were successful, for example.[115] However, the labor laws that passed in the 1910s were not quite the blows the NAM had feared. The Clayton Antitrust Act in particular proved a weak crutch. Although Samuel Gompers hailed it as the "Industrial Magna Carta," its real impact was minimal. It began boldly enough by declaring that labor is not a commodity and went on to forbid the use of injunctions in a broad swath of labor cases. But it ended with a clause declaring that all the preceding could be ignored if faced with "severe danger." Thus, courts continued to issue injunctions as before; in fact, in the 1920s more injunctions were issued than in the two previous decades combined.[116]

Moreover, the years of delay that the NAM had engineered mattered: they had successfully curbed labor's momentum and legitimacy. Had the labor bills passed in 1902, when the NAM first started its lobbying campaign, the situation might have been very different. If contemporary assessments by the NAM and by labor sources were correct, the bills would have enjoyed such large bipartisan majorities that no roll call would have been required.

The AFL could have chalked up a major victory within only a few years of beginning its serious lobbying campaign. The content of the bills, particularly of the anti-injunction bill, might also have been different—with a perception of broader support, the Congress might not have felt it necessary to open the "severe danger" back door to injunctions. Legislative successes might also have raised the credibility of the AFL's political line among workers, thus perhaps inspiring more workers to keep their status as workers in mind at the ballot box. And a congressional endorsement of AFL demands might have lent greater legitimacy to union organizing in general. Instead, in these crucial years the AFL was constantly on the defensive, neither its lobbying nor its electioneering producing very impressive results. The enthusiasm with which the AFL greeted its successes with the state in the 1910s probably had at least as much to do with the complete lack of legislative accomplishments it had faced for a decade as it had with the significance of the new appointments and laws.

7 The Battle over Public Opinion

Half the lies they tell about me aren't true.
—Attributed to Yogi Berra

"A Capitalistic Judge Takes Another Step Toward Czardom," a subheadline on the first page of *The Wageworker* declared in 1905. "Time Has Come to Make a Stand for American Rights," the headline continued.[1] *The Wageworker* was talking about the injunction upheld by Judge Jesse Holdom against the striking printers in Chicago. The injunction was indeed sweeping, forbidding the strikers from "interfering" in any way with the nonunion workmen hired by Chicago printers or with the print shops themselves, including picketing, speaking to the strikebreakers, or contacting the shops' customers. "By court order the right to free speech is denied," seethed *The Wageworker*.[2]

The famously antiunion *Los Angeles Times*, by contrast, saw no problem with the injunction. "Why do the trades-unionists object to injunctions to restrain them from committing crime, unless they intend to commit crime?" the paper asked in an editorial entitled "Meddlers Enjoined."[3] Later, when the printers held a meeting to rally opposition to the injunction, the paper's correspondent wired from Chicago that the meeting gave voice to many "utterances bordering on the revolutionary." The front-page article was ominously headlined "Printers Talk of Cold Lead."[4]

Most stories about the injunction were not so unabashedly partisan. The Associated Press report, which was probably the most commonly read source about the injunction, mainly confined itself to the key news points: that Holdom was upholding an injunction issued a week earlier by a lower court and that in explaining the grounds for his decision, he declared the closed shop and the eight-hour day "unlawful when it is attempted to force the employer to enter into it against his will."[5]

In an era before radio or film (not to mention television or the internet), the press was the key tool of mass communication; it also amplified any other forms of publicity, such as speeches and rallies. Hard as it was to know the state of "public opinion" in an era when well-designed public opinion polling was still decades in the future, both labor and employers cared about what appeared in the newspapers and magazines of the day. Overall, publicity was a growing business in the early twentieth century, and shaping news coverage was of increasing concern to both politicians and corporations.[6]

The public's support mattered for several reasons. Support from members of the general public might manifest itself in very direct ways. As consumers, they might back a labor union boycott of "unfair" goods—or they might ignore it. As members of a community, they might be recruited as participants in a street protest in support of a strike—or sworn in as members of a sheriff's posse to suppress a strike. And as voters, they might support a politician with a prolabor record—or consider that record a reason to vote against him. Given the growing web of state presence in the early twentieth century, this last point made publicity politically ever more salient. The state made decisions on many key questions regarding labor. Would courts uphold or deny the legality of labor union strategies? Would the state use its coercive power to break strikes, as it had often done? Would legislatures pass laws that forced the parties to labor disputes to arbitrate? Would the state enforce the results of such arbitration? Would state agencies investigate conditions of labor or regulate hours of work? Both labor unions and employer organizations considered the answers to such questions vital. How the different branches of the state answered those questions depended at least in part on public opinion.

Labor and employer organizations asked somewhat different things of the public. Employers mainly needed to convince ordinary Americans that there was no dire problem to address, or if there was, then unions and the remedies they proposed were not the answer. Employers' goal was to maintain the status quo—to prevent new prolabor legislation, to hamper workers' efforts to change the power dynamics at the workplace, to check challenges to employers' managerial authority and freedom. Achieving that goal did not require the public to do anything; employers could rely on their financial clout and personal contacts to pursue their political goals. For labor, by contrast, the goal was to achieve change, and the public's active support was crucial for reaching that goal. Labor's main—perhaps its only—advantage lay in numbers. Only by mobilizing a meaningful number of workers, consumers, or voters could labor threaten a business with a loss in income or hold out the promise of votes to a politician. This in itself was a publicity advantage for employers. Employers could accomplish many of their goals out of the public eye and therefore with less exposure to public critique. Labor, by contrast, had to engage in the fundamental and very public activities of a democratic process: arguing, wheedling, exhorting, organizing.

Labor was not without advantages with regard to the public. Most obviously, it could garner underdog sympathies. Moreover, much of "the public" consisted of workers and their families. Especially in places with substantial union penetration, there was obvious social pressure to support union demands, and the benefits of union achievements were clear enough to fellow workers. Union wages supported the local economy, union work rules made fathers more likely to come home at the end of a shift rather than being injured on the job, union halls were places of gathering.[7] However, labor organizing, particularly strikes, also regularly inconvenienced people of all classes who had no part in the dispute. Streetcars might stand still, deliveries of goods might not take place, services might be unavailable. Even when a strike was limited to a specific factory, the normal life of the town where the factory stood might be disrupted if the company brought in replacement workers and strikers resisted their employment. The public might well also perceive social unrest as threatening: this was an era with regular and dramatic labor confrontations and significant radical movements. Unsurprisingly, open-shop employers, including those in the National Association of Manufacturers, focused much of their publicity message on highlighting these inconveniences and arguing that labor unions imposed them on communities for reasons that were selfish and frivolous. Moderate labor unions like the American Federation of Labor and their middle-class allies like the leadership of the National Civic Federation sometimes countered that unions formed the best bulwark against the chaos that might erupt if labor's legitimate demands were ignored.

This chapter discusses the forces that shaped reporting about labor in newspapers and magazines. It starts by examining the labor press, focusing on a computational analysis of the content of selected labor newspapers and comparing it to the mainstream press. It next turns to the open-shop employers, particularly the NAM's publicity campaigns, and explores how the infrastructure and economics of the early twentieth-century press offered an opening to employers to use their financial clout to influence what Americans read. Finally, it examines the NCF's substantial publicity efforts. The NCF's explicit focus was on conciliating the conflict between labor and capital, and especially early on its officers conducted much publicity on behalf of finding formal accord between organized labor and organized employers as a cure for radical tendencies in the society. Yet both the personal inclinations of its secretary, Ralph Easley, and the NCF's dependence on funding from its business members pushed it to prioritize the antiradicalism portion of its message over the prounion part.

Labor Papers and Labor News

The turn of the twentieth century was in many ways the heyday of American newspaper and magazine journalism. Tens of thousands of newspapers and magazines served a highly literate readership: there were several dozen times more newspapers in 1900–1910 than there were at the turn of the twenty-first century. Most of these newspapers were what were known as "country week-lies," small-town or rural newspapers that came out once a week. Purchasing or setting up such a paper could be done for as little as $500 (the equivalent of about $15,000 in 2020 dollars), though larger operations could require a few thousand dollars. Even small towns of a few thousand residents might have two or three weekly papers. In total, there were some thirty thousand weeklies in the United States in the early twentieth century and about five thousand dailies. (For comparison, in the early 2000s, the number of dailies was just over thirteen hundred, and it has been falling rapidly since.)[8]

Newspapers with a specific agenda were common. Although journalism in the early twentieth century developed an increasingly professional identity that began to emphasize objectivity as a core value, a large number of newspapers remained explicitly affiliated with political parties.[9] The paper often proudly proclaimed its party affiliation in its title, calling itself something like the *Taney County Republican*, the *Ripley County Democrat*, or even the *Alaska Socialist*. Or it might declare a specific political position in a slogan placed prominently on the front page; for example, issues of the *Forest City Press* in South Dakota announced the paper's motto right under the newspaper title: "The Saloon Is the Enemy of the Home: May America Protect Her Homes."[10]

Labor-affiliated newspapers abounded in the early twentieth century, even if one considers only "bona fide" newspapers and ignores the official union journals (i.e., such publications as the *American Federationist* and the *Shoeworkers' Journal*). Through the first two decades of the twentieth century (and beyond), newspapers affiliated with labor, with the Socialist Party, or more loosely with working-class concerns proliferated throughout the United States.[11] Though labor papers were often short-lived and small-scale, there were hundreds of them. Labor news also came in multiple languages; alongside the English-language labor press, there existed a lively immigrant working-class newspaper landscape. These papers offered a different set of news stories and a different take on the news of the day to a significant slice of the American working class.[12] The readership of labor papers constituted a community widely dispersed in geography but limited to those who identified as (union) workers. The cultivation of such a community was deliberate. The union halls and "labor temples" that were erected in dozens of cities around the turn of the century were well-stocked with labor papers from across the country, providing visitors with information and a sense of the strength of the movement.[13] Labor papers were also often much more participatory than mainstream ones: much of the content came from readers' voluntary contributions and from the movement's organizers. To an extent, this was making a virtue out of necessity, as few labor papers could afford a standard wire service, and as such services were in any case unlikely to provide the kind of news they wanted to print. But to an extent, it was also a question of basic philosophy: Why should a labor paper operate in the top-down manner of a capitalist news dissemination service when the movement was all about organizing and involving workers in their own uplift?[14]

An important function of labor papers was to provide the news that the mainstream media slighted and to offer analysis from an alternative viewpoint. Labor was generally very dissatisfied with the portrayal of worker movements in the mainstream press. To be sure, the "labor question" loomed sufficiently large among the issues of the day that newspapers contained a fair amount of reporting on various aspects of the labor movement. Many newspapers also ran columns that gathered very brief updates on union activity under such headers as "Organized Labor at Home and Abroad," "News of the Labor World," and "Labor and Industry."[15] Nevertheless, unions alleged bias in labor coverage. The press, unions argued, printed accusations by organized antiunion employers of corruption among union men without giving unions a chance to respond, even when the accusations concerned specific individuals. Meanwhile, organizing successes went unremarked, thus robbing labor of the optimism such successes might have inspired in workers who read about them.[16]

Accordingly, labor papers made news that mattered to unionists a priority. They also framed news in ways that set labor actions in a much more positive context than was usually the case in the mainstream press while providing much more critique of industry and capitalism. The differences between labor papers and nonlabor small-town papers with either a mainstream political affiliation or no affiliation become strikingly clear through a computational analysis comparing the vocabulary and topics in both sets of papers. The computational analysis discussed here is based on a sample of four labor papers and twelve mainstream papers for the years 1909–1911 (see table 3).[17]

If one examines the vocabulary of these papers comparatively (labor papers vs. nonlabor papers), one soon notes that they are quite far apart from each other. Even simple counts of words reveal obvious differences. Most strikingly, the word *capitalism* occurred only *once* in the mainstream material for roughly *every 675 times* it appeared in the labor material—and indeed,

Table 3. Newspapers in the data set.

Paper affiliation	Title	Publication frequency	Place of publication
Democrat	*Valentine Democrat*	Weekly	Valentine, NE
Democrat	*Little Falls Herald*	Weekly	Little Falls, MN
GOP	*Fairmont West Virginian*	Daily	Fairmont, WV
GOP	*Omaha Daily Bee*	Daily	Omaha, NE
GOP	*Clarksburg Telegram*	Weekly	Clarksburg, WV
GOP	*Bemidji Daily Pioneer*	Daily	Bemidji, MN
GOP	*McCook Tribune*	Triweekly	McCook, NE
GOP	*Colfax Gazette*	Weekly	Colfax, WA
Labor	*Labor Journal*	Weekly	Everett, WA
Labor	*Labor World*	Biweekly	Duluth, MN
Labor	*Labor Argus*	Weekly	Charleston, WV
Labor	*The Wageworker*	Weekly	Lincoln, NE
Unaffiliated	*Princeton Union*	Weekly	Princeton, MN
Unaffiliated	*Leavenworth Echo*	Weekly	Leavenworth, WA
Unaffiliated	*Ellensburg Dawn*	Weekly	Ellensburg, WA
Unaffiliated	*Lynden Tribune*	Weekly	Lynden, WA

Note: The set contains 25,897 pages (about 56 million words) and represents the full runs of these papers for 1909-11.
Source: Chronicling America, http://chroniclingamerica.loc.gov/.

only once for roughly every fifty times the mainstream material mentioned *socialism*. The mainstream press, it seems, took capitalism as the water it swam in, something that required no mention, while the labor press invested considerable effort in discussing it.

In addition to simply counting word frequencies, one can also examine and compare word meaning. This draws on so-called word embeddings: representing a word's "meaning" using its context words (i.e., a *bank* is clearly a different thing if surrounded by words like *money*, *cash*, and *bill* than if surrounded by words like *river*, *mud*, and *picnic*). These representations can be converted into vectors of numbers; doing so makes calculations of difference between two meanings possible.[18] For example, the word *capitalist*, which did occur with regularity in the mainstream material, takes on a very different meaning in the mainstream press than in the labor press. In the labor press, as one might expect, *capitalist* was used in similar contexts as words like *class*, *trusts*, *nation*, *masses*, *masters*, and *greed*; it was surrounded by words like *system*, *power*, and *struggle*. By contrast, in the mainstream material, *capitalist* was similar to such words as *financier*, *magnate*, and *philanthropist* and was surrounded by words referring to places (New York and Chicago) and words like *dead*, *died*, *estate*, *home*, and *son*. What this indicates is that in the mainstream material, *capitalist* mainly appeared in obituaries, where the deceased was identified as a "capitalist" as a neutral or positive appellation, as in this headline from a *New York Times* obituary: "Theodore G. Montague Dead: A Leading Capitalist and Iron Manufacturer of Chattanooga."[19]

Words like *socialism, socialist,* and *strikers* also show clear differences in usage between the labor and the mainstream papers. The mainstream press discussed *socialism* as a doctrinal issue rather similar to a religious belief, while the word *socialist* mainly appeared in reporting about elections and was used in ways similar to reporting about populist-flavored political campaigns. Thus, *socialism* was similar to such words as *doctrine* and *believer* and *propaganda*, while *socialist* was similar to words like *Hearst* and *Bryan*, referring to the newspaper owner William Randolph Hearst, who had run unsuccessfully for mayor of New York in 1905 on a platform of municipal ownership of public utilities, and William Jennings Bryan, the four-time Democratic presidential candidate who had also received endorsements from the People's Party.[20] In the labor material, too, *socialist* is used in the context of electoral campaigns, while *socialism* is used similarly to *unionism* or *democracy,* that is, in contexts discussing politics and governance, as is also indicated by the context words, which include *state, lecture, party,* and *antitrust.* Finally, a noteworthy difference can be seen in the word *strikers.* In the mainstream material, *strikers* appears in the same contexts as *foreigners* and *riot.* Given that the context words in both materials clearly indicate labor disputes, this indicates that stories in the mainstream material were likely to characterize strikers as foreign and to associate strikes with riots.

The differences between labor and mainstream papers are even more obvious if one compares the topics that are prominent in each rather than the specific ways in which some key words are used. Topics are analyzed here using a technique called topic modeling, which automatically identifies the requested number of topics in a set of texts based on word co-occurrence and calculates the "weight" or prominence of each topic (roughly, how much of the material falls under that topic).[21] The most obvious difference in topics between the labor and mainstream papers was the prevalence of news about strikes in the labor papers (see figure 10, which shows the topics most consistently appearing in the labor papers so that the most prominent topics are at the top of the list). That topic tops the list of prominent topics in labor papers and is well represented in each of the labor papers in the set. The other sets of news material that are clearly much more prevalent in the labor papers than in the mainstream papers are the "analysis, principles, ideals" category, news about socialists and socialism, and the category of "political demands." The first, when examined more closely, proves to contain a mix of editorial-type material, reports of speeches, and the like that cultivates the fairly flowery language often common in explication of political principles.[22] The second is fairly self-explanatory, and its clear prominence in specifically the *Labor Argus* is hardly surprising, as the *Argus* had a history of supporting workers' efforts to self-organize both politically and economically and became an explicitly Socialist paper in 1911 under the editorship of Charles H. Boswell.[23] The third contains material such as Socialist Party platforms, political demands of state labor federations, and political demands of the AFL.

By contrast, neither the strikes topic nor the socialism topic makes it onto a list of the top topics in the mainstream material (see figure 11); indeed, the socialism topic is at the very bottom, while the strikes topic is about two-thirds of the way down the list. The topics most prominent in the mainstream material are also very different from the top topics in the labor material. The two most common topics are "personal news" (local society pages reporting on such tidbits as Mrs. Kinnicaid's New York cousin being in town or the Misses Nelson having gone to visit their aunt in Seattle) and fiction or other entertaining narratives. Both are more about amusement and local gossip than news. Other important topics include advertisements of various kinds, including for local professional services; railroad timetables; official notices of various sorts; ads and news about farming; and news about state legislation, crime, and accidents.

While we usually focus on news and editorials when using historical newspapers in historical research, the fact is that the newspaper was always about much more than the news.[24] In the form of personal news notices, it provided the local gossip—that Mrs. Jones's nephew was visiting from New Orleans or that an excellent time had been had by all at the picnic thrown by Mr. and Mrs. Smith for their daughter's birthday. In the classified columns and advertisements, one could find a new job or a place to live, find a cow for sale or a handyman for a job, learn that the YMCA was hosting a lecturer on the wonders of Niagara Falls, or find out what time the local Elks lodge was meeting. In the local news, one could read about the Labor Day picnic or the latest theater performance. In addition, one could check the train timetables, enjoy a fiction story, or perhaps get new recipe ideas. All this minutiae of local life and bland entertainment, mundane as it seems, made the local small-town paper a community staple and a community glue. It is also the kind of material that shines by its absence in labor papers.

Figures 12 and 13, on the topics least prominent in and least characteristic of the labor material, underline the absences in the labor papers.[25] As they show, the labor material contains virtually no personal news; similarly absent are classified ads such as those for housing, notices of church and Sunday school meetings, advertisements by local doctors and other professionals, and practical information like railway timetables. In regular news, topics that are common in mainstream material, such as sports news, news about (local) government, and news about accidents and fires, are much less prevalent in the labor papers.

This "alternative" role of the labor papers both underlines their importance and signals their marginality. The labor press did not really serve the regular nonnews functions of the local press; it also provided less of the "ordinary" daily news. It was explicitly *in addition to* rather than *in lieu of* the regular newspaper. A reader who wanted the usual newspaper fare of classifieds, personal items, and news about accidents, government, and local goings-on could not simply subscribe to a labor paper, even a local one. He or she would need to get the local paper for general news and the labor paper for labor news. That did not diminish the value of the labor paper; indeed, if anything, it increased it. The written word was a crucial component in the formation of the early twentieth-century labor movement and in the development of working-class interpretations of the world. The role of socialist and radical periodicals and book publishers constituted a key part of the intellectual life of working-class movements. By the 1910s and 1920s labor was taking very seriously the need to educate workers to become, among other things, labor journalists.[26] But the alternative nature of labor papers did mean that the papers' reach was practically limited to those who were willing to deliberately subscribe to a publication providing the labor viewpoint. To an extent, then, labor papers were inevitably preaching to the choir rather than gaining a hearing for their viewpoint among the general population.

By the same token, the fact that news about strikes or about socialism was downplayed in the regular press meant that people who did not subscribe to a dedicated labor paper simply did not hear much about those topics. Despite the association of newspapers with self-education and rationality, the presence of the newspaper in a household probably depended heavily on the utility of the nonnews categories. Readership studies of the role of newspapers are scarce, but one study from the early 1950s focusing on weekly newspapers (which formed the vast majority of early twentieth-century newspapers) notes that although the average reader read a larger percentage of the paper's news items than of all items, and although items on the front page were about twice as likely to get read as items anywhere else in the paper, the categories read by more than half the readers did not include news but did include classified advertising, personal ads, and human interest stories.[27] Thus, one's news was in some ways served "on the side" of other useful information. What news those "side dishes" included largely determined the type of information a general reader got. Labor's systematic publicity efforts lagged a decade or two behind the corporate discovery of "public relations."[28] Where labor emphasized interpreting the world to its constituency, employers focused on shaping the content of mainstream reporting—and enjoyed significant structural advantages in doing so.

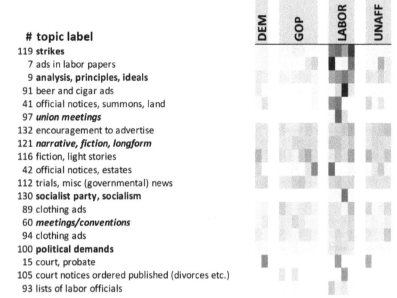

# topic label	DEM	GOP	LABOR	UNAFF
119 **strikes**				
7 ads in labor papers				
9 **analysis, principles, ideals**				
91 beer and cigar ads				
41 official notices, summons, land				
97 *union meetings*				
132 encouragement to advertise				
121 *narrative, fiction, longform*				
116 fiction, light stories				
42 official notices, estates				
112 trials, misc (governmental) news				
130 **socialist party, socialism**				
89 clothing ads				
60 *meetings/conventions*				
94 clothing ads				
100 **political demands**				
15 court, probate				
105 court notices ordered published (divorces etc.)				
93 lists of labor officials				

Figure 10: Topics most prominent in the labor material. Note especially the starkly disproportionate reporting on strikes in labor papers and the near absence of the topic from mainstream papers. Note also the prominence of the "analysis, principles, ideals" category. News and editorial topics in bold, topics containing a mix of notices/advertising and news/editorials in bold italic. Each square represents the strength of a topic in a particular newspaper title; the darker the square, the more prominent the topic was in that title. The labor papers represented by the squares are (from left to right) *Labor Journal*, *Labor World*, *Labor Argus*, and *The Wageworker*. Incoherent topics and topics representing OCR (optical character recognition) errors have been culled.

The NAM: Planted Stories, Publicity Stunts, and Press Agentry

Organizations like the NAM fully expected that newspapers would bend to their publicity campaigns: as the NAM secretary, Marshall Cushing, wrote to another officer, "If you will show [the papers] how to suppress matter and even print matter in a way that will not be unsafe for them . . . they will do it."[29] Publicity professionals confirmed this assumption: in 1907, when the NAM hired a publicity bureau to "conduct a campaign of education" on labor and on other questions, such as tariff revision, the bureau explained that newspapers that would refuse "campaign" material were "comparatively few," so that with "a sufficient fund at hand," most of the country's newspapers could be reached. The source of such material, the bureau emphasized, should be kept hidden. If it was identified with the NAM, it would be revealed as "more

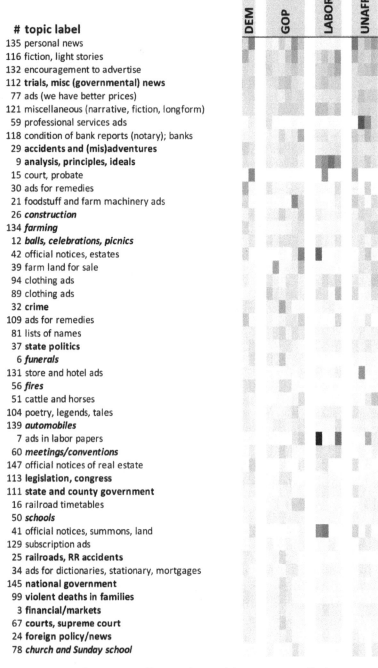

#	topic label	DEM	GOP	LABOR	UNAFF
135	personal news				
116	fiction, light stories				
132	encouragement to advertise				
112	**trials, misc (governmental) news**				
77	ads (we have better prices)				
121	miscellaneous (narrative, fiction, longform)				
59	professional services ads				
118	condition of bank reports (notary); banks				
29	**accidents and (mis)adventures**				
9	**analysis, principles, ideals**				
15	court, probate				
30	ads for remedies				
21	foodstuff and farm machinery ads				
26	*construction*				
134	*farming*				
12	*balls, celebrations, picnics*				
42	official notices, estates				
39	farm land for sale				
94	clothing ads				
89	clothing ads				
32	crime				
109	ads for remedies				
81	lists of names				
37	**state politics**				
6	*funerals*				
131	store and hotel ads				
56	*fires*				
51	cattle and horses				
104	poetry, legends, tales				
139	*automobiles*				
7	*ads in labor papers*				
60	*meetings/conventions*				
147	official notices of real estate				
113	**legislation, congress**				
111	**state and county government**				
16	railroad timetables				
50	*schools*				
41	official notices, summons, land				
129	subscription ads				
25	**railroads, RR accidents**				
34	ads for dictionaries, stationary, mortgages				
145	**national government**				
99	**violent deaths in families**				
3	**financial/markets**				
67	**courts, supreme court**				
24	**foreign policy/news**				
78	*church and Sunday school*				

Figure 11: Top topics by average in all material except labor. Note especially the prominence of personal news in nonlabor material and its almost complete absence in labor material. News and editorial topics in bold, topics containing a mix of notices/advertising and news/editorials in bold italic. Each square represents the strength of a topic in a particular newspaper title; the darker the square, the more prominent the topic was in that title. Topic number is simply a unique ID. Incoherent topics and topics representing OCR (optical character recognition) errors have been culled.

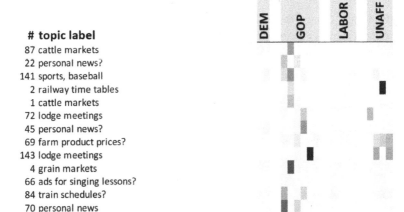

#	topic label	DEM	GOP	LABOR	UNAFF
87	cattle markets				
22	personal news?				
141	sports, baseball				
2	railway time tables				
1	cattle markets				
72	lodge meetings				
45	personal news?				
69	farm product prices?				
143	lodge meetings				
4	grain markets				
66	ads for singing lessons?				
84	train schedules?				
70	personal news				

Figure 12: Topics least prominent in the labor material.

Note: The least prominent topic appears on top. For more explanation, see the caption of figure 10 and endnote 25.

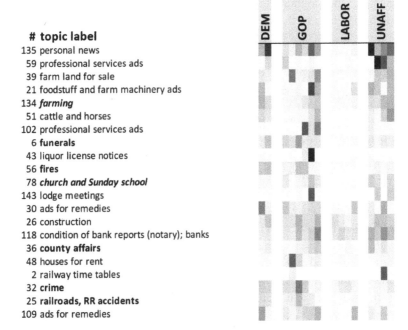

#	topic label	DEM	GOP	LABOR	UNAFF
135	personal news				
59	professional services ads				
39	farm land for sale				
21	foodstuff and farm machinery ads				
134	*farming*				
51	cattle and horses				
102	professional services ads				
6	**funerals**				
43	liquor license notices				
56	**fires**				
78	***church and Sunday school***				
143	lodge meetings				
30	ads for remedies				
26	construction				
118	condition of bank reports (notary); banks				
36	**county affairs**				
48	houses for rent				
2	railway time tables				
32	**crime**				
25	**railroads, RR accidents**				
109	ads for remedies				

Figure 13: Topics least characteristic of the labor material.

Note: The least characteristic topic appears on top. For more explanation, see the caption of figure 10 and endnote 25.

or less partisan propaganda": the campaign would be of little use "unless the matter that is caused to appear all over the country comes with the utmost naturalness, and without the evidence of any inspiration."[30]

While publicity agents naturally had an interest in exaggerating their ability to insert material in the country's newspapers, the structure of the newspaper industry offered a variety of openings for influencing the content of papers. In particular, the same economics that enabled small towns to have multiple papers also enabled the "planting" of news stories. The vast majority of the country's papers were small country weeklies that operated on a shoestring budget. A large part of the costs of producing a paper came from typesetting, which was well-paid skilled work, and few country editors could have borne the expense of paying for typesetting or found the time to do it all themselves. What made the existence of most country weeklies possible was the significant savings in typesetting costs ensured by the infrastructure of readyprint and boilerplate.

Readyprint (also known as auxiliary service, patent insides, or patent outsides) was newsprint preprinted on one side with national news, fiction, and the like. The publisher would then print the local news on the other side.[31] Readyprint that contained advertising, which was what most papers used, could be had for practically the same price as blank newsprint paper, representing significant cost savings for the publisher and not quite such a sacrifice in content as one might imagine: one could request content that, for example, emphasized regional news or excluded particular types of advertising, such as liquor ads.[32] The idea behind boilerplate was similar, though it offered the newspaper editor more choice. Boilerplate, more commonly known as plate matter, consisted of pretypeset thin metal sheets that could be cut and rearranged by the publisher by story or even by paragraph.[33] The newspaper paid for the stories it decided to use or agreed to print advertisements sent by the supplier of the plate in exchange for regular news plate.[34] Both types of material were widely used, and many papers made use of both. By the eve of World War I, one contemporary student of journalism claimed that the "great bulk of the matter in the country newspaper, outside of the local news and editorials, comes in the form of stereotypes [boilerplate]," while up to half of "the general and telegraphic news appearing in the daily newspapers, published outside the large centers," was plate matter.[35]

Both readyprint and plate matter offered opportunities to place material before the country's newspaper readers without the readers knowing that the material was paid for by someone with an agenda. For a premium price, a company could opt to replace or supplement "display advertisements" with "reading notices," advertising material masquerading as news; these would be "sandwiched between items of pure reading matter set in same type."[36]

To get such notices in readyprint, advertisers would simply select which region or regions they wanted to target, and the reading notice would appear in dozens, hundreds, or thousands of "family weekly newspapers of the better class."[37] In plate matter, the use of "free," or sponsored, plate was acknowledged openly by the directors of the companies that produced it. As they explained, their companies regularly sent to editors proofs of plates that were paid for by a third party hoping to disseminate a particular story. However, even if an editor carefully considered all material before printing it, the reader might still be left in the dark. When editors used sponsored plate they often omitted to inform their readers of its original source. Nor did editors always know much about who actually had paid for the plate, as the purported sponsor might be a "front" that revealed little about the interests actually behind the material.[38] For example, one of the first modern-style publicity bureaus, the Municipal Ownership Publicity Bureau, regularly placed material in the newspapers. According to an early article on publicity techniques, the bureau represented a number of utility companies opposed to municipal ownership of utilities. The bureau sternly advised the companies not to try to place material in newspapers themselves. Instead, they should work through the bureau, which could ensure that "the company does not appear in the matter at all."[39]

Readyprint and boilerplate, then, made it not just feasible but unremarkable for an organization like the NAM to place material in newspapers. The Century Syndicate, the publicity bureau hired by the NAM in 1907, recommended an essentially three-pronged strategy for conducting a publicity campaign: small news articles, magazine articles, and editorials. The short news items, the publicity agent explained, formed "the infantry in such a campaign": their role was to "[keep] the subject constantly before the people in news paragraphs without comment." The "heavy artillery" was "in the magazine field," where talented writers should be contracted to craft persuasive articles based on data supplied by the NAM. Editorials were less useful, though they too had their place. Moreover, the publicity agent emphasized, "attention should be continually directed to the subject under discussion for the creation of news" through events, interviews, and speeches by "prominent men," which would then be reported in the papers.[40]

The NAM had already applied a similar logic to the pages of its own magazine. The content of *American Industries* illustrates the respective roles of the news item "infantry" and the "heavy artillery" of longer stories. The short news items in *American Industries* kept up a constant patter of small anecdotes that made labor unionists appear corrupt, fanatical, and ridiculous. They recounted incidents that in themselves mattered little but whose very insignificance may in fact have made them that much more effective. A

story about a miner who abandoned his fiancée when she rode on boycotted streetcars, a note about a burglar who reported overhearing union plans
for the assassination of mine operators and federal officials, an item about
a unionized theater ensemble that considered not playing to nonunionized
audiences—these were entertaining anecdotes, not something that would
prompt a reader to engage in critical analysis and evaluation.[41] The story stood
on its own, a small, apparently objective factoid that nevertheless implied a
particular view of unions. Having been primed by such "infantry" of news
items, the reader might be more receptive to the longer articles detailing
how the NAM viewed the closed shop or the boycott, liberally sprinkled
with quotes from judicial, religious, and academic authorities ("prominent
men") to highlight the mainstream nature of the NAM's views.

Though the NAM's records are spotty on its purchases of publicity and the
Century Syndicate's records appear not to have survived, it seems that the
NAM sponsored material that was in fact widely printed in the weekly (and
possibly also daily) papers. It also at least planned to sponsor "a half-page
story regarding the general uprising against the methods of organized labor"
through boilerplate and to place an editorial smearing the president of the
AFL (entitled "Gompers Incites to Treason") in thousands of papers. The
publicity agent noted that the boilerplate story would cost three dollars per
paper for the papers that decided to run it; he estimated that probably around
a hundred papers might pick it up. The anti-Gompers editorial would cost
$1,400 (apparently inserted in readyprint, given the firm price) and would
be run in nearly five thousand country weeklies in the Midwest. These sums
were not negligible: in 2020 dollars, $1,400 comes to about $40,000. Sensitive
to his expense-conscious customers, the Century Syndicate's representative
noted that the editorial might not be the best use of the money, and it appears
that it was never printed. However, the representative did confirm that some
matter ordered by the NAM was being printed at a rate of "about 30 [papers]
a day."[42]

As for the "artillery" of magazine stories, the NAM sometimes managed to
get major magazines to publish articles that either supported the NAM's labor
views without acknowledging the article's NAM provenance or were openly
attributed to the NAM's officers and thereby helped them position themselves
as experts on labor questions. For example, Henry Harrison Lewis, editor of
American Industries, published an article in the *North American Review* in
1908 that closely followed the NAM line on unions and made no mention of
Lewis's affiliation with the NAM.[43] Often rapport with the editors of magazines was key to access: for example, the friendship of the NAM's counsel,
James Emery, with S. S. McClure of the iconic Progressive Era publication
McClure's Magazine resulted in at least one article that supported the NAM

position and drew on NAM-supplied information without the NAM's influence being acknowledged.[44] Similarly, the good relations between two successive NAM presidents and John A. Sleicher, editor of *Leslie's Weekly*, led the magazine to give "considerable space to affairs of the National Association of Manufacturers" both by commissioning articles by its officers and by printing editorials in support of the NAM (and even, perhaps, written by its officers). Thus, in July 1908 NAM president James W. Van Cleave was asked to supply an article titled "Duty of Business Men of the Country in the Presidential Campaign," while an editorial later the same year praised the NAM's firmness in standing up against labor's demands in Congress.[45] NAM officers' friendships with editors were, of course, also an indication of the leanings of newspaper editors in general: in 1900 over half of the editors of the country's largest dailies were the sons of businessmen, and the NAM in fact counted at least one newspaper publisher among its active members.[46]

In the field of the "creation of news," the NAM made significant use of the courts. As discussed in chapter 1, injunctions forbidding union picketing and other activities were prominently publicized in the NAM's trade magazine, *American Industries*, and they also provided excellent newspaper copy that would get plenty of play even when the NAM did nothing to explicitly exhort newspapers to report on them. Even if *The Wageworker* might report on a story like the one that opened this chapter in terms that favored labor, most newspaper readers who read even an impartial report of it might well interpret it as casting a pall on unions. A judge—a respectable representative of legal authority—had, after all, reprimanded the union and declared its aims illegal to boot.

The NAM also conducted some rather outlandish publicity stunts. One was a classic "planted" story that appeared in the *Los Angeles Times* in late 1907. An organization of workers, the paper reported, had awarded "a handsome walking stick" to NAM president Van Cleave to recognize his work "in the preservation of harmony between the fairminded workingman and the fairminded employer."[47] The article identified both the association and the person presenting the award: the Workingmen's Protective Association, represented by one M. M. Mulhall. It did not add, however, that Mulhall had been on the NAM's payroll more or less formally since 1902 nor that the Workingmen's Protective Association was a semipolitical organization mostly created by Mulhall and with close ties to the NAM.[48] Whether the event ever took place beyond the newspaper page is less than clear.

In an even more bizarre episode, earlier the same year the NAM put into operation a scheme to discredit the AFL president Samuel Gompers. The story is convoluted and not fully documented; it was apparently hatched by the Century Syndicate, though agreed to by President Van Cleave and other NAM officials. First, the NAM had Gompers followed in an effort to find material for a scandal. Failing in this, it then tried to bribe him to leave the labor movement. Apparently, the ultimate aim was to then publicize his acceptance of the bribe, with the idea that this would discredit Gompers personally while also casting a pall on the integrity of labor leaders in general. The execution of the plan was almost farcically incompetent, and in the end only last-minute cold feet saved Van Cleave from being caught in the act of offering the bribe. As for Gompers, he recounted the story at the American Federation of Labor's annual convention in 1907, with the result that he received a unanimous vote of confidence, even getting a special show of support from Victor Berger, the Socialist leader usually opposed to Gompers's presidency.[49]

In a bid to provide more sustained reporting unfavorable to labor unions, the NAM also sponsored the creation of "astroturf" worker organizations—organizations funded and initiated by employers but purporting to be the spontaneous creations of workers opposed to unions. Some of these organizations served as providers of strikebreakers, but another important function they had was to provide fodder for news stories.[50] At about the same time as the employer open-shop drive was getting off the ground, a series of stories cropped up in newspapers about organizations of "independent workmen" who asserted their "right to sell their labor to whom they choose" and planned "to compel organized labor to obey the law."[51] In 1903–4 a number of such organizations were reported in different parts of the country, from New York to Indiana to Washington. Always, however, these organizations made claims to being "independent" in language identical to that of the open-shop employers. Often, the stories noted explicit connections to the open-shop drive, such as when the *New York Sun* praised NAM president D. M. Parry for having "done valiant work in assisting these organizations" in Indiana.[52] Sometimes these organizations were tied to electoral campaigns: for example, in the campaign to reelect Charles Littlefield in Maine, the NAM had Mulhall coordinate organizing the "Independent Labor League," which held a number of events in support of Littlefield and some of whose purported members received payments from the NAM.[53] These events aimed to create an appearance of labor support for Littlefield. As a Republican paper crowed, the Democratic papers seemed to take Gompers's stumping against Littlefield as proof that labor opposed Littlefield unanimously, but "they seem not to have heard that the Independent Labor League of Rockland has endorsed Mr Littlefield."[54]

Fairly quickly, however, the NAM came to doubt whether these campaigns produced sufficient results to warrant the effort and expense. Purchasing publicity and sponsoring astroturf organizations could be an endless sinkhole of money, and it was hard to tell what return one really got for the money poured into boilerplate, Century Syndicate fees, and similar ventures.[55] Moreover, no matter how much material the NAM produced, the newspapers and magazines themselves always produced more. It was imperative, therefore, to stay abreast of what newspapers and magazines were writing on labor questions and to try to direct them "toward right industrial thought."[56] Early in its antiunion campaign, the NAM therefore exhorted its members to refuse to advertise in papers that made employers look bad.[57] It also instructed them to appoint a press committee to see what the local paper wrote about labor. If the paper showed signs of being too friendly to labor, the committee should protest to the business manager of the paper. The business manager, the NAM publication predicted, "will make a *bee line* to the office of the publisher" and point out to him "the danger of offending the employing and property-owning 'class.'"[58]

All newspaper publishers and reporters were keenly aware that advertisers could and did use their power to influence the news. By the turn of the twentieth century, advertising had come to form over half—and in some cases much more—of newspaper and periodical revenue.[59] The papers hurt worst by advertisers' political preferences, unsurprisingly, were those catering to the working class. The *Chicago Daily Socialist*, for instance, could not get many advertisers even when its circulation in 1912 topped that of the other Chicago English-language papers combined. Similarly, the Scripps newspapers, which tried to find a market niche among the working class by being attentive and sympathetic to labor news, constantly battled advertisers and frequently had to forgo revenue to maintain their editorial independence.[60]

Advertisers also policed run-of-the-mill papers and withdrew their ads when displeased. In a political context, the best-known of such instances is probably the decision of many companies to withdraw their advertising from newspapers that endorsed the left-leaning Democrat William Jennings Bryan for president in 1896. More generally, reporters' memoirs recount incidents like being forbidden to report on the misdeeds of the local department store magnate or his family members, and everyone in the news business was familiar with the concept of a "business office must," that is, news copy that had to be printed to please an advertiser.[61] Of course, one should not exaggerate the willingness of companies to pressure newspapers, especially to consider political rather than business benefits in deciding where to advertise. For example, when an anti-socialist activist connected with the NCF tried to exhort a number of prominent companies to pressure *The Metropolitan* magazine to show less favor to "socialist articles," many of the responses commented that it was the magazine's own business what it printed—what interested the company was that the readers could afford to buy the company's products.[62] On the other hand, some companies' responses did show more inclination to use their advertising dollars to shape the magazine's editorial policy.[63]

Individual newspaper staff, too, could be susceptible to the attractions of money. Even on most big-city dailies, journalism remained a poorly paid job rather than a professional career, and newspaper reporting paid such a pittance that staying in the business for the long term was simply not an option for most reporters. Many journalists, then, were susceptible both to actual bribes and to the more subtle influence of potential extra income or future stable employment. As communications scholar Ted Smythe points out, it was common for reporters to "continue a career elsewhere after having gained *experience* and *contacts* in newspaper work."[64] Like other employer organizations, the NAM's staff included a cadre of secretaries, lobbyists, and press agents—positions for which journalists with their newspaper and other contacts were well suited. In fact, the NAM's secretary in the first years of its antilabor campaign, the indomitable Marshall Cushing, had a background as a correspondent on New York and Washington, DC, papers, besides having worked as the private secretary of a number of influential politicians.[65]

There were, however, limits to what could be accomplished with money alone or even with a few friends among magazine editors. The NAM's rhetoric was not a particularly good match with the tone of larger metropolitan newspapers that increasingly prided themselves on professional reporting, nor did it mesh well with the magazines publishing stories by investigative reporters. In such publications, the NAM rarely got prominent mention, nor were its officers often published or quoted as authorities.[66] Perhaps partly as a result of this, the NAM in about 1908 began to shift its press publicity toward a more "progressive" position. While the pamphlets the NAM distributed itself continued to cultivate "freely-flowing anathema against organized labor," as a content study of the pamphlets puts it, publicity directed at the press began to emphasize workplace safety, industrial education, and insurance compensating workers for injuries sustained on the job.[67] As James Emery phrased it, "The trap must be baited for the game," and the "bait" of frothing-at-the-mouth antiunion rhetoric may not have been the most suitable one for the "game" of the general magazine audience of the Progressive Era.[68] Emery may, in fact, have learned to pay closer attention to audience preferences from the NAM's work with the Century Syndicate: the developing advertising profession regularly attempted to convince businessmen that it was not the businessmen's tastes but the tastes of their customers that should determine advertising strategy.[69]

The new line, though it gained NAM officers articles in such magazines as *Harper's Weekly* and *The Survey,* hardly proved a panacea in getting the desired results.[70] The Progressive Era magazine landscape tended toward critical exposés and a faith in experts with academic credentials, not dour pronouncements by stolid business types. It was far more amenable to the type of publicity efforts cultivated by the NAM's rival as the voice of business regarding labor: the National Civic Federation.

The NCF: Expertise and Glamour

In contrast to the NAM, the NCF cared little about small country dailies or about manufacturing sordid stories about its "enemies"—such strategies were neither necessary nor well-suited to the federation's purposes. As the NCF's ideologue and general factotum Ralph Easley explained, "The only kind of [newspaper] publicity worth much to us is that of the large daily papers" because they reached a far greater number of employers and employees than did the small country papers that relied on readyprint and boilerplate material.[71] Large dailies and major magazines were also more in keeping with the image of soundness, respectability, and rationality that the NCF so carefully cultivated. Access to such media was far more difficult to buy than boilerplate stories, but then again, outright buying of attention was hardly a necessity for the NCF. The prestige of the people associated with it and the timeliness of its project of building labor-management concord ensured substantial (and mostly favorable) publicity.

In many ways, the NCF strove not so much to create story hooks as to *be* one. In this, it largely succeeded: the presence of high-wattage guests at its functions and the slight oddness of the spectacle of labor unionists dining at the home of an Andrew Carnegie or a Mrs. J. Borden Harriman got the NCF noticed while underlining its conciliatory message.[72] The apparent ease with which the NCF got into the press aroused even the admiration of the NAM, which noted that the NCF's "skillful adaptation of persons and things to desired ends" was a model worth studying.[73] The NAM was right that the publicity was carefully engineered: Ralph Easley was a proficient and tireless promoter. Like the NAM's Marshall Cushing, Easley had begun his career in the newspaper business, first as the owner-editor of a Kansas newspaper and then as a supervisor at the *Chicago Inter-Ocean.* At the NCF, Easley almost single-handedly produced the federation's official organ, the *National Civic Federation Review.*[74] The *Review* was then sent to various magazines and newspapers so they could use it as a source. In more concrete terms, Easley and other NCF functionaries produced piles of magazine articles on the work of the NCF and on related topics. This gained the NCF visibility in many of the major general-interest magazines of the day, including *The Independent*, *McClure's Magazine*, and *Harper's Weekly*.[75]

In addition to directly producing material, the NCF courted the friendship of editors and publishers. For instance, it invited them to join one of its many departments, especially the Advisory Council and the Industrial Economics Department. Such membership involved little obligation and no fees; instead, the invitation and its acceptance constituted something like a mutual nod of approval and recognition and, in the case of the Industrial Economics Department, a more or less vague commitment to attempt to attend quarterly dinners where various industrial and labor-related topics were considered.[76] The number and prominence of the editors and publishers who agreed to either type of membership is an indication of the general favor with which the NCF was viewed in the print media. The Industrial Economics Department counted among its members Lawrence Abbott of *The Outlook*, Hamilton Holt of *The Independent*, and Bradford Merrill of *The World*, while the Advisory Council included Sereno S. Pratt of Dow Jones & Company and Herman Ridder of the *New Yorker Staats-Zeitung*. Others associated with the NCF in different capacities included Albert Shaw of the *American Monthly Review of Reviews* and Charles H. Taylor of the *Boston Globe*.[77] Such contacts were useful when the NCF wished to either gain publicity for its official doings or get specific material published; at the very least, they established an opening for the NCF to send material and inquiries to the editors.[78]

The extent of the NCF's contacts with prominent editors and the eager interest that the press displayed in the organization's activities indicate that the NCF could have played a major role in supporting the efforts of moderate union leaders like Gompers and United Mine Workers president John Mitchell to raise awareness of what they viewed as labor's legitimate grievances. Explicit NCF backing could have lent these leaders some of the respectability they so desired and opened doors for them at major magazines and newspapers. To be sure, the annual conventions and hosted discussion dinners organized by the NCF provided a forum at which figures like Gompers and Mitchell could present their views on various topics, including the closed shop and the courts' use of injunctions in labor cases, both of which businessmen generally severely frowned upon.[79] Such statements would surely have gained added weight had they received clearer flank support from the NCF's official statements and proceedings. That, however, was hard to secure, given business preferences and the fact that the NCF got its funding in donations from its business members. For example, the NCF arranged for a commission to study the issue of injunctions, but it never took any action: business members found the issue too important to compromise on, and thus the NCF's hands were tied.[80]

This is not to say that the NCF did nothing to support unions in its publicity. Ralph Easley frequently argued that unions had a crucial role to play in ensuring the well-being and development of the nation and indeed in safeguarding the future of democracy from socialists. NCF publications often emphasized that strident antiunionism of the type that the NAM cultivated only paved the way for revolution by refusing to redress legitimate grievances workers raised. Organization was the order of the day, and, Easley argued, the NAM was inconsistent in exhorting employers to band together against labor while telling laborers to remain "independent."[81] (The NAM shot back that the NCF was "a menace to free American industrialism" in its naivete about the true character of unions.)[82]

The NCF also supported the trade agreement unequivocally, and Easley defended both the trade agreement and even the closed shop in public as well as in private.[83] This was important and probably forms a major part of the explanation for why Gompers, Mitchell, and others like them remained affiliated with the NCF even as they were criticized by the rank and file of the labor movement for doing so. Few middle-class reformers understood the role of the closed shop in the trade agreement system as clearly as Easley did. Yet in its publicity, the NCF focused on the calming influence of unions and trade agreements, not on their transformative potential. In a set of articles written during the height of the NCF's conciliatory work, Easley painted a picture of unions that emphasized restraint rather than vigorous action. His goal, clearly, was to "sell" unions to the magazine audience by emphasizing the limits of the challenge they posed to the existing order. He especially zeroed in on the firm stance the unions affiliated with the NCF took on the sacredness of the contract between the union and the employer(s). Rank-and-file members or unorganized workers, Easley argued, might act rashly when dissatisfied with labor conditions, but the leaders of large unions operating on "business principles" would understand the value of reliability. The leaders would, therefore, check their members' militancy. In this spirit, Easley recounted several instances where prominent union leaders had gone to great lengths to bring the hotheaded membership into line, including revoking the local union's charter and bringing in strikebreakers to protect the sanctity of the national union's contract.[84]

In keeping with the emphasis on union conservatism, much of the NCF's praise of unions emphasized them as a bulwark against the threat of a socialist future. That role, of course, was not always unwelcome to those labor leaders who, like Samuel Gompers, themselves faced challenges to their leadership from socialists and radical industrial unions.[85] In the early years, the NCF's emphasis on the threat of socialism and radicalism mainly served as a whip to get unions and employers into the negotiating room.[86] However, it quickly became an end unto itself, and overall the NCF's emphasis shifted away from the trade agreement and toward antiradicalism.[87] When the NCF created the Department of Industrial Economics in 1906, a memorandum describing it stated that its aim was "to mitigate social and industrial unrest" through both "the study of subjects which are purely industrial in character" and "the organization of a broad and effective plan of publicity to counteract the present influences which tend to create social unrest." Most of the memorandum, though, focused on specific ways of counteracting the "sensational rubbish" of socialists with critiques and "forceful statements of the good in our present institutions." Only at the very end did it note that "it may also be deemed wise to urge the passage of laws to meet the reasonable demands of labor" because "better wages, hours of work, etc." would reduce and even eliminate "the incentive toward socialism."[88]

In its antisocialist campaign, the NCF also expanded its publicity strategy to one of more active recruitment. Realizing that an organization whose membership was dotted with prominent capitalists might not be the most credible or engaging voice against socialists, the NCF recruited religious leaders to speak against Christian socialism, labor leaders to speak against socialism in the unions, and ex-members of the Socialist Party to generally expose the alleged iniquities of the movement.[89] Thus, it worked with, for instance, F. G. R. Gordon, a former Socialist Party member and officer of the Boot and Shoe Workers' Union, and with Martha Avery, another former Socialist. Besides publishing their antisocialist writings in the *National Civic Federation Review*, Easley promoted their articles in newspapers and magazines and recommended them as antisocialist speakers. He also tried to interest Henry Holt & Company in publishing a book by Avery.[90] The NCF financed the work of these labor antisocialists and tried to secure their income in other ways.[91] The NCF also monitored the popular press for socialist writings, socialist-leaning editorials, and similar items and, on finding such, facilitated the publishing of a response by one of its labor writers or other antisocialist affiliates. Often, the responses were sent to the paper in question via the NCF, although the NCF affiliation of the author was not explicitly displayed in the piece if it was published; sometimes, the pieces were published anonymously.[92] The NCF's secret coordination of these antisocialist responses sometimes led to awkward situations, as when both Easley and Gordon sent a response under Gordon's name to a piece that had appeared in the *New York Tribune*, prompting Easley to exhort Gordon to send the *Tribune* staff a plausible explanation.[93]

Easley's concern with socialism was never solely about the labor movement; he thought that leftist challenges to traditional women's roles and sexual mores were at least as pernicious, and thus he cultivated conservative and antisuffrage women writers and expostulated against "the Socialist doctrine of 'free love.'"[94] However, even as he devoted more time to inveighing against radicalism, Easley did not waver in his presentation of Gompers and the AFL as upstanding examples of American values and reliable bulwarks against socialism, even when they were under fire.[95] Repeatedly and proudly—and correctly—Easley emphasized that the AFL's leadership shared his antiradicalism, noting that, for example, he counted on Gompers's help in drafting his anti-Socialist writings.[96] One might imagine that had the promotion of the trade agreement and of AFL perspectives on workplace issues received equal billing with antiradicalism in the NCF's publicity, this line might well have bolstered the AFL's standing in the public eye. This, however, was not the case, and thus the NCF was not as effective as it might have been in countering the open-shop employers' basic contention that there was barely any difference between unionism and socialism.

As they had in politics, employer voices had a definite advantage over labor ones in the battle for public opinion. The influence of employers' power as advertisers, their ability to outright buy stories, and the class sympathies of newspaper editors meant that both the NAM's antilabor position and the NCF's softer message emphasizing conciliation found greater prominence in the press than did the views of even the most moderate and respectable labor unionists. At the same time, the newspaper landscape of early twentieth-century America was in some ways broad and complex enough to provide an opening to labor voices. Notably, low production costs, which allowed diversity, were far more responsible for this opening than the developing journalistic ethic of "objectivity." Labor found a foothold in the raucous, advocacy-oriented niche labor press, not in the most professional major dailies. Indeed, Richard Kaplan has argued that the rise of the ethic of objectivity had some counterintuitive effects: without its previous partisan moorings, the press lost its interpretive mandate and became prone to providing a "deferential narration of the views of legitimate authorities from formal political society."[97] In such a narration, the NCF's experts might fare well. Labor unionists were less likely to do so.

8 Defending the Status Quo Ante Bellum

The beatings will continue until morale improves.
—Anonymous

In the early summer of 1914, Magnus Alexander, employment manager at General Electric, wrote to Walter Drew, head of the National Erectors' Association and an open-shop activist, with an idea for a retreat of important businessmen. He wanted, he said, to invite "a dozen men [for] a trip into the Maine woods . . . for a week's pleasurable outing and discussion of the industrial problem."[1] Over the course of the next year, this idea solidified into a plan and then a reality. Alexander and Drew recruited James Emery, counsel for the National Association of Manufacturers, to help with planning and organization. Instead of the Maine woods, the retreat was to be held at Yama Farms Inn in the Catskill Mountains, which offered all the trappings of an upper-class country resort, from excellent dining and trout fishing to such spiritual delights as a "resident American Indian chief who sat before a teepee in full Indian dress and dispensed words of wisdom."[2] The first of what became known as the "Yama conferences" was held in June 1915 and included twenty-three participants, divided roughly evenly between representatives of employer associations and executives of fairly sizable firms.[3] Over the course of the next year, the Yama conferences gave birth to a new business group, the National Industrial Conference Board (NICB), with much the same organizational membership as the first Yama conference and an ambition of becoming "the supreme court on industrial matters, the officially-recognized voice of the business man and employer." The NICB, Drew explained, would investigate and deliberate on important matters and thereby acquire a "dignity and authority that will put it on a higher level" than mere "crusades and propaganda."[4]

The creation of the NICB and its aspiration to be seen as a respected, professional voice in the discussion regarding industrial relations marked a growing acceptance of the permanence of the "labor question." The crusade-style open-shop campaigns of the early twentieth century, though they had hampered the growth of unions and obstructed the legislative projects of the American Federation of Labor, had not eliminated labor agitation. Meanwhile, by the eve of World War I, the reform projects and investigations of the Progressive Era had cast business in a decidedly unfavorable light. A posture that strove for "dignity" rather than vociferousness might therefore be prudent.

Neither employers' increasing acceptance that the labor movement could not be quickly vanquished nor their interest in organizations such as the NICB with its loftier tone should be confused with an actual acceptance of the permanence of organized labor. The social-reform tenor of the prewar years and especially the wartime emergency forced employers to tone down their rhetoric but not to change their views. Most employers did not see negotiation with labor in the war years as a new order of things. They viewed it as a temporary cessation of hostilities—made necessary by hostilities of a different order. They made this clear both by their wartime planning and by their immediate postwar actions.

This chapter starts by examining how the immediate prewar years demonstrated both a new labor militancy and a growing acceptance among middle-class reformers that labor had legitimate and urgent grievances. It then turns to the special circumstances of wartime, arguing that while employers considered it politic to rein in their rhetoric and, sometimes, to acquiesce to labor's demands, they never accepted the new situation. Finally, it considers the period immediately following the end of the war, focusing particularly on what became known as the President's Industrial Conference, which Woodrow Wilson had called together to try to create a policy framework for the future, and on the absolute employer refusal at that conference to endorse labor's right to organize.

The Persistence of the Labor Question

For a few years at the very beginning of the twentieth century, it had seemed that labor organizations and collective bargaining might become a permanent and accepted feature of the industrial landscape. Unions grew rapidly, while the trade agreement was hailed as the harbinger of rational, orderly labor relations. The National Civic Federation had thrown itself into the work of "conciliation," helping broker agreements between unions and employers. To underline the new, modern, cooperative spirit, it had also arranged fancy dinners that brought representatives of the AFL together with top-dog capitalists like Andrew Carnegie. Yet within only a few years, any such dreams of harmony seemed ephemeral indeed.

Disenchantment with the NCF message of cooperation and trade agreements had gripped even many of the AFL unionists who had been closely involved in the NCF's work. As the general secretary of the United Brotherhood of Carpenters and Joiners explained in 1908, "We do not believe in agreements between employers and employees as much as we did years ago" because employers seemed to have little compunction about breaking such agreements.[5] Other unionists echoed this sentiment: although the NCF's employer members professed cooperation, one noted, many of them were acting in ways that could only be explained by assuming that they were either "in league" with antiunion employers or "as weak as circus lemonade."[6]

Meanwhile, new groups of workers took the stage in a series of strikes. Indeed, estimates based on state labor bureau data indicate that while the number of strikes remained flat, the size of strikes grew to the extent that a record number of workers went on strike in 1910, followed by new records in 1912 and 1913.[7] Women, immigrants, the unskilled—groups often ignored by the AFL's focus on skilled craft workers—walked out of garment factories, steel works, and textile mills. Often, they received help from radicals affiliated with the Socialist Party or the Industrial Workers of the World. They were met with determined employer resistance and, often, violence; sometimes, they took to violent tactics themselves.

These strikes made headlines—company recalcitrance, violence, radical leadership, and, often, the involvement and suffering of women and children offered dramatic newspaper copy. A strike by mainly unskilled eastern European immigrant workers at the Pressed Steel Car Company in McKees Rocks, Pennsylvania, for example, made the front page of the *New York Times* at least nineteen times between July and September 1909. The strike involved violent confrontations between the strikers and the replacement workers brought in by the infamous "king of the strikebreakers," Pearl Bergoff, as well as a scandal when some of the strikebreakers alleged that the company had held them in stockades against their will, barely feeding them and forcing them to work. Some of the immigrant strikebreakers escaped and got their consuls involved, prompting a peonage investigation of the company.[8] A few months later, newspaper headlines erupted with tidings of the "Uprising of the 20,000," the "girl army" of young Russian Jewish and Italian immigrant workers who had walked off their jobs in New York's garment factories. The

organizers' youth and gender lent them an air of innocence that attracted reporters' attention, especially when contrasted with the brutal police response
to their picket lines. The copy got even better once the Women's Trade Union
League (WTUL) invited college students and upper-class women to walk
the line, resulting in embarrassing situations for police who were not always
aware of their targets' high social status. As the WTUL had intended, arrests
and violence diminished as the police began to worry about arresting one of
the "mink brigade" by mistake. The resolution of the strike was ambiguous,
however, and a little over a year later, one of the garment factories least willing to negotiate and most resistant to the women's demands of better safety
procedures was in the headlines for a very different sort of conflagration.
The Triangle Shirtwaist Fire in March 1911 killed 146 people, most of them
young women workers trapped inside as the factory went up in flames.[9]

Violence visited upon women and children also featured in two of the era's
most famous strikes, a 1912 textile strike in Lawrence, Massachusetts, and
a 1914 strike in the coal fields of Colorado. In Lawrence the strike exposed
the squalid conditions in which mill families tried to survive. It also created
dramatic scenes as police tried to prevent strikers from sending their children
to New York to be housed with supporters for the duration of the strike—a
move partly motivated by the dwindling strike coffers, which made feeding
the strikers and their families genuinely difficult, and partly executed as a
conscious publicity maneuver.[10] In Ludlow, Colorado, a tent city inhabited
by strikers evicted from company housing burned, suffocating eleven children and two women hiding in a dugout under one of the tents. The Ludlow
Massacre, as it became known, was only the most horrifying in a series of
violent incidents that had accompanied the strike; most accounts attributed
the deaths to the deliberate actions of the militiamen who had entered the
camp and, witnesses insisted, set fire to the tents.[11]

Company intransigence and the suffering of women and children may have
elicited sympathy from newspaper reporters and readers, but workers were
not always cast in the role of victims in the era's labor violence. The deaths at
Ludlow, for example, precipitated a ten-day armed conflict between strikers
and Colorado forces that was only quelled when federal troops intervened.
By then, thirty more people were dead.[12] And if the Colorado Ten Days' War
at least had a clear catalyst in the deaths of the women and children, some
violence was more calculated, a deliberate act to enforce the strikers' will
rather than an emotional, desperate reaction. The most famous such case
of the era was the dynamiting of the building of the notoriously antiunion
Los Angeles Times around 1:00 a.m. on October 1, 1910. The explosion killed
twenty people. Later the same day, explosives were discovered at the homes

of the paper's owner, Harrison Gray Otis, and the secretary of a local employer association (neither was hurt). In April of the following year John and James McNamara, officials of a structural iron workers' union then engaged in a protracted strike in Los Angeles, were arrested for the bombings. The McNamaras proclaimed their innocence, and the labor movement, as well as many Progressive reformers, rallied to their cause, collecting money for their defense. Faced with overwhelming evidence, however, in December 1911 the McNamaras changed their plea to guilty and were convicted.[13]

Violent acts initiated by labor gave employers prime ammunition in their efforts to portray all unions as coercive and vicious—especially as the Mc-Namaras represented "mainstream" unionism rather than left-wing radicals. Thus, in the wake of the McNamaras' conviction, NAM president John Kirby gloated that although he had been the target of critique for arguing that the AFL was "as great, if not a greater menace to society than the Ku Klux Klan, the Molly Maguires, the Mafias, and the Black Hand societies," now "every newspaper in the country is saying the same and more."[14] Militant strikes worried even middle-class observers not particularly eager to condemn unions. For example, the annual meeting of the National Civic Federation in the spring of 1912 demonstrated a renewed sense of urgency about the labor question. As a contemporary account of the meeting noted, "It is hardly possible to convey the conviction permeating the whole meeting that the industrial problem has reached a crisis demanding instant treatment."[15]

What seemed perhaps most ominous to the proponents of labor conciliation like those gathered in the NCF was the increasingly political bent of labor, particularly the appeal of socialism. In the 1912 presidential election the Socialist Party candidate and labor leader, Eugene Debs, polled nearly 6 percent of the popular vote, the best showing of a Socialist presidential candidate before or since. This followed on the heels of a string of municipal elections in 1910 and 1911 that put Socialists in control in such cities as Milwaukee, Wisconsin, and Schenectady, New York, as well as successes for socialists in the unions: in 1911 the International Association of Machinists, one of the most important unions in the American Federation of Labor, elected a socialist as its president.[16]

Yet many reformers, although they worried about violence and radicalism, believed that both raised more systemic questions. Progressive journalist Lincoln Steffens, for instance, argued that although the McNamaras were guilty of the dynamiting they were accused of, it was unproductive to treat their acts as individual criminal incidents. Rather, one should view them as symptomatic of a larger pattern of social resentment rooted in the wrongs experienced by labor.[17] Similarly, in the aftermath of the Lawrence strike, writer and social commentator Walter Weyl called for examining the root causes of radicalism. "It is easy to say that these strike leaders are incendiaries, anarchists, and revolutionaries," Weyl said. "But why do the mass of workmen and workwomen follow such leaders? What conditions have we allowed to grow up in Massachusetts and in other states to render such an allegiance possible or conceivable?"[18]

A sense that labor had legitimate grievances reached beyond a narrow group of reformers to an increasing slice of the larger public. For example, labor causes and unionism received substantial support from both Catholic and Protestant divines. Many clergymen had been drawn to the reform ideas of the social gospel; many also worried that workers were abandoning churchgoing. This offered a fertile ground for a campaign by local and national labor organizations to promote a more prolabor attitude in the churches. By 1910 thousands of Americans attending church the Sunday before Labor Day were hearing a "Labor Sunday" sermon with a proworker and often prounion message, sometimes preached by a worker. Newspaper reports of the sermons delivered the message to many more who had not heard it firsthand. Labor Sunday was endorsed and promoted by the AFL, and at the AFL's request it was also advocated by the Federal Council of Churches (FCC), an umbrella organization of thirty Protestant denominations. At its 1909 convention, the council unanimously adopted the AFL's resolution calling for Labor Sunday sermons on the labor question and recommended to churches "a hearty compliance" with the Labor Sunday idea, with the request going out to the ministerial associations of over 650 cities.[19] In the following years, despite the new militancy and violent incidents like the *Los Angeles Times* bombing, the Federal Council of Churches strengthened its links with the labor movement. The council's new Men and Religion Forward movement signaled a renewed emphasis on social issues, and council members involved themselves in supporting the strikers in Lawrence and in investigating the Ludlow Massacre.[20]

The growing mainstream acceptance that there were legitimate labor grievances in need of solution became visible in politics as well. Social and industrial reform was not the sole province of the Socialist Party. Within mainstream politics, the AFL had achieved a number of legislative victories it had worked for since the turn of the century, such as an eight-hour day on government contract work (1912) and restrictions on courts' ability to issue injunctions that had hampered such basic labor protest tactics as picketing (1914).[21] Progressive reform had also been a major theme of the 1912 presidential election, which had seen the incumbent, the employer favorite William Howard Taft, left behind both by the Democrat Woodrow Wilson and by Theodore Roosevelt, who had campaigned on a third-party Progressive Republican platform that explicitly emphasized the welfare of ordinary people.[22]

Many reformers, despite their fears of where agitation might lead, recognized the role that protest and even radicalism played in raising awareness. "A few months ago," Walter Weyl acknowledged, "we knew nothing about conditions at Lawrence." Legislators had only become interested in investigating the lives of mill workers after the strike had caused a crisis. The lesson, Weyl argued, was that one should not wait "to discuss fire protection" until "the house is already ablaze"; one should "know in advance."[23] Accordingly, a group of the leading lights of Progressive reform suggested that a new special commission be appointed to conduct a new and comprehensive investigation of the state of industrial relations. The commission was to have a tripartite structure, with three representatives each to labor, employers, and the public, and it would conduct research as well as hold public hearings. Congress passed the bill creating the US Commission on Industrial Relations in 1912; after delays resulting from disagreements about its composition, the commission got to work in 1914.[24]

The NAM showed its new desire to cultivate a pose of expertise by supporting the creation of the USCIR and suggesting nominees to serve on it. One of the NAM's priorities was to get proemployer conservatives rather than what it termed "erratic college professors" appointed as the representatives of the public on the USCIR. Another was to get one of its own people among the representatives of the employers. Realizing that its most vocally antiunion employers would be unlikely to receive approval, the NAM instead put forward its vice president, Ferdinand Schwedtman, the man in charge of the NAM's recent campaigns regarding workplace safety and workmen's compensation. An engineer genuinely interested in investigation and problem-solving who was also a longtime leader in the NAM and the open-shop movement, Schwedtman represented both the NAM's new aspirations to being seen as a source of constructive information on labor relations and its commitment to opposing a larger role for unions.[25]

President Taft did in fact include Schwedtman among the employer representatives he nominated, living up to the NAM's conviction that he was "as keenly determined to protect [the USCIR] from weedy-headed individuals" as the NAM itself.[26] The NAM saw the appointment as a significant recognition of its growing societal stature. As the NAM counsel noted, Schwedtman's nomination was the first time that the NAM had received "high public recognition" on a "government body . . . of prime importance"—a treat that was perhaps doubly sweet because both the National Civic Federation and "the college element" had been sidelined.[27]

Taft's appointments, however, prompted enough dissatisfaction among the reformers who had originally proposed the commission that they success-fully delayed confirmation of the nominees until President Wilson, elected in 1912, could appoint a new commission. On that commission, the NAM was no longer represented, while the reformers' main protests about the lack of a sociologist or economist among the members had been addressed by the appointment of prominent labor economist John R. Commons.[28] The USCIR also had a new chair, Frank Walsh, a Kansas reformer and lawyer who wanted to use the hearings to call public attention to the problems that laborers faced and to dig deep into the injustices of the industrial system. Walsh worried little about angering the powers that be, insisting that "if our investigation results in placing our whole industrial system upon trial and endorsing or condemning it," the USCIR should not shrink away from doing so.[29]

For much of 1914 and early 1915, the USCIR's work became the focal point of public attention. Over the course of 154 days of hearings in 1914–15 the USCIR heard over seven hundred witnesses, from radicals to industrial mag-nates. True to Walsh's determination to thoroughly air the dirty laundry of American industry, the hearings subjected even the high and mighty to tough questioning. In one of the most spectacular and best-known parts of the hearings, Walsh for three days grilled John D. Rockefeller Jr., who owned a substantial interest in the Colorado Fuel and Iron Company (CF&I), the target of the strike that culminated in the Ludlow Massacre.[30] Walsh's ques-tioning had a double thrust: on the one hand, to demonstrate that Rockefeller did not care enough about the workers toiling for his profit to bother to learn about the workers' lives, how his companies treated them, or about labor matters in general, and on the other, to show that the CF&I exercised undue and undemocratic power over the lives of its workers and in Colorado more generally.[31]

The popularity of the USCIR hearings and of Frank Walsh himself un-derlined the shift in public opinion that was taking place in the 1910s. Even the NAM, which rarely admitted that the public might have sympathy for labor, retrospectively viewed the period as one when "public sentiment was . . . quite decidedly more in favor of the closed shop" and presumably of labor unionism in general than early in the century.[32] And indeed, a significant slice of popular opinion seemed to agree with the USCIR's final conclusion that "the only hope for the solution of the tremendous problems created by the industrial relationship lies in the effective use of our democratic institutions and in the rapid extension of the principles of democracy to industry."[33]

The concept of "industrial democracy" seemed to suddenly be everywhere (see figure 14).[34] Even more than the trade agreement at the opening of the twentieth century, the idea of industrial democracy as it was advanced on the cusp of World War I seemed to capture an exhilarating prospect of bringing the nation's economic life in line with its political ideals. As Joseph McCartin has argued, it is easy to forget "just how fertile and fluid was the progressive moment before the Great War," when the assumption that businessmen should run their companies as they pleased was increasingly challenged not merely by demands for regulation but by demands for democracy in industry.[35] Many reformers saw the lack of democratic control of industry as one of the fundamental problems that reform should address. For instance, Walter Weyl, the reformer quoted above on the meanings of the Lawrence strike, published a long treatise on the rising "new democracy." This new democracy, he predicted, would involve far more regulation and socialization of industry, accompanied by a democratization of government, so that the people's voice would be heard in industry at least indirectly. Weyl also defended the demand for union recognition and the closed shop on the grounds that it represented "the nearest possible approach to a real industrial democracy" in the existing circumstances.[36] Others concurred. For example, Victor Yarros, a Russian-born former anarchist, a longtime resident of Jane Addams's Hull-House, and a law partner of Clarence Darrow, thought industrial democracy practically a foregone conclusion. It was simply not realistic to expect any other future—any "sober-minded, studious observer" had to recognize the "signs and portents" in the United States and abroad. Industrial democracy would of course be at least as challenging a problem as the management of any industrial system, but the sooner everyone realized that it was "inevitable and right," the sooner the country could get to the task of figuring out how to best go about it.[37]

Yet even as the demands for industrial democracy grew in popularity, their meaning hardly became clearer. Nor was there much agreement about the means of achieving better industrial relations. Indeed, as Shelton Stromquist has pointed out, even "Progressive reformers divided sharply over the work and substantive conclusions of the USCIR."[38] Frank Walsh emphasized reckoning with the class divisions in American society through public— and well-publicized—hearings. By contrast, John R. Commons, who was in charge of the USCIR's research branch, believed that only careful study and private conversation between conflicting parties could result in actionable knowledge. Commons had worked closely with Ralph Easley and the NCF on conciliation and trade agreements in the early years of the century, and he continued to believe that the thorny questions of industrial relations would best be solved by an NCF-like approach: investigate, discuss, find common ground, formulate agreements. The language of industrial democracy,

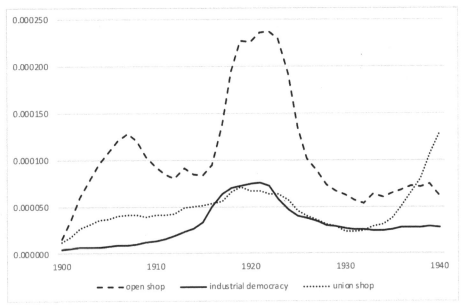

Figure 14: Google Ngram of the bigrams "open shop," "industrial democracy," and "union shop." The graph shows the frequency with which these bigrams (two-word phrases) have appeared in Google's corpus of American English (consisting of millions of books and magazines published in English in the United States). They are represented as a proportion of all bigrams in a given year. Note that although "open shop" is clearly a more popular term than "industrial democracy," "industrial democracy" overtakes "union shop" between 1916 and 1923. Of course, given the limitations of Google Books Ngrams, one should not read too much into the graph, especially the exact dating of changes. For data and documentation, see https://github.com/vhulden/bossesunion/.

Commons believed, was pulling labor unions toward politics and socialism, whereas what was needed was strengthening collective bargaining. Indeed, in the end Commons authored a separate final report outlining a government-facilitated collective bargaining system. Although the labor members of the commission joined the report endorsed by Walsh, Commons saw his own report as the one that really encapsulated the AFL's and Samuel Gompers's "own ideals of American unionism."[39]

Neither the NAM nor the NCF found the commission's work satisfactory. When the USCIR concluded its work, the NAM's publication, *American Industries,* dismissed the whole endeavor as a waste of time and money that had merely indulged uneducated workers in airing "their maudlin tales of wrong and fancied wrong" to the eager attention of the "metropolitan press."[40] The NCF, too, had soured on the commission after some initial optimism.

At first, the NCF had praised the USCIR and invited Frank Walsh, whom it called "a determined fighter for civic reforms and a worker for social welfare," to speak at its annual meeting.[41] But by May 1915—that is, as the USCIR was concluding its hearings—Ralph Easley was complaining of being slighted. The NCF, Easley grumbled in a letter, was the only organization in the country with real expertise on industrial relations, so "one would think they [the US-CIR] would naturally have come first to the Federation to get its materials."[42] That the USCIR had neither asked for materials nor invited Easley himself to testify was, Easley thought, an indication of its overly radical bent.[43]

The commission's general popularity and the attention it garnered indicated, however, that the political realities had shifted. The NCF's emphasis on "conservative" reform seemed increasingly anachronistic in a time when even the very staid and upper-crust Woodrow Wilson felt he had to describe himself as a radical to secure the presidency. While the USCIR was gearing up for its plunge into the darkest recesses of American industry, Easley was busy orchestrating an ambitious survey to track "the social, industrial and civic progress of the last fifty years."[44] That survey was to provide an "antidote to the revolutionary talk of the Socialist Party" by showing that things had, in fact, improved substantially.[45] Although many of his correspondents warned Easley that "to make a catalogue of our virtues" might look like whitewash rather than investigation, Easley forged on. In his view, conditions in the country were basically sound and had indeed significantly improved, which meant that the real problem was radical exaggeration that whipped people into an unnecessary frenzy. The survey, however, made little progress, and the NCF itself rather faded from its prime position in the public eye.[46]

If the NCF's insistent antiradicalism and defense of the status quo seemed increasingly stodgy, the NAM's blustery intransigence looked even more out of place in a climate that had become more sympathetic to labor as well as more oriented toward an emphasis on investigation and bureaucratic procedure. As if to underline that the NAM's accustomed political tactics had become outdated, in the summer of 1913 its longtime political operative, M. M. Mulhall, responded to being fired by spilling the whole sorry tale of the shadiest parts of the NAM's lobbying and antiunion work. "Operations of Vicious Lobby Laid Wide Open," screamed an above-the-fold headline of a story taking up half the front page in the Sunday, June 29, *Chicago Daily Tribune*. "Secret Agent Tells of Men of Prominence He Bought and Their Price," it added.[47] The resulting congressional investigation subpoenaed the NAM's accounts and correspondence and grilled the association's officials at hearings where the NAM's counsel felt the investigating legislators had adopted "the attitude of prosecutors."[48] Newspapers reported how Mulhall, apparently with great relish, recounted that the NAM gave bribes to labor union officials to spy on their own organizations, funded politicians in exchange for favors, and kept congressional employees on its payroll to gain inside information on Congress's actions.[49] Although no NAM officers were actually prosecuted, the hearings cast the association in an ugly light that seemed to vindicate all labor union accusations against it over the years. The NAM itself was keenly aware that the "false representations" had tarnished its reputation and made it "necessary . . . to carefully weigh and analyse every Association activity" with a view toward the new realities of public opinion.[50] As Julie Greene has put it, "Between the NAM investigations and Walsh's Commission on Industrial Relations, American employers had never looked so bad."[51]

Perhaps somewhat unexpectedly, in the end the NAM and its open-shop allies arguably managed the trough of business prestige rather better than the NCF. On the one hand, Easley's increasingly obsessive anti-Socialism pulled the NCF further away from constructive work; on the other, as the state itself got more involved in brokering labor relations in the war years, it to some extent superseded the NCF's role as mediator. The NAM, by contrast, sailed into wartime and beyond with a new wariness but with its conviction of its own importance fully intact.

Holding the Line in Wartime

Even before the United States became a belligerent in the Great War, as it was then called, the war had begun to alter the dynamic of labor relations. It strengthened labor's hand by heightening the demand for labor and drastically curbing immigration flows while fanning worker dissatisfaction by pushing up inflation. Once the United States entered the war in April 1917, employers added to this discontent by using the wartime atmosphere to further repress workers' rights, call for military-style work reserves or corps, and demand loyalty oaths that included refraining from in any way damaging the company. On the other hand, some workers also took the wartime employment of women or African Americans as an affront that prompted them to strike or exploited wartime anti-immigrant sentiment to violently drive out immigrant workers. The result of all this was a significant strike wave: in the first six months of the war, there were more than three thousand strikes, a majority of them in war-related industries.[52]

A major concern for the Wilson administration, of course, was to ensure the smooth operation of industrial production so the war effort could proceed apace. One step in this process was the explicit suppression of dissent, ranging from censorship of the press and of the mails to the raiding of the offices of radical labor unions like the Industrial Workers of the World and prosecuting their officials for seditious conspiracy. However, having courted the Left in the 1916 campaign and being in the midst of fighting a war to "make the world safe for democracy," Wilson also needed to secure support among unions and the Left. Otherwise, coercive tactics might backfire by pushing moderates away from the administration and toward the radicals and further fanning already considerable antiwar sentiment among American workers. Thus, the administration included in its plans the wing of the AFL that supported war and preparedness.[53]

Although Samuel Gompers initially expressed horror at the outbreak of war, he quickly came to believe that US entry in the war was both inevitable and necessary; therefore, he moved to consolidate the AFL's position with the Wilson administration. Convincing the AFL's executive council to support Wilson's preparedness program, Gompers in 1916 reaped the reward of being nominated a civilian advisor to the Council of National Defense, the newly created federal organization that was tasked with coordinating production and resources in the service of war preparedness. In the spring of 1917, just before the United States became a belligerent, Gompers coaxed first the AFL executive council and then a special conference of seventy-nine AFL-affiliated organizations to endorse a statement called "American Labor's Position in Peace or in War." The statement stopped short of endorsing US entry into the war, but it made clear that labor would not oppose a war effort and called for the inclusion of organized labor in the bureaucracy of war. That same summer, Gompers created the American Alliance for Labor and Democracy, which explicitly backed the war effort and soon received funding from the Committee on Public Information, the governmental wartime propaganda agency.[54]

Gompers's defense of US involvement in the war, his efforts to promote support for the war among organized workers, and his support for government suppression of dissent met with considerable opposition within the ranks of the AFL, not to mention within the broader labor Left. As Elizabeth McKillen points out, Gompers's actions also precluded a democratic decision on the war among organized workers, which, given the widespread antiwar sentiment, might have resulted in a joint labor demand for a popular referendum on US involvement in the war.[55] In more narrow terms, however, the decision paid off. It secured a place for the AFL in the governmental machinery steering the war effort, and it apparently convinced Wilson to put the weight of the government behind the decisions made by that machinery, even over employer opposition.

Employers, though, were maintaining a vigilant eye on ways to prevent wartime developments from shifting the power balance. As Howard Gitelman notes, maintaining the status quo ante bellum was an explicit goal for the employers who had in 1915 convened at the Yama conferences in the Catskills and eventually created the National Industrial Conference Board. They believed that the impact of the war on labor policy should be temporary, not a harbinger of things to come. If business allowed the shorter hours and higher wages of wartime to continue in the postwar era, costs would rise. Allowing costs to rise, in turn, would impede the ability of American business to compete in the postwar world.[56] Perhaps because the NICB was not as strident as the NAM but was more representative of manufacturing than the newly created US Chamber of Commerce, on January 28, 1918, the Wilson administration asked it to name five representatives to the War Labor Conference Board (WLCB), which was to create a framework for labor policy during the war.[57] The day after, the NICB created its own Committee on Principles.[58]

The NICB Committee on Principles was tasked with putting "in terse and concise language" what the board viewed as "fundamental economic principles." Tellingly, the Committee on Principles was instructed to take as its starting point a number of propositions put forth by Leonor F. Loree, a railroad executive whom the NICB also named to the WLCB. The first of these propositions made clear the NICB's attitude toward unions, proclaiming that "it is intolerable in any government to have a force grow up within the country which sets at defiance the country as a whole, such as the labor union movement now is."[59]

Yet, given wartime demands of production and wartime emphasis on unity, employers doubted that all-out intransigence would win them the results they desired. They therefore participated in the work of the War Labor Conference Board. In March 1918 the WLCB issued its principles, which both the employer and the worker representatives endorsed. Among other things, the principles called for no strikes during wartime, no coercive measures by unions to gain members or bargaining rights, and the maintenance of either open-shop or union-shop conditions in accordance with the prewar status quo at each establishment. They also affirmed workers' and employers' right to organize and explicitly stated that "employers should not discharge workers for membership in trade unions nor for legitimate trade union activities."[60] The WLCB was then transformed into a permanent wartime agency, the National War Labor Board (NWLB), charged with resolving disputes in accordance with the principles issued. The reformer Frank P. Walsh, known for his leadership of the USCIR, and former president William Howard Taft were elected cochairs by the worker and employer representatives, respectively.[61]

If the men of the NICB had assumed that the principles would not significantly curtail antiunion policies, they soon found out otherwise—at least temporarily. In the summer of 1918 the NWLB considered the case of Western Union and Postal Telegraph, which had discharged some eight hundred of its employees for union membership. The president of the company, Newcomb Carlton, insisted that Western Union employees "must choose employment with the company or membership in [the union]."[62] The NWLB deemed this unacceptable under the principles agreed to in March: as Taft explained to Carlton, "I do not think our principles include the closed non-union shop in the status quo to be maintained."[63] When Carlton refused to budge and a telegraph strike loomed, President Wilson called on Congress to act swiftly to pass government control of the wires, and after considerable debate, Congress agreed. The dismissed unionists were reinstated, and Western Union employees gained a 10 percent wage increase.[64]

All five employer members of the NWLB had voted against the report that found Carlton in the wrong. Even so, the employers continued to participate in the board's work. Key NICB members estimated that it was worth cooperating with the NWLB to head off something more radical. "I believe," explained Walter Drew to Magnus Alexander about a month after the Western Union decision and a few days after President Wilson had made it clear that he proposed emergency nationalization of telephone and telegraph services, "the War Labor Board is a safer institution than [Felix] Frankfurter's [President's Mediation Commission], and that by backing it up we can get conditions and precedents established which will greatly minimize the danger from Frankfurter and his crowd." Drew explained that the board's rejection of the nonunion shop was less dangerous than it sounded, since the report had also acknowledged that the employer was not required to recognize or deal with the union. This, Drew surmised, "takes away very largely any incentive to organize." Moreover, in a subsequent decision on a labor dispute in Bridgeport, Connecticut, the NWLB had solidified its primacy as the arbiter in labor matters, which in Drew's view presaged the "lessening of union influence," because "if all the employers and workers in Bridgeport look to the War Labor Board in all labor matters, what object is there in paying dues to a union?"[65]

Moreover, in Drew's view the actual award in the Bridgeport case undermined union authority in two crucial ways. First, because it granted wage increases to workers who were not organized, it "tended to show to workers generally that it was not necessary to agitate and strike, or even to be members of a union, in order to get consideration from the War Labor Board." And second, it did not endorse the union's demand for union wage classifications—in Drew's view, a key feature differentiating an "open shop" from a "union shop." Whereas in a union shop a union was able to impose a high minimum wage for different types of jobs and thus enforce collective rather than individual wage setting, in an open shop an employer could determine wages (or at least a premium) based on his judgment of the merit of each worker. Thus the employer could improve "efficiency and output," as well as steer workers away from solidarity and "[holding] together for joint action."[66]

The NICB's Committee on Principles and Drew's analysis of the benefits of working with the NWLB illustrate that employers' cooperation with wartime labor agencies was skin-deep at best. Organized employers had not abandoned or even significantly mitigated their opposition to unions. In fact, even as they realized the necessity of formal cooperation, the NWLB's employer members frequently voted as a unit against the board's more union-friendly decisions. That the board was able to function to the extent it did was due not to a newfound cooperative spirit among employers but to the choices of two presidents. The sitting president, Woodrow Wilson, was willing to put the weight of the administration behind the NWLB's decisions, as exemplified by the decision to nationalize Western Union. And in contradiction of his substantial record of antiunionism, former president William Howard Taft acquitted his role as cochair of the NWLB in a much more labor-friendly fashion than the employers who had selected him for the role had expected. As McCartin notes, to everyone's surprise Taft generally sided with Walsh and the labor representatives and smoothed over disagreements between warring parties. The employer members of the board were not just surprised; they were infuriated.[67]

Right to Manage Reasserted: The President's Industrial Conference

For the duration of the actual hostilities, Taft's and Wilson's actions, Walsh's leadership, and the enthusiasm for self-government of the workers who brought their cases before the NWLB made the board reasonably effective. Indeed, under its short tenure, it gained the trust of a large number of workers and caused many Progressives to express hopes that it might become the forerunner of an effective peacetime labor relations board. Few employers, however, planned to countenance any such development. On the contrary, what they saw as the NWLB's consistent friendliness to labor made them increasingly obstructionist. As soon as the wartime exigency was over, any pretense at cooperation crumbled: the employer members on the NWLB focused their energies on engineering delays rather than on resolving disputes, and companies that were subject to NWLB awards simply ignored the awards—or flaunted them explicitly. By December 1918 Walsh had resigned in frustration.[68] As the country moved into peacetime, employers got ready to claw back any concessions made and to reestablish their own primacy in industrial relations.

In March 1919 the NICB formed the Committee on a Labor Policies Program, to be composed of twelve manufacturers from within and without the NICB and receiving legal advice from Walter Drew and James Emery.[69] The first principle in an early draft produced by the committee was entitled "Freedom of Contract" and stated that both workers and employers should be "at liberty individually or collectively to make *or to refuse to make* any contractual relationship with the other." The third principle, "Freedom of the Individual," further elaborated that even if either workers or employers associated, that "confers no authority over and must not deny any right of those who do not so desire to associate themselves," and individuals "must be protected against unreasonable subjection by collective action."[70] In other words, employers were to remain at liberty to refuse to deal with unions, which could not gain any say over workers who declined union membership. The wording changed over multiple drafts, but this basic principle remained the same.[71] It also captured the attitude that the NICB carried into the postwar industrial conference that President Wilson had been induced to organize, and it was the position the employer group at that conference reiterated in the statement of principles it presented to the conference.[72]

In the period after the armistice, Wilson quickly backpedaled on his support for labor. He showed no willingness to undertake tangible action and restricted himself to occasional rhetorical favors more calculated, noted one contemporary observer, to keep the AFL within the Democratic fold and undermine "the national demand for a Labor Party" than to accomplish any concrete reforms.[73] The conference itself—which, due to Wilson being ill and the presence of other pressing concerns, convened without a clear agenda or rules—underscored this. It was organized in a tripartite structure, with an employer group, a labor group, and a public group. The public group, though it also included socialist John Spargo and muckraking journalist Charles Edward Russell, was generally well-stocked with men notorious for their antiunionism, such as Elbert Gary of U.S. Steel, Harvard president Charles Eliot, and John D. Rockefeller Jr.[74] The labor group consisted of various representatives of organized labor, and the employer group contained members representing the US Chamber of Commerce, the Investment Bankers' Association, the US Railroad Administration, the National Industrial Conference Board, and, somewhat incongruously, farmers' organizations (a point that caused some dissatisfaction among employers, as the farmers did not see themselves as employers). Under the rules the conference set for itself, each group could propose resolutions by majority vote within the group, but no statement by the conference would be issued unless all three groups agreed.[75]

Although collective bargaining was from the beginning clearly an issue that the conference would need to reckon with, it took several days for the conferees to set up procedures for how they would consider and vote on the resolutions presented. On the eighth day, the committee tasked with handling resolutions reported a straightforward resolution in support of unions formulated on the basis of an earlier set of propositions drafted by the labor group and agreed to by the labor and the public groups: "The right of wage-earners to organize in trade and labor unions, to bargain collectively, to be represented by representatives of their own choosing in negotiations and adjustments with employers, and in respect to wages, hours of labor, and relations and conditions of employment is recognized."[76] To ensure that it was not trampling individual rights, the committee added a clause to the resolution that read: "This must not be understood as limiting the right of any wage earner to refrain from joining any organization or to deal directly with his employer if he so chooses."[77] This latter clause represented a major concession from the labor representatives. After all, at least in principle, it opened the door to the elimination of the closed shop. Samuel Gompers explained later in the conference that neither he nor many of his colleagues would have approved it "under ordinary circumstances," but the occasion seemed momentous enough that they had decided to compromise so as to help "[bring] about some constructive program" that would be in everyone's best interest.[78] The employer group, however, refused to endorse the proposition. It objected that the resolution limited workers to organizing only into labor unions, as opposed to some other organizations, and that it did not protect the employer from being "coerced into bargaining collectively with his employees through an agent of labor unions who is not one of his employees."[79] After a full day of discussion on the resolution by the entire conference, the employers' group the next morning offered a substitute resolution that (in double the number of words of the labor resolution) hedged the right to organize in multiple ways and in addition affirmed "the right of the employer to deal or not to deal with men or groups of men who are not his employees and chosen by and from among them."[80] Unsurprisingly, the employer resolution went nowhere. Nor did the labor proposal. Nor did various attempts to reconcile the two.

Throughout the conference, the employer group made clear "its objection to a resolution which might compel an employer, even in an open shop, to deal with his employees through outside agencies"—that is, through unions. The employers' resolution sought to make explicit that "collective bargaining" should encompass employer "negotiation" with any "lawful form of association" and leave the employer free to refuse to deal with union representatives not in his employ. In other words, employers insisted that if employers were to accept it, the concept of "collective bargaining" had to explicitly include company unions—employee organizations created and/or approved by employers and not affiliated with organizations beyond the company. Such organizations had a deeply tarnished reputation as the tools of employers wishing to create an illusion of employee representation while refusing any dealings with trade unions. Well aware of this and concluding that the employers wanted "shop organizations, the employers' union," the labor group voted down any construction of the collective bargaining resolution that would admit company unions as legitimate parties to a contract, including rejecting a formulation that modified the original resolution by merely adding "and other organizations" after "trade and labor unions." The employers went further: they, too, voted against that modified resolution, insisting on an explicit declaration of employers' right to refuse to negotiate with representatives who were not their employees.[81]

In a final push, on the twelfth day of the conference (October 22), Samuel Gompers introduced a version of the collective bargaining resolution that made no direct reference to trade unions but merely affirmed workers' right to organize "without discrimination" and "to be represented by representatives of their own choosing in negotiations and adjustments with employers." The employer group torpedoed that resolution as well, leading the labor group to withdraw from the conference. Employers had made clear their position: they argued that a vote for Gompers's final proposition would look like endorsement by employers of "the kind of collective bargaining that the labor unions insist upon as distinguished from other kinds."[82] That, of course, was precisely what the labor group was looking for: a recognition of collective bargaining where workers had an actual say and were represented by their own organizations, not by employer-created ones. This the employer group would not grant. Yet in his summary of the conference for the NICB, Magnus Alexander piously declared that "the Conference split, not on the issue of collective bargaining, the principle of which had been accepted by the

Employers' Group," but on the definition of collective bargaining as requiring negotiation with specifically a labor union—or, as the employers put it, "an outside labor union agent."[83]

Organized employers, then, came out of World War I the way they had entered it: determined not to budge. They remained fundamentally opposed to the concept of collective bargaining with representatives of organized labor, and they had no intention of letting either labor unions or public opinion shift them from that position. Given the exigencies of the prewar Progressive atmosphere and the war to "make the world safe for democracy," though, they had learned to temper their rhetoric. In the 1920s, without in the least modifying their refusal to allow workers to choose their own representatives, they began to apply a language that better reflected the nationalist postwar atmosphere and dovetailed with a more "modern" and bureaucratic personnel management style.

9 The Gift That Keeps on Giving

Institutionalizing the Open-Shop Ideal in the 1920s

Jos työ herkkua olisi, niin herrathan sen tekisivät.
—Finnish proverb

At its 1920 convention, the National Association of Manufacturers unanimously adopted a comprehensive "Platform for American Industry," which it presented to both party conventions that summer and distributed at considerable expense in pamphlet form.[1] The preamble, authored mainly by NAM counsel James Emery, bore hardly a trace of the early NAM's vituperative language. Instead, it struck a note of sober patriotism and judicious defense of common goals. It offered "a fervent appeal for a national revival of study, discussion and personal understanding of the nature, purpose and history of American government." It contained a section on the "fundamentals of our Republic" that emphasized the foundation of the country upon the "recognition of the moral worth and practical value of the individual." And, acknowledging that "the modern system of production and distribution makes us to an ever-increasing degree inter-dependent," it gestured toward an acceptance of the necessity of reasonable rules. Balancing individual rights and the legitimate functions of collective action and government was, it recognized, "constantly a more difficult practical problem." Thus, in the name of "public interest," the platform called for government regulation of "all combinations."[2]

Quickly, however, the platform proceeded to modifications to such even-handed and universally applicable regulatory ideas. It explained that business combinations were already overregulated and taxed excessively. The real necessity was for the greater regulation of unions. In particular, the platform urged that the right to strike be "defined and limited" so as to prohibit strikes by government employees and employees of public utilities. It also called for unions to be made legally accountable, a reference to the NAM's longtime demand that unions incorporate and become legal entities that could be sued or fined. The platform did not explicitly mention the closed shop, though it referred to it indirectly. One of "the primary dut[ies] of government," the platform asserted, was "to protect each person in his liberty to select and pursue any lawful business or occupation without molestation." This was a reference to the unions' system of apprenticeships, another persistent object of NAM critique. And, the platform added in the next sentence, employment "without respect to the membership or non-membership . . . in any organization" was part of everyone's "personal freedom." In other words, without quite saying so, the platform implied that the government ought to make the closed shop illegal.[3]

Both the universalist, reasonable language and the underlying continuity of the antiunion line of the "Platform for American Industry" were emblematic of the broader shape of the open-shop campaign in the postwar years. Open-shop activists understood that there was a need for change in rhetoric and procedure but remained committed to the prewar principle of unwavering resistance to organized labor.[4]

The disruption of the war years and the intensity of the postwar open-shop push that followed caused some contemporaries, as well as some later scholars, to interpret the postwar open-shop campaign in reactionary terms. Former president William Howard Taft, for example, argued in 1921 that the blame for employer antiunionism lay with union overreach, especially the massive strike wave after the war. Although he condemned "Bourbon employers" who "misuse[d]" the term "open shop" to disguise their recalcitrant antiunionism, Taft also insisted that union leaders' successes during the war had made them "swollen with pride and blind in their obduracy" so that they now refused to see reason. As a direct result, Taft claimed, "the iron entered the souls of the employers, and they were led, many of them, into this fight to end labor unionism."[5]

Taft was wrong. Employers were not reacting to new circumstances; instead, they were draping some new window-dressing on a campaign they were relaunching along well-established principles. Even before the war, many in the open-shop movement had understood that there was no quick fix to the labor problem; despite its successes, the first open-shop campaign had not vanquished organized labor. The open-shop position therefore needed a stronger institutional expression. As Walter Drew had put it in the planning for the National Industrial Conference Board before the war, what was needed was an employer-dominated "supreme court on industrial matters" rather than a "crusade."[6] Crusading, after all, makes one look a bit fanatical. It invites critique and ridicule. At least as importantly, it is also exhausting. A crusade-based movement is not sustainable. If the goal of decisively vanquishing labor unions could not be achieved in the short term, it was necessary to modify one's approach.

The NICB had been one effort in a new direction; during and after the war, it produced reams of reports on such topics as wages, labor conditions in Europe, works councils, workmen's compensation, and profit sharing.[7] After the war, the NAM, too, fashioned a number of new internal structures to promote a fresh expertise-oriented public image and a stronger institutional structure to support it. The NAM created first a new Open Shop Committee and then, on the recommendation of that committee, a new Open Shop Department. This department was tasked with cooperating with other organizations and collecting and disseminating information in favor of the open shop. The NAM also started a new regular pamphlet called *Open Shop Bulletin*, sent out to local open-shop associations and others, and invested more resources in specifically promoting the open shop.[8] It hoped to go about its new plans in a way that was more methodical and thoughtful than its earlier efforts. In particular, the architects of the 1920s campaign believed that open-shop advocates needed to be more discreet, do more to avoid looking like hypocrites, and think more long-term.

In a memo from roughly 1921, the NAM laid out its vision for the open-shop campaigns of the future. To start with, the memo rejected the idea of a new national open-shop organization, as previous efforts in that vein had invited charges of a "capitalistic conspiracy." Unless the public believed "the actions of employer associations to be spontaneous and absolutely necessary," it might withdraw its support and instead back the union side.[9] In addition, campaigns needed to sound convincing. In the past, open-shop proponents had contradicted themselves too flagrantly, praising the open shop as nondiscriminating in one sentence and vowing never to employ union members in the next. Open-shop advocates had also pretended to be above self-interest, hammering unconvincingly on employers' desire to protect workers' individual rights while avoiding any mention of the dent in employer profits that unions represented. Now, the economic advantages of the open shop would be acknowledged, and their (alleged) benefits to the society at large would be made a selling point. Finally, open-shop advocates had earlier failed to take the long view; now, more attention would be focused on efforts that might not pay off the next day but that would bear plentiful fruit in the years and decades to come.[10]

This chapter opens by considering the postwar political and societal landscape and employers' analysis of it. It next turns to shifts in how employers dealt with their workers, exploring modern personnel management, welfare programs, and company unions; to an extent, the NAM advocated such programs to try to lend its language of fair dealing some ballast. Finally, the chapter examines the segment of the open-shop campaign that formed the bulk of the NAM's expenditures of time and money: publicity. The 1920s publicity push, in accordance with the new emphasis on preparing for the long haul, aimed at entrenching employer ideas everywhere from churches to colleges. In this, it presaged the sophisticated and far-reaching campaigns of the post–World War II era.[11]

The Business of America Is Business?

At the opening of the 1920s it was not at all obvious that the decade would be remembered for people sitting on top of flagpoles, "flaming youth" dancing the Charleston powered by bathtub gin, and President Calvin Coolidge declaring that "the business of America is business."[12] On the contrary. Overall union membership in 1920 stood at a record five million workers. In 1919 a larger number of workers than ever before had participated in strikes: a general strike in Seattle put workers in control of the city of over three hundred thousand people for nearly a week in February, and in late September and early October some quarter of a million steelworkers walked out in a strike that, in David Brody's words, "exceeded in magnitude and scope anything in the nation's experience."[13] Added to such unprecedented rank-and-file militancy was a wave of something even more alarming: bombs. In late April 1919 two mail bombs were delivered and over thirty more were discovered at the post office before they reached their recipients; the targets were politicians and industrialists, mainly of a particularly antiradical bent. In June more bombs exploded, including one at the home of Attorney General A. Mitchell Palmer. From the timing of the bombs, their targets, and—in at least the Palmer case—literature found at the site, the authorities and the press rapidly drew the conclusion that anarchists and other radicals were the culprits.[14]

The large-scale strikes and especially the bombings raised the specter of labor conflict spilling over into organized left-wing terrorism. The intensity and often violent confrontations that had attended labor disputes in the preceding decades seemed to many to make such fears plausible. Indeed, Beverly Gage has argued that violent radical resistance to the political and industrial order had formed a remarkably unremarkable part of the American experience for the first two decades of the twentieth century. Americans of that era "identified this sort of violence as part of an ongoing crisis—one that thrust the country perilously close to anarchy and civil war." To be sure, the numbers hardly warranted such an interpretation, but as Gage points out, neither do the numbers killed in terrorist attacks in the twenty-first century warrant Americans' fear of such attacks or the lengths to which the society is willing to go to make them less feasible.[15]

That radicals and labor activists were much more likely to be on the receiving end of violence than its instigators did not necessarily allay general fears of radicalism. Like court injunctions forbidding picketing that turned a picket line into a scene of arrests and thereby made the striking workers look like criminals, the vicious state and vigilante attacks on groups like the Industrial Workers of the World throughout the war or on Socialist parades on May Day 1919 tarred their targets more than their perpetrators. Their perpetrators, after all, were soldiers, upstanding citizens, and members of conservative and respectable groups like the American Legion, and the attacks often enjoyed the acquiescence if not the approval of labor reformers and of unions that belonged to the American Federation of Labor. If men like this thought it a good idea to raid the offices of a labor or political organization, the logic seemed to go, they must have had a reason.[16]

The National Civic Federation, of course, had since the opening of the century argued that if labor did not get its due, if employers refused to negotiate with moderate unions, radicals would take over. Now, it seemed, radicalism had reached new heights. Wasn't this proof that the NCF had been right, and it was now high time for employers to drop their intransigence? That continued to be the argument of both the NCF's Ralph Easley and AFL president Samuel Gompers. Easley, for example, praised the AFL for its patriotism, which he contrasted with what he said was the willingness of European unions to support the overthrow of government—but to limited effect, as the NCF was more and more focused on direct attacks on radicals.[17] At the Industrial Conference convened by President Wilson in 1919, Gompers sounded the warning explicitly. Employers' radical rejection of negotiation, he said, was the same line as that taken by the IWW—the "Bolshevists of America"—and the consequences of employer intransigence would be further radicalism.[18]

The dangers of "Bolshevism" also came up a handful of times at the NAM's 1919 annual convention, held in mid-May. One of the guest speakers was Seattle mayor Ole Hanson, the man whom the national press hailed as a hero for having suppressed the general strike in his city. Hanson gave a talk entitled "Bolshevism and Readjustment," in which he excoriated the Seattle general strikers and the IWW. He also offered some words of praise to the AFL for its antiradicalism and emphasized the need for the government and businessmen to ensure prosperity and high wages to ward off revolution.[19] However, such mitigating measures formed a minor theme in Hanson's speech, and the convention overall gave no sense that manufacturers found radicalism more of a threat than the AFL. Similarly, the employers' group at the President's Industrial Conference did not echo Gompers's warnings about "Bolshevists"; indeed, the labor men seem to have been the only ones at the conference to bring up the problem of radicals. Employers who were inclined toward the open shop focused, as before, on the problem of unions. As the labor men disapprovingly remarked, they had heard some in the employer group state that "if we just defeat the A.F. of L. we can take care of the bolshevik or anything else."[20]

Rather in the way that it viewed moderate labor unions as a road to radicalism, not an antidote to it, the NAM considered social reform not as the alternative but the path to socialism. Thus, the NAM took the passage of the 1921 Sheppard-Towner Maternity Act, which provided federal funding for maternity clinics in an effort to reduce high rates of infant mortality, as a sign of the insidious influence of the "Feminist Lobby." The Women's Joint Congressional Committee (that "feminist lobby"), the NAM claimed, was dotted with radicals, as were many of the other "interlocking directorates" of women's organizations. Their leaders, the NAM warned, included self-proclaimed socialists and communists. As evidence of their radicalism, the NAM cited such facts as that Jane Addams and several others held pacifist beliefs, that Madeline Doty was married to the head of the American Civil Liberties Union, and that Florence Kelley had corresponded with Friedrich Engels. Such leaders had "carefully permeated the legitimate organizations of women." The NAM should work to prevent "sincere women" from being lured onto "paths of error" by such radicals.[21]

Though it found it useful to point to the radical credentials of the women reformers, for the NAM, it was quite bad enough to advocate any kind of social legislation. Overall, the NAM suspected that the new reality of woman suffrage might lead to more agitation for such legislation, since women were "naturally, and rightfully, interested in measures to improve the living and working conditions" of everyone, especially women and children, and therefore susceptible to ideas about social reform.[22] At the same time, NAM president John Edgerton explained, "few even of our most intelligent women understand much about the problems of industry." The NAM, therefore, needed to see to it that the "new great body of enfranchised women shall have proper information upon which to cast intelligent ballots."[23] Women's clubs and organizations, accordingly, became a standard target of the NAM's publicity efforts: *American Industries* published remarks by "representative" women to show that important women agreed with the open-shop principle, and in 1926 the NAM organized the Woman's Bureau to recognize the new role of women in both industry and politics.[24]

The NAM's reactions to the radicalism of 1919–20 and to new realities like woman suffrage seem to indicate that it believed it needed to take them into account in its political calculations but that there was little cause for alarm. Such an interpretation was, perhaps, unsurprising, given the strength of the antiradical consensus among the political classes of the country. In the fall and winter of 1919–20 a wave of state suppression was directed at radical groups, whether they had any involvement with violent incidents or not. The famous Palmer raids (named for their architect, Attorney General A. Mitchell Palmer) led to the arrest of thousands of leftists. Similarly, Democrats and Republicans in Congress united in refusing to seat Victor Berger, who had been elected in 1918 on a Socialist Party ticket as a representative from Wisconsin. That the Wisconsinites reaffirmed their decision in the new election that was prompted by Congress's decision to exclude him gave the congressmen no pause, and they proceeded to exclude him again.[25]

An internal NAM memo that was probably written sometime in early 1922 approached the postwar situation and future prospects with equanimity. Although it blamed employers for having "become overconfident and self-satisfied" before the war, so that public opinion had swung toward support for the closed shop, it did not seem particularly alarmed. Instead, though it noted the "necessity of the intensive work that began in 1919," it estimated that from "1919 to 1922, the sentiment of the public has been very strongly in favor of the open shop." It also listed the many successes of the open-shop movement's postwar iteration. The first victory, in fact, had been the defeat of the Seattle general strike and the "resulting overthrow of closed shop conditions in that city." This was followed by further victories for the open shop in San Francisco and throughout the Southwest.[26]

The NAM's view that there was little cause for alarm but that vigilance was warranted was shared by its peers. In September 1923 the NAM sent out a survey about the likelihood of radical gains in the 1924 elections to eighty-three industrial associations. In the 1922 elections, after all, the Democrats had made significant gains in both the House and the Senate, the Farmer-Labor Party had elected one senator and two representatives from Minnesota, and even the twice-refused Socialist Victor Berger now entered the House. Moreover, with the constraints of wartime conformity now in the past, there seemed to be an overall revival of Progressive politics and talk of a broader Farmer-Labor coalition for 1924.[27] The NAM therefore wanted to gauge business assessments of the situation as well as potential business support for a campaign to "counteract such [radical] tendencies." The results were reassuring: from the fifty-three replies it received, the NAM concluded that most businessmen did not see radicalism as a "serious and permanent danger." They did, however, consider "anti-radical activity a form of 'insurance'" that they thought it necessary for the NAM to pursue and that they were willing to support.[28]

On the whole, then, the NAM's 1920s political line was a fairly direct continuation of its prewar views. Despite the upheavals that ushered in the new decade, the NAM registered little worry about extremists; its main goal, as before the war, was to protect the right to manage from its mainstream challengers.

A Softer Touch: Personnel Management and Company Unions

In keeping with the effort to infuse its open-shop rhetoric with credibility by demonstrating its goodwill toward workers, the NAM took a new interest in personnel management. The promotion of personnel management held a central position among the early recommendations of the NAM's Open Shop Committee. Indeed, in the first set of recommendations the committee made, three out of the four recommendations concerned improving personnel management. They emphasized the need "to stimulate a wider appreciation among employers of their obligation with respect to the human factor in industry," to exercise care in the selection of foremen and other supervisory personnel so as to impart the right "spirit" to relations with workers, and "to encourage . . . better methods of employment and allocation of men in industry."[29] Of particular importance in this effort to make employment practices at once more humane and more scientific was the role of the foreman. Framed as a question of efficiency, duty, and good public relations, foreman training aimed to smooth things between workers and management: foremen "must interpret the spirit of the management to the workers" and should do so with care, because "if they are unfair and autocratic the workers will assume that the management possesses these same characteristics."[30]

The NAM's new emphasis on foreman training and "the human factor in industry" fit into a broader effort across industry to modernize personnel management. By the early 1920s the language of management had become imbued with the idea that "professional" and thought-out personnel policies were the modern way, while the autocratic foreman represented the unenlightened past. Proper modern employment relations involved "understanding" and some variant of consulting with one's employees, or at least appearing to do so.[31] These ideas had multiple roots, among them workers' demand for unions and industrial democracy, worker welfare plans (themselves often developed in response to union threats), and efficiency-oriented scientific management theories. Moreover, in the 1920s, "modernity" itself was a selling point, while the corporation, newly dominant, was badly in need of a humanizing touch. Better, more humane personnel management potentially provided the answer to multiple problems.[32]

Ideas about worker services and professional personnel departments had been percolating in some quarters for a while. During World War I, practical considerations made employers look at these ideas with new interest. Labor scarcity made it harder to extract production from workers and to maintain discipline: labor turnover increased, productivity plummeted, and absenteeism skyrocketed. Perhaps, after all, professionals could institute measures that would increase worker satisfaction and ameliorate such problems. By 1920 a quarter of firms employing 250 or more workers had a personnel department, a significant increase. Similarly, the number of professional personnel managers grew manifold.[33] Even more directly, the war promoted employee representation. The National War Labor Board had required that employees be allowed representation but had stopped short of requiring that such representation consist of bona fide unions. Thus, hundreds of companies had instituted employee representation plans. When the war ended, the existence of such plans allowed employers to claim that they were all for employees having a voice and only opposed the outside interference of unions.[34]

Employee representation plans—plans that offered workers a route to participation without relinquishing management control—also allowed companies to lay claim to the newly popular language of "industrial democracy" (see chapter 8). That language, amorphous as it was, seemed to legitimize the idea that industry was not the sole domain of the businessman but a joint project subject to some kind of democratic influence. That might mean unions; it might even mean state control. Quite self-consciously, management therefore set about instituting forms of democracy of its own.

Perhaps the best-known of these plans was the one at Goodyear Tire & Rubber Company, hailed in the popular press as the "broad-minded, humane, sensible and statesmanlike conception" of industrial relations that "marks a new era in American industrial life."[35] As was often the case, the Goodyear employee representation plan was part of a comprehensive human relations approach involving a modern personnel division and a comprehensive welfare program, including a large selection of classes on business and industry, a gymnasium and an athletic field, and a sizable factory hospital.[36] Most remarkably, however, it had an elaborate structure that imitated the US government in a none-too-subtle effort to underline its democratic credentials.

The Goodyear employee representation plan, called the Industrians, provided for an Industrial Assembly, divided into a Senate and House of

Representatives. The Goodyear factory was divided into forty "precincts," each of which got to elect one representative to the House; four precincts made up a "district," which got to elect two senators. Every worker who was an American citizen, was over eighteen, and had worked at Goodyear for six months had a vote. The Industrial Assembly had "legislative power" to make changes in wages and working conditions and adjust grievances; the manager had veto power but could be overridden by two-thirds of both houses.[37]

Of course, the plan made sure that management retained the final say. It reserved for management all executive power that was not specifically given to the assembly. It also apparently did not accord the assembly any control over hiring and firing.[38] After all, Goodyear executives argued, as long as workers did not risk their capital, management retained the right to make the decisions that could affect capital. A prerequisite for a functioning "industrial republic" was management's ability to "careful[ly] select its working force" to ensure that its workers had a fair and cooperative spirit (which ideally would also characterize those who put up the capital).[39]

Goodyear, like many of the companies with the most prominent welfare and employee representation plans, was a member of the NAM.[40] The NAM had in 1914 decided to create the Committee on Industrial Betterment, partly to amplify its work on such "constructive" projects as accident prevention and partly to keep an eye on social legislation in the states.[41] Over time, the committee modestly endorsed various welfare ideas. At the 1919 NAM convention, the committee suggested offering benefits like group life insurance as "a constructive demonstration of the employer's interest in his employes and their families" and reported on efforts on accident prevention and re-employment of those injured at work or in the war. It also reported favorably on implementing employee representation plans in large companies.[42]

Yet the NAM's enthusiasm for employee representation plans as well as for other measures of worker involvement, such as profit sharing and including workers on company boards, was distinctly limited. Many of its members worried that representation plans might make workers arrogant and eventually lead to strikes; that they would not be welcomed by workers, who preferred to leave management to managers; that they would be abused by workers who would only look after workers' interests on boards; or that workers would simply spend their profit-sharing earnings on extravagances.[43] Besides, there was a danger in promoting even management-led employee representation: it seemed to imply that employees were, in fact, entitled to representation. That might be taken by labor unions or the public as an endorsement of the need for organized labor. At the 1919 convention, William P. White, one of the members of the Committee on Industrial Betterment, raised precisely this point, insisting that the committee report should not be misconstrued as an endorsement of labor unions and proceeding to offer lengthy remarks on the evils of organized labor.[44]

Fears that employee representation might be more trouble than it was worth were perhaps not entirely misplaced. Workers were sometimes able to use the representational structures provided by such plans to wrest important concessions from the company.[45] Moreover, the very fact of a representative structure that was to be consulted about certain management decisions posed some risk: in submitting its proposal to a deliberative body, management invited discussion and therefore dissent. Even if it could then override the representative assembly's decision, having to do so would rather defeat the purpose of using representation to gain greater harmony through cooperation.[46]

In the NAM's activities, personnel management and foreman training quickly faded into the background. While they came up in occasional speeches held at the annual conventions, they never formed a prominent topic in, for example, *American Industries* or the NAM's other materials. More generally, too, the enthusiasm for employee representation plans faded. The proliferation of employee representation plans peaked in the mid-1920s; after that, the tenor of the times turned more conservative, and as the AFL's power waned (helped along, of course, by the NAM's open-shop drive), company-managed representation no longer seemed as attractive. Although the popularity of the plans among large companies meant that the number of workers covered kept growing through the 1920s, Bruce Nissen points out that "by 1928, more companies were discontinuing plans than were instituting them."[47]

The brief prominence of the question of personnel management and employee representation in the NAM's deliberations is a testament to the uncertainty of the postwar moment. As one manufacturer noted at the 1919 convention, "It is a time of readjustment, and that readjustment must come slowly and gradually." Convinced as he was that strict antiunionism was "the sentiment of a very great majority of the manufacturers of this Association," he nevertheless felt that "it may not be politic at this time" to give public expression to it.[48] Better to focus on the softer themes of personnel management. In fact, although recommendations two through four in the Open Shop Committee's first set of recommendations concerned personnel management, recommendation number one concerned the tone that should be adopted in publicity work.[49]

No amount of advertising employer benevolence, however, could quite allay public suspicions if employers failed too flagrantly to live up to their professed ideals of treating their workers well and not discriminating on the basis of union membership. Many in the NAM leadership and among its professional staff were aware of this problem.[50] As some speakers at the NAM's Open Shop Conference in 1922 somewhat wryly noted, the NAM's Open Shop Department should perhaps try harder to "educate the employer to his duties to worker and public—to make the Open Shop in practice actually what it claims to be."[51] But that was easier said than done; indeed, it was even difficult for many NAM leaders to be consistent in their claims about what the open shop really meant with regard to unions. For example, John Edgerton, elected NAM president the previous year, had in the first months of his presidency given statements emphasizing that refusing to hire union men contradicted the open-shop principle and "gives comfort to those who falsely claim" that the open shop equaled antiunionism.[52] As the NAM's 1922 convention discussed the report of the Open Shop Committee, however, Edgerton openly contradicted the committee's tone. The committee had insisted that the open shop ought to be combined with "constructive methods" and had "urge[d] . . . that those entrusted with the guidance of the affairs" of the NAM "give earnest consideration" to the committee's earlier resolutions on promoting the "human factor" in industry. When Edgerton rose to give "the views of your President on this subject," however, he offered a ringing defense of his right to refuse to hire unionists, complete with disease metaphors almost identical to those employed by David Parry in launching the open-shop offensive almost two decades before. Where Parry had compared unions to typhoid fever, sneaky yet deadly, Edgerton compared his right to not hire a union man to his right to not let someone with leprosy or tuberculosis work alongside his employees. It was not a question of "denying the right to that man to have leprosy or tuberculosis" but of being obliged to "protect [the other employees] against infection."[53]

As Edgerton's language indicated, the new line on modern personnel management wobbled badly under the weight of old-line antiunionism. In fact, in these remarks Edgerton arguably went even further than had been traditional among open-shop proponents, who had generally insisted that an open-shop employer did not inquire about a man's union membership any more than about his membership in the Masons or about his religious affiliation. Edgerton, by contrast, argued for an explicit right to discriminate on any basis whatsoever, admitting that he would refuse to hire a person whose religious or doctrinal views he found objectionable. With regard to unions, Edgerton (who was from Tennessee) professed his satisfaction that there were few unionists in his part of the world—but, he declared, "I do not hesitate for one moment to say to you that if it comes to choosing between a union man and a non-union man, all other things being equal, I will select the non-union man every time."[54]

Entrenching the Business Viewpoint

As it had been before the war, publicity was one of the least friction-prone and most agreeable pursuits for the NAM. Unlike new personnel policies, publicity required little more than money. And where new ideas on personnel management might point toward a need for self-criticism, publicity was all about showing how right the manufacturers were.

In the postwar era, the NAM was much better aware of the challenges of publicity than it had been early in the century. Its experiences with press work had apparently taught it that getting into mainstream, wide-circulation magazines was "easier said than done" and that trying to bully local newspapers into printing what the advertisers liked could easily "boomerang."[55] Newspaper publicity was therefore not a primary objective of the Open Shop Department—though it reported that it could also "claim credit" for "145 3/4 columns" worth of it in 1921, plus that it had assisted several magazine writers with material for their articles.[56] To have a long-term impact on general opinion, however, the NAM was convinced that it had to gain a better foothold among the opinion-makers of the country. A key component in the NAM's publicity strategy in the postwar era, therefore, was cultivating better interlocutors for the employer point of view. The open-shop message would be far more appealing if it could be funneled through those who already possessed moral and intellectual authority.

One group that the NAM particularly targeted was the clergy. "The furnishing of sound information to the clergy" mattered for two reasons. First, the clergy had significant moral authority and stature as a "molder of public opinion"—increased, in the NAM's view, by the fact of woman suffrage.[57] Second, the NAM worried that the clergy had begun to lean toward labor. In the years before the war, Labor Sunday—the practice of giving prolabor sermons at churches on the Sunday before Labor Day—had grown in popularity, and the Federal Council of Churches (FCC) had involved itself in investigating strikes (see chapter 8). After the war, the churches seemed only to be shifting in a more prolabor direction. The council's Social Service Commission participated in the Interchurch World Movement (IWM) to bring together the many Protestant denominations, to help them raise funds, and to do its own fundraising to enhance church influence in a variety of social questions. When the Great Steel Strike of 1919 brought out hundreds of thousands of largely immigrant workers, the IWM's Industrial Relations Department decided to investigate the strike. The report that it issued the next year vindicated the strikers. It documented the antiunion practices of U.S. Steel, highlighted the dangerous working conditions and twelve-hour shifts that steelworkers endured, and dismissed as steel company propaganda claims that the workers were radicals or Communist dupes. In its "Christian Findings," the report recommended the eight-hour day and the right to unionize. It also called for establishing minimum wage commissions and starting a federal investigation of the use of detective agencies in labor disputes. Finally, the report pointedly "recommend[ed] to the press that it free itself of the often all too well founded charge of bias, favoring capital as against labor."[58] A few months after the steel strike report came out, the Federal Council of Churches warned "Christian employers" against the open-shop campaign, which, it said, gave the impression of being "inspired in many quarters by . . . antagonism to union labor."[59]

The open-shop employers were, to put it mildly, upset. The NAM and other employers accused the IWM of timing the steel strike report strategically so as to provide fodder for the 1920 Labor Sunday sermons. They also objected to the open-shop statement issued by the FCC. While employers acknowledged that the statement also condemned the closed shop as "inimical . . . coercion," they complained that that condemnation was not stated prominently enough and that the council's ideas of the open shop were rooted in ignorance. The clergymen, employers said, should come visit factories and talk to employers to learn the true state of affairs.[60]

Shifting the FCC toward its own views became an explicit NAM goal, and it cooperated with local employer groups to supply clergy with more appropriate literature to inspire their Labor Day sermons. By 1922 the NAM's Open Shop Department claimed that it had succeeded in the "modification of the antagonistic attitude" of the council, though it admitted lack of "similar success with the National Catholic Welfare Council."[61] Claims of success may have been rather premature; the FCC continued to speak in favor of labor, and the tradition of Labor Sunday continued and even strengthened.[62] Open-shop advocates did, however, manage to block Labor Sunday speakers in specific locations and perhaps succeeded in shifting the views or at least the practices of individual clergy. In Detroit in the fall of 1926, for example, invitations to labor speakers to preach from the city's pulpits in conjunction with the AFL annual convention were canceled by local churches as a result of a campaign by the Board of Commerce and the Building Trades Association.[63] And financial pressure took its toll: the IWM folded within a few years due to a decline in donations in the wake of its steel strike report, at least in part because many businessmen withdrew their funding.[64]

Another group the NAM believed it important to influence was students and especially educators. University-level educators, like clergy, were "molders of public opinion." Even more importantly, every day they shaped the "social philosophy" that thousands of future teachers imbibed in university classes on economics, government, and sociology.[65] This effort to educate the educators highlights the way in which the 1920s campaign differed from the cruder publicity efforts of the open-shop campaign's early years. It was the NAM's most deliberately farsighted publicity effort; as an Open Shop Department report noted, "We feel that even though several years may be necessary for the carrying out of this plan, . . . the benefits obtained, indirect as they may be, will prove highly beneficial."[66]

The NAM opened its campaign to target educators and students with a major undertaking, the compilation and distribution of the *Open Shop Encyclopedia for Debaters*, first published in February 1921 and revised twice by May of the following year. By the third edition, the encyclopedia ran to over three hundred pages and provided the prospective debater with anything but impartial information and arguments on strikes, union apprenticeship rules, and the "irresponsibility of unions."[67] The encyclopedia took advantage of the enthusiasm for competitive debating among high school and university students. Beginning in the 1890s, college debating had grown from intramural debating clubs to intercollegiate competitive debates, inaugurated by an 1892 debate between Harvard and Yale. By World War I debating had spread across the country, and the immediate postwar years saw intense growth in collegiate debating, as well as the spread of the contests to high schools and junior colleges. Though some, such as Theodore Roosevelt, condemned debating as training for glibness without principle, debaters had a certain stature on campuses, and at least some debates were held before enthusiastic and sizable audiences. Coached by experts in the new discipline of public speaking, members of debating teams could spend months in intense research to prepare for a competitive debate.[68] Either the encyclopedia or other pro-open-shop material was sent to thousands of debaters, and the debating teams of a handful of universities, including Princeton and Harvard, received personal visits from NAM officers. As a result, the NAM claimed, the side advocating the open shop won three-quarters of the debates, which were "heard by millions of people."[69]

In the immediate postwar years, the question of the closed versus open shop was prominent among topics of competitive debates. Overall, the topics reflected the burning domestic and foreign political questions of the day: in 1922, for instance, the eight subjects selected as "representative" and "sure to be of interest to debaters for some time to come" by the *University Debaters' Annual* included the Kansas Court of Industrial Relations, unemployment insurance, the sales tax, independence for the Philippines, recognition of Soviet Russia, naval disarmament, government ownership and operation of coal mines—and the closed shop. Indeed, the closed or open shop made the list of eight in 1920, 1921, and 1922.[70]

University educators were an even more important target than debaters. In a debate, after all, each position is by definition at least worth considering. Even if the open-shop side won the majority of debates, that still allowed the closed-shop side to emerge victorious at some debates and probably left at least some listeners of the debates convinced of the value of the closed shop even at the debates won by the open-shop side. Unlike debaters, university educators had the power to make the open shop a matter of common sense and standard theory. Thus, the NAM worked to put its materials and people at the disposal of university educators. By 1922 the NAM's Open Shop Department reported that "practically all of the college and university teachers of sociology, government and economics receive our publications," and in many states the material supplied by the NAM was also being lent out by universities to schools across the state.[71] At Harvard's Graduate School of Business Administration, "students of labor problems" were, according to the NAM, required to read its open-shop literature.[72]

Getting educators to use the NAM's open-shop literature required, of course, that that literature actually look like information rather than vitriol. That indeed was the NAM's goal in the new iteration of the open-shop campaign. As James Emery explained at the opening of the decade, the NAM should strive to get beyond "abstract argument on the principles involved" and instead "overwhelmingly demonstrat[e] by facts and figures that the open shop condition secures a larger return to the worker, a lower cost to the consumer and a greater opportunity for American production to enlarge its facilities, better its services, expand its competition with other nations," and generally provide regular Americans with more "comforts and luxuries."[73] The open shop, in other words, was simply good for everyone.

In addition to printed matter, the Open Shop Department sent its personnel to give speeches at universities and associations. The 1922 report noted that the department manager, Noel Sargent, had that year given a total of forty-three addresses on the open shop: eighteen at universities and the rest at meetings of organizations ranging from the Economic Club of Pittsburgh to the American Economic Association. Not without glee, the department pointed out that the American Federation of Labor had "declared it was absolutely necessary to counteract our work in educational institutions."[74]

The NAM's publicity campaign in the 1920s reflected trends it had begun pursuing before the war; it was also a harbinger of things to come. In a development that had begun with the NAM's focus on accident prevention around 1908–9, the organization increasingly, though somewhat intermittently, tried to position itself as a reliable, creditable source of information. As was the case with the issue of personnel management, though, efforts to soften or professionalize the publicity campaign ran up against reality. The goal, it was clear, was to promote the open shop. To do so it might be politic to not be too vociferous in the open shop's defense, and it might be politic to bring the realities at the workplace more in line with the professed ideals. But most of the membership had limited interest in changing their workplace procedures, and many of them were unwilling to curb their rhetoric. The more research-oriented staff of the NAM, as well as some of its members, mostly labored in vain to convince the old-line open-shoppers that change was needed.

After about 1922 the intense phase of the open-shop campaign seems to have died down, and in 1925 the NAM replaced its Open Shop Department with the more neutrally named Industrial Relations Department.[75] However, when that department attempted to tone down the combative language of the Declaration of Labor Principles, originally drafted in 1903 at the start of the first open-shop campaign, the effort failed.[76] Whether the advocates of a softer line were correct in their assumption that a more neutral position would make the NAM more effective, however, is far from clear. In the early twentieth century its hardcore opposition to labor had served it well; in the 1920s, too, there were indications that a hard line was more efficacious against labor than soft-pedaling. Lizabeth Cohen, for instance, has argued that welfare programs and representation plans, intended to pacify workers and convince them of corporate benevolence and labor-capital harmony, potentially backfired on employers, convincing workers that a "fair employer should take responsibility for the welfare of his work force" while providing those workers with little evidence that their employer was actually doing so. Employers had inadvertently legitimized standards they were not able or willing to meet.[77]

In the 1930s new organizations of industrial workers and the alliances of those organizations with political parties and the state presented employers with unprecedented challenges. As the Great Depression gnawed at the prestige of capitalism, and labor and the New Deal redoubled the challenge to business authority, the NAM recommitted itself to its vociferous antiunionism and opposition to state intervention on workers' behalf. It was soon clear that this line again served the NAM well: its ideological clarity appealed to a significant segment of the business community, and the NAM's membership, as well as its income, soared.[78]

Coda

The Working Class and the Prerequisites of Power

So it goes.
—Kurt Vonnegut, *Slaughterhouse-Five*

Early on in the National Civic Federation's work, Ralph Easley penned a letter to an old acquaintance who had drifted away from efforts at labor-capital cooperation and closer to the open-shop movement. The acquaintance had criticized the NCF for its seeming inability to convince its labor members of the misguidedness of many of their actions. To this, Easley replied that great changes could not be wrought overnight. "You, doubtless, have attended Hagenbach's [*sic*] animal show," Easley wrote. "I imagine it took a great deal of time and patience to get the lion and the lamb, the jaguar and the kangaroo, et al., to gambol together yet preserve themselves, respectively, intact."[1]

Carl Hagenbeck was a German animal merchant and trainer who created the modern zoo. His show of trained exotic animals performing circus tricks—which was a big draw at the World's Columbian Exposition in Chicago in 1893—was widely interpreted as a triumph of "the human spirit over the animal's mind and brute strength."[2] It was not, however, merely human assertion of dominance over animals that attracted people to such performances as lions riding horses and boarhounds leaping over living hurdles of lions. Rather, "what seems to have repeatedly struck visitors to the Hagenbeck arena . . . were the performances in which diverse animals, though popularly conceived to be mortal enemies, performed together with apparently no enmity between them."[3]

The allure of the Hagenbeck animal show lay in the strange spectacle of the lion gamboling with the lamb (or at least the horse). Easley likely chose the metaphor because it underlined the triumph of rationality and civilization over reflexive, narrow self-interest. Yet, unwittingly, the choice of metaphor revealed the fundamental flaw in the NCF's project. It underlined that harmony was utopian, not real. The Hagenbeck animal show had not in fact transcended the lion's desire to dine on the lamb. Rather, it offered a carefully constructed illusion of having done so. That illusion relied on continual oversight by a party above the fray.

Hagenbeck understood that if the gamboling was to continue, he or his trainers had to continually keep the lion in check. Even after considerable training, Hagenbeck said, "there is . . . always a chance of some savage outburst of temper, and the teacher has to watch with a never-tiring eye for the smallest indication of any change in behaviour of any of his fearsome pupils."[4] Easley, to the extent that he recognized that the interests of labor and capital conflicted, saw the NCF as Hagenbeck—the force that brought the beasts to the arena and made them behave like tame pets. In reality, though, the NCF had no such power. It was not impartial: its funds came entirely from its business members, and thus Easley ultimately served at their pleasure. Nor did it have the means to enforce its will on the contending parties. As the outcomes of strikes at NCF-affiliated companies attested, on the NCF's watch the lion repeatedly imposed its own kind of peace.

The closed shop represented one form of a working-class claim to a different interpretation of industrial relations. That interpretation took as its metaphor not utopian harmony but government, and it relied not so much on the impartial master of ceremonies as on countervailing power: on uniting the flock of lambs so they could hold their own against the lion. The closed shop was not the only worker solution to the dilemma—others included proposals for worker influence through the state, cooperatives and other working-class institutions that put workers directly in charge of their economic lives, and various revolutionary philosophies that envisioned radical resistance in the present and actual power at some future date. Common to all worker visions, however, was real power wielded by workers themselves.

In this sense, the closed shop was a radical demand, despite being favored by unions that were deemed "moderate." Against employers' insistence on the right to manage and middle-class solutions relying on middle-class expertise rather than worker power, the unions in the American Federation of Labor asserted that the right to govern in the workplace was, at least in part, theirs. They knew, though, that this vision clashed with the narrative of American democracy that prized individual rights while naturalizing the economic structures that effectively governed the exercise of such rights. That made the vision difficult to champion. Indeed, the frequent tiptoeing around what unions actually wanted provoked the famous lawyer Clarence Darrow, one of labor's staunchest and most perceptive reformer friends, to snort that unions were "afraid to defend their own doctrine" regarding the closed shop, and so "the enemy runs away with all the editorials and most of the language."[5]

Darrow, always keenly suspicious of power and never one to mince words, had little sympathy for efforts to tone down critique or pursue respectability.[6] The closed shop, Darrow acknowledged, was a "harsh and arbitrary and in many ways a dangerous power." In an ideal world, perhaps nobody should have such power, and unions had better "give some very good reason" for wielding it. If they did not, people would stick with the employer, because the employer could position himself as "the man who's fighting for individual liberty." The employer would be able to maintain that advantage as long as unions danced around their purpose instead of stating it honestly. As things were, unions claimed that they did not attempt to limit output, curb the number of apprentices, or coerce the nonunionist to join—but in saying these things, "they lie." Instead, they needed to forthrightly admit that of course these were union goals. The purpose of unions was to resist capital's efforts to push down the price of labor; the purpose of the closed shop was to give them the power to do so. That, of course, was precisely why employers objected to it.[7]

It was no use, Darrow said, to discuss the question of open versus closed shop "as if the brotherhood of man had come." In that imaginary world, the closed shop would of course be illegitimate because individuals would be on an equal footing and capable of exercising that much-vaunted individual liberty. In the real world, though, the closed shop was justified because it functioned as an equalizer by amassing the power of the workers. Only by being honest about this could unions point out the dishonesty of complaining about it. After all, professionals had their own mechanisms to restrict membership. One could only practice law if one fulfilled the legal requirements for doing so—or, as Darrow put it, "We [lawyers] have enforced our trade union by the statutes of every State in the Union." And employers had their own organizations, having "made up their minds that they'd better not cut each other's throats; they'd better cut somebody else's throat."[8] Organization was power, and the struggle between labor and capital was a contest over power. Why pretend otherwise?

But many middle-class observers wished to pretend otherwise. Although unionists like Samuel Gompers and John Mitchell sometimes drew the same parallels Darrow did—that doctors, lawyers, and preachers had their own versions of the closed shop, and their associations exercised power in much the same way as unions did—the impact was limited. Even those middle-class allies who understood the functions of union governance, such as Ralph Easley, could not bring themselves to acknowledge that workers' lack of real power sunk the whole enterprise of reforming labor relations. Without real power, workers could not be true partners in workplace rulemaking, and without worker partners, reformers would be reduced to pleading for mutual understanding and goodwill.

The New Deal legislative framework that responded to the next wave of massive labor unrest in the 1930s attempted to guarantee a worker voice by implementing a bureaucratic regime that formalized how union contracts were achieved and administered. That framework—which in principle remains the law of the land, though one might often be forgiven for not noticing—did offer real power. As Jack Metzgar has eloquently argued, for all its boring bureaucratic detail, it created a "workplace rule of law" that was a world away from what preceded it. In the pre–New Deal workplace, the foreman could exercise near-absolute power. Getting decent work shifts or even full-time work might require blandishments that at best chafed against one's sense of dignity and at worst flew in the face of one's basic morals. In the former category was, say, a foreman's implicit expectation that one would bring him a weekly supply of nice homemade kielbasa prepared by one's wife. In the latter category was, for example, a foreman's veiled demand for a date with one's sixteen-year-old daughter. That the latter kind of demand was rare made the power that it implied no less repulsive. In the new world of union work rules, such powers were reined in by the very feature of the New Deal labor regime that has been the most frequent target of critique: its tendency to bureaucratize the work relationship. In real ways, Metzgar says, "the very impersonality of the labor contract as a binding document was the foundation of . . . freedom and dignity."[9]

The New Deal, in an unprecedented way, put the state in the role of Hagenbeck. That mattered. Yet as the erosion of workers' position in recent decades indicates, giving the state a role could not maintain a permanent balance between workers and employers.[10] There is no truly impartial umpire; the state, too, acts only in response to the power of different parties to apply pressure on it. Inserting the state into the equation does not eliminate the need for ordinary people to be able to exert organized power. One can, of course, debate what form labor law or union practice should take, how much union discipline is too much, how much bureaucracy saps the labor movement's grassroots spirit, or even whether labor unions, specifically, are the best form of organized grassroots power. If we claim to value democracy, however, we cannot get away from the fact that grassroots organization is a necessity, not a luxury. As Mark E. Warren and many other scholars have noted, in recent decades democratic participation has—at least in the West—largely shrunk to the act of voting, while the term "democracy" itself has come to be almost synonymous with periodic elections.[11] Yet, a democracy consisting only of periodic elections, scholars have argued, is a "diminished democracy"; it lacks the fundamental democratic apparatus of civic participation in intermediary organizations that can percolate local concerns and local activism up to the national level and vice versa. Political scientist Theda Skocpol, in particular, has lamented the replacement of voluntary membership organizations possessing a real local grassroots base with professionally managed advocacy organizations where actual input by ordinary people is nearly nonexistent.[12] Increasingly, such "grassroots" organizations as exist are managed top-down and involve their members via what union organizer and scholar Jane McAlevey has called "mobilization" rather than "organization." In other words, their policies are made at the top by those who supposedly know better; the role of the general membership is merely to show up when commanded. This model has become widespread among unions as well, as McAlevey points out.[13]

The shift away from membership organizations and toward top-down structures perhaps reflects the same elite concerns as early twentieth-century reformers had about unions. Can ordinary people really be allowed to wield power on their own account without elite tutelage? Are ordinary people really capable of self-government? In some ways, doubts about ordinary people's capacities have in recent decades only strengthened. As Michael Sandel, for instance, has argued, credentialism is "the last acceptable prejudice." The well-educated offer education as the primary answer to inequality, look down upon those who do not pursue it, and evaluate even politicians by their educational credentials rather than by whether they speak for or listen to their constituents. Meanwhile, access to elected office has become practically restricted to the college-educated: whereas in the 1960s about a quarter of senators and representatives did not possess a college degree, now everyone in the Senate and nearly everyone in the House has one. What all this says to the majority of citizens who do not possess—and perhaps, horror of horrors, do not care to possess—a college degree is rarely discussed.[14]

Once upon a time, labor unions formed an intermediary organizational level that offered a grassroots route to participation in the common affairs of the society; they could, in principle, fulfill that role again.[15] Such participation was grounded in real power; it was not merely a civic charade. It mattered on multiple social and personal levels. As union activist Grace Clements explained to the famous oral historian Studs Terkel in the early 1970s, "Before the union came in, all I did was do my eight hours, collect my paycheck, and go home, did my housework, took care of my daughter, and went back to work. I had no outside interests. You just lived to live. Since I became active in the union, I've become active in the community, in legislative problems. I've been to Washington on one or two trips. I've been to Springfield. That has given me more of an incentive for life."[16] Clements's comments show that the union was not, for her, merely about an individual calculation of economic benefit. Indeed, James Pope has noted that portraying unions solely as an economic calculation is a key technique of antiunion consultants, who are well aware of the need "to deromanticize the union." An antiunion consultant wants "to move his audience from a narrative model of rights and solidarity to one of profits and self-interested calculation."[17] Such a model is not particularly conducive to collective action, especially not of a kind that may involve taking real risks in pursuit of uncertain reward. Dreams are a necessary part of collective action.

At the same time, no movement survives on dreams alone; just as we expect institutional sticks and carrots to be necessary in a corporation or a state, they are necessary in maintaining a workers' organization. Why should workers, after all, live up to more idealism and altruism than we expect of anyone else?

Abbreviations

AABA	American Anti-Boycott Association
AFL	American Federation of Labor
AFL-CIO	American Federation of Labor and Congress of Industrial Organizations
ANPA	American Newspaper Publishers Association
ARU	American Railway Union
ASE	Amalgamated Society of Engineers [Great Britain]
BML	Business Men's League [St. Louis]
BSTL	*The Book of St. Louisans*
BTEA	Building Trades Employer Association
CA	Citizens' Association [Chicago]
CCF	Chicago Civic Federation
CF&I	Colorado Fuel and Iron Company
CIA	Citizens' Industrial Association [there are several local ones]
CIAA	Citizens' Industrial Association of America
IAM	International Association of Machinists
ILGWU	International Ladies' Garment Workers' Union
IMU	Iron (later International) Molders' Union
ITU	International Typographical Union
IWM	Interchurch World Movement
IWW	Industrial Workers of the World (also known as the Wobblies)
KOL	Knights of Labor
NAM	National Association of Manufacturers
NCF	National Civic Federation
NCR	National Cash Register [company]
NFA	National Founders' Association
NICB	National Industrial Conference Board
NMTA	National Metal Trades Association
NWLB	National War Labor Board

SFNDA	Stove Founders' National Defense Association
SPD	Social Democratic Party [Germany]
UMWA	United Mine Workers of America
USCIR	US Commission on Industrial Relations
UTA	United Typothetae of America
WLCB	War Labor Conference Board
WPA	Workingmen's Protective Association
WTUL	Women's Trade Union League

A Note on Sources and Methods

Nearly all contemporary newspapers and magazines cited here have been consulted in digitized form in online databases, in most cases either ProQuest Historical Newspapers (a subscription database) or Chronicling America (open-access, at https://chroniclingamerica.loc.gov/). Some newspapers also came from the Colorado Historic Newspapers Collection (open-access, https://www.coloradohistoricnewspapers.org/) and a few from the Google News archival collection (open-access, https://news.google.com/newspapers). Congressional hearings and other congressional documents were accessed through the ProQuest Congressional database (formerly Lexis-Nexis), a subscription service. For magazines I have mostly relied on Readers' Guide Retrospective (an EBSCOHost subscription database) and American Periodicals Online (a ProQuest subscription database). Many contemporary magazines, trade journals, government reports, biographical compendia, and other publications were also consulted through the HathiTrust Digital Library (mainly open-access, https://www.hathitrust.org/).

All conversions of historical to modern dollar amounts in this book are to 2020 dollars and use the purchasing power calculator based on the consumer price index described and implemented in Samuel H. Williamson, "Seven Ways to Compute the Relative Value of a U.S. Dollar Amount, 1790 to Present," Measuring Worth, accessed November 22, 2021, https://www.measuringworth.com/calculators/uscompare/. In places in the manuscript, I have made extensive use of various computational methods and data I have extracted or developed from sources ranging from newspapers to biographical compendia. These computational methods and data are discussed in some detail at https://github.com/vhulden/bossesunion, where one can also download the data and code.

Archival Collections

AFL-CIO Papers, George Meany Memorial AFL-CIO Archive, University of Maryland, College Park.

Drew, Walter, Papers, accession number 9616 Aa2, microform, Bentley Historical Library, University of Michigan, Ann Arbor.

Mitchell, John, Papers, accession number 1629, microform, Hagley Museum and Library, Wilmington, DE.

National Association of Manufacturers Records, accession number 1411, Hagley Museum and Library, Wilmington, DE.

National Civic Federation Records, 1894–1949, Manuscripts and Archives Division, New York Public Library, New York.

National Founders' Association Records, accession number LR001292, Walter P. Reuther Library, Detroit, MI.

National Industrial Conference Board Records, accession number 1057, Hagley Museum and Library, Wilmington, DE.

Records of the Committee on Labor, Records of the US House of Representatives, Record Group 233, 57th–63rd Congresses, National Archives, Washington, DC.

Records of the Committee on the Judiciary, Records of the US House of Representatives, Record Group 233, 57th-63rd Congresses, National Archives, Washington, DC.

Records of the United States Senate, Record Group 46, 57th–63rd Congresses, National Archives, Washington, DC.

Tompkins, Daniel Augustus, Papers, accession number 724, microform, Southern Historical Collection, University of North Carolina Library, Chapel Hill.

In addition, a major source of NAM correspondence and records for the early years of the open-shop campaign is the subpoenaed NAM material, reprinted as an appendix to the 1913 congressional hearings investigating lobbying: US Congress, Senate, Subcommittee of the Committee on the Judiciary, *Maintenance of a Lobby to Influence Legislation: Appendix: Exhibits Introduced during the Hearings*, 63rd Cong., 1st sess., 1913.

Notes

Introduction

1. Industrial Commission, *Final Report of the Industrial Commission*, vol. 19 of the commission's reports (Washington, DC: GPO, 1902), 805.

2. For a recent analysis of the labor question and its intellectual and social context, see Rosanne Currarino, *The Labor Question in America: Economic Democracy in the Gilded Age* (Urbana: University of Illinois Press, 2011).

3. Elizabeth Anderson, *Private Government: How Employers Rule Our Lives (and Why We Don't Talk about It)* (Princeton, NJ: Princeton University Press, 2017), 37–40.

4. Michael Roach and Henry Sauermann, "A Taste for Science? PhD Scientists' Academic Orientation and Self-Selection into Research Careers in Industry," *Research Policy* 39, no. 3 (April 2010): 422–34.

5. Peter Howley, "The Happy Farmer: The Effect of Nonpecuniary Benefits on Behavior," *American Journal of Agricultural Economics* 97, no. 4 (July 2015): 1072–86.

6. Matthias Benz and Bruno S. Frey, "The Value of Doing What You Like: Evidence from the Self-Employed in 23 Countries," *Journal of Economic Behavior & Organization* 68, no. 3 (December 2008): 445–55.

7. Richard Barry Freeman and Joel Rogers, *What Workers Want* (Ithaca, NY: Cornell University Press, 2006), introduction and table 3.5 on 76–77. The original survey was conducted in 1994–95; in the updated edition, the authors argue that other surveys show that their results on what workers want still largely hold, though it seems that workers had also become more convinced that what they had was not what they wanted.

8. Freeman and Rogers, *What Workers Want*, 26.

9. Freeman and Rogers, *What Workers Want*, 139–41. The authors note that employee involvement (EI) does reduce worker desire for a union, but, on the other hand, EI programs are more popular and deemed to work better at unionized workplaces, where they also increase workers' satisfaction with the union.

10. Howell John Harris, "Between Convergence and Exceptionalism: Americans and the British Model of Labor Relations, c. 1867–1920," *Labor History* 48, no. 2 (May 2007): 148 (emphasis in original).

11. The shift to a distinction between a pre- or posthiring membership requirement happened in conjunction with the more comprehensive legislative definition of labor relations during the 1930s and 1940s. For example, a 1939 article still uses the terms interchangeably; by 1942 the Bureau of Labor refers to the distinction between the terms as a fait accompli. Leon M. Despres, "The Collective Agreement for the Union Shop," *University of Chicago Law Review* 7, no. 1 (December 1939): 24–57; US Department of Labor, Bureau of Labor Statistics, *Union Agreement Provisions*, Bulletin No. 686, 1942. The Taft-Hartley Act (the Labor Management Relations Act of 1947) prohibited the preentry closed shop, besides generally establishing the bureaucratic transformation of labor relations so that the whole subject of union membership requirements had "become highly technical and complex." Robert J. Rosenthal, "Union Security under the Taft-Hartley Act," *Monthly Labor Review* 77, no. 4 (April 1954): 391–96.

12. Thomas Ashton to R. M. Easley, September 18, 1903, box 4, folder 4, National Civic Federation Records, 1894–1949, Manuscripts and Archives Division, New York Public Library, New York. Hereafter cited as NCF Records.

13. Against characterizations of business unionism as cold or opportunistic, Philip Taft defends it as "no late nineteenth-century import, but the first type of cooperative activity carried on by workers in the United States," the basic model on which workers had organized since the late eighteenth century. "On the Origins of Business Unionism," *Industrial and Labor Relations Review* 17, no. 1 (October 1963): 20–38, quote on 37. Whatever the case may be, the term came into widespread use in the first years of the twentieth century specifically in the context of the AFL's more streamlined and bureaucratic organization.

14. All quotes are from a brief item in the NAM's trade publication: "One Uses Politics, the Other Direct Coercion: The Only Difference between Socialism and Unionism," *American Industries*, February 15, 1904, 11. See also the speech of John Kirby (later to become NAM president) at the 1904 NAM convention, in which he repeatedly used "socialism" and "unions" more or less interchangeably and explicitly argued that the labor movement "has fallen a complete victim to your foreign socialist. Some of the labor leaders deny they are socialists, but while saying they are not socialists they are at the same time constantly preaching socialism." National Association of Manufacturers, *Proceedings of the Ninth Annual Convention*, Pittsburgh, PA, May 17–19, 1904 (New York: Issued from the Secretary's Office), 108.

15. Randall Bartlett, *Economic Foundations of Political Power* (New York: Free Press, 1973), 147.

16. Marshall Cushing to Dear Sir, March 28, 1906, US Congress, Senate, Subcommittee of the Committee on the Judiciary, *Maintenance of a Lobby to Influence Legislation: Appendix: Exhibits Introduced during the Hearings*, 63rd Cong., 1st sess., 1913, 619–20. Hereafter cited as *Maintenance Appendix*.

17. Joseph A. McCartin, *Labor's Great War: The Struggle for Industrial Democracy and the Origins of Modern American Labor Relations, 1912–1921* (Chapel Hill: University of North Carolina Press, 1997).

18. Or, as Howell John Harris notes, middle-class attitudes toward unions in the early twentieth century and beyond were vacillating, tending to end up in a "synthesis" that basically contended that "trade unions were a good thing, in theory, and industrial democracy, in the abstract, desirable, though nobody really knew what it meant; but that

union power was in practice suspect whenever it showed itself." "Industrial Democracy and Liberal Capitalism, 1890–1925," in *Industrial Democracy in America: The Ambiguous Promise*, ed. Nelson Lichtenstein and Howell John Harris (New York: Cambridge University Press, 1993), 54.

19. See the discussion on this in Rosanne Currarino, "The Politics of 'More': The Labor Question and the Idea of Economic Liberty in Industrial America," *Journal of American History* 93, no. 1 (June 2006): 17–36.

20. Howard B. Rock, *Artisans of the New Republic: The Tradesmen of New York City in the Age of Jefferson* (New York: New York University Press, 1984); Bruce Laurie, *Artisans into Workers: Labor in Nineteenth-Century America* (New York: Hill and Wang, 1989); Sean Wilentz, *Chants Democratic: New York City & the Rise of the American Working Class* (New York: Oxford University Press, 1984). For a modern argument for one model of including workers in firm governance, see Isabelle Ferreras, *Firms as Political Entities: Saving Democracy through Economic Bicameralism* (New York: Cambridge University Press, 2017).

21. Andrew W. Cohen, *The Racketeer's Progress: Chicago and the Struggle for the Modern American Economy, 1900–1940* (New York: Cambridge University Press, 2004).

22. Shelton Stromquist, *Reinventing "the People": The Progressive Movement, the Class Problem, and the Origins of Modern Liberalism* (Urbana: University of Illinois Press, 2006). On Progressive reformers, see also Michael McGerr, *A Fierce Discontent: The Rise and Fall of the Progressive Movement in America, 1870–1920* (New York: Oxford University Press, 2003). On repression of the IWW, see Ahmed A. White, *Under the Iron Heel: The Wobblies and the Capitalist War on Radical Unionism* (Berkeley: University of California Press, 2022).

23. As William G. Roy has pointed out with regard to understanding the rise of the corporation, we are often strangely obsessed with evaluating the morality and motivations of famous individual businessmen. Was Andrew Carnegie's philanthropy genuinely meant? Was John D. Rockefeller a true Christian? Yet as Roy argues, whether industrial magnates "were motivated by greed, order, or charity is less important" than "the economic resources they could draw on, the economic relationships that states enforced, and the institutional forms they could adopt to achieve wealth, order, or charity." *Socializing Capital: The Rise of the Large Industrial Corporation in America* (Princeton, NJ: Princeton University Press, 1997), 262.

24. Howell John Harris, *Bloodless Victories: The Rise and Fall of the Open Shop in the Philadelphia Metal Trades, 1890–1940* (New York: Cambridge University Press, 2000); Sidney Fine, *"Without Blare of Trumpets": Walter Drew, the National Erectors' Association, and the Open Shop Movement, 1903–57* (Ann Arbor: University of Michigan Press, 1995); William Millikan, *Union against Unions: The Minneapolis Citizens Alliance and Its Fights against Organized Labor, 1903–1947* (St. Paul: Minnesota Historical Society Press, 2001). For an earlier period, see Sven Beckert, *The Monied Metropolis: New York City and the Consolidation of the American Bourgeoisie, 1850–1896* (New York: Cambridge University Press, 2001).

25. Jeffrey Haydu, *Citizen Employers: Business Communities and Labor in Cincinnati and San Francisco, 1870–1916* (Ithaca, NY: Cornell University Press, 2008), and Haydu's other work cited in the chapters that follow.

26. Elizabeth Fones-Wolf, *Selling Free Enterprise: The Business Assault on Labor and Liberalism, 1945–60* (Urbana: University of Illinois Press, 1995).

27. Julie Greene, *Pure and Simple Politics: The American Federation of Labor and Political Activism, 1881–1917* (New York: Cambridge University Press, 1998), especially chapter 3; see also Greene, "Dinner-Pail Politics: Employers, Workers, and Partisan Culture in the Progressive Era," in *Labor Histories: Class, Politics and the Working-Class Experience*, ed. Eric Arnesen, Julie Greene, and Bruce Laurie (Urbana: University of Illinois Press, 1998), 71–96. For another labor history that pays plenty of attention to employers, see David Montgomery, *The Fall of the House of Labor: The Workplace, the State, and American Labor Activism, 1865–1925* (Cambridge: Cambridge University Press, 1987), especially chapter 6.

28. Chad Pearson, *Reform or Repression: Organizing America's Anti-union Movement* (Philadelphia: University of Pennsylvania Press, 2015) (which I originally encountered in its dissertation form).

29. Jennifer Delton, *The Industrialists: How the National Association of Manufacturers Shaped American Capitalism* (Princeton, NJ: Princeton University Press, 2020). Before Delton's work, the only monograph explicitly on the NAM was Albert K. Steigerwalt, *The National Association of Manufacturers: A Study in Business Leadership, 1895–1914* (Ann Arbor: Bureau of Business Research, Graduate School of Business Administration, University of Michigan, 1964), which, besides being rather dated, has a somewhat hagiographic tone. Steigerwalt was involved in the NAM's abortive history project in the 1940s and 1950s; he was allowed access to the association's files after the NAM determined that although he could not be expected to "suppress any information on the Association," he did have "a free-enterprise mind." Vada Horsch to Earl Bunting, July 20, 1949, series I, box 43, National Association of Manufacturers Records, accession number 1411, Hagley Museum and Library, Wilmington, DE. Hereafter cited as NAM Records.

30. Kim Phillips-Fein, *Invisible Hands: The Making of the Conservative Movement from the New Deal to Reagan* (New York: W. W. Norton, 2009); Tami J. Friedman, "Exploiting the North–South Differential: Corporate Power, Southern Politics, and the Decline of Organized Labor after World War II," *Journal of American History* 95, no. 2 (September 2008): 323–48; Elizabeth Tandy Shermer, *Sunbelt Capitalism: Phoenix and the Transformation of American Politics* (Philadelphia: University of Pennsylvania Press, 2013); Nancy MacLean, *Democracy in Chains: The Deep History of the Radical Right's Stealth Plan for America* (New York: Penguin Books, 2018); Lawrence B. Glickman, *Free Enterprise: An American History* (New Haven, CT: Yale University Press, 2019). See also Amy C. Wallhermfechtel, "Shaping the Right to Work: The Cecil B. DeMille Foundation's Role in State and National Right to Work Campaigns" (PhD diss., Saint Louis University, 2014). For yet a newer wave of employer resistance, see Lane Windham, *Knocking on Labor's Door: Union Organizing in the 1970s and the Roots of a New Economic Divide* (Chapel Hill: University of North Carolina Press, 2017).

31. Christopher L. Tomlins, *Law, Labor, and Ideology in the Early American Republic* (New York: Cambridge University Press, 1993); William E. Forbath, "The Ambiguities of Free Labor: Labor and the Law in the Gilded Age," *Wisconsin Law Review* 767 (1985): 767–817; Victoria Hattam, *Labor Visions and State Power: The Origins of Business Unionism in the United States* (Princeton, NJ: Princeton University Press, 1993).

Chapter 1. *The Invention of the Closed Shop*

1. *Daily Picayune*, April 15, 1903, 4. About the epigraph: The translation is "Remember the old police maxim: Who profits from the crime?" The English-language version of the album (Land of Black Gold) was translated by Leslie Lonsdale-Cooper and Michael Turner.

2. For more on the rise of the modern labor movement, see chapters 2 and 3. See also David Montgomery, *Workers' Control in America: Studies in the History of Work, Technology and Labor Struggles* (New York: Cambridge University Press, 1979), especially chapters 1 and 4; and William E. Forbath, *Law and the Shaping of the American Labor Movement* (Cambridge, MA: Harvard University Press, 1991). The boycott was an especially powerful weapon locally or with products mainly bought by workers. For example, NAM president James Van Cleave found that his business was severely endangered by a boycott resulting from a fight he had picked with the molders' union. His company, Buck's Stove and Range, was put on the AFL's unfair list in 1907, and order cancellations flowed in from all parts of the country. As a union member had warned Van Cleave, "Your class of people are not buying your stoves. . . . They have steam heat and the working men are using the Stoves." Quoted in Daniel R. Ernst, *Lawyers against Labor: From Individual Rights to Corporate Liberalism* (Urbana: University of Illinois Press, 1995), 128–29.

3. On precirculation, see, for example, "National Association of Manufacturers Will Meet," *American Artisan and Hardware Record*, April 11, 1903, 21; and *Daily Picayune*, April 15, 1903, 4.

4. Report of David M. Parry quoted in the *Daily Picayune*, April 16, 1903, 14; and in the *New York Times*, April 15, 1903, 3.

5. Chapter 2 delves deeper into the history of the membership requirement.

6. Mancur Olson, *The Logic of Collective Action: Public Goods and the Theory of Groups* (Cambridge, MA: Harvard University Press, 1965), 12–13.

7. James King in National Association of Manufacturers, *Proceedings of the Eighth Annual Convention*, New Orleans, LA, April 14–16, 1903 (New York: Issued from the Secretary's Office), 246. At this convention the NAM considered a graded fee based on the number of employees or some other measure but ultimately rejected the idea. Conversion from Samuel H. Williamson, "Seven Ways to Compute the Relative Value of a U.S. Dollar Amount, 1790 to Present," Measuring Worth, accessed November 22, 2021, https://www.measuringworth.com/calculators/uscompare/.

8. Hayes Robbins, "Freeing San Francisco," *Public Policy* 11, no. 23 (December 1904): 272.

9. Millikan, *Union against Unions*, 38.

10. On AABA, see Ernst, *Lawyers against Labor*, 50. The NAM's foreign department, which included translation and credit report services, was the largest item in its budget in 1905; see "Treasurer's Annual Report," in National Association of Manufacturers, *Proceedings of the Tenth Annual Convention*, Atlanta, GA, May 16–18, 1905 (New York: Issued from the Secretary's Office), 102–6. On NFA, see "Pink Bulletin," May 19, 1908, box 1, folder 3, National Founders' Association Records, accession number LR001292, Walter P. Reuther Library, Detroit, MI; extracts from the report of the commissioner (O. P. Briggs) at the NFA annual convention in the *Iron Age*, November 23, 1905, 1382–84.

See also Pearson, *Reform or Repression*, 46, 76–77, 98, 149–50, 163–65; Fine, *"Without Blare of Trumpets,"* 39.

11. Beyond Mulhall's own report, there is evidence in the correspondence that he did in fact send money to be delivered to labor leaders in Portsmouth, and the strike was originally called off everywhere but at one company on the same date as the checks reached Portsmouth. See unsigned [Mulhall] to Ferdinand [Schwedtman], April 21, 1909; unsigned [Mulhall] to Mitchell Jordan, April 21, 1909; unsigned [Mulhall] to J. P. Bird, April 28, 1909; H. T. Bannon to M. M. Mulhall, April 29, 1909; M. M. Mulhall to Ferdinand [Schwedtman], May 5, 1909; George D. Selby to Martin M. Mulhall, May 6, 1909, all in *Maintenance Appendix*, 2818–23, 2825, 2837–38, 2841, 2856, 2857. See also "Selby Shoe Company" in State of Ohio, Board of Arbitration, *Seventeenth Annual Report to the Governor of the State of Ohio for the Year Ending December 31, 1909* (Columbus, OH: F. J. Heer Printing Company, 1911), 8–21. One of the Knights of Labor leaders later denied that the strike had been called off because of Mulhall's activities but confirmed that Mulhall had strewn bribes about him and had claimed that the NAM would pay a $1,000 "donation" to the shoe workers' relief fund if the strike was called off. C. A. Ackley to Senator [William] Hughes, n.d. [ca. July 1913], 63A-F15, box 98, Records of the United States Senate, Record Group 46, 57th–63rd Congresses, National Archives, Washington, DC. Hereafter cited as Senate Records, RG 46.

12. For some examples, see Jeffrey Haydu, "Two Logics of Class Formation? Collective Identities among Proprietary Employers, 1880–1900," *Politics & Society* 27, no. 4 (December 1999): 511.

13. William G. Roy and Rachel Parker-Gwin, "How Many Logics of Collective Action?," *Theory and Society* 28, no. 2 (April 1999): 203–37. Richard W. Gable notes the NAM's efforts to "enliven the spark of group consciousness through indoctrination and member services programs." "A Political Analysis of an Employers' Association: The National Association of Manufacturers" (PhD diss., University of Chicago, 1950), 282. See also Arthur J. McIvor, *Organised Capital: Employers' Associations and Industrial Relations in Northern England, 1880–1939* (Cambridge: Cambridge University Press, 2002), which notes the role of British "employers' associations . . . in bolstering solidarity" (81).

14. James Emery, the NAM's chief counsel, spoke in twenty-four major cities in 1910, while President Kirby spoke in ten; a large portion of the venues were business organizations. Sarah Lyons Watts, *Order against Chaos: Business Culture and Labor Ideology in America, 1880–1915* (New York: Greenwood Press, 1991), 146. For the term "revival meetings" (which Watts quotes as well), see J. Kirby Jr. to Ferdinand Schwedtman, April 23, 1909, *Maintenance Appendix*, 2829: "Am glad to hear of your successful revival meetings, which of course means converts."

15. *American Industries*, October 1, 1903, 1; for a similar account of successful and united employer resistance, this one against the type founders, see *American Industries*, March 1, 1904, 3. For a story about a national organization, see the letter to the editor by Berkley R. Merwin, president of the National Association of Merchant Tailors, *American Industries*, September 1, 1903, 4.

16. *American Industries*, September 15, 1903, 6.

17. *American Industries*, September 1, 1905, 6.

18. See, for example, Pearson, *Reform or Repression*, 161–63. NAM annual meetings were also, of course, accompanied by the usual receptions and outings; for example, the

1905 convention in Atlanta included a barbecue and receptions at the Capital City Club and the Driving Club. NAM, *Proceedings* (1905), 16–17.

19. *American Industries*, September 1, 1902, 6.

20. *American Industries*, April 1, 1903, 3; *American Industries*, October 1, 1903, 1–2.

21. *American Industries*, March 15, 1903, 1–3.

22. NAM, *Proceedings* (1903), 167–73; Marnie Jones, *Holy Toledo: Religion and Politics in the Life of "Golden Rule" Jones* (Lexington: University Press of Kentucky, 2014).

23. For instance, William McCarroll (a New York leather manufacturer and NAM vice president for New York from 1902 through 1905) emphasized that David Parry and his successor James Van Cleave had practically given their lives to the movement for the open shop. Seconding the views of McCarroll, John Kirby (NAM president from 1909 through 1913) underlined that he had never been interested in the NAM's work at all until David Parry had turned the organization toward organized labor. Remarks of Mr. William McCarroll and remarks of Mr. John Kirby Jr., both in National Association of Manufacturers, *Proceedings of the Twenty-Fifth Annual Convention*, New York City, May 17–19, 1920 (New York: Issued from the Secretary's Office), 44–53.

24. Gerald Friedman, *State-Making and Labor Movements: France and the United States, 1876–1914* (Ithaca, NY: Cornell University Press, 1998), especially chapter 1, quote on 33.

25. Editorial entitled "For Peace, by Fighting," *American Industries*, October 15, 1903, 6.

26. Secretary's annual report, NAM, *Proceedings* (1903), 98; secretary's annual report, NAM, *Proceedings* (1904), 34; Gable, "A Political Analysis," 191–97. Between the manufacturing censuses of 1900 and 1914, the number of manufacturing establishments (excluding hand and neighborhood industries) grew only by about a third. US Department of Commerce, Bureau of the Census, *Census of Manufactures 1914* (Washington, DC: GPO, 1919), 2:17.

27. Troy Rondinone, *The Great Industrial War: Framing Class Conflict in the Media, 1865–1950* (New Brunswick, NJ: Rutgers University Press, 2009); Eric Foner, *Reconstruction: America's Unfinished Revolution, 1863–1877* (New York: Harper & Row, 1988), chapter 11.

28. Mark Aldrich, "Tariffs and Trusts, Profiteers and Middlemen: Popular Explanations for the High Cost of Living, 1897–1920," *History of Political Economy* 45, no. 4 (November 2013): 693–746; David Nasaw, "Gilded Age Gospels," and Alan Dawley, "The Abortive Rule of Big Money," both in *Ruling America: A History of Wealth and Power in a Democracy*, ed. Steve Fraser and Gary Gerstle (Cambridge, MA: Harvard University Press, 2005), 123–48, 149–80 (quote about the Senate as the "Millionaires' Club" on 155). On the theme of industry, civilization, and evolution, see Daniel E. Bender, *American Abyss: Savagery and Civilization in the Age of Industry* (Ithaca, NY: Cornell University Press, 2009).

29. On middle-class reform and the question of class in the Progressive Era, see Stromquist, *Reinventing "the People."* See also McGerr, *A Fierce Discontent*; Mary O. Furner, "Knowing Capitalism: Public Investigation and the Labor Question in the Long Progressive Era," in *The State and Economic Knowledge: The American and British Experiences*, ed. Mary O. Furner and Barry Supple (New York: Press Syndicate of the University of Cambridge, 1990), 241–86; Mark Pittenger, *Class Unknown: Undercover Investigations of American Work and Poverty from the Progressive Era to the Present* (New York: New York University Press, 2012).

30. Kathleen Brady, *Ida Tarbell: Portrait of a Muckraker* (New York: Seaview/Putnam, 1984), chapter 7.

31. Address by Mr. John Kirby Jr. at a meeting of the Citizens' Industrial Association of St. Louis, printed in *The Exponent* 3, no. 2 (February 1906): 16.

32. Pearson, *Reform or Repression*, 66–72.

33. On streetcar strikes, see Scott Molloy, *Trolley Wars: Streetcar Workers on the Line* (Lebanon: University of New Hampshire Press, 1996), which is very useful for understanding streetcar workers even though it is limited in scope to Rhode Island, and Stephen H. Norwood, *Strikebreaking & Intimidation: Mercenaries and Masculinity in Twentieth-Century America* (Chapel Hill: University of North Carolina Press, 2002), chapter 2.

34. "Declaration of Principles," NAM, *Proceedings* (1903), 165.

35. Any issue of the NAM's *American Industries* in the early twentieth century, especially between roughly 1903 and 1908, furnishes ample examples. There is some variation in the specifics. Some articles rejected all union demands as violations of the rights of the employer; see, for example, Thomas Shaw, "Fundamentals in Regard to Labor," *American Industries*, March 1, 1904, 9. Others implied that workers had the right to form organizations to demand higher wages; see, for example, W. B. Flickinger, "How the Community Organization Restores the Industrial Equilibrium," *American Industries*, November 1, 1904, 13, which stated that "if capital demands the right to combine and organize for the purpose of fixing the selling price of its product, then labor has the same right." However, Flickinger thought that mostly unions should focus on such projects as "general moral uplifting by lecturers" and "encouragement of industry, of thrift, of sobriety."

36. For a few examples, see the *American Industries* issues of March 15, 1903, October 15, 1903, and May 15, 1906. For funeral-related news items, see *American Industries*, March 2, 1903, 15; *American Industries*, August 1, 1903, 16; and *American Industries*, January 1, 1904, 16.

37. "F. E. Myers' Address," *Iron Age*, November 17, 1904, 57–58; *American Industries*, January 1, 1906, 2.

38. E. F. Du Brul to James O'Connell, October 22, 1903, box 5, folder 2, NCF Records. By contrast, employers credited themselves with efforts "to promote the vital interests of the American boy by advancing him to independence in industrial life." "To Educate Men: Detroit Employers' Association and Board of Education Co-operate," *American Employer* 1, no. 5 (December 1912): 303–4. See also Elizabeth Fones-Wolf, "The Politics of Vocationalism: Coalitions and Industrial Education in the Progressive Era," *Historian* 46, no. 1 (1983): 39–55.

39. For particularly good examples of hyperbole on the dangers of the closed shop, see W. C. Shepherd, "Open Shops, Freedom, Opportunity, Progress, Fellowship," *American Industries*, January 15, 1904, 1.

40. Examples abound in *American Industries*; for one article making this point along with many of the other standard ones, see H. T. Newcomb, "Some Recent Phases of the Labor Problem," eight-page supplement, *American Industries*, October 1, 1904, 1.

41. Samuel Gompers, *The Union Shop and Its Antithesis* (Washington, DC: American Federation of Labor, 1920), 7.

42. President Parry's annual address, NAM, *Proceedings* (1905), 46.

43. On southern white victimization narratives, see Ted Tunnell, "Creating 'the Propaganda of History': Southern Editors and the Origins of 'Carpetbagger and Scalawag,'"

Journal of Southern History 72, no. 4 (November 2006): 789–82; and Anne S. Rubin, *A Shattered Nation: The Rise and Fall of the Confederacy, 1861–1868* (Chapel Hill: University of North Carolina Press, 2005), 142–45, 243–45. For more discussion of NAM members' self-made self-image versus reality, see chapter 4.

44. Report of President Gompers, American Federation of Labor, *Report of Proceedings of the Twenty-Second Annual Convention of the American Federation of Labor*, New Orleans, Louisiana, November 13–22, 1902 (Washington, DC: Law Reporter Printing Company, 1902), 9, 11, 23–24; *Albuquerque Daily Citizen*, November 12, 1901, 1.

45. *American Federationist* 10, no. 3 (March 1903): 173; *American Federationist* 10, no. 4 (April 1903): 266–68; *American Federationist* 10, no. 5 (May 1903): 365. Although the dismissive attitude was likely partly posturing, the AFL's initial unconcern is perhaps underlined by the fact that only after the 1903 convention did the *Federationist* get Parry's initials right; the first two articles referred to him as "I. M. Parry."

46. Editorial in *American Federationist*, November 1903, reprinted in the pamphlet *Open Shop Editorials* by Samuel Gompers, RG 98-002, 41/14, AFL-CIO Papers, George Meany Memorial AFL-CIO Archive, University of Maryland, College Park.

47. William English Walling, "Open Shops Mean the Destruction of the Unions" (reprinted from *The Independent*), *American Industries*, open-shop supplement, September 1, 1904, 7.

48. Frank T. Stockton, *The Closed Shop in American Trade Unions* (Baltimore, MD: Johns Hopkins Press, 1911), 9.

49. Google's n-grams are described at https://books.google.com/ngrams/info and presented in Jean-Baptiste Michel et al., "Quantitative Analysis of Culture Using Millions of Digitized Books," *Science*, January 14, 2011, 176–82.

50. Nate Holdren, *Injury Impoverished: Workplace Accidents, Capitalism, and Law in the Progressive Era* (New York: Cambridge University Press, 2020); Hugh D. Hindman, *Child Labor: An American History* (New York: M. E. Sharpe, 2002). The average weekly work time in manufacturing in 1900 was about fifty-five hours. Ethel B. Jones, "New Estimates of Hours of Work per Week and Hourly Earnings, 1900–1957," *Review of Economics and Statistics* 45, no. 4 (November 1963): 374–85.

51. "A Glimpse at the Officers' Reports," *Typographical Journal* 25, no. 2 (August 1904): 110.

52. Robert H. Wiebe, "The Anthracite Strike of 1902: A Record of Confusion," *Mississippi Valley Historical Review* 48, no. 2 (September 1961): 229–51. Anthracite Coal Strike Commission quoted in Pearson, *Reform or Repression*, 60.

53. Theodore Roosevelt to George Cortelyou, July 14, 1903, in *Addresses and Presidential Messages of Theodore Roosevelt, 1902–1904*, by Theodore Roosevelt (New York: G. P. Putnam's Sons, 1904), 274–75.

54. Ray Stannard Baker, "The Right to Work: The Story of the Non-striking Miners," *McClure's Magazine* 20, no. 3 (January 1903): 323 ff.

55. Craig Phelan, "John Mitchell and the Politics of the Trade Agreement, 1898–1917," in *The United Mine Workers of America: A Model of Industrial Solidarity?* (University Park: Pennsylvania State University Press, 1996), 72–103; Wiebe, "The Anthracite Strike." On violence, see Rhodri Jeffreys-Jones, *Violence and Reform in American History* (New York: New Viewpoints, 1978). Because of the complexities in how the miners were paid, whether their pay was "fair" or even comparable to that of workers with similar skill

levels in other industries was not a simple question; indeed, the Anthracite Coal Strike Commission's final report bleakly concluded that "it is impossible to be accurate in this matter." *Report to the President on the Anthracite Coal Strike, May–October 1902*, S. Doc. No. 6, 58th Cong., special session, 1902, 49.

56. Dimitra Doukas, "Corporate Capitalism on Trial: The Hearings of the Anthracite Coal Strike Commission, 1902–1903," *Identities* 3, no. 3 (1997): 367–98.

57. Statement of Lewis G. Hines, national legislative representative of the American Federation of Labor, in debate with Congressman Clare Hoffman over station WGN, Chicago, Illinois, December 15, 1946, at 6:00 p.m., RG 98-002, 41/16, AFL-CIO Papers.

58. Nelson Lichtenstein, "Taft-Hartley: A Slave-Labor Law?," *Catholic University Law Review* 47, no. 763 (1998): 765.

59. Reuel Schiller, "Singing 'the Right-to-Work Blues': The Politics of Race in the Campaign for 'Voluntary Unionism' in Postwar California," in *The Right and Labor in America: Politics, Ideology, and Imagination*, ed. Nelson Lichtenstein and Elizabeth Tandy Shermer (Philadelphia: University of Pennsylvania Press, 2016), 139–59.

60. National Right to Work Legal Defense Foundation, "Right to Work Frequently-Asked Questions," accessed April 20, 2019, https://www.nrtw.org/right-to-work-frequently -asked-questions.

61. National Right to Work Committee, "About the National Right to Work Committee," accessed April 20, 2019, https://nrtwc.org/about/. (Note that the phrasing has since eliminated the David and Goliath language, but the 2019 version can still be accessed through the Wayback Machine: https://web.archive.org/web/20190831184558/https://nrtwc.org/ about/). The National Right to Work Legal Defense Foundation and the National Right to Work Committee are technically separate organizations, but the websites share much of the exact same language. On the history and funding of the National Right to Work Committee and similar organizations, see Sophia Z. Lee, "Whose Rights? Litigating the Right to Work, 1940–1980," in Lichtenstein and Shermer, *The Right and Labor*, 160–80; Celine McNicholas, Zane Mokhiber, and Marni von Wilpert, "Janus and Fair Share Fees: The Organizations Financing the Attack on Unions' Ability to Represent Workers," Economic Policy Institute, February 21, 2018, https://www.epi.org/publication/janus-and-fair-share -fees-the-organizations-financing-the-attack-on-unions-ability-to-represent-workers/.

Chapter 2. The Deep History of the Closed or Union Shop

1. Editorial in *American Federationist*, November 1903, reprinted in the pamphlet *Open Shop Editorials* by Samuel Gompers, RG 98-002, 41/14, AFL-CIO Papers.

2. *American Industries*, January 15, 1904, 14.

3. Anthony Ittner, "Apprentices and Trade Schools," *American Industries*, July 1, 1904, 9; W. C. Shepherd, "Americanism the Living Issue," *American Industries*, July 1, 1904, 13.

4. William Clerkin to John J. Kirby Jr., March 7, 1912, reprinted in "Two Actual Instances of the Failure of the Closed Shop," *Square Deal* 10 (May 1912): 329–33. The sentiment was echoed by employers affiliated with the National Civic Federation, which was attempting to promote negotiations between organized labor and employers. For example, Charles L. Eidlitz of the Building Trades Employer Association of New York, who was involved in the NCF, used almost identical language to enshrine individual rights and condemn

union coercion: he insisted that it was no more right for the employer to ask about union membership than about "whether he is a Catholic or Protestant or a Republican or a Democrat or a Mason." Eidlitz quoted in the *New York Times*, December 20, 1903, 5.

5. J. Maddison to R. M. Easley, September 23, 1903, box 6, folder 3, NCF Records.

6. See, for example, Shaw, "Fundamentals."

7. Heather Swanson, "The Illusion of Economic Structure: Craft Guilds in Late Medieval English Towns," *Past and Present*, no. 121 (November 1988): 29–48; Robert Darnton, *The Literary Underground of the Old Regime* (Cambridge, MA: Harvard University Press, 1982), chapter 5; Catharina Lis and Hugo Soly, *Worthy Efforts: Attitudes to Work and Workers in Pre-Industrial Europe* (Leiden: Brill, 2012), 430. In the United States, too, rules about apprenticeships and who could practice a craft were never entirely firm and were fraying by the time of the revolution; see Richard B. Morris, *Government and Labor in Early America* (New York: Columbia University Press, 1946), chapter 3.

8. Wilentz, *Chants Democratic*, 28; O. F. Hamouda and B. B. Price, "The Justice of the Just Price," *European Journal of the History of Economic Thought* 4, no. 2 (Summer 1997): 191–216, esp. 198–200. Note that setting the price of work by custom did not always mean that the workers benefited: Eric Hobsbawm, for instance, argues that customary price could also mean that employers were able to pay less than market price for labor. E. J. Hobsbawm, "Custom, Wages and Work-Load," in *Labouring Men: Studies in the History of Labour* (New York: Basic Books, 1964), 347–48. On the involvement of (master) artisans in various aspects of commercial life and on variance between journeymen's prospects in different trades in early nineteenth-century New York, see Rock, *Artisans*, chapters 6 and 7.

9. Wilentz, *Chants Democratic*, 30–32, 50, 56–60. For an overview of the transition from artisan to wage work and the development of the labor movement in the nineteenth-century United States, see Laurie, *Artisans into Workers*.

10. Jerome L. Toner, *The Closed Shop* (Washington, DC: American Council on Public Affairs, 1944), 58–63.

11. See, for example, David Bensman, *The Practice of Solidarity: American Hat Finishers in the Nineteenth Century* (Urbana: University of Illinois Press, 1985), chapter 4.

12. Sidney Webb and Beatrice Webb, *Industrial Democracy* (London: Longmans, Green, 1902), 167–70.

13. Walter Nelles, "The First American Labor Case," *Yale Law Journal* 41, no. 2 (December 1931): 167.

14. Stockton, *The Closed Shop*, 21.

15. Stockton, *The Closed Shop*, 21, 25–27.

16. Stockton, *The Closed Shop*, 23.

17. For example, rather than imposing a universal closed-shop rule, Maryland cigarmakers in the 1850s required men who had worked in cities where an organization existed to be members of such organizations, while the 1858 annual convention of the glassblowers adopted a resolution forbidding members to work with anyone working below union scale. Stockton, *The Closed Shop*, 27–29.

18. For a discussion of the strength of such practices of secrecy, as well as of the depth of craft identity even in the late nineteenth century, see, for example, Bensman, *The Practice of Solidarity*, 44–45. Bensman notes that "the hatters' exclusive fellowship was bounded by a wall of silence; hatters were sticklers for secrecy."

19. The prosecutor in the case *Commonwealth v. Hunt*, quoted in Christopher L. Tomlins, *The State and the Unions: Labor Relations, Law, and the Organized Labor Movement in America, 1880–1960* (New York: Cambridge University Press, 1984), 43. Hugh Armstrong Clegg, *Trade Unionism under Collective Bargaining* (Oxford: Basil Blackwell, 1976), 7, makes the argument for vagueness as prudent for early British craft unions.

20. The traditional powerful unit among hatters was the local, which attempted to control work practices in shops within a particular town. In the 1850s, in response to increasing interregional competition in the hat industry, the hatters created a national organization, the Hat Finishers' National Trade Association. The new organization established by the silk hatters in the late 1860s was the Silk and Fur Hat Finishers' National Association. Bensman, *The Practice of Solidarity*, 22–25.

21. Wilentz, *Chants Democratic*, 58–59.

22. Quoted in E. P. Thompson, "The Moral Economy of the English Crowd in the Eighteenth Century," *Past & Present*, no. 50 (February 1971): 86.

23. E. P. Thompson, *Customs in Common: Studies in Traditional Popular Culture* (New York: New Press, 1993), 1, 6.

24. Terry Bouton, *Taming Democracy: "The People," the Founders, and the Struggle over the American Revolution* (New York: Oxford University Press, 2007), 218; on hierarchy and the forces weakening it, see, for example, Gordon S. Wood, *The Radicalism of the American Revolution* (New York: Vintage Books, 1991), especially chapters 7, 8, and 15.

25. The scholarship on ordinary people during and after the American Revolution and on their economic demands, assertions of moral economy arguments, and insistence on the necessity of curbing economic inequality if popular, republican government was to survive has grown quite sizable; see, for example, Woody Holton, *Forced Founders: Indians, Debtors, Slaves, and the Making of the American Revolution in Virginia* (Chapel Hill: University of North Carolina Press, 1999); Gary Nash, *The Unknown American Revolution: The Unruly Birth of Democracy and the Struggle to Create America* (New York: Viking, 2005); Michael A. McDonnell, "Class War? Class Struggles during the American Revolution in Virginia," *William and Mary Quarterly* 63, no. 2 (April 2006): 305–44; Bouton, *Taming Democracy*. Quote from Woody Holton, "An 'Excess of Democracy'—or a Shortage? The Federalists' Earliest Adversaries," *Journal of the Early Republic* 25, no. 3 (October 2005): 363. The name "Pennsylvania Regulation" is from Bouton, who notes that the name "Whiskey Rebellion" was what Alexander Hamilton, its biggest opponent, called it and that "the term implicitly ridicules the protest, much as Hamilton intended" (218).

26. Eric Foner, *Tom Paine and Revolutionary America* (New York: Oxford University Press, 1976), chapter 2.

27. William J. Novak, *The People's Welfare: Law and Regulation in Nineteenth-Century America* (Chapel Hill: University of North Carolina Press, 1996), 19; for examples of lists of regulations, see, for example, 3–6, 15–16.

28. Novak, *The People's Welfare*, chapter 3, quote on 90; R. H. Britnell, "Forstall, Forestalling and the Statute of Forestallers," *English Historical Review* 102, no. 402 (January 1987): 89–102. The assize of bread had deep roots in early medieval times and was a serious matter: the assize was adjusted (sometimes as often as weekly) according to the price of wheat, bailiffs regularly checked that it was being followed, and "infractions were

severely punished, offenders being fined, exposed upon the pillory, thrust into prison, or suspended from their occupation." Alan S. C. Ross, "The Assize of Bread," *Economic History Review* 9, no. 2 (1956): 334.

29. Kate Masur, "The People's Welfare, Police Powers, and the Rights of Free People of African Descent," *American Journal of Legal History* 57, no. 2 (June 2017): 242.

30. Tomlins, *The State and the Unions*, 36.

31. Ely Moore quoted in Tomlins, *Law, Labor, and Ideology*, 156, footnote 85; see also more generally 152–60.

32. Gerald S. Henig, "The Jacksonian Attitude toward Abolitionism in the 1830's," *Tennessee Historical Quarterly* 28, no. 1 (Spring 1969): 42–56.

33. Forbath, "The Ambiguities of Free Labor." I have used the formulation "his labor" since, though many women did in fact work for pay, the discourse of free labor definitely imagined the canonical free worker as male, and the freedom of contract was one badge of his difference from dependents like women or slaves.

34. Quoted in Forbath, "The Ambiguities of Free Labor," 785.

35. William Graham Sumner, for instance, argued in this vein in his 1883 *What the Social Classes Owe Each Other*, equating subjection and claims to sustenance and insisting that "in escaping from subjection they [the former slaves] have lost their claims" but obviously are the better off for it. Quoted in Jonathan Levy, *Freaks of Fortune: The Emerging World of Capitalism and Risk in America* (Cambridge, MA: Harvard University Press, 2014), 193.

36. Quoted in Amy Dru Stanley, *From Bondage to Contract: Wage Labor, Marriage, and the Market in the Age of Slave Emancipation* (New York: Cambridge University Press, 1998), 88–89.

37. *Chicago Daily Tribune*, November 19, 1871, 2; Tomlins, *The State and the Unions*, 46.

38. Stanley, *From Bondage to Contract*, 91–97.

39. Currarino, *The Labor Question*, 24.

40. Eric Foner, *Free Soil, Free Labor, Free Men: The Ideology of the Republican Party before the Civil War* (New York: Oxford University Press, 1970), especially chapters 1 and 2. On this theme, see also Cedric De Leon, *Origins of Right to Work: Antilabor Democracy in Nineteenth-Century Chicago* (Ithaca, NY: Cornell University Press, 2015), which emphasizes the creation of an "antilabor democracy" in the post–Civil War decades.

41. Recorder Moses Levy presiding over the case, quoted in Tomlins, *The State and the Unions*, 37.

42. Philadelphia Cordwainers, *Commonwealth v. Pullis*, 1806, in *A Documentary History of American Industrial Society*, vol. 3, *Labor Conspiracy Cases*, ed. John R. Commons et al. (New York: Russell & Russell, 1958), 70–71.

43. Tomlins, *The State and the Unions*, 40.

44. Horatio Woodman, ed., *Reports of Criminal Cases: Tried in the Municipal Court of the City of Boston, before Peter Oxenbridge Thacher [1823–1842]* (Boston: Charles C. Little and James Brown, 1845), 611; Walter Nelles, "Commonwealth v. Hunt," *Columbia Law Review* 32 (1932): 1134, note 21.

45. Nelles, "Commonwealth v. Hunt," 1132–33; Woodman, *Reports of Criminal Cases*, 619.

46. Woodman, *Reports of Criminal Cases*, 613–14.

47. Tomlins, *The State and the Unions*, 48–49.

48. *Journal of Commerce*, April 7, 1835, reprinted in Joseph P. Thompson, ed., *Memoir of David Hale: Late Editor of the Journal of Commerce*, 2nd ed. (Hartford, CT: E. Hunt, 1850), 414–16.

49. Levy, *Freaks of Fortune*, 7–12.

50. Forbath, "The Ambiguities of Free Labor," 795–99.

51. An 1871 decision quoted in Karen Orren, *Belated Feudalism: Labor, the Law, and Liberal Development in the United States* (New York: Cambridge University Press, 1991), 123. Orren discusses several cases relying on this logic from the 1880s and even notes that "the vast majority of judges continued to restrain strikes under the doctrine of enticement" well into the twentieth century (134).

52. David Montgomery, *Citizen Worker: The Experience of Workers in the United States with Democracy and the Free Market during the Nineteenth Century* (New York: Cambridge University Press, 1993), 47.

53. Quoted in Leon Fink, *Workingmen's Democracy: The Knights of Labor in American Politics* (Urbana: University of Illinois Press, 1985), 4. On organizational growth, see Kim Voss, *The Making of American Exceptionalism: The Knights of Labor and Class Formation in the Nineteenth Century* (Ithaca, NY: Cornell University Press, 1993), 73–76.

54. Fink, *Workingmen's Democracy*, 6–13, quote on 8.

55. Voss, *The Making of American Exceptionalism*, 76; Fink, *Workingmen's Democracy*, chapter 1.

56. Philip Taft, *The A. F. of L. in the Time of Gompers* (New York: Harper, 1957), chapters 2 and 5.

57. Voss, *The Making of American Exceptionalism*, 75–76; Shelton Stromquist, *A Generation of Boomers: The Pattern of Railroad Labor Conflict in Nineteenth-Century America* (Urbana: University of Illinois Press, 1987), 61–69. On the KOL's support for and use of the closed shop, see Toner, *The Closed Shop*, 69–71. For an early and particularly crisp statement of the business unionist rejection of theory and insistence on immediate and practical results, see the exchange between Adolph Strasser of the Cigarmakers and Senator Henry Blair at the hearings of the Senate Committee on Labor and Capital in 1883, quoted in Fink, *Workingmen's Democracy*, 8.

58. Shelton Stromquist, "The Crisis of 1894 and the Legacies of Producerism," in *The Pullman Strike and the Crisis of the 1890s: Essays on Labor and Politics*, ed. Richard Schneirov, Shelton Stromquist, and Nick Salvatore (Urbana: University of Illinois Press, 1999), 181.

59. Stromquist, *A Generation of Boomers*, table 7 on 114.

60. Lawrence Goodwyn, *The Populist Moment: A Short History of the Agrarian Revolt in America*, abridged ed. (New York: Oxford University Press, 1978), vii.

61. See Matthew Hild, *Greenbackers, Knights of Labor, and Populists: Farmer-Labor Insurgency in the Late-Nineteenth-Century South* (Athens: University of Georgia Press, 2007), chapter 4.

62. Greene, *Pure and Simple Politics*, 61–64, quote reproducing plank 10 on 62.

63. On the AFL's political stance and its evolution in the late nineteenth and early twentieth centuries, see generally Greene, *Pure and Simple Politics*. See also Robin Archer, *Why Is There No Labor Party in the United States?* (Princeton, NJ: Princeton University Press, 2010).

64. Goodwyn, *The Populist Moment*, 282; Thomas Ferguson, *Golden Rule: The Investment Theory of Party Competition and the Logic of Money-Driven Political Systems* (Chicago: University of Chicago Press, 1995), 74–76.

65. Hild, *Greenbackers*, chapter 4 and 201–4.

66. Richard Schneirov, Shelton Stromquist, and Nick Salvatore, introduction to Schneirov, Stromquist, and Salvatore, *The Pullman Strike*, 1–20; Greene, *Pure and Simple Politics*, 64–68.

67. Friedman, *State-Making*, 302, emphasis added. Robin Archer, in *Why Is There No Labor Party*, makes a similar point in discussing the 1894 AFL convention's decision to not endorse a labor party, noting that while this decision "made no sense to those unionists whose organizations had already been destroyed, or almost destroyed, in the wake of repression," it seemed prudent to the leadership of those unions that "still had something to lose." Archer, though, goes on to discuss the threat that politics posed to unions mainly in terms of exacerbating internal rifts (239–40). For an account that emphasizes the depth of workers' support for political action, see Michael Cain Pierce, *Striking with the Ballot: Ohio Labor and the Populist Party* (DeKalb: Northern Illinois University Press, 2010).

68. For an overview of socialist politics and working-class organizations in Europe, see Geoff Eley, *Forging Democracy: The History of the Left in Europe, 1850–2000* (New York: Oxford University Press, 2002), chapters 3 and 4. For an overview of the absence of the closed shop in most western European countries (except Great Britain), see Everett M. Kassalow, "The Closed and Union Shop in Western Europe: An American Perspective," *Journal of Labor Research* 1, no. 2 (Autumn 1980): 323–39.

69. See, for example, Elizabeth Jameson, *All That Glitters: Class, Conflict, and Community in Cripple Creek* (Urbana: University of Illinois Press, 1998); Tony Michels, *A Fire in Their Hearts: Yiddish Socialists in New York* (Cambridge, MA: Harvard University Press, 2009). On the AFL unions, Elizabeth Fones-Wolf and Ken Fones-Wolf, "Rank-and-File Rebellions and AFL Interference in the Affairs of National Unions: The Gompers Era," *Labor History* 35, no. 2 (March 1994): 237–59, note that rank-and-file rebellions, often pushed by unionists with a more radical outlook or a greater emphasis on industrial rather than craft-based organizing, succeeded in challenging high-handed or otherwise unresponsive leadership in several AFL unions in the 1890s and 1900s.

70. Orren, *Belated Feudalism*, 128.

Chapter 3. The Potential and Limitations of the Trade Agreement

1. Unsigned [Gertrude Beeks] to Ralph Easley, May 13, 1901, box 488, folder 4, NCF Records.

2. Joshua L. Rosenbloom, "Union Membership: 1880–1999. Table Ba4783–479," and Joshua L. Rosenbloom, "Work Stoppages, Workers Involved, Average Duration, and Person-Days Idle: 1881–1998. Table Ba4954–4964," both in *Historical Statistics of the United States, Earliest Times to the Present: Millennial Edition Online*, ed. Susan B. Carter et al. (New York: Cambridge University Press, 2006).

3. Stanley, *From Bondage to Contract*, 81–82.

4. Currarino, *The Labor Question*, 63–66; Furner, "Knowing Capitalism," 251–56. These works also provide a detailed discussion of the shift in economic thinking that took place in the late nineteenth century.

5. The 1870s and 1890s depressions were severe: in both, thousands of businesses failed, and millions were thrown out of work; indeed, the 1870s depression had alarmed observers for the first time into trying to count the unemployed, and their findings indicated that perhaps a third of Massachusetts workers were out of work. Nell Irvin Painter, *Standing at Armageddon: United States, 1877–1919* (New York: W. W. Norton, 1987). On corporate mergers, see Naomi R. Lamoreaux, *The Great Merger Movement in American Business, 1895–1904* (New York: Cambridge University Press, 1985). Generally on the sense of chaos and the need for creating order, see Painter's book, as well as Robert H. Wiebe, *The Search for Order, 1877–1920* (New York: Hill and Wang, 1967). On various reform projects, see McGerr, *A Fierce Discontent*.

6. Unsigned [Gertrude Beeks] to Ralph Easley, May 13, 1901, box 488, folder 4, NCF Records.

7. Easley's businessmen friends, upon hearing of the doctor's recommendation, promptly set up a collection among themselves to fund such a trip. John Hays Hammond and Marcus M. Marks to Dear Sir, August 3, 1909, box 488, folder 2, NCF Records.

8. Kathryn Kish Sklar, "Hull House in the 1890s: A Community of Women Reformers," *Signs* 10, no. 4 (Summer 1985): 658–77; Sklar, *Florence Kelley & the Nation's Work: The Rise of Women's Political Culture, 1830–1900* (New Haven, CT: Yale University Press, 1997); Ellen Carol DuBois, "Working Women, Class Relations, and Suffrage Militance: Harriot Stanton Blatch and the New York Woman Suffrage Movement, 1894–1909," *Journal of American History* 74, no. 1 (June 1987): 34–58; see also Stromquist, *Reinventing "the People."*

9. Currarino, *The Labor Question*, chapter 4; Furner, "Knowing Capitalism."

10. Stanley, *From Bondage to Contract*, 81–84.

11. US Strike Commission quoted in Paul Michel Taillon, *Good, Reliable, White Men: Railroad Brotherhoods, 1877–1917* (Urbana: University of Illinois Press, 2009), 111.

12. Industrial Commission, *Final Report*, 844, 845.

13. Industrial Commission, *Final Report*, 833–43, quote on 834.

14. David Montgomery, "Industrial Democracy or Democracy in Industry? The Theory and Practice of the Labor Movement, 1870–1925," in *Industrial Democracy in America: The Ambiguous Promise*, ed. Nelson Lichtenstein and Howell John Harris (New York: Cambridge University Press, 1993), 29; Sidney Webb and Beatrice Webb, "The Method of Collective Bargaining," *Economic Journal* 6, no. 21 (March 1896): 19, 25.

15. Though the commission acknowledged that arbitration was sometimes prescribed as the remedy for failed negotiations, the commission—again following the Webbs—felt that neither employers nor workers were likely to accept the verdict of an outside body or individual regarding the major contours of the conditions of employment. See Industrial Commission, *Final Report*, 833–37; Webb and Webb, *Industrial Democracy*, 224–25.

16. Gompers speaking at the Boston Monday Evening Club in 1899, quoted in Currarino, "Politics of 'More,'" 26.

17. Quoted in Hattam, *Labor Visions*, 137.

18. The brotherhoods also updated their membership initiation rituals and built much larger staffs and skyscraper offices. Taillon, *Good, Reliable, White Men*, 126–29.

19. Ethelbert Stewart, "Trade Agreements," *Annals of the American Academy of Political and Social Science* 36, no. 2 (September 1910): 67. Stewart's article is a good summary of the case made for the trade agreement in the early twentieth century.

20. Industrial Commission, *Reports of the Industrial Commission on Labor Organizations, Labor Disputes, and Arbitration, and on Railway Labor*, vol. 17 of the commission's reports (Washington, DC, 1901), xc–xci. For more detailed treatments of the development of collective bargaining and trade agreements in various industries, besides the rest of this report, see, for example, Ken Fones-Wolf, *Glass Towns: Industry, Labor, and Political Economy in Appalachia, 1890–1930s* (Chicago: University of Illinois Press, 2007); David Brody, *Steelworkers in America: The Nonunion Era*, Illini Books ed. (1960; repr., Urbana: University of Illinois Press, 1998); Montgomery, *Fall of the House of Labor*; William Graebner, "Great Expectations: The Search for Order in Bituminous Coal, 1890–1917," *Business History Review* 48, no. 1 (Spring 1974): 49–72; Montgomery, "Industrial Democracy."

21. Howard Stanger, "Cooperation, Conciliation, and Continuity: The Evolution of a Modern Grievance Procedure in the Columbus Typographical Union No. 5, 1859–1959" (PhD diss., Ohio State University, 1994), 115–24, 252–53; Emily Clark Brown, "Book and Job Printing," in *How Collective Bargaining Works: A Survey of Experience in Leading American Industries*, ed. Harry A. Millis (New York: Twentieth Century Fund, 1942), 126–28.

22. Brody, *Steelworkers in America*, 64–48; see also Fones-Wolf, *Glass Towns*, 27, noting that the commission was witnessing "an industry at the precipice of dramatic change" and that "beneath [the] calm, potential conflict swirled."

23. "The Trade Agreement in Five Great Industries," *NCF Review* 2, no. 10 (August 1906): 10.

24. Industrial Commission, *Final Report*, 835, 844; Ralph M. Easley, "The Work of the National Civic Federation," *Harper's Weekly*, November 26, 1904, 1899.

25. Unsigned [NCF office] to Samuel Gompers, December 5, 1903, box 5, folder 4, NCF Records. The letter writer (in all likelihood Easley) surmised that, given present depressed conditions, "the textile industry, metal trades, building trades and public service corporation interests, I believe, are ripe for rational treatment."

26. Marguerite Green, *The National Civic Federation and the American Labor Movement, 1900–1925* (Westport, CT: Greenwood Press, 1956), 56, 67–69.

27. "The Trade Agreement."

28. David Brian Robertson, *Capital, Labor and State: The Battle for American Labor Markets from the Civil War to the New Deal* (Lanham, MD: Rowman & Littlefield Publishers, 2000), 73–76; Cohen, *Racketeer's Progress*, 151–54.

29. Some European unions also offered selective benefits, such as additional unemployment insurance, that made membership attractive. In addition, some unions rejected the closed shop because they feared that their organization would only be weakened by the induction of members who neither knew nor cared much about the union. See, for example, Kassalow, "The Closed and Union Shop"; E. Cordova and M. Ozaki, "Union Security Arrangements: An International Overview," *International Labour Review* 119, no. 1 (January–February 1980): 19–38. Historical work on the union-shop/closed-shop question specifically is scarce.

30. "'Open Shop' versus 'Closed Shop,'" *Bridgemen's Magazine* 5, no. 5 (December 1905): 6–9 (quote); Edward A. Moffett, "A Comparison of the Union Shop and the 'Open Shop':

Reproduction of an Address before the National Civic Federation, Chicago, October 15, 1903," *Official Journal of the Amalgamated Meat Cutters and the Butcher Workmen of America* 2, no. 50 (November 1903): 16.

31. Horace Traubel, "Through the Closed Shop to the Open World," *Journal of the Switchmen's Union* 11, no. 2 (December 1908): 929.

32. "Letter from W. P. Shutt," *Railroad Telegrapher* 26, no. 1 (January 1909): 72–73.

33. Moffett, "A Comparison of the Union Shop and the 'Open Shop,'" 16, 19.

34. Recorder Moses Levy presiding over the case, quoted in Tomlins, *The State and the Unions*, 37. For more, see chapter 2.

35. Montgomery, *Workers' Control*, 12; see also Montgomery, *Fall of the House of Labor*, chapter 1.

36. The process of professionalization in different scientific, academic, and professional fields is of course a complex one and has its own literature; I do not mean to imply that the question of who makes the rules in those fields is straightforward or simple. For the social sciences, see Mary O. Furner, *Advocacy & Objectivity: A Crisis in the Professionalization of American Social Science, 1865–1905* (Lexington: University Press of Kentucky, 1975); on the issue of faculty governance specifically, see Larry G. Gerber, *The Rise and Decline of Faculty Governance: Professionalization and the Modern American University* (Baltimore, MD: Johns Hopkins University Press, 2014).

37. Clayton Sinyai, *Schools of Democracy: A Political History of the American Labor Movement* (Ithaca, NY: ILR Press, 2006), 28–35. The phrase "schools of democracy" comes from an article in the AFL's journal *American Federationist*: "Unions are the schools of the workers where they learned the lessons of democracy and independence" (quoted on 33).

38. Ralph M. Easley, "What Organized Labor Has Learned: A Measure of the Progress of Trades-Unionism in the United States," *McClure's Magazine* 19 (October 1902): 483 ff.

39. Ralph Easley to Marcus M. Marks, February 11, 1911, quoted in Green, *The National Civic Federation*, 303. To be sure, some Progressive Era reformers did see the logic of the union shop and the necessary protection that it afforded unions; see, for example, Walling, "Open Shops."

40. Craig Phelan, *Divided Loyalties: The Public and Private Life of Labor Leader John Mitchell* (Albany: State University of New York Press, 1994), xi.

41. Unsigned [Ralph Easley] to C. A. Chadwick, December 31, 1903, box 4, folder 7, NCF Records. The themes of talking to representatives of labor as individuals and of emphasizing conservative leadership are discussed further below.

42. David Montgomery, "Strikes of Machinists in the United States, 1870–1920," in *Strikes, Wars, and Revolutions in an International Perspective*, ed. Leopold H. Haimson and Charles Tilly (Cambridge: Cambridge University Press, 1989), 272. Montgomery bases the story on a 1926 autobiography by Charles Steltzle.

43. For a concise account of the Homestead strike, see Paul Kahan, *The Homestead Strike: Labor, Violence, and American Industry* (New York: Routledge, 2014); on McKees Rocks, see John N. Ingham, "A Strike in the Progressive Era: McKees Rocks, 1909," *Pennsylvania Magazine of History and Biography* 90, no. 3 (July 1966): 353–77.

44. H. M. Gitelman, "Perspectives on American Industrial Violence," *Business History Review* 47, no. 1 (March 1973): 1–23, especially 11–12; Paul F. Lipold and Larry W. Isaac, "Striking Deaths: Lethal Contestation and the 'Exceptional' Character of the American

Labor Movement, 1870–1970," *International Review of Social History* 54, no. 2 (August 2009): 167–205.

45. Richard N. Price, "The Other Face of Respectability: Violence in the Manchester Brickmaking Trade, 1859–1870," *Past & Present*, no. 66 (February 1975): 126–28.

46. Lipold and Isaac, "Striking Deaths," 199. On vigilante businessmen, see Vilja Hulden and Chad Pearson, "The Wild West of Employer Anti-unionism: Individualism, Vigilantism, and the Glorification of Organized Anti-union Leagues in the Early-Twentieth-Century United States," in *Corporate Policing, Yellow Unionism, and Strikebreaking, 1890–1930: In Defence of Freedom*, ed. Matteo Millan and Alessandro Saluppo (London: Routledge, 2021).

47. William M. Tuttle, "Labor Conflict and Racial Violence: The Black Worker in Chicago, 1894–1919," *Labor History* 10, no. 3 (June 1969): 408–32. Tuttle recounts incidents ranging from pelting African American drivers with bricks and stones to stabbing out the eyes of African American packinghouse workers and even murdering African American strikebreakers.

48. Price, "The Other Face," 130.

49. Quoted in Tuttle, "Labor Conflict," 416. For the original of the quote, see *Chicago Daily Tribune*, May 5, 1905, 2.

50. Samuel Gompers, "Labor's Differences with Mr. Marcus M. Marks et al.," *American Federationist* 17, no. 10 (October 1910): 885. See also, for example, Report of Treasurer, American Federation of Labor, *Report of Proceedings of the Twenty-Fourth Annual Convention of the American Federation of Labor*, San Francisco, California, November 14–26, inclusive (Washington, DC: Law Reporter Printing Company, 1904), 59–60; Report of the General Secretary John B. Lennon, "Proceedings of the Eighth Convention of the Journeymen Tailors' Union of North America," held at Bloomington, Illinois, February 6–10, *The Tailor* 15, no. 7 (February 1905): 4.

51. Some examples of this phraseology, with greater or lesser openness, include "Trade unions are open. Nearly all are wide open to any man or woman qualified at the occupation organized," "No Shop Is Closed," *American Federationist* 28, no. 2 (February 1911): 117–18; "Anyone except a rank scab can go to work anywhere if he is not a member. All we can do is to ask him to join us, and should he say no we give him the cold shoulder," Charles D. Smith, "Correspondence from Branch No. 30, St. Louis, Mo," *Leather Workers' Journal* 8, no. 8 (April 1906): 428–29.

52. Taillon, *Good, Reliable, White Men*, 73, 87.

53. Opponent of federation quoted in Taillon, *Good, Reliable, White Men*, 100.

54. William M. Dick, *Labor and Socialism in America: The Gompers Era* (Washington, NY: Kennikat Press, 1972), 90.

55. "Appeal by San Francisco Labor Council," *American Federationist* 14, no. 2 (February 1907): 117–18.

56. John Mitchell, "Protect the Workman," *American Federationist* 16, no. 10 (October 1909): 859–63, quote on 861. On the complex construction of the semiracial "coolie" category, see Moon-Ho Jung, *Coolies and Cane: Race, Labor, and Sugar in the Age of Emancipation* (Baltimore, MD: Johns Hopkins University Press, 2008).

57. Most Asians were prohibited from immigrating in 1917 with the creation of an "Asiatic barred zone"; Japan was ascendant as a nation, so for foreign policy reasons the

Japanese were treated somewhat more diplomatically until the exclusion in the 1924 act. On race in the Immigration Act of 1924 (a.k.a. the National Origins Act or the Quota Act), see especially Mae M. Ngai, "The Architecture of Race in American Immigration Law: A Reexamination of the Immigration Act of 1924," *Journal of American History* 86, no. 1 (June 1999): 67–92.

58. Albert S. Ashmead, "Japanese Atavism," *American Federationist* 14, no. 10 (October 1907): 781–83.

59. Samuel Gompers, "More Open Shop Hypocrisy," editorial, *American Federationist* 11, no. 10 (June 1904): 490–92.

60. Eva McDonald Valesh, "Child Labor," *American Federationist* 14, no. 3 (March 1907): 157–73, quote on 158.

61. Eva McDonald Valesh, "An Instructive Exhibit," *American Federationist* 14, no. 9 (September 1907): 681–89, quote on 687.

62. Edwin R. A. Seligman, "Liberty, Democracy, Productivity and the Closed Shop," *National Civic Federation Review* 1, no. 5 (July 1904): 9.

63. Even within a mostly immigrant union, suspicion and condescending attitudes between different ethnic groups could complicate matters. For example, in the ILGWU, Italian workers often felt they were sidelined and condescended to by the union and particularly by Jewish workers. Charles Anthony Zappia, "Unionism and the Italian American Worker: A History of the New York City 'Italian Locals' in the International Ladies' Garment Workers' Union, 1900–1934" (PhD diss., University of California, Berkeley, 1994), chapter 3.

64. W. E. B. Du Bois, *The Negro Artisan: A Social Study* (Atlanta, GA: Atlanta University Press, 1902), 153–79.

65. Philip S. Foner, *Organized Labor and the Black Worker, 1619–1981* (New York: International Publishers, 1982), 64–74.

66. Du Bois, *The Negro Artisan*, 173–74.

67. Eric Arnesen, "Following the Color Line of Labor: Black Workers and the Labor Movement before 1930," *Radical History Review* 55 (Winter 1993): 60, 63.

68. Eric Arnesen, "Specter of the Black Strikebreaker: Race, Employment, and Labor Activism in the Industrial Era," *Labor History* 44, no. 3 (August 2003): 319–35. There is, of course, a substantial literature on unions cold-shouldering racial and ethnic minorities and immigrants and the ways in which racism and nativism undermined solidarity. See, for example, David R. Roediger, *The Wages of Whiteness: Race and the Making of the American Working Class* (New York: Verso, 1999); Gwendolyn Mink, *Old Labor and New Immigrants in American Political Development: Union, Party, and State, 1875–1920* (Ithaca, NY: Cornell University Press, 1986).

69. For a discussion on the complexities of the sexual division of labor and of labor unions' role with regard to it, see Ruth Milkman, *On Gender, Labor, and Inequality* (Urbana: University of Illinois Press, 2016), especially chapter 3.

70. Dorothy Sue Cobble, "Rethinking Troubled Relations between Women and Unions: Craft Unionism and Female Activism," *Feminist Studies* 16, no. 3 (Autumn 1990): 519. Interestingly, Cobble argues that the craft structure of the AFL-affiliated Hotel Employees and Restaurant Employees International Union made women's locals more efficacious than in most unions because they were also cohesive by craft and because sexual division

coincided with craft division, leading the international to treat women's locals like "any other craft-based local" (522).

71. For example, M. E. J. Kelley argued that women's involvement in the Knights of Labor had surged in the early years but quickly dropped off to nearly nothing, showing women's tendency to "plan and dream glorious things and act rashly" instead of engaging in sustained unionism, of which further evidence were estimates that workingwomen's rate of unionization was only 1 percent to workingmen's 10. Kelley's piece aimed to make the case for paying more attention to women as consumers, which she thought was their "more important capacity." "Women and the Labor Movement," *North American Review* 166, no. 497 (April 1898): 408–17.

72. Annelise Orleck, *Common Sense and a Little Fire: Women and Working-Class Politics in the United States, 1900–1965* (Chapel Hill: University of North Carolina Press, 1995), 45–58. For an overview of women in the workforce and in unions, see Alice Kessler-Harris, *Women Have Always Worked: A Concise History*, 2nd ed. (1981; repr., University of Illinois Press, 2018), especially chapter 3.

73. "Open Shop," *International Wood Worker* 14, no. 3 (March 1904): 116.

74. Samuel Gompers, "Report of President Samuel Gompers to the Twenty-Third Annual Convention of the American Federation of Labor," *American Federationist* 10, no. 12 (December 1903): 1282.

75. C. L. Baine, "Is the Closed Shop Just?," reproduction of a letter to the editor of the *Boston Globe*, September 3, 1905, *Shoeworkers' Journal* 6, no. 9 (September 1905): 16.

76. Currarino, "Politics of 'More,'" 26.

77. Richard Hyman, *Industrial Relations: A Marxist Introduction* (London: Macmillan, 1975), 194–95, emphasis in original.

78. Quoted in Melvyn Dubofsky, *We Shall Be All: A History of the Industrial Workers of the World*, 2nd ed. (Urbana: University of Illinois Press, 1988), 33.

79. Quoted in A. Ross McCormack, *Reformers, Rebels, and Revolutionaries: The Western Canadian Radical Movement 1899–1919* (Toronto, ON: University of Toronto Press, 1977), 102.

80. Bruno Ramirez, *When Workers Fight: The Politics of Industrial Relations in the Progressive Era, 1898–1916* (Westport, CT: Greenwood Press, 1978), chapter 11.

81. Dubofsky, *We Shall Be All*, especially chapters 6 and 12. On repression, see especially White, *Under the Iron Heel*.

82. Peter Cole, *Wobblies on the Waterfront: Interracial Unionism in Progressive-Era Philadelphia* (Urbana: University of Illinois Press, 2007), 42, 55, 63–64, 95, 113.

83. John Laslett, *Labor and the Left: A Study of Socialist and Radical Influences in the American Labor Movement, 1881–1924* (New York: Basic Books, 1970), 153.

84. See, for example, Montgomery, *Fall of the House of Labor*, 168, on textile and shoe workers in Massachusetts.

85. American Federation of Labor, *Report of Proceedings of the Thirty-First Annual Convention of the American Federation of Labor*, Atlanta, Georgia, November 13–25, inclusive (Washington, DC: Law Reporter Printing Company, 1911), 217–38.

86. Gompers and Hillquit both cross-examined each other at the hearings. Gompers mainly focused on demonstrating that the Socialists got nothing done, while Hillquit endeavored to establish that the AFL shared nearly all the Socialists' goals but was made

ineffectual by its refusal to enter into politics and by its cooperation with capitalists. Testimony of Morris Hillquit, May 21, 1914, and testimony of Samuel Gompers, May 22, 1914, US Commission on Industrial Relations, *Final Report and Testimony Submitted to Congress by the Commission on Industrial Relations*, 64th Cong., 1st sess., 1914, 1462–92, 1492–1549.

87. James Lynch of the International Typographical Union made this point particularly insistently, noting that Harrison Gray Otis of the *Los Angeles Times*, a notorious antiunion activist, remained a member of the American Newspaper Publishers Association, but that did not prevent the ITU from winning contracts that improved its members' lives through its relations with the ANPA. American Federation of Labor, *Report of Proceedings of the Thirty-First Annual Convention*, 240.

88. Testimony of Samuel Gompers, 1540–42; *New York Times*, May 23, 1914, 20; *Boston Daily Globe*, May 23, 1914, 8.

89. Testimony of Samuel Gompers, 1547.

90. General Secretary [Easley] to Samuel Mather, February 4, 1904, box 6, folder 3, NCF Records.

Chapter 4. *The Range and Roots of Employer Positions on Labor*

1. Ferdinand Schwedtman to Ralph M. Easley, February 16, 1903, box 7, folder 1, NCF Records.

2. Ferdinand Schwedtman to Ralph M. Easley, March 19, 1904, box 7, folder 1, NCF Records.

3. Circular letter, April 28, 1904, box 7, folder 1, NCF Records; "Civic Federation Is Solution of Labor and Capital Problem," *NCF Review* 1, no. 2 (June 1903): 20.

4. Ralph M. Easley to John Mitchell, July 1, 1903, box 6, folder 4, Ferdinand Schwedtman to Ralph M. Easley, September 30, 1903, and other letters in the same folder, box 7, folder 1; F. N. Judson to R. M. Easley, February 26, 1904, box 9, folder 2; all in NCF Records. On the change of tune after the world's fair and on Schwedtman's background and company, see Rosemary Feurer, *Radical Unionism in the Midwest, 1900–1950* (Urbana: University of Illinois Press, 2006), 7–12.

5. The first letters in preserved NAM correspondence from Schwedtman in his capacity as CIA secretary and open-shop activist are exchanges in April 1904 with NAM secretary Marshall Cushing praising Cushing for his "splendid work" in Washington; see Secretary [Cushing] to F. C. Schwedtman, April 8, 1904, and Fred C. Schwedtman to Marshall Cushing, April 14, 1904, *Maintenance Appendix*, 313, 328.

6. Quoted in Feurer, *Radical Unionism*, 9.

7. Edwin Freegard, "No Peace except with the Open Shop," *American Industries*, December 1, 1904, 13.

8. Clarence E. Bonnett, *Employers' Associations in the United States: A Study of Typical Associations* (New York: Macmillan Company, 1922), 14.

9. Robert H. Wiebe, *Businessmen and Reform: A Study of the Progressive Movement* (Chicago: Ivan R. Dee, 1962), 165.

10. James Weinstein, *The Corporate Ideal in the Liberal State, 1900–1918* (Boston: Beacon Press, 1968), ix. See also Gabriel Kolko, *The Triumph of Conservatism: A Reinterpretation of American History, 1900–1960* (New York: Free Press, 1963); and Martin J. Sklar, *The*

Corporate Reconstruction of American Capitalism, 1890–1916: The Market, the Law, and Politics (New York: Cambridge University Press, 1988).

11. James Weinstein, "Gompers and the New Liberalism," in *For a New America: Essays in History and Politics from Studies on the Left, 1959–1967*, ed. James Weinstein and D. W. Eakins (New York: Random House, 1970), 121, 111.

12. Weinstein, *Corporate Ideal*, 15–18.

13. As Easley explained to Daniel Ripley of the U.S. Glass Company, the NCF believed that the key effort was "stem[ming] the Socialist tide" but that "Socialism can only be met by the laboring classes themselves" through nonsocialist unions. By contrast, the NAM "believes that the Unionist is as bad as the Socialist . . ., and their hatred for one is about as great as for the other." Daniel C. Ripley to James W. Van Cleave, October 5, 1906, and Chairman Executive Council [Easley] to Daniel C. Ripley, October 6, 1906, both in box 185, folder 4, NCF Records.

14. Cohen, *The Racketeer's Progress*, 16–17, 33–34.

15. As the NCF office explained to an ally whose help it was trying to enlist in its recruitment efforts, "We cannot say to such men that we will not ask them to give any time if they will permit the use of their names," as it was their names that "would aid very materially in promoting this work," but perhaps that message could be conveyed diplomatically by a fellow businessman. Unsigned to Cyrus H. McCormick, January 15, 1904, box 9, folder 4, NCF Records. The chief source for demographic data about the NCF is Gordon Maurice Jensen, "The National Civic Federation: American Business in an Age of Social Change and Social Reform, 1900–1910" (PhD diss., Princeton University, 1956). See also the database referred to in note 63. NCF executive committee members are listed in the *NCF Review*; see the following issues: April 1903, July 1904, November 1905, July/August 1906, March/April 1907, February 1908, November 1909, and March 1910. Appendix B in Hulden, "Employers, Unite!," also contains a full list of the men who sat as employer representatives on the NCF executive council between the years 1903 and 1910.

16. Williamson, "Seven Ways."

17. "Robbins, Francis Le Baron," in *The National Cyclopaedia of American Biography, Supplement 1* (James T. White & Company, 1910), 498; Montgomery, *Fall of the House of Labor*, 341–42.

18. Francis L. Robbins, speech titled "Trade Agreements and Individual Liberty," reported in *NCF Review* 2, no. 2 (May 1905): 16–17; Francis L. Robbins quoted in "An Historic Gathering to Promote Industrial Peace," *NCF Review* 1, no. 20 (January 1905): 9.

19. Robbins in *NCF Review* 2, no. 2 (May 1904): 1, 17. Robbins could not attend the meeting, so his address was read by Ralph Easley. See also Montgomery, *Fall of the House of Labor*, 341–42.

20. For example: "As there may be underhand competition in the individual 'Open Shop' in the matter of wages, so may one 'Open Shop' compete in this way with another to the point of cut-throat competition. Under the union shop policy the employers have the common advantage of stability in price of the largest item of cost—the matter of wages." Moffett, "A Comparison of the Union Shop and the 'Open Shop,'" 17.

21. Graebner, "Great Expectations," 51–54; see also Curtis Seltzer, *Fire in the Hole: Miners and Managers in the American Coal Industry* (Lexington: University Press of Kentucky, 1985), chapter 1.

22. Robertson, *Capital, Labor and State*, 131.

23. "Strike Story in Three Chapters," *Search-Light*, March 10, 1906, 147; Jerry Bruce Thomas, "Davis, Henry Gassaway," American National Biography Online (Oxford University Press, February 2000), http://www.anb.org/articles/04/04-00298.html; John A. Williams, *West Virginia and the Captains of Industry*, revised ed. (1976; repr., Morgantown: West Virginia University Press, 2003), especially chapter 1.

24. Thomas A. Klug, "The Roots of the Open Shop: Employers, Trade Unions, and Craft Labor Markets in Detroit, 1859–1907" (PhD diss., Wayne State University, 1993), 442–62, quote on 482.

25. "Stove Founders and Iron Molders Agree," *NCF Review* 2, no. 8 (June 1905): 14; "Trade Agreement Conference," *NCF Review* 1, no. 4 (June 1904): 11.

26. Fine, *"Without Blare of Trumpets,"* 15–19.

27. "The Great Conflict in the Building Industry Ended," *NCF Review* 2, no. 2 (May 1905): 9; "An Unprecedented Opportunity," *NCF Review* 2, no. 2 (May 1905): 10.

28. Quotes from the *New York Times*, May 16, 1903, 1. The headline of the story was "Employers Decide on Organized War."

29. Testimony of Otto M. Eidlitz, US Commission on Industrial Relations, Final Report and Testimony Submitted to Congress by the Commission on Industrial Relations, 64th Cong., 1st sess., 1914, 644–59 (quote on 647).

30. *New York Times*, December 20, 1903, 5. On the Eidlitzes' work in arbitration and with unions, see Otto M. Eidlitz, "How Can Voluntary Arbitration in Case of Labor Disputes Be Made Effective?," reprinted from *New York Journal*, October 5, 1901, *Building Trades Association Bulletin* 2, no. 5 (October 1901): 103–6; and Eidlitz, "Voluntary Arbitration: Experience in the Building Trades," in *Labor and Capital: A Discussion of the Relations of Employer and Employed*, ed. John P. Peters (New York: G. P. Putnam's Sons, 1902). On the Eidlitzes' background and position in the building industry, see Kathryn E. Holliday, *Leopold Eidlitz: Architecture and Idealism in the Gilded Age* (New York: W. W. Norton, 2008), 30–31; *New York Times*, October 31, 1928, 30; "An Historic Firm," *Architectural Record* 5, no. 4 (April–June 1896): 454–55.

31. On open shop: for example, Charles Eidlitz participated in the 1904 annual convention of the Citizens' Industrial Association of America, an umbrella organization of multi-industry, antiunion Citizens' Alliances. See *New York Times*, November 30, 1904, 7. On enduring NCF affiliation, see, for example, the list of executive committee members, including Otto Eidlitz, in *NCF Review* 4, no. 6 (December 1918).

32. Pearson, *Reform or Repression*, 27–34; "The Trade Agreement Enthusiastically Endorsed," *NCF Review* 2, no. 2 (May 1905): 5 ff.; Bonnett, *Employers' Associations*, 67.

33. Jensen, "The National Civic Federation," 148–65.

34. Andrea Tone, *The Business of Benevolence: Industrial Paternalism in Progressive America* (Ithaca, NY: Cornell University Press, 1997), 66–70.

35. For a detailed account of the 1901 strike and its impact, see Daniel Nelson, "The New Factory System and the Unions: The National Cash Register Company Dispute of 1901," *Labor History* 15, no. 2 (1974): 163–78.

36. National Civic Federation, Welfare Department, *Conference on Welfare Work*, Held at the Waldorf Astoria, New York City, March 16, 1904, under the Auspices of the Welfare Department of the National Civic Federation (New York: Press of Andrew H. Kellogg Company, 1904), 118. See also an article by the new NCR welfare director in the *NCF*

Review 1, no. 11 (February 1905): 14. The NCR itself reported favorably on the NCF's aim to "secure the absolute rights for employer and employe as well" and its own Labor Bureau's close cooperation with the NCF in its company magazine, *The N.C.R.*, March 15, 1902, 167–71.

37. Brody, *Steelworkers in America*, 128–29.

38. John Rogers Commons, *Myself, the Autobiography of John R. Commons* (Madison: University of Wisconsin Press, 1963), 88.

39. For an account of the NCF's role in the 1901 steel strike, see Philip S. Foner, *History of the Labor Movement in the United States. Vol. 3: The Policies and Practices of the American Federation of Labor, 1900–1909* (New York: International Publishers, 1964), 78–86. For a vigorous argument that makes the case that labor leaders not only became less militant but in fact used the NCF for their own purposes in crushing radicalism, see John Zerzan, "Understanding the Anti-radicalism of the National Civic Federation," *International Review of Social History* [Netherlands] 19, no. 2 (August 1974): 194–210.

40. J. Maddison to R. M. Easley, September 23, 1903, box 6, folder 3, NCF Records.

41. On the various versions of Vanderbilt's 1882 "public be damned" outburst, see Scott M. Cutlip, *Public Relations History: From the 17th to the 20th Century. The Antecedents* (Hillsdale, NJ: Lawrence Erlbaum Associates, 1995), 188–90.

42. According to Gordon Jensen, though smaller businesses were not entirely unrepresented in the NCF, over half of "more active" NCF business corporations were capitalized at $25 million or more (about $750 million in 2020 dollars); other NCF business members included trust companies, banks, and insurance companies with assets usually well in excess of that, however. Jensen's definition of "more active" business affiliates is fairly broad; details in Jensen, "The National Civic Federation," 344n32, capitalization figures on 378–79. See also Williamson, "Seven Ways."

43. Roland Marchand, *Creating the Corporate Soul: The Rise of Public Relations and Corporate Imagery in American Big Business* (Berkeley: University of California Press, 1998), especially chapter 1.

44. National Civic Federation, *Industrial Conciliation: Report of the Proceedings of the Conference*, Held under the Auspices of the National Civic Federation, December 16 and 17, 1901 (New York: G. P. Putnam's Sons, 1902); "Banker's Wife Dines Labor Delegates," *New York Times*, August 19, 1909, 1; "An Evening of Industrial Peace," *New York Observer and Chronicle*, April 11, 1907, 478.

45. "Declaration of Principles of the Social Democracy of America: Adopted at the Special Convention Held under the Auspices of the American Railway Union, June 15, 16, 17, 18, 19, and 21, 1897," published in the *Social Democrat* [Terre Haute, IN], July 1, 1897, 1, 4, 2, https://www.marxists.org/history/usa/parties/spusa/1897/0618-sda-declofpriciples.pdf.

46. Greene, *Pure and Simple Politics*, 61–64, quote reproducing plank 10 on 62.

47. "The 'Omaha Platform' of the People's Party (1892)," *American Yawp Reader*, http://www.americanyawp.com/reader/16-capital-and-labor/the-omaha-platform-of-the-peoples-party-1892/.

48. Richard T. Ely, "Natural Monopolies and the Workingman: A Programme of Social Reform," *North American Review* 158, no. 448 (1894): 296.

49. Jack Ross, "Socialist Party Elected Officials 1901–1960," Mapping American Social Movements, accessed July 19, 2020, http://depts.washington.edu/moves/SP_map-elected

.shtml; see also James Gregory, "Socialist Party Votes by Counties and States 1904–1948," *Mapping American Social Movements*, accessed July 19, 2020, http://depts.washington .edu/moves/SP_map-votes.shtml; and James N. Gregory, "Remapping the American Left," *Labor* 17, no. 2 (May 2020): 11–45.

50. Gail Radford, "From Municipal Socialism to Public Authorities: Institutional Factors in the Shaping of American Public Enterprise," *Journal of American History* 90, no. 3 (December 2003): 863–90, quote on 869.

51. For some examples of newspaper stories on these topics, see, "The Story of Bribery," *Washington Post*, June 14, 1890, 1; "Railroads Fleecing Farmers" (editorial), *Chicago Daily Tribune*, August 9, 1896, 28; "Railroad Graft Next Scandal?," *Chicago Daily Tribune*, October 14, 1905, 7; "Life Insurance Graft," *Chicago Daily Tribune*, February 22, 1906, A2. For Cortelyou, see Jensen, "The National Civic Federation," 226. See also Viviana A. Rotman Zelizer, *Morals and Markets: The Development of Life Insurance in the United States* (New York: Columbia University Press, 1979); Radford, "From Municipal Socialism."

52. "An International Investigation of Public Ownership," *NCF Review* 2, no. 7 (December 1905): 5.

53. Jensen, "The National Civic Federation," 234–38.

54. The quote is from an exchange with economist Edwin R. A. Seligman, who had claimed that a particular speaker, Professor Mussey, whom Easley had denounced as a socialist, was not in fact a socialist and denied being one. Easley explained that one could not trust people's statements on this and added, "You may remember I was sharply called down by Mrs. J. G. Phelps Stokes and Mr. Robert Hunter for stating a year ago that they were Socialists. I believe it was only a year afterwards that they came out in the open." Unsigned (Easley) to Edwin R. A. Seligman, December 5, 1908, box 185, folder 4, NCF Records. Seligman's statements denying that Mussey was a socialist and that Mussey himself "expressly denied being one" are in Edwin R. A. Seligman to R. M. Easley, November 30, 1908, and December 7, 1908, box 185, folder 4, both in NCF Records.

55. Unsigned [Easley] to Andrew Carnegie, May 20, 1913, box 186, folder 6, NCF Records. The "large men" included, for example, such figures as Cyrus H. McCormick, August Belmont, John Hays Hammond, and Frederick D. Underwood.

56. Unsigned [Easley] to George Eastman, May 8, 1913, box 187, folder 2, and R. M. Easley to John Grier Hibben [president of Princeton], November 6, 1912, box 187, folder 7, both in NCF Records. Easley repeatedly underlined that "there is certainly nothing more important than to get these future captains of industry educated along the [antisocialist] line." Unsigned [Easley] to John Hays Hammond, May 7, 1913, box 187, folder 6, NCF Records.

57. Unsigned [Easley] to George Eastman, May 8, 1913, box 187, folder 2, NCF Records.

58. The Woman's Department was first organized as an auxiliary to the Welfare Department. "Women Organize to Help Workers," *New York Times*, August 9, 1908, SM7; Cyphers, *The National Civic Federation*, chapter 3. Quote from unsigned [NCF office] to Franklin MacVeagh, January 6, 1907, box 21, folder 5, NCF Records. Jane Addams, Mary McDowell, and Florence Kelley all worked at Chicago's famous Hull-House settlement and shared an interest in reform, as well as some radical leanings; Kelley was also a self-described socialist. See, for example, Sklar, "Hull House"; Sklar, *Florence Kelley*.

59. Unsigned [Easley?] to Mrs. J. Medill McCormick, March 10, 1908, box 21, folder 5, NCF Records. Katherine Mackay was president of the Equal Suffrage Society, which she founded in 1908 and which "will take the organized work more into the ranks of society than it has yet been." Harriot Stanton Blatch was also a member of the society. See *New York Times*, December 24, 1908. Clarence Mackay attended suffragist meetings with his wife, so it is unclear to what extent he shared the NCF's assessment of his wife's radicalism; they were divorced a few years later. *New York Times*, February 17, 1910, 9, and May 7, 1914, 1; *Washington Post*, January 22, 1911, 8.

60. Unsigned [Easley] to Cyrus H. McCormick, April 18, 1913, box 188, folder 2, and unsigned [Easley] to John Hays Hammond, April 23, 1913, box 187, folder 6, both in NCF Records.

61. Unsigned [Easley] to Samuel Lewisohn, April 18, 1913, box 188, folder 1, NCF Records. For a reference to Easley's writing to Vreeland, see unsigned [Easley] to John Hays Hammond, April 24, 1913, box 187, folder 6, unsigned [Easley] to Andrew Carnegie, May 20, 1913, box 186, folder 6, and unsigned [Easley] to Cyrus H. McCormick, September 22, 1914, box 188, folder 2, all in NCF Records. The NCF also coached Vincent Astor in his reply to an open letter from the Socialist Upton Sinclair that emphasized the injustice of some being as rich as Astor while others starved. See *The Sinclair–Astor Letters: Famous Correspondence between Socialist and Millionaire* (Girard, KS: Appeal to Reason, 1914).

62. Extract from an address by Edward A. Filene at the Economic Club, reprinted in *NCF Review* 1, no. 11 (February 1905), 7.

63. Augustus Waldo Drury, *History of the City of Dayton and Montgomery County, Ohio* (Chicago: S. J. Clarke Publishing Company, 1909), 2:608–13. There had, of course, been locally based employer organizations before, as well as other local organizations targeting unionists. For example, Kim Voss argues that employer counterorganization had a significant impact on the demise of Knights of Labor locals in 1880s New Jersey, and Chad Pearson has noted that many law-and-order leagues in the American West emerged in response to the 1886 Southwest Railway Strike and functioned as antiunion organizations. Voss, *The Making of American Exceptionalism*; Chad Pearson, "Plenary: The History of Right to Work from the First Gilded Age to Janus," *Journal of Collective Bargaining in the Academy*, article 11, https://thekeep.eiu.edu/jcba/vol0/iss14/11 (2019).

64. Address of John Kirby, NAM, *Proceedings* (1903), 227.

65. For example, Kirby explained in 1909 that the NAM represented the "great army of men of wealth and influence" who had climbed to those positions "from the humblest conditions in which men are born." Quoted in Pamela Walker Laird, "How Business Historians Can Save the World—from the Fallacy of Self-Made Success," *Business History* 59, no. 8 (November 2017): 1201–17, 1204.

66. My dissertation, from which this work grew, attempted a more detailed demographic examination of the politically active members as defined by their frequent appearance in the association's preserved correspondence prior to 1913. I was particularly interested in NAM members who were actively involved in the association rather than just paying membership dues in order to have access to translation services, for example. A spreadsheet version of the resulting database along with some discussion can be found at https://github.com/vhulden/bossesunion/. For more demographic details, see Hulden, "Employers, Unite!"

67. The figure is 1.7 percent for 1870 and 3 percent for 1890; by contrast, in the 1960s, for instance, the figure was about 40 percent. John Seiler Brubacher and Willis Rudy, *Higher Education in Transition: A History of American Colleges and Universities*, 4th ed. (New Brunswick, NJ: Transaction Publishers, 1997), 257.

68. There are numerous examples of the significance of tangible and intangible family inheritance for the success of NAM members. To take just a few: Charles S. Keith, an important NAM member from Missouri, was from the start groomed to take over his father's coal and coke company, which by the time of his father's death had ten thousand employees. Francis Stillman, an NAM officer and the first president of the National Metal Trades Association, got his start in business through his stepfather. Alfred E. Cox, treasurer and general manager at the boiler and marine engine manufacturer Atlantic Works, was the son of a dyer and laster who had started to work at a young age, but his family nevertheless had long roots in Massachusetts politics that probably smoothed his rise in both business and politics; by the time he was in his forties, he was being talked about as a potential successor to Henry Cabot Lodge's House of Representatives seat. On Keith, see Walter Barlow Stevens, *Missouri the Center State: 1821–1915* (Chicago: S. J. Clarke Publishing Company, 1915), 3:580–83; on Stillman, see *New York Times*, February 19, 1912 (obituary); "Francis H. Stillman: A Biographical Sketch," *Cassier's Magazine* 33, no. 6 (April 1908): 684; John William Leonard, ed., *Who's Who in Finance, Banking and Insurance: A Biographical Dictionary of Contemporary Bankers, Capitalists and Others Engaged in Financial Activities in the United States and Canada* (New York: Joseph & Sefton, 1911), 1:693; on Cox, see William Richard Cutter, ed., *Historic Homes and Places and Genealogical and Personal Memoirs Relating to the Families of Middlesex County, Massachusetts* (New York: Lewis Historical Publishing Company, 1908), 1:367–69; Daniel P. Toomey and Thomas C. Quinn, eds., *Massachusetts of Today: A Memorial of the State, Historical and Biographical, Issued for the World's Columbian Exposition at Chicago* (Boston: Columbia Publishing Company, 1892), 426.

69. The Hinde & Dauch Paper Co. to J. A. Norton, December 15, 1902, HR57A-H15.2, Records of the Committee on Labor, Records of the US House of Representatives, Record Group 233, 57th–63rd Congs., National Archives, Washington, DC.

70. *American Industries*, May 15, 1906, 7; Walter Drew to Norman Hapgood, March 30, 1904, reel 1, Walter Drew Papers, Accession number 9616 Aa2, microform, Bentley Historical Library, University of Michigan, Ann Arbor; editorial in *American Industries*, December 1, 1904, 8.

71. Larry J. Griffin, Michael E. Wallace, and Beth A. Rubin note that the business failure rate between 1890 and 1928 was double that of the post–World War II rate and particularly affected small firms unable to modernize their production processes, that is, the types of firms often drawn to the NAM. Using a complicated statistical analysis, they then tentatively conclude that unions perhaps increased the risk of failure: "Increases in unit labor costs resulted in a larger number of failures and a higher failure rate than might otherwise be predicted" and "this increase was due, indirectly, to unionization." "Capitalist Resistance to the Organization of Labor before the New Deal: Why? How? Success?," *American Sociological Review* 51, no. 2 (April 1986): 154.

72. While this was not the first time that the Sherman Antitrust Act had been used against unions, Daniel Ernst notes that it was the first time that the Supreme Court had

"unambiguously held that the Sherman Act reached organized labor." *Lawyers against Labor*, 17–19, 113, 152, quote on 168.

73. Ernst, *Lawyers against Labor*, 17–18.

74. Montgomery, *Fall of the House of Labor*, 260–66, 275; Jeffrey Haydu, "Employers, Unions, and American Exceptionalism: Pre–World War I Open Shops in the Machine Trades in Comparative Perspective," *International Review of Social History* 33 (December 1988): 30–33; Laslett, *Labor and the Left*, chapter 5.

75. Klug, "The Roots of the Open Shop," chapter 13.

76. See Harris, *Bloodless Victories*, 32–36; and Philip Scranton, "Diversity in Diversity: Flexible Production and American Industrialization, 1880–1930," *Business History Review* 65, no. 1 (Spring 1991): 66–68.

77. Scranton, "Diversity in Diversity."

78. Table 5 in US Department of Labor, Bureau of Apprenticeship, *The Skilled Labor Force: A Study of Census Data on the Craftsman Population of the United States, 1870–1950*, Technical Bulletin No. T-140, 1954, 24.

79. In 1909 foundry and machine shop workers brought home an average hourly wage of $0.22, or 118 percent of the average hourly wage in manufacturing; see Robert A. Margo, "Annual and Hourly Earnings in Manufacturing, by Industry: 1889–1914," table Ba4298-4313, in *Historical Statistics of the United States, Earliest Times to the Present: Millennial Edition Online*, ed. Susan B. Carter et al. (New York: Cambridge University Press, 2000).

80. All numbers in the table are rounded (to the closest thousand, million, or whole percent, as indicated in the table header). The "aggregate expenses" category in the census contains the total payroll (including officials and clerks, as well as wage earners), materials, fuel, rent, taxes, contract work, and a residual "other" category. The wages figure in the table is the "wage earners" category of payroll ("services"). The "cars and general shop construction by steam railroad companies" industry does not appear among NAM members because NAM membership, being limited to manufacturers, does not include railroads (it was apparently a fully integrated part of the railroad industry, as its value of product matches its aggregate expenses, i.e., it has no margin of profit).

81. For example, in the US canning industry, canning machines successfully and dramatically reduced the need for (and power of) craft labor, increased the productivity of unskilled labor, and pushed down overall labor needs and per-unit labor costs simultaneously. See Martin Brown and Peter Philips, "Craft Labor and Mechanization in Nineteenth-Century American Canning," *Journal of Economic History* 46, no. 3 (September 1986): 743–46.

82. Charles Babbage, *On the Economy of Machinery and Manufactures*, 4th, enlarged ed. (1835; repr., New York: Augustus M. Kelley, Bookseller, 1903), chapter 19. The classic work on deskilling is Harry Braverman, *Labor and Monopoly Capital: The Degradation of Work in the Twentieth Century*, 25th anniversary ed. (1974; repr., New York: Monthly Review Press, 1998), though Braverman is more concerned with the impact on the worker than with the benefits to the corporation. Braverman discusses Babbage's division of labor on 55–58.

83. Howell John Harris, "The Rocky Road to Mass Production: Change and Continuity in the U.S. Foundry Industry, 1890–1940," *Enterprise & Society* 1 (June 2000): 391–437.

84. Montgomery, *Fall of the House of Labor*, chapter 1.

85. See table 2; for molders, see figure 3.1. in Harris, *Bloodless Victories*, 83.

86. While the diagrams and stopwatches are the best-known part of Taylor's work, many foundry and machine shop proprietors were probably also impressed by Taylor's actual engineering experiments, which had led to new discoveries in the hardening of steel and to new tools and processes that were widely adopted. Montgomery, *Fall of the House of Labor*, 222–24, 230–31.

87. Montgomery, *Fall of the House of Labor*, 208; see also John N. Ingham, "Towne, Henry Robinson," in *Biographical Dictionary of American Business Leaders*, 4 vols. (Westport, CT: Greenwood Press, 1983), 4:1473–75.

88. "Second Vice President Holmes' Report," *Machinists' Monthly Journal* 16, no. 5 (May 1904): 418–19; "Business Agents' Reports, District No. 3," *Machinists' Monthly Journal* 16, no. 12 (December 1904): 1097; "Business Agents' Reports, Syracuse, NY," *Machinists' Monthly Journal* 17, no. 11 (November 1905): 1042–43.

89. George D. Babcock, *The Taylor System in Franklin Management*, 2nd ed. (New York: Engineering Magazine Company, 1918).

90. Frederic Parkhurst, *Applied Methods of Scientific Management*, 2nd ed. (New York: John Wiley & Sons, 1917), 325–26.

91. Parkhurst, *Applied Methods*, 325–26.

92. Data on union densities is notoriously poor, and thus these figures should be taken as roughly indicative rather than exact. My source for numbers of union members is Leo Wolman, *The Growth of American Trade Unions, 1880–1923* (National Bureau of Economic Research, 1924), 110–19. Wolman lists unions and their memberships by industrial category, and I have tried to match these figures to census categories; the figure for "total workers" is the "average number of workers" listed in the census, rounded to the nearest thousand. The census's "average number" was a number adjusted for fluctuations in turnover and seasonality with the assumption that the number reflected "the number who would have been required to perform the work done if all had worked for a full year." US Department of Commerce, Bureau of the Census, *Thirteenth Census of the United States, 1910*, vol. 8, *Manufactures* (Washington, DC: GPO, 1913), 459. The year 1909 was chosen because for that year, the census lists average numbers of wage workers by midlevel industrial categories such as "foundry and machine shop products"; in the 1900 census, only broad categories ("food and kindred products") and individualized headings ("liquors, malt") are listed. The leather industry union membership figure is Wolman's figure for that category minus the memberships of the Boot and Shoe Workers' Union and the Shoe Workers' Protective Union, which together form the union membership figure for the boot and shoe industry category. The category "iron and steel, elaborated" is a catchall. The union figures here represent Wolman's category of "Metal, Machinery and Shipbuilding" minus the Iron, Steel, and Tin Workers' Union, which forms the union membership figure for the "iron and steel, crude" category. It was impossible to get a union density figure for the foundry and machine shop industry separately, as one would then need to know the percentage of machinists, metalworkers, and molders who worked at a foundry and machine shop as opposed to those who worked in another elaborated metal trade such as a typewriter factory. Furthermore, the density figure is probably somewhat inflated because the union membership figure includes at least parts of some categories (shipbuilding, jewelry, and, most importantly, railroad repair shop work, also performed

by machinists and the like) that are listed separately in the census. Even including the average number of railroad repair shop workers ("cars and general shop construction by steam RR") in table 1 in the total number of elaborated iron and steel workers, however, one gets a union density figure of 18 percent. For the clothing industry, the union membership is formed by the United Garment Workers, Ladies' Garment Workers, and Tailors (the Amalgamated Clothing Workers, which became big later, was not yet established in 1909). The average number of workers is the census categories of workers in men's and women's clothing trades added together. The union figures for the printing and publishing industry are Wolman's category for "Paper, Printing, and Bookbinding" minus the unions Paper Makers, Paper Box Workers, Pulp and Paper Mill Workers, and Wall Paper Crafts, which together form the union membership figure for the paper and wood pulp industry. Lumber and timber, as well as textiles, are straightforward category totals for both union and census figures; the reason I am using "textiles" rather than the more specific "cotton goods" category here is that the largest of the small unions in the textile industry were not organized by material.

93. Partly the low union density is an artificial effect of the census category, which bundles together everything from logging to planing mill products like doors and sashes. Even if the figures remained fairly low in all lumber trades, union membership was much more common in planing mill production than it was in logging or sawmill work. Calculating a union density figure for 1909 for planing mill production alone with the same method as in table 2 and using the union membership figures for the Wood Carvers' Union and Amalgamated Wood Workers results in a union density figure of 5 percent. However, as Wolman's table shows, the Amalgamated Wood Workers had lost a substantial number of members in the years immediately preceding 1909; if one were to use the figures from 1906, union density would be 15 percent. Both figures, however, are somewhat exaggerated, since members of both unions also worked in wood box and furniture factories and probably also in the building trades.

94. See, for example, C. A. Smith Timber Company to Jas. A. Tawney, January 25, 1904, *Maintenance Appendix*, 210–11.

95. See Secretary [Cushing] to Geo. K. Smith, February 12, 1904, and James Emery to J. P. Bird, May 23, 1911, both in *Maintenance Appendix*, 247, 3867–68.

96. Chewing and smoking tobacco manufacturing were no longer high-labor-cost industries by the turn of the twentieth century. Mechanization and concentration had proceeded much faster in the "manufactured tobacco" category—plug, chewing, pipe, fine cut—as well as in cigarettes and snuff than it had in cigar manufacture. By 1905 labor made up only about 5 percent of the total costs in these simpler forms, whereas it represented some 20 percent of the costs in cigar manufacturing; similarly, in the 1910 census the average size of an establishment manufacturing the simpler sorts of tobacco was fifty-nine workers, while cigar manufactories only averaged nine workers. Meyer Jacobstein, *The Tobacco Industry in the United States* (New York: Cambridge University Press, 1907), 91–92; US Department of the Interior, Bureau of the Census, *Thirteenth Census*, 8:470.

97. If one removes contract work (which is listed in the census as a separate category) from the total expenses and then calculates wages as percentage of this new total, the figure is 24 percent for women's clothing and 23 percent for men's clothing; by contrast,

the same procedure for foundry and machine shop products, for example, would not change the rounded percentage, as the change is only 0.2 percent.

98. Daniel Soyer, "Class Conscious Workers as Immigrant Entrepreneurs: The Ambiguity of Class among Eastern European Jewish Immigrants to the United States at the Turn of the Twentieth Century," *Labor History* 42, no. 1 (February 2001): 59.

99. In 1906 only 2 percent of cigar factories employed more than thirty workers. See Patricia Ann Cooper, *Once a Cigar Maker: Men, Women, and Work Culture in American Cigar Factories, 1900–1919* (Urbana: University of Illinois Press, 1987), 29. The annual membership fee of the NAM was $50, which was quite a bit of money at the time; in 2020 dollars the equivalent is about $1,500. NAM, *Proceedings* (1903), 248; Williamson, "Seven Ways."

100. For a concise and informative essay on the historiography of gendering labor history, see Ava Baron, "Gender and Labor History: Learning from the Past, Looking to the Future," in *Work Engendered: Toward a New History of American Labor*, ed. Ava Baron (Ithaca, NY: Cornell University Press, 1991), 1–46; for good examples of the cultural interpretations imposed on women's work, see also the other essays in that collection and Sonya O. Rose, *Limited Livelihoods: Gender and Class in Nineteenth-Century England* (London: Routledge, 1992).

101. Patricia Ann Cooper, "'What This Country Needs Is a Good Five-Cent Cigar,'" *Technology and Culture* 29, no. 4 (October 1988): 779–807.

102. US Department of the Interior, Bureau of the Census, *Thirteenth Census*, 8:186.

103. The example here is Theodore McFerson of McFerson & Foster.

104. This has been my finding in researching NAM members, but it is also borne out by older work on the NAM, such as Wiebe, *The Search for Order*. For more on the pattern of managerial control, see Howell Harris's work on Philadelphia; Harris notes that "proprietary capitalism prevailed irrespective of firm size" and that "a break in proprietary control, or even a company's acquisition of the status of an incorporated business under Pennsylvania's laws, did not necessary entail any fundamental alteration in its character." *Bloodless Victories*, 37, 39.

105. Klug, "The Roots," 513–14.

106. Ernst, *Lawyers against Labor*, 128–46; *Chicago Daily Tribune*, July 20, 1910, 1. My thanks to Howell Harris for providing me with the latter reference.

107. Harris, *Bloodless Victories*, 124.

108. For more on both the social aspects and the practical assistance like strikebreaking that employer organizations provided their members, see Pearson, *Reform or Repression*.

109. For a sampling of the more interesting contributions to this debate, see Aristide R. Zolberg, "How Many Exceptionalisms?," in *How Many Exceptionalisms? Explorations in Comparative Macroanalysis* (1986; repr., Philadelphia: Temple University Press, 2008); Archer, *Why Is There No Labor Party*; Larry G. Gerber, "Shifting Perspectives on American Exceptionalism: Recent Literature on American Labor Relations and Labor Politics," *Journal of American Studies* 31, no. 2 (August 1997): 253–74. Gerber's essay is also a good guide to the sizable literature on the topic. For a fairly recent effort to argue for exceptionalism along rather classical lines, see Seymour Martin Lipset and Gary Marks, *It Didn't Happen Here: Why Socialism Failed in the United States* (New York: W. W. Norton & Co., 2000).

110. Sanford Jacoby, "American Exceptionalism Revisited: The Importance of Management," in *Masters to Managers: Historical and Comparative Perspectives on American Employers*, ed. Sanford Jacoby (New York: Columbia University Press, 1991), 176.

111. Haydu, "Employers, Unions," 26.

112. Haydu, "Employers, Unions," 35–36.

113. Alessandro Saluppo, "Strikebreaking and Anti-unionism on the Waterfront: The Shipping Federation, 1890–1914," *European History Quarterly* 49, no. 4 (October 2019): 570–96.

114. Haydu, "Employers, Unions," 30.

115. Excerpts from Sebastian Ziani de Ferranti's speech on December 31, 1897, reprinted in Eric Wigham, *The Power to Manage: A History of the Engineering Employers' Federation* (London: Macmillan, 1973), appendix C.

116. See McIvor, *Organised Capital*, 125–31; and Haydu, "Employers, Unions."

117. Danish Employers' Confederation (DA, Dansk Arbejdsgiverforening) in 1899, quoted in Jesper Due, Jørgen Madsen, and Carsten Jensen, "The 'September Compromise': A Strategic Choice by Danish Employers in 1899," trans. Séan Martin, *Historical Studies in Industrial Relations*, no. 10 (Autumn 2000): 55.

118. Due, Madsen, and Jensen, "The 'September Compromise.'" For a Scandinavia-wide comparison that also argues for the roots of central agreements in employers' efforts to resist rising union power, see Peter Swenson, "Bringing Capital Back In, or Social Democracy Reconsidered: Employer Power, Cross-Class Alliances, and Centralization of Industrial Relations in Denmark and Sweden," *World Politics* 43, no. 4 (July 1991): 513–44.

119. Alexander G. Kuo, "Explaining Historical Employer Coordination: Evidence from Germany," *Comparative Politics* 48, no. 1 (October 2015): 87–106.

120. Haydu, "Employers, Unions," 37–38.

121. Michael Kazin, *Barons of Labor: The San Francisco Building Trades and Union Power in the Progressive Era*, Illini Books ed. (1987; repr., Urbana: University of Illinois Press, 1989), 13–27, quote on 14.

122. Haydu, *Citizen Employers*, 75–78, 87–89.

Chapter 5. Employers, Unite?

1. *Reunion of the Commercial Clubs of Boston, Chicago, St. Louis and Cincinnati*, Cincinnati, OH, May 27–28, 1897, report prepared by Douglas A. Brown, official stenographer, 1897, https://hdl.handle.net/2027/hvd.hboolm, guest lists on opening pages, races on 25–27, menu on insert preceding 43. On the Joe Hill epigram: The legendary Swedish-American labor organizer and IWW member Joe Hill did not actually use this specific form of the quote, but that's the form that became canonical. The quip is adapted from a telegram to William "Big Bill" Haywood that Hill sent on November 18, 1915, the day before Hill's execution for a murder he denied committing. The quote in full is actually "Don't waste any time mourning. Organize." Peter Carlson, *Roughneck: The Life and Times of Big Bill Haywood* (New York: W. W. Norton, 1983), 235.

2. *Reunion of the Commercial Clubs*, Jones quoted on 47, Glessner quoted on 48–49.

3. David W. Blight, *Race and Reunion: The Civil War in American Memory* (Cambridge, MA: Belknap Press of Harvard University Press, 2001), 137–39; Foner, *Reconstruction*, especially chapter 11.

4. Blight, *Race and Reunion*, especially chapter 6, Grady quoted on 200.

5. See, for example, William Cronon, *Nature's Metropolis: Chicago and the Great West* (New York: W. W. Norton & Company, 1991).

6. Beckert, *Monied Metropolis*, 145–53; Lamoreaux, *Great Merger Movement*, 2; Richard Franklin Bensel, *The Political Economy of American Industrialization, 1877–1900* (New York: Cambridge University Press, 2000), 454–55.

7. Beckert, *Monied Metropolis*; Bradley Hansen, "Commercial Associations and the Creation of a National Economy: The Demand for Federal Bankruptcy Law," *Business History Review* 72, no. 1 (Spring 1998): 86–113; Sam Mitrani, "Reforming Repression: Labor, Anarchy, and Reform in the Shaping of the Chicago Police Department, 1879–1888," *Labor: Studies in Working-Class History of the Americas* 6, no. 2 (Summer 2009): 73–96; Haydu, *Citizen Employers*.

8. Haydu, "Two Logics"; Haydu, *Citizen Employers*, 54–58, 103–4, quote on 104. Antebellum harmony should of course not be exaggerated (as is clear from chapter 2 as well), and in some ways the line between employers and workers was stark and getting starker much before the Civil War. See, for example, Paul E. Johnson, *A Shopkeeper's Millennium: Society and Revivals in Rochester, New York, 1815–1837* (New York: Hill and Wang, 1978); Peter Way, *Common Labour: Workers and the Digging of North American Canals, 1780–1860* (New York: Cambridge University Press, 1993); Peter Linebaugh and Marcus Rediker, *The Many-Headed Hydra: Sailors, Slaves, Commoners, and the Hidden History of the Revolutionary Atlantic* (Boston: Beacon Press, 2000).

9. Montgomery, *Fall of the House of Labor*, especially 179–91.

10. Montgomery, *Fall of the House of Labor*, 210–13, 252–55.

11. Kenneth T. Jackson, *Crabgrass Frontier: The Suburbanization of the United States* (New York: Oxford University Press, 1985), chapters 4 and 5.

12. Francis A. Walker in 1899, quoted in Joseph M. Hawes, "Social Scientists and Immigration Restriction: Highlights of a Debate, 1890–1924," *Cahiers d'Histoire Mondiale* 11, no. 3 (1968): 470. On the rise of anti-immigrant sentiment, the classic work is John Higham, *Strangers in the Land: Patterns of American Nativism, 1860–1924*, 2nd ed. (New Brunswick, NJ: Rutgers University Press, 1988); for a work that explicitly connects immigration restriction and worries about labor radicalism, see Kitty Calavita, *U.S. Immigration Law and the Control of Labor: 1820–1924* (Orlando: Academic Press, 1984). On New England patricians in particular, see Barbara Miller Solomon, *Ancestors and Immigrants: A Changing New England Tradition* (Chicago: University of Chicago Press, 1972). On shifting sources: for example, over three hundred thousand Italians arrived in the 1880s, as opposed to only fifty-five thousand in the 1870s, a nearly sixfold increase. In aggregate numbers, the proportion of southern and eastern Europeans grew substantially in the postbellum years and surpassed northern and western European migrants by 1900–1920. Roger Daniels, *Coming to America: A History of Immigration and Ethnicity in American Life* (New York: HarperPerennial, 1990), 122, 188–89.

13. Bender, *American Abyss*, 124–28.

14. See generally Calavita, *U.S. Immigration Law*. Employers in the South and West in particular griped that they were, as Rosemary Feurer notes for St. Louis employers, "at a disadvantage because the city did not have a low-wage labor supply of new immigrants to the extent that other cities did." *Radical Unionism*, 7.

15. While detailed accounts of any of these developments are beyond the scope of this book, see chapter 2 for slightly more discussion of late nineteenth-century labor and Left politics. For an overview of the era's upheavals, see Painter, *Standing at Armageddon*. For the Populists, see Goodwyn, *The Populist Moment*.

16. Haydu, *Citizen Employers*, 54–58, 103–4.

17. Wiebe, *Search for Order*.

18. David Roediger, "'Not Only the Ruling Classes to Overcome, but Also the So-Called Mob': Class, Skill and Community in the St. Louis General Strike of 1877," *Journal of Social History* 19, no. 2 (Winter 1985). 215–17.

19. Beckert, *Monied Metropolis*, 220–21, 233. The rules for voting eligibility for the board were that one had to have taxable property worth at least $500 or pay rent of at least $250; for comparison, skilled workers made $400–$600 annually. Had the amendment passed (it did not), about a third of the city's population would have been disenfranchised according to contemporary estimates, though Beckert estimates the proportion to be closer to two-thirds. This effort preceded the 1877 strike.

20. Sam Mitrani, *The Rise of the Chicago Police Department: Class and Conflict, 1850–1894* (Urbana: University of Illinois Press, 2013), 116–18, 131.

21. Bensel, *Political Economy*, 87–91, 453–55, quote on 517.

22. Undated memo by the Citizens' Industrial Association, *Maintenance Appendix*, 508–9, emphasis in original; see also Greene, *Pure and Simple Politics*, 92.

23. Quote from J. W. Van Cleave to J. P. Bird, June 23, 1908, *Maintenance Appendix*, 748. On tariff and conflict, see Paul Wolman, *Most Favored Nation: The Republican Revisionists and U.S. Tariff Policy, 1897–1912* (Chapel Hill: University of North Carolina Press, 1992), xix–xx, 2–3, 96, 138; President [Van Cleave] to H. E. Miles, January 11, 1909, *Maintenance Appendix*, 2497–2501.

24. For illustrative local-level case studies, see Pearson, *Reform or Repression*.

25. For an interesting analysis (though for a rather more elevated level of businessman) of the ways in which networks engender trust, facilitate economic transactions, and generate influence, see Susie Pak, *Gentlemen Bankers: The World of J. P. Morgan* (Cambridge, MA: Harvard University Press, 2013). A classic in the field of "power structure research" with a focus on a specific city is E. Digby Baltzell, *Philadelphia Gentlemen: The Making of a National Upper Class* (Glencoe, IL: Free Press, 1958).

26. NAM members from National Association of Manufacturers, *American Trade Index: Descriptive and Classified Membership Directory of the National Association of Manufacturers of the United States, Arranged for the Convenience of Foreign Buyers* (New York: Published for the National Association of Manufacturers, 1906); National Association of Manufacturers, *American Trade Index: Descriptive and Classified Membership Directory of the National Association of Manufacturers of the United States, Arranged for the Convenience of Foreign Buyers* (New York: Published for the National Association of Manufacturers, 1913).

27. *Maintenance Appendix*, 1062, 1089, 1100, WPA bylaws on 1355–63. On the CIA, see, for example, "How St. Louis Citizens Imposed a Reign of Law and Freedom," *American Industries*, September 15, 1904, 5. The local branch was headed by Van Cleave.

28. Dina M. Young, "The St. Louis Streetcar Strike of 1900: Pivotal Politics at the Century's Dawn," *Gateway Heritage* 12 (Summer 1991): 10–11.

29. John W. Leonard, ed., *The Book of St. Louisans: A Biographical Dictionary of the Leading Living Men of the City of St. Louis and Vicinity* (St. Louis: St. Louis Republic, 1906); Albert Nelson Marquis, ed., *The Book of St. Louisans: A Biographical Dictionary of the Leading Living Men of the City of St. Louis and Vicinity*, 2nd ed. (Chicago: A. N. Marquis & Company, 1912); *Gould's Blue Book for the City of St. Louis* (St. Louis: Gould Directory Company, 1913).

30. Documentation of the computational analyses, along with additional images, can be found at https://github.com/vhulden/bossesunion.

31. James Neal Primm, *Lion of the Valley: St. Louis, Missouri, 1764–1980* (St. Louis: Missouri History Museum, 1998); Patricia Cleary, "Contested Terrain: Environmental Agendas and Settlement Choices in Colonial St. Louis," in *Common Fields: An Environmental History of St. Louis*, ed. Andrew Hurley (St. Louis: Missouri Historical Society Press, 1997), 58–72.

32. Primm, *Lion of the Valley*; Jeffrey S. Adler, *Yankee Merchants and the Making of the Urban West: The Rise and Fall of Antebellum St. Louis* (New York: Cambridge University Press, 2002), chapters 6 and 7.

33. Primm, *Lion of the Valley*, 347.

34. Horbury L. Wayman, "Central West End," History of St. Louis Neighborhoods, accessed July 26, 2020, https://www.stlouis-mo.gov/archive/neighborhood-histories -norbury-wayman/cwe/subdivisions8.htm.

35. Primm, *Lion of the Valley*, quote on 347.

36. Where not otherwise noted, the discussion below relies on computational analysis of data extracted from Leonard, *Book of St. Louisans*; Marquis, *Book of St. Louisans*; *Gould's Blue Book*.

37. The Noonday Club had been founded in 1893; the incorporators included, for example, Rolla Wells, the future mayor of St. Louis and heir to the Missouri Railroad Company, which owned the St. Louis streetcar system, and John R. Lionberger, the scion of a wealthy family with multiple business enterprises, including significant shares in the Missouri Railroad Company. William Hyde and Howard L. Conard, eds., *Encyclopedia of the History of St. Louis: A Compendium of History and Biography for Ready Reference* (New York: Southern History Company, 1899), 3:1653; James Cox, *Old and New St. Louis: A Concise History of the Metropolis of the West and Southwest, with a Review of Its Present Greatness and Immediate Prospects. With a Biographical Appendix* (St. Louis: Central Biographical Publishing Company, 1894), 225; Lawrence O. Christensen, William E. Foley, and Gary Kremer, *Dictionary of Missouri Biography* (Columbia: University of Missouri Press, 1999), 789.

38. Howard Louis Conard, ed., *Encyclopedia of the History of Missouri: A Compendium of History and Biography for Ready Reference* (New York: Southern History Company, Haldeman, Conard & Co., 1901), 3:204; price conversion from Williamson, "Seven Ways."

39. Many of these clubs continue to exist and continue to be highly exclusive, although those not quite at the top have found themselves forced to open up membership to a broader swath of the population in order to survive. The St. Louis Country Club, Westwood, Old Warson, and Bellerive are considered the top of the present-day hierarchy and are known as the Big Four. Two of these, the St. Louis Country Club and Bellerive, were among the core clubs in the early twentieth century; Old Warson was only organized in 1953; and Westwood's Jewish membership separated it from the core in the early twentieth century. The initiation fee for the St. Louis Country Club, at $50,000, continues to guarantee that its members have substantial financial wherewithal, while the Log Cabin Club won't disclose its membership fee or any other information: a reporter writing a story on the state of St. Louis social clubs got the short reply, "We don't want to be in your article. You'll need to remove us." Jeannette Cooperman, "Dinner at the Club, Darling?," *St. Louis Magazine*, July 31, 2006.

40. Over a third of Glen Echo's members also belonged to the Mercantile Club, which was founded in 1889 in response to a perceived lack of a downtown club that would serve busy businessmen. While often described as "exclusive," at almost one thousand, its membership far exceeded that of, for example, the Commercial Club, organized in 1880 to bring the city's most prominent businessmen together socially. The Glen Echo Country Club was founded in 1901 and was soon accompanied by the adjacent development of Glen Echo Park, "an inexpensive but attractive home place in the country" that nevertheless was a "restricted residence" only "sold to refined people." Although it of course also served the usual social purposes of a country club, Glen Echo was serious about its golf course, which hosted the Olympic golf championship in 1904. Julius K. Hunter, *Westmoreland and Portland Places: The History and Architecture of America's Premier Private Streets, 1888–1988* (St. Louis: University of Missouri Press, 1988), 43; Hyde and Conard, *History of St. Louis*, 3:1441. Quotes from an advertisement for Glen Echo Park homes in the *Reality Record and Builder* 15, no. 4 (April 1908): 101–3.

41. Peter Hernon and Terry Ganey, *Under the Influence: The Unauthorized Story of the Anheuser-Busch Dynasty* (New York: Simon & Schuster, 1991), 120; the authors note that a popular adjective for "gaudy displays of wealth and privilege" in fancy St. Louis society was "Buschy."

42. About 28 percent of the Sunset Hill Country Club's members also belonged to the Racquet Club, while 26 percent of Cuivre Club members and 40 percent of Log Cabin Club members belonged to the Sunset Hill Country Club. Sunset Hill was also connected, though less strongly, to the Noonday Club, the St. Louis Club, and Glen Echo.

43. About 37 percent of Westwood Country Club members belonged to the Columbian Club. Considered differently, individuals belonging to both clubs represented about 18 percent of the combined membership of the two clubs. Westwood had been founded in 1907 and was financially quite exclusive; see Peter Levine, "The 'American Hebrew' Looks at 'Our Crowd': The Jewish Country Club in the 1920s," *American Jewish History* 83, no. 1 (March 1995): 27–49.

44. Hyde and Conard, *History of St. Louis*, 3:1653.

45. The newspaper editor was Charles Knapp of the *St. Louis Republic*, who was also on the board of directors of the Associated Press and the ANPA. The candidate for senator was Thomas K. Niedringhaus. The mayor of St. Louis was Rolla Wells.

46. Distribution, though, continued to play a major role in the city's economy, with a wholesale trade worth more than $200 million (over $6 billion in 2020 dollars) and retail, wholesale, and transportation employing over 30 percent of the city's population. See Primm, *Lion of the Valley*, 333, 338; Williamson, "Seven Ways."

47. Membership in the BML, MFA, and CIA is derived from the biographies in the *BSTL*.

48. Wayman, "Central West End."

49. In the interests of transparency, it is perhaps worth emphasizing that this is not a comprehensive view of the St. Louis business landscape, only of the individuals who had an entry in the *BSTL* and who declared a membership in one of the business organizations—and, for connections based on clubs, whose entry listed their club memberships. Not being mentioned in the *BSTL* is plausibly an indication of lower social status; not listing social clubs might also indicate lower status (though it could also simply be that the individual in question did not care for clubs or did not bother to list his member-

ships). The organized businessmen who appear in the *BSTL* and the network graph, then, represent only a slice of the St. Louis business community and only a slice even of the members of St. Louis business organizations. Of the 107 member companies of the NAM in St. Louis, for instance, 53 are represented in the *BSTL* data. The *BSTL* (1906 and 1912 editions) contains biographies of some 140 individuals connected with these companies as owners or upper management. The representation percentage for the other organizations might be even lower: the Business Men's League of St. Louis, for instance, claimed a membership of 803 in 1911 and the Manufacturer's Association a membership of 200, while the network contains only 331 members of both associations combined. It is, however, possible that the claimed membership figures are inflated to exaggerate the importance of the associations; for example, a letter between NAM officials clarifying membership numbers in the NAM's National Council for Industrial Defense noted both that those numbers contained a lot of "hot-air stories" but that, "compared with some of the stories I am telling every day about the Citizens' Industrial Association of St. Louis," that "inconsistency is very trifling." Secretary to J. P. Bird and James Emery, December 17, 1908, *Maintenance Appendix*, 2447. The Manufacturers' Association was properly called the Missouri Manufacturers' Association, which was later (after a merger with the Latin American and Foreign Trade Association) changed to the Manufacturers' and Exporters' Association. See Civic League of Saint Louis, *Directory of Civic and Business Associations of Saint Louis* (St. Louis, MO: Nixon-Jones Printing Company, 1911), 19, 20, 25, supplement p. 10.

50. The underlying data, extracted by a combination of manual and automated methods from the biographies in the *BSTL*, is not entirely clean and may include some duplicates. On the other hand, connections are also undercounted: not every biography lists club memberships, some connections were missed due to spelling errors, and so on. For further discussion and to download the data, see https://github.com/vhulden/bossesunion.

51. The geolocating of addresses was done with the Census Geocoder, https://geocoding. geo.census.gov/. Historical addresses do not, of course, always map exactly onto current addresses, so inevitably there will be some errors. To minimize errors, only exact matches returned by the geocoder were used, in addition to some manually added ones.

52. With a looser standard of a single shared club membership or residence within 0.1 miles of each other, 370 of the 472 members of NAM or the three local business organizations in the *BSTL* were connected into a single network.

53. The business-related connections that are the most feasible to extract from the biographies in the *BSTL* are interlocking directorates. St. Louis was home to a number of trusts and large enterprises whose boards of directors brought together the business (and, to an extent, political) class of the city. Especially the Mercantile Trust Company, the Mississippi Valley Trust Company, the St. Louis Union Trust Company, and the Commonwealth Trust Company brought together the St. Louis greats, but, equally importantly, directorates of dry goods and manufacturing firms forged additional ties between businessmen.

54. Biographical information from the *BSTL*; see also Hunter, *Westmoreland and Portland Places*, chapters 3 and 4; *St. Louis Republic*, April 8, 1900, 42 (page 4 of the magazine section); *St. Louis Republic*, February 1, 1902, 3.

55. Roediger, "'Not Only the Ruling Classes.'"

56. Primm, *Lion of the Valley*, 312–14; Roediger, "'Not Only the Ruling Classes.'"

57. Theresa A. Case notes that the KOL had thirty-four locals in St. Louis by 1884 and that through the 1880s in St. Louis "an average of one hundred workers struck every working day." *The Great Southwest Railroad Strike and Free Labor* (College Station: Texas A&M University Press, 2010), 128, 28.

58. Hunter, *Westmoreland and Portland Places*, 31; Young, "The St. Louis Streetcar Strike"; Leonard, *Book of St. Louisans*.

59. Young, "The St. Louis Streetcar Strike"; "Personal—Mr. George W. Baumhoff," *Street Railway Review*, April 15, 1900, 226. Baumhoff does not appear in the *BSTL* or in *Gould's Blue Book*, so it seems he did not belong to any of the major clubs. He lived at 2908 Washington Avenue, clearly farther east (closer to the industrial district) than the manufacturers and businessmen listed in the directories. A decade later, though, he had become the president of the Aerial Electric and Manufacturing Company and moved to Kirkwood. *Gould's St. Louis City Directory for 1904* and *Gould's St. Louis City Directory for 1916*, in Ancestry.com, *U.S. City Directories, 1822–1995* [online database] (Provo, UT: Ancestry.com Operations, 2011).

60. *St. Louis Republic*, June 27, 1900, 4.

61. Young, "The St. Louis Streetcar Strike"; *St. Louis Republic*, May 31, 1900, 3; *St. Louis Republic*, June 1, 1900, 3.

62. *St. Louis Republic*, June 6, 1900, 3. The story reports that fifteen union members were dismissed for refusing to ride a streetcar; the colonel in charge stated that he respected their decision but insisted that he needed to have his men "obey implicitly." On June 10, a further forty-three deputies were discharged for being union members. *St. Louis Republic*, June 11, 1900, 2.

63. *St. Louis Republic*, June 10, 1900, 29 (page 1 of the magazine section); *St. Louis Republic*, June 13, 1900, 2; *St. Louis Republic*, June 19, 1900, 5; *St. Louis Republic*, June 27, 1900, 3. Quote from the article on June 13, in which Sheriff Pohlmann expressed his indignation regarding accusations that the posse employed Pinkertons or transit company employees, insisting instead that there was "nobody on this posse who is not a citizen of St. Louis, and the most of them are taxpayers and represent the very best element of our citizens"; indeed, "most of them are leading businessmen." (Pohlman does not have an entry in *The Book of St. Louisans* and only appears as a member of the not-very-elite St. Louis Amateur Athletic Association in *Gould's Blue Book*.)

64. *St. Louis Republic*, June 2, 1900, part 2, 1; *St. Louis Republic*, June 4, 1900, 12.

65. *St. Louis Republic*, June 10, 1900, 29 (page 1 of the magazine section), headlined "How the Posse Comitatus Proceeds with Its Organization and Duties—the Personal Side Considered."

66. *St. Louis Republic*, June 11, 1900, 1.

67. Both incidents are reported in the *St. Louis Republic*, June 11, 1900, 1. See also Young, "The St. Louis Streetcar Strike."

68. *St. Louis Republic*, June 11, 1900, 2.

69. Young, "The St. Louis Streetcar Strike," 15–16.

70. Young, "The St. Louis Streetcar Strike," also notes that the strike prompted city leaders to try to uproot entrenched corruption and clean up St. Louis's reputation.

71. Printing ranked sixth nationally in value of products. See US Department of Commerce, Bureau of the Census, *Thirteenth Census*, 8:49.

72. Memo entitled "Rough suggestions for candidates and campaign managers" (probably by Secretary Cushing), n.d. (1906?), *Maintenance Appendix*, 563–65.

73. Leona M. Powell, *The History of the United Typothetae of America* (Chicago: University of Chicago Press, 1926), 40–41; Bonnett, *Employers' Associations*, 238 and chapters 8 and 9; M. E. J. Kelley, "The Union Label," *North American Review* 165, no. 488 (July 1897): 26–36.

74. Wm. B. Becktold to Marshall Cushing, December 15, 1903, *Maintenance Appendix*, 158. The Chicago, Dayton, Kansas City, Milwaukee, St. Louis, and St. Paul Typothetae were among the founding members of the Citizens' Industrial Association, an umbrella group formed in 1903 to bring together all antiunion employers and their supporters. Powell, *History of the United Typothetae*, 667.

75. For one example, see the description of how the master printers of Camden, New Jersey, managed to wrest substantial concessions from the union because "the employers were a unit in opposition to the signing of any such contracts" as the ones the union had presented. "If the employing printers in every city would only stir themselves up more on this question and get together," similar benefits could be achieved anywhere. "A Lesson in Labor Contracts," *American Printer* 37, no. 1 (September 1903): 56–57.

76. Leona M. Powell, "Typothetae and the Eight-Hour Day," *Journal of Political Economy* 33, no. 6 (December 1925): 679.

77. *Typographical Journal* 27, no. 4 (October 1905): 288, 409–10. Striking when a contract was in force, of course, would have violated that contract; the ITU (along with other printing trades unions) was quite scrupulous in avoiding the breaking of contracts.

78. Powell, "Typothetae," 676–77.

79. Secretary [Marshall Cushing] to F. C. Nunemacher, September 15, 1905, *Maintenance Appendix*, 505; minutes of the meeting of the board of directors, September 15, 1905, series III, box 199, reel 1, NAM Records; *American Industries*, September 15, 1905, 5, 8. For the circulars, see Secretary [Cushing] to Dear Sir (marked "To 3,000 members NAM"), September 25, 1905. The same letter was also sent to "400 advertisers (not members of NAM) in selected journals," October 10, 1905. Marshall Cushing to Dear Sir (marked "To 250 Presidents of Railroads, Editorial Reprint of Sept 15 enclosed"), September 23, 1905. A follow-up letter noted that the International Association of Machinists was planning to strike for the eight-hour day on the railroads and expostulated: "You see, if you give them an inch they immediately reach out for a mile; and they will never quit until they find some opposing force." Secretary [Cushing] to Dear Sir (marked "To same 250 Presidents of Railroads"). See also Marshall Cushing to Dear Sirs (marked "To paper mfrs members of NAM"), December 4, 1905. The letter notes that a similar one was sent to 750 nonmember paper manufacturers and asks member manufacturers to contact these further. All circulars in reel 2, Daniel Augustus Tompkins Papers, accession number 724, microform, Southern Historical Collection, University of North Carolina Library, Chapel Hill.

80. "Letter specially typewritten in each case and specially signed to 225 members of American Newspaper Publishers' Ass'n, each accompanied by reprint of editorial of September 15," September 23, 1905. The same text was sent on NAM letterhead to twenty-five hundred daily newspapers, October 7, 1905. See Marshall Cushing to Dear Sir (marked "Daily Newspapers"), December 5, 1905; Marshall Cushing to Dear Sir (marked "Brady

List"), December 5, 1905; Marshall Cushing to Dear Sir (marked "Advertisers in this publication"), December 20, 1905, all in reel 2, Tompkins Papers.

81. *American Industries*, May 1, 1906; *American Industries*, October 2, 1905, 4, 8; *American Industries*, October 16, 1905, 1–2, 6–7; *American Industries*, November 1, 1905; *American Industries*, November 15, 1905, 4; *American Industries*, December 1, 1905, 4; *American Industries*, January 15, 1906, 5, 6; *American Industries*, February 1, 1906, 3, 9. On replacement workers, see telegram, *Augusta Chronicle* to Marshall Cushing, December 29, 1905; telegram, Marshall Cushing to *Augusta Chronicle*, December 29, 1905; editor / business manager of *Augusta Chronicle* [name illegible] to D. A. Tompkins, December 29, 1905, all in reel 2, Tompkins Papers. There is no record of whether D. A. Tompkins (who owned the *Charlotte Observer*) provided the *Augusta Chronicle* with workers, but as he had promised to do so in other cases and was vehemently for the employing printers, he probably did. See unsigned [D. A. Tompkins] to D. M. Parry, December 23, 1905, and [illegible, of *Greenville News*] to D. A. Tompkins, December 16, 1905, both in reel 2, Tompkins Papers.

82. For example, W. H. Cowles, editor of the *Spokesman-Review* of Spokane Falls, Washington, was an NAM ally, and as early as October 1903 *American Industries* had reported (under the headline "No Words Adequate to Describe This Typographical Union Perfidy") on his labor troubles and exhorted the ANPA to take a firmer stance against the union. *American Industries*, October 15, 1903, 14.

83. Secretary [Cushing] to Ferdinand C. Schwedtman, July 31, 1906, *Maintenance Appendix*, 754–56.

84. See *Typographical Journal* 27, no. 1 (July 1905): 49–50; *Typographical Journal* 31, no. 3 (September 1907): 288–89. Some typical *Philadelphia Inquirer* headlines included "Typothetae Ranks Stand Unbroken" (January 3, 1906, 16); "Further Gains for the Master Printers" (January 5, 1906, 11); "Typothetae Gain against Strikers: Advocates of Open Shop Have Grown Stronger after First Week of Labor Trouble" (January 7, 1906, 4). These were clearly more positive toward the Typothetae than, for example, headlines in the *New York Times* or the *Chicago Daily Tribune*. However, nothing ever came of the project to convince newspaper publishers to join the fight; only a few individual newspapers (some of them owned by NAM members) used the occasion as a springboard to defeat the union in their shops. One such newspaper was the *Greenville News*, owned by NAM board of directors member Daniel A. Tompkins; see [illegible signature] to D. A. Tompkins, December 16, 1905, reel 2, Tompkins Papers.

85. On Mulhall's Philadelphia contacts, see his testimony in US Congress, Senate, Subcommittee of the Committee on the Judiciary, *Maintenance of a Lobby to Influence Legislation: Hearings*, 63rd Cong., 1st sess., 1913, 2435–37. Hereafter cited as *Maintenance Hearings*. On nonunion printers in Philadelphia and ITU worries about the threat they would pose, see the report of the Committee on Appeals and letters reprinted in International Typographical Union, *Reports of Officers and Proceedings of the Fifty-First Session of the International Typographical Union*, Toronto, Canada, August 14–19, 1905 (supplement to the *Typographical Journal* 27, no. 4 (October 1905): 179 ff. The journal even went so far as to call Philadelphia "a hotbed of non-unionism." *Typographical Journal* 31, no. 2 (August 1907): 144.

86. On Mulhall's appointment, see Marshall Cushing to Col. Mulhall, February 20, 1906; on the Philadelphia excursion, see "Meeting between the committees of the Manufactur-

ers' organization and the Central Labor Union," both in *Maintenance Appendix*, 566–81. On the New York trip, see *Typographical Journal* 29, no. 2 (August 1906): 181–82.

87. Williamson, "Seven Ways"; US Department of Commerce, Bureau of the Census, *Thirteenth Census*, 8:40–45, 518–63.

88. Documents show that Mulhall did engage labor spies, that the UTA supported or commissioned his work, and that he did at least convince the UTA that his work was producing results. There are several reports on union meetings from at least three different workers; some of these workers also explicitly referred to Mulhall's payments to them. There are also letters from UTA officials praising Mulhall's work. See Mulhall's testimony in *Maintenance Hearings*, 2521–23; for examples of the reports sent to Mulhall, see unsigned to M. M. Mulhall, March 25, 1906; D. Sibole to Col. Mulhall, April 28, 1906; Michael Collins to Col. Mulhall, April 22, 1906; Michael Collins to M. M. Mulhall, July 15, 1906; unsigned [Joseph Pfeiffer?] to M. M. Mulhall, May 7, 1906; and Joseph H. Pfeiffer to unidentified [Mulhall], May 22, 1906, all in *Maintenance Appendix*, 614, 660, 654–55, 731–32, 663, 677. For letters between Mulhall and UTA officials and UTA letters regarding Mulhall, see John Macintyre [secretary of the UTA] to M. M. Mulhall, April 13, 1906; unsigned [Mulhall] to John F. Macintyre, April 17, 1906; John Macintyre to Martin M. Mulhall, May 25, 1906; John C. Winston Co. to Marshall Cushing, March 21, 1906; and Joseph Hays to M. M. Mulhall, January 21, 1907, all in *Maintenance Appendix*, 643, 648, 680, 611, 892.

89. See, for example, *New York Times*, September 1, 1905, 5; *New York Times*, January 11, 1906, 6; *Washington Post*, December 15, 1905, A1; *Philadelphia Inquirer*, January 16, 1906, 16; *Philadelphia Inquirer*, February 7, 1906, 2.

90. *Chicago Daily Tribune*, January 5, 1906, 4; *Chicago Daily Tribune*, May 17, 1906; *New York Times*, January 9, 1906, 16; *Washington Post*, January 16, 1906; *Washington Post*, October 4, 1906.

91. *Typographical Journal* 29, no. 2 (August 1906): 159–63.

92. Quoted in Powell, *History of the United Typothetae*, 102–3. On membership, Powell states that, notably enough, the UTA would not even keep figures on membership in 1905 and 1906 but that between 1904 and 1908 UTA membership plummeted from over 1,300 to 729; see "Typothetae," 679. For a somewhat different interpretation of the strike, emphasizing an injunction handed down in Chicago by the (in)famous judge Jesse Holdom and how that injunction—issued as it was against a conservative union careful to avoid violence—contributed toward pushing Samuel Gompers and the AFL toward greater political involvement, see Greene, *Pure and Simple Politics*, 102–4.

93. George E. Barnett, "The Printers: A Study in American Trade Unionism," *American Economic Association Quarterly*, 3rd series, 10, no. 3 (October 1909): 157.

94. The strike in Philadelphia began in November 1905, and still in August 1906 Philadelphia had only 467 of its 1,300 ITU members working eight hours a day, leaving 833 on strike rolls. In other words, only 35 percent of Philadelphia ITU members had achieved the eight-hour day in almost a year of fighting; by contrast, that figure for New York (where Typographical Union No. 6 was quite powerful) was 91 percent. As late as December 1907 (over two years into the strike), 297 ITU members remained on the strike roll in Philadelphia. See *Typographical Journal* 31, no. 6 (December 1907): 665.

95. On Philadelphia, see *Typographical Journal* 27, no. 3 (September 1905): 278–82; "Report of President," International Typographical Union, *Reports of Officers and Proceedings of the Fifty-Third Session of the International Typographical Union,* Hot Springs, Arkansas, August 12–17, 1907 (supplement to the *Typographical Journal* 31, no. 4 (October 1907): 5; for quote, see Powell, "Typothetae," 678. Moreover, the ITU's membership losses were mostly due to very small locals leaving the union and were in any case hardly comparable to the 50 percent losses suffered by the Typothetae. See Barnett, "Printers," 157. Despite their doubts, the employing printers were prepared to credit Mulhall with averting a sympathetic strike and hoped to enlist his services in the future. Recording Secretary [Joseph Hays] to Marshall Cushing, March 22, 1906, and John Macintyre to M. M. Mulhall, November 13, 1906, both in *Maintenance Appendix*, 611.

96. Powell, *History of the Union Typothetae,* 67–69, 99; *New York Times,* January 3, 1906, 4. (The story was headlined "1,200 Printers Begin a Most Peaceful Strike.")

97. Barnett, "Printers," 27–32; Ronald Mendel, *"A Broad and Ennobling Spirit": Workers and Their Unions in Late Gilded Age New York and Brooklyn, 1886–1898* (Westport, CT: Praeger, 2003), 57–62. In addition to the ITU, the main printing unions were the International Printing Pressmen's Union and the Lithographers' Protective Association.

98. Much of the newspaper industry was already using the eight-hour day by the time of the 1905 strike. Powell, *History of the Union Typothetae,* 21–22, 51.

99. For more on the later history of the UTA, see Howard Stanger, "A Moderate Employers' Association in a 'House Divided': The Case of the Employing Printers of Columbus, Ohio, 1887–1987," in *Against Labor: How U.S. Employers Organized to Defeat Union Activism,* ed. Rosemary Feurer and Chad Pearson (Urbana: University of Illinois Press, 2017), 184–211.

Chapter 6. The Battle over the State

1. US Congress, Senate, Committee on Education and Labor, *The Eight-Hour Law: Report to Accompany H.R. 3076,* 57th Cong., 1st sess., Senate Report No. 2321, 1902, 2, 14.

2. Greene, *Pure and Simple Politics;* on incorporation, see, for example, Bernard D. Meltzer, "The Brandeis-Gompers Debate on 'Incorporation' of Labor Unions," *Green Bag* 1, no. 3 (Spring 1998): 299–305, and the reprints of Brandeis's and Gompers's debate speeches in the same volume.

3. David Vogel, "Why Businessmen Distrust Their State: The Political Consciousness of American Corporate Executives," *British Journal of Political Science* 8, no. 1 (January 1978): 45–78.

4. State legislatures are barely discussed in this chapter; most of my source material comes from records that focus heavily on the national level. However, both labor and business obviously paid attention to state legislatures. State legislatures passed more, and more comprehensive, labor laws than did the national Congress (see, e.g., Robertson, *Capital, Labor and State,* especially chapter 2). The NCF created the Department of Uniform State Legislation in 1909 and organized the Conference on Uniform State Legislation the following year; its aim was mainly to square the circle of the necessity of harmonizing legislation on everything from divorce rules to commercial regulation without increas-

ing the power of the national government unacceptably. See Cyphers, *The National Civic Federation*, especially chapter 6. The NAM, too, though its main concern was obviously to coordinate efforts at the national level, considered the state level important. D. M. Parry mentioned state legislatures in his (extraordinarily long) 1903 NAM convention remarks, which in a way officially launched the open-shop campaign, noting that "there are many measures hurtful to employers" at the state and municipal levels and that "there is as much reason for having a watchful eye on these bodies as upon Congress." Accordingly, the NAM did monitor state legislation; in 1913, for example, one NAM official reported on trying to combat anti-injunction legislation in several state legislatures. "Annual Report of President," NAM, *Proceedings* (1903), 14–87, quote on 58; unsigned [probably James Emery] to F. C. Schwedtman, March 28, 1913, *Maintenance Appendix*, 4148–49.

5. Delton, *The Industrialists*, chapter 1. Note also one member's defense of the NAM's relatively high membership fee on these grounds: "We all know for what this organization was created—to influence national legislation—and when you want any thing you ask the members to correspond with the senators and representatives at Washington, and we want the men with us that have the greatest influence." S. O. Bigney in NAM, *Proceedings* (1903), 252.

6. Greene, *Pure and Simple Politics*, 93–97.

7. John Elrick, "Social Conflict and the Politics of Reform: Mayor James D. Phelan and the San Francisco Waterfront Strike of 1901," *California History* 88, no. 2 (2011): 8.

8. David Witwer, "Unionized Teamsters and the Struggle over the Streets of the Early-Twentieth-Century City," *Social Science History* 24, no. 1 (Spring 2000): 191.

9. The year range is simply a period for which the New York Bureau of Labor kept records on the matter. Harry W. Laidler, *Boycotts and the Labor Struggle* (New York: John Lane Company, 1913), 73–75, 85–95, 162–64.

10. Forbath, *Law and the Shaping*, 83.

11. Forbath, *Law and the Shaping*, 83–84.

12. Cohen, *Racketeer's Progress*, chapter 2, quote on 93. Cohen also discusses the use of the boycott in these trades in the same chapter.

13. *Courier-Journal* (Louisville, KY), July 1, 1902, 8.

14. *Nashville American*, July 12, 1902, 1.

15. *New York Times*, July 27, 1902, 1.

16. See, for example, Millikan, *Union against Unions*; J. C. Craig, *The History of the Strike That Brought the Citizen's Alliance of Denver, Colo. into Existence*, From George's Weekly, 1903, Western History Collection, Denver Public Library.

17. For a particularly detailed analysis of the CIAA, its composition, and its symbolism, see Pearson, *Reform or Repression*, chapter 2.

18. Mark H. Haller, "Historical Roots of Police Behavior: Chicago, 1890–1925," *Law & Society Review* 10, no. 2 (Winter 1975): 305.

19. "Statement of Mr. J. C. Craig, president of the Citizens' Alliance of Denver, Colo.," US Congress, House, Committee on the Judiciary, *Anti-Injunction Bill: Complete Hearings on the Bill (H.R. 89) Entitled "A Bill to Limit the Meaning of the Word 'Conspiracy' and the Use of 'Restraining Orders and Injunctions' in Certain Cases,"* 58th Cong., 2nd sess., January 13–March 22, 1904, 256–79, quote on 261.

20. Mitrani, *Rise of the Chicago Police Department*, especially chapters 5 and 6.

21. Sidney L. Harring, *Policing a Class Society: The Experience of American Cities, 1865–1915* (New Brunswick, NJ: Rutgers University Press, 1983), 136–38; Thomas R. Clark, *Defending Rights: Law, Labor Politics, and the State in California, 1890–1925* (Detroit, MI: Wayne State University Press, 2002), 33.

22. Robert M. Smith, *From Blackjacks to Briefcases: A History of Commercialized Strike breaking and Unionbusting in the United States* (Athens: Ohio University Press, 2003), 14–19; Elaine S. Frantz, "The Homestead Strike and the Weakening of the First US National Paramilitary System," *Global South* 12, no. 2 (Fall 2018): 45–63.

23. Smith, *From Blackjacks to Briefcases*, 14–21; see also Frantz, "The Homestead Strike"; and Robert P. Weiss, "Private Detective Agencies and Labour Discipline in the United States, 1855–1946," *Historical Journal* 29, no. 1 (March 1986): 87–107.

24. The price that Henry Frick, president of Carnegie Steel, agreed to pay for the Pinkertons was $5 per man per day, or $1,500 per day for the services of three hundred men. In 2020 dollars, $1,500 is about $44,000—not a sum every manufacturer might be prepared to shell out on a daily basis. At Homestead, though, the monthly payroll exceeded $200,000 (about $5.9 million in 2020 dollars), so even if the Pinkerton expense ran to multiple days, it was fairly insignificant by comparison. US Congress, House, Committee on the Judiciary, *Employment of Pinkerton Detectives*, 52nd Cong., 2nd sess., House Report No. 2447, 1892, 3, 7. For another measure of the expense of strikebreaking, when three of his hired men died in a strike at McKees Rocks, Pennsylvania, in 1909, the "king of strikebreakers," Pearl Bergoff, commented that having to pay "four or five thousand dollars" compensation per man was no problem: "The income was so large that this expense made no difference." Quoted in Smith, *From Blackjacks to Briefcases*, 61.

25. *American Industries*, March 1914, 10.

26. Harring, *Policing a Class Society*, 141–43; Marilynn S. Johnson, *Street Justice: A History of Police Violence in New York City* (Boston: Beacon Press, 2003), 33–34.

27. Quoted in Clark, *Defending Rights*, 31.

28. See, for example, Elrick, "Social Conflict." Mayor Phelan initially refused to increase police presence in a labor conflict between Teamsters and the San Francisco Employers' Association, despite an appeal from the president of the Police Commission, who also happened to be a member of the chamber of commerce.

29. This point is made with reference to the behavior of the Ohio police in the Pope-Toledo Motor Car Company strike in 1906 versus their behavior in the Cleveland garment worker strike of 1911 in Harring, *Policing a Class Society*, 136. Both Cleveland and Toledo had in the 1900s been applying a "Golden Rule" police policy that emphasized lenience toward minor offenders and a socioeconomic explanation of crime; it also incorporated a heavy critique of economic inequality and of the encouragement of profit-seeking over the protection of the common good. See Robert H. Bremner, "The Civic Revival in Ohio: Police, Penal and Parole Policies in Cleveland and Toledo," *American Journal of Economics and Sociology* 14, no. 4 (July 1955): 387–98.

30. E. F. Du Brul to J. B. Foraker, March 4, 1902, SEN57A-K2, box 198, Senate Records, RG 46.

31. Forbath also notes that since the early nineteenth century, equity could only apply to property questions, leading to some convoluted reasoning as to what was "property." Courts ended up asserting that employers had a property right in the labor they had

purchased or that the entrepreneur's right to pursue his business was a form of a property right that, for example, a boycott could endanger. Forbath, *Law and the Shaping*, 84–88 and appendix B.

32. Edwin Emil Witte, *The Government in Labor Disputes* (New York: Arno & the New York Times, 1969), 85–90.

33. Forbath, *Law and the Shaping*, 103–4.

34. Herbert George to John W. Jenkins, March 7, 1906, HR59A-F21.2, box 357, Records of the Committee on the Judiciary, Records of the US House of Representatives, Record Group 233, 57th–63rd Congs., National Archives, Washington, DC.

35. Clark, *Defending Rights*, 73.

36. Clark, *Defending Rights*, 72–74; Williamson, "Seven Ways."

37. Forbath, *Law and the Shaping*, 103–5 (quotes), 193–98 (figures).

38. Final decree, *H. N. Strait Manufacturing Company v. The Iron Molders' Union No. 162 (et al.),* in the Circuit Court of the United States for the District of Kansas, first division, No. 8487. H. N. Strait Manufacturing Company was a member of the NAM. See also the very similar decree in another NAM member case: injunction, July 16, 1910, *American Blower Company v. Timothy Molone et al.*, in the Circuit Court for the County of Wayne, No. 37090; both reproduced in SEN62A-F13, box 87, Senate Records, RG 46.

39. Harris, *Bloodless Victories*, 135. Harris states that only fourteen persons were targeted by the injunction; this seems contradictory with the language of the injunction, which, after listing the names of union officials, goes on: "your agents, servants, associates and confederates and all others acting under or with you." Nevertheless, Harris's point regarding the particularly difficult situation of the leadership stands. The text of the injunction, along with the full bill of complaint and affidavits, can be found in *Niles Bement Pond Company v. The Iron Molders' Union of North America, et al.,* in the Circuit Court of the United States, Eastern District of Pennsylvania, No. 32, October sessions 1905, reproduced in SEN62A-F13, box 87, Senate Records, RG 46. Niles-Bement-Pond Company was also a member of the NAM.

40. Forbath, *Law and the Shaping*, 125–26.

41. Bill of complaint, *H. N. Strait Manufacturing Company v. The Iron Molders' Union No. 162 (et al.),* in SEN62A-F13, box 87, Senate Records, RG 46.

42. State of Colorado, City and County of Denver, District Court, order, *D. C. Coates et al.,* plaintiffs, *v. The Citizens' Alliance et al.*, defendants, May 14, 1903, No. 35652 DIV 2, Colorado State Archives, Denver. (Thanks to University of Colorado history librarian Frederick Carey for tracking down this source.) For the Citizens' Alliance perspective, see Craig, *The History of the Strike.*

43. Edwin E. Witte, "Labor's Resort to Injunctions," *Yale Law Journal* 39, no. 3 (January 1930): 374–75.

44. For example, labor tried to make use of injunctions to prevent San Francisco open-shop advocates from forcing all building contractors to operate on an open-shop basis. The chamber of commerce and the Building Trade Exchange in San Francisco had instituted a permit system: to get access to materials from participating suppliers or loans from participating banks, building contractors had to operate on an open-shop basis. The AFL never approved of these campaigns, viewing them as legitimizing injunctions, though the United Mine Workers and the Amalgamated Clothing Workers thought them justified. Clark, *Defending Rights*, chapter 6.

45. Forbath, *Law and the Shaping*, 103–9, quote on 109.

46. Robertson, *Capital, Labor and State*, 38–55, quote on 54.

47. Hattam, *Labor Visions*, chapter 4, quote on 147, from a judicial opinion in the 1886 New York case *People v. Wilzig*; the other cases were *People v. Kostka* under the same judge in 1886 in New York, and the last is an unnamed Pennsylvania case in 1881 stemming from a coal miners' strike at the Waverly Coal and Coke Company.

48. See, for example, *American Industries*, August 15, 1902, 10; *American Industries*, March 2, 1903, 8; *American Industries*, April 15, 1903, 12; *American Industries*, December 15, 1904, 3.

49. *American Industries*, September 1, 1905, 6; *American Industries*, November 16, 1903, 13.

50. John M. Maxwell, "Relief for Manufacturers in United States Courts," *American Industries*, June 15, 1903, 11.

51. Quoted in the *Chicago Daily Tribune*, October 18, 1905, 6. The limitation at issue in *Lochner* was to ten hours, however, not eight, as described in the news story.

52. *American Industries*, February 15, 1903, 8.

53. Robbins, "Freeing San Francisco."

54. The case that came closest was *Christensen v. People*, which arose from an injunction granted in a 1903 strike at the Kellogg Switchboard & Supply Company. In that decision, Judge Frances Adams argued not only that the strikers' picketing and other tactics were unlawful but also that the closed-shop agreements they demanded would be illegal in themselves. The open-shop employers were jubilant. The NAM published selections from Adams's opinion in a pamphlet, which it then encouraged its members to distribute among their friends and their employees; the National Metal Trades Association hailed it as "the death knell of the closed shop." As things turned out, however, subsequent court decisions did not take *Christensen v. People* as the kind of precedent the open-shop employers had expected. See Ernst, *Lawyers against Labor*, 95–99. For the NAM pamphlet, see Marshall Cushing to Dear Sirs, July 7, 1904, series I, box 43, NAM Records.

55. *Chicago Daily Tribune*, February 21, 1906, 7. See also Powell, *History of the United Typothetae*, 67–70. The scope of the injunction is reproduced in Commonwealth of Massachusetts, Bureau of Statistics of Labor, *Labor Bulletin*, ed. Charles F. Pidgin (Boston: Wright & Potter Printing Co., State Printers, 1905), 38:332–33.

56. Injunctions were issued in the 1920s with even greater frequency than previously; roughly the same number were issued in the 1920s as in the decades of the 1890s, 1900s, and 1910s combined. See Forbath, *Law and the Shaping*, 158–60, 193. The Norris-LaGuardia Act issued a straightforward prohibition, stating that "no court . . . shall have jurisdiction to issue any restraining order or temporary or permanent injunction in a case involving or growing out of a labor dispute." A court could only intervene if it first heard "the testimony of witnesses in open court (with opportunity for cross-examination) in support of the allegations of a complaint made under oath, and testimony in opposition thereto, if offered" that satisfactorily established the existence of a fairly strict set of circumstances, including evidence of lawful acts, irreparable injury, and the absence of other remedies at law. The act also prohibited contracts that required workers to agree not to join a union (popularly known as "yellow-dog contracts") and provided that courts could not prohibit workers from such acts as refusing to work, joining a union, publicizing a labor dispute, or urging others to do so. "Act of March 23, 1932," Pub. L. No. 65, 47 Stat. 70, 70–71.

57. E. P. Thompson, *Whigs and Hunters: The Origins of the Black Act* (New York: Pantheon Books, 1975), 262–63.

58. There was some disagreement between manufacturers and the proponents of the bill as to how broadly it would apply: the language of the bill excluded from it such goods as could "usually be bought on the open market, whether made to conform to particular specifications or not, or for the purchase of supplies by the Government whether manufactured to conform to particular specifications or not." US Congress, Senate, Committee on Education and Labor, *The Eight-Hour Law: Report to Accompany H.R. 3076*, 57th Cong., 1st sess., Senate Report No. 2321, 1902, 2. Both the definition of goods that could be "bought on the open market" and the definition of "supplies" caused some confusion, with the bill's sponsor in the Senate, for example, repeatedly insisting that almost none of the manufacturers who appeared before him would come under the provisions of the act and the manufacturers insisting that the way they read the bill they could not see how they could avoid its provisions. For one example, see the exchange between Senator McComas and Fuller E. Callaway, a NAM member manufacturing cotton duck: McComas insisted that the only things the act really would apply to were large items like trains, vessels, and marine engines, while Callaway complained that he could not see how his goods would not come under the act, as he manufactured mailbag duck, something that he only produced because the government ordered it and that could not be bought off the shelf anywhere. Argument of Fuller E. Callaway, Esq., of LaGrange, GA, US Congress, Senate, Committee on Education and Labor, *Senate Bill 489, Eight Hours for Laborers on Government Work: Arguments*, 58th Cong., 2nd sess., March 15–April 6, 1904, 108–14.

59. Sklar, *Corporate Reconstruction*, 223–26.

60. The quote is from Marshall Cushing to Dear Sir, June 8, 1906, *Maintenance Appendix*, 706, emphasis in original. The congressman was Charles Littlefield, a member of the House Judiciary Committee. See Greene, *Pure and Simple Politics*, 96.

61. The Sherman Antitrust Act had been applied to unions in several cases since its passage in 1890, but the 1908 decision in the *Loewe v. Lawlor* (Danbury Hatters) case seemed much more far-reaching than previous ones. According to Martin Sklar, "Labor leaders understood the Court's ruling to mean that . . . not only were boycotts illegal, but so were strikes and union contracts with employers that provided for union recognition and that set wages and conditions over a period of time." *Corporate Reconstruction*, 224.

62. Executive committee members listed in *NCF Review* 1, no. 10 (January 1905): 8; Jensen, "The National Civic Federation," 27–28; Philip H. Burch, *Elites in American History*, vol. 2, *The Civil War to the New Deal* (New York: Holmes & Meier Publishers, 1981), 154–55, 167.

63. Jensen, "The National Civic Federation," 211.

64. Sklar, *Corporate Reconstruction*, 228–85, examines the drafting and fate of the Hepburn bill in great detail. Sklar attributes the weakening of the labor provisions to Theodore Roosevelt's insistence that the bill be redrafted to his preferences (255). Sklar notes that when introduced in Congress, the Hepburn bill became known as the Hepburn amendments to the Sherman Act; in the House its designation was H.R. 19745 and in the Senate S. 6440 (238 and 239n83).

65. See, for example, *American Industries*, September 15, 1904, 11; *American Industries*, February 15, 1906.

66. Oliver Crosby to Marshall Cushing, March 11, 1907; unaddressed letter by M. C. [Cushing], April 19, 1906, *Maintenance Appendix*, 91–92, 650. See also D. M. Parry to Fred C. Schwedtman, October 17, 1908: "Of course we all know how cowardly our politicians are when they come up against any sort of a labor proposition." *Maintenance Appendix*, 2230–31.

67. Unaddressed letter by M. C. [Cushing], April 19, 1906, *Maintenance Appendix*, 650.

68. C. C. Hanch to Marshall Cushing, March 11, 1907; C. C. Hanch to James W. Van Cleave, January 14, 1908, *Maintenance Appendix*, 922, 1290–92.

69. Secretary [Cushing] to H. W. Stegall, April 29, 1904, *Maintenance Appendix*, 341.

70. James A. Emery to Ferdinand C. Schwedtman, June 24, 1910, *Maintenance Appendix*, 3636.

71. See, for example, E. T. Gilbert, Michigan Bolt and Nut Works [NAM member], to James McMillan, April 2, 1900, SEN56A-F8, box 81, Senate Records, RG 46. The argument regarding the eight-hour day destroying prosperity was made over and over again; for one example, see E. S. Douglas, Secretary of Businessmen's Association of St. Joseph, Missouri, to L. E. McComas, March 9, 1904, reprinted in US Congress, Senate, Committee on Education and Labor, *Senate Bill 489, Eight Hours for Laborers on Government Work: Matter in Support and Opposition*, 58th Cong., 2nd sess., 1904, 397–98.

72. *Free Conspiracy, Free Riot*, pamphlet, n.d. (1903?), series I, box 43, NAM Records.

73. "Statement of Mr. E. S. Gary," US Congress, House, Committee on Labor, *Hearings on H.R. 6882, Hours of Labor for Workmen, Mechanics, etc., Employed upon Public Works of the U.S.*, 56th Cong., 1st sess., February 15–April 12, 1900, 316–17; "Statement of W. B. Cowles," US Congress, House, Committee on Labor, *Hearings on H.R. 11651, Eight Hours on Government Work*, 59th Cong., 1st sess., May 3–29, 1906, 129–35; "Statement of Frank C. B. Page," US Congress, Senate, Committee on Education and Labor, *Hearings on H.R. 9061, Eight-Hour Law*, 62nd Cong., 2nd sess., January 9–March 16, 1912, 200–211.

74. G. N. Bierce, Stilwell Bierce & Smith-Vaile Co. [NAM member], to J. B. Foraker, May 25, 1900, SEN56A-F8, box 81, Senate Records, RG 46; Charles E. Ellicott, Ellicott Machine Company, to Louis E. McComas, December 9, 1902; and Charles M. Jarvis, American Hardware Corporation [NAM member], to Louis E. McComas, December 9, 1902, both in SEN57A-F7, box 94, Senate Records, RG 46.

75. The "entering wedge" argument was repeated frequently; for some examples, see Alfred E. Cox, treasurer of Atlantic Works [NAM member], to L. E. McComas, December 9, 1902; and Jno. G. Hetzell & Son to L. E. McComas, December 9, 1902, both in SEN57A-F7, box 94, Senate Records, RG 46; John S. Farrell, J. S. Farrell & Co., to Albert J. Beveridge, January 23, 1904, SEN58A-J14, box 100, Senate Records, RG 46.

76. On the Senate Steering Committee and the procedural intricacies of the Senate in this period, see, for example, Robert C. Byrd, *The Senate, 1789–1989: Addresses on the History of the United States Senate* (Washington, DC: GPO, 1988), 362–68.

77. See, for example, Secretary [Cushing] to George A. Draper, December 31, 1903; Secretary to George K. Smith, February 17, 1904; unsigned to J. M. Manley, February 16, 1912, *Maintenance Appendix*, 181, 252–53, 4016–18. The obstructionist tactics were not, of course, invented by the NAM and were used also at the state level; Frederic Howe, for example, complained that progressive legislation in Ohio was killed simply by not letting it move forward: "Our bills never came to a vote; they were blocked at some stage of the proceedings." Quoted in Pierce, *Striking with the Ballot*, 219.

78. For examples of NAM exhorting manufacturers to write to congressmen and of the resulting letters (which are particularly common in the first year or two of the association's lobbying activism), see, for example, D. M. Parry and Marshall Cushing to Dear Sirs, February 11, 1903 (exhorting recipients to write to Senator William B. Allison to keep the eight-hour bill off the Senate calendar); Secretary [Cushing] to J. A. J. Shultz, December 1, 1903 (about writing and speaking to Senator Stone [?] of Missouri to keep him from supporting the eight-hour bill); Julius F. Kurtz to John Dalzell, June 2, 1906 (letter to congressman urging him to try to prevent the passage of the eight-hour bill). Sometimes congressmen received so many of these letters that they asked their manufacturer contacts to stop sending them: see Charles M. Jarvis to Marshall Cushing, January 30, 1903. All in *Maintenance Appendix*, 78–79, 136–37, 693–94, 75.

79. James Van Cleave quoted in Greene, *Pure and Simple Politics*, 96. The reproduction of the letter is in *Maintenance Appendix*, 128. See also Cushing's thanks to August Busch (Adolphus's son and vice president of the company) for ensuring that Bartholdt did the "right thing" in committee: Secretary [Cushing] to Aug. A. Busch, April 8, 1904, *Maintenance Appendix*, 317.

80. Greene, *Pure and Simple Politics*, 96.

81. Richard Bartholdt, *From Steerage to Congress: Reminiscences and Recollections* (Philadelphia: Dorrance, 1930), chapter 6.

82. Secretary [Cushing] to Dear Sirs, November 21, 1903, *Maintenance Appendix*, 120. What may have made the NAM even more worried about Stone was that there was substantial opposition to him within the ranks of Missouri Democrats, as a reformist wing of the party was gaining ascendancy at the time; see Ruth Warner Towne, *Senator William J. Stone and the Politics of Compromise* (New York: Kennikat Press, 1979), 68–73.

83. Marshall Cushing to John S. Brittain, November 24, 1903, *Maintenance Appendix*, 125.

84. E. S. Douglas to Marshall Cushing, March 15, 1904; E. J. Douglas to Marshall Cushing, April 12, 1904, both in *Maintenance Appendix*, 284, 326 (note that despite the different initials the letters are from the same person, the secretary of the St. Joseph Businessmen's Association). Other influential businessmen whom the NAM recruited to pressure Stone included August A. Busch, as well as a personal acquaintance of Stone, J. A. J. Shultz of the Shultz Belting Company of St. Louis; see Secretary [Cushing] to Aug. A. Busch, April 8, 1904; and J. A. J. Shultz to Marshall Cushing, April 6, 1904, both in *Maintenance Appendix*, 317, 309.

85. For instance, the manager of the International Harvester Company deliberately got Cyrus H. McCormick to personally sign a letter to House Speaker Joseph Cannon against the eight-hour bill, "thinking such [a] letter would carry more weight than it might otherwise." C. S. Fink to Marshall Cushing, February 4, 1906, *Maintenance Appendix*, 539.

86. Secretary [Cushing] to Ferdinand C. Schwedtman, April 16, 1904, *Maintenance Appendix*, 330–31. As Cushing explains in the letter, Stone acquiesced to the NAM's pressure only to the extent of not opposing the NAM's plan, not to the extent of actually going on record to support it. Instead of voting for referring the bill for further study, as the NAM wished, Stone merely stayed away from the committee meeting at which the vote was to take place. Up until the last minute, the NAM feared he might attend the meeting and vote against further delay in the consideration of the bill. As it was, Stone's decision to

avoid the crucial committee meeting made the vote 4–3 for referral, hardly a comfortable margin.

87. See Marshall Cushing's detailed report on the fate of the eight-hour bill in the spring of 1903, Secretary to Mr. Parry, March 14, 1903, *Maintenance Appendix*, 88–92. In the report, Cushing also noted that Senator Quay of Pennsylvania kept another bill on the floor for an extended period to prevent there being time for consideration of the eight-hour bill; Quay was a personal friend of an important and high-prestige NAM member from Pennsylvania, A. B. Farquhar. See A. B. Farquhar to D. M. Parry, February 2, 1903, *Maintenance Appendix*, 75–76.

88. Secretary [Cushing] to Mr. Parry, March 14, 1903. See also, for example, Secretary [Cushing] to Charles M. Jarvis, January 14, 1903, and January 22, 1903; A. B. Farquhar to D. M. Parry, February 2, 1903, all in *Maintenance Appendix*, 89, 69–70, 72, 75–76.

89. Greene, *Pure and Simple Politics*, 97.

90. As the secretary, Marshall Cushing, put it in 1903 regarding the "part of the Secretary's work" that was "involved in attending to legislative affairs, from the very nature of all this not much can be written." "Annual Report of Secretary, April 1, 1902 to March 31, 1903," NAM, *Proceedings* (1903), 88–108, quote on 104.

91. Secretary to the President [Ferdinand Schwedtman] to Henry Harrison Lewis, November 18, 1907. The letter is in response to Henry Harrison Lewis to Ferd C. Schwedtman, November 15, 1907, in which Lewis had suggested that the NAM ask congressmen to publicly rescind their pledges to support the AFL's anti-injunction bill. Both in *Maintenance Appendix*, 1139, 1146–47.

92. Secretary [Cushing] to Charles K. McDowell, March 25, 1904, *Maintenance Appendix*, 300. The congressman about whom the NAM was particularly concerned was George Gilbert (referred to in the letter to McDowell as "Mr. G."); he had earlier voted favorably on the bill. Secretary [Cushing] to N. F. Thompson, March 7, 1904, *Maintenance Appendix*, 270–72.

93. Quote is from Marshall Cushing to Dear Sir, July 24, 1905, *Maintenance Appendix*, 499–500. On getting the bill referred, see Marshall Cushing, "Organized Labor's Greatest Knockout Blow," April 3, 1904, *Maintenance Appendix*, 307–8. The report itself is US Congress, House, Committee on Labor, *Eight Hours for Laborers on Government Work. Report by the Hon. Victor H. Metcalf, Secretary, Department of Commerce and Labor, on H.R. 4064 (Eight-Hour Bill)*, 58th Cong., 3rd sess., January 27, 1905. The NAM had actually been instrumental in the creation of the Department of Commerce and Labor and in torpedoing labor's demands for a separate cabinet-level Department of Labor. While promotion of foreign trade was the NAM's main motivation for wanting a Department of Commerce, the effort to keep Labor within the same fold probably stemmed from a desire to prevent an independent labor voice at the highest levels (as labor feared it did). Once the combined department was created in early 1903, the NAM did its best to stay in close touch with the secretary and to influence the appointment of assistant secretaries and other department functionaries to strengthen the department's ties with business. The very day that George B. Cortelyou was appointed the first secretary of commerce and labor, the NAM's secretary wrote him and recommended that a "plain, straight-forward businessman" should receive the post of assistant secretary. Secretary [Cushing] to George B. Cortelyou, February 16, 1903, *Maintenance Appendix*, 81–82. For the NAM's role in the

creation of the department, see "A Sketch of the Purposes and Activities of the Organization, Prepared for the Extension Department," n.d., series I, box 43, NAM Records; and "Statement of John W. Ela, of Chicago," US Congress, House, Committee on Interstate and Foreign Commerce, *Hearings on H.R. 4364, to Establish a Department of Commerce and Industry*, unpublished hearings, 55th Cong., 2nd sess., February 4, 1898, 6–7. For labor fears of a combined department, see "Statement of Mr. H. R. Fuller, Representing the Brotherhood of Locomotive Engineers, the Brotherhood of Locomotive Firemen, the Order of Railway Conductors, the Brotherhood of Railroad Trainmen, and the Order of Railroad Telegraphers"; "Statement of Mr. A. Furuseth, Representing the Seamen's Union." See also "Statement of John W. Hayes, General Secretary of the Knights of Labor," which shows that the Knights of Labor, although it would have preferred a separate Department of Labor, supported the bill creating the combined department on the grounds that at least having a cabinet member whose responsibilities included labor was better than not having one at all. All statements in US Congress, House, Committee on Interstate and Foreign Commerce, *Hearing on Senate Bill 569 and House Bills 14, 95 and 2026, to Establish a Department of Commerce and Labor, Industries, and Manufactures*, 57th Cong., 1st sess., March 25–April 11, 1902, 39–61, 104–8, 90–104.

94. As Van Cleave explained to John Kirby, Cushing was not suitable for work with multiple organizations, because he had a tendency to "consider his judgment superior to the judgment" of everyone else combined. Kirby agreed, replying that "I feel just as you do about Mr. Cushing and am awful sorry that he possesses such a strong disposition to over-ride everybody but *Marshall Cushing*." President [Van Cleave] to John Kirby Jr., June 22, 1907; J. Kirby Jr. to James W. Van Cleave, June 25, 1907 (emphasis in original), both in *Maintenance Appendix*, 982–85, 990–91. On support for Cushing within the NAM and the broader open-shop movement, see Unsigned [D. A. Tompkins] to Marshall Cushing, September 13, 1907; Marshall Cushing to D. A. Tompkins, September 17, 1907; Richard C. Jenkinson to D. A. Tompkins, September 20, 1907; all in reel 8, Tompkins Papers. See also O. P. Briggs to J. Kirby Jr., June 15, 1907, *Maintenance Appendix*, 972–973. See also Wiebe, *Businessmen and Reform*, 26, 28–29.

95. As one NAM officer put it, Emery was an excellent lobbyist for the new multiorganization Council, since "he is a splendid mixer; can always get an audience with the biggest of men; is thoroughly posted on the labor situation; can make a splendid address at any time and place, and above all I believe he is absolutely sincere and loyal to the cause in which he is engaged." Unsigned [Schwedtman?] to O. P. Briggs, June 19, 1907. *Maintenance Appendix*, 977–78. On Emery's appointment and the NAM's resources being places at his disposal, see President [Van Cleave] to E. Lawrence Fell, November 28, 1907; Ferd. C. Schwedtman to James A. Emery, December 2, 1907; J. W. Van Cleave to F. C. Schwedtman, December 19, 1907; all in *Maintenance Appendix*, 1166–67, 1179, 1224–25. On Emery and Davenport, see Ernst, *Lawyers against Labor*, 53.

96. J. P. Bird to Henry B. Joy, April 2, 1910, *Maintenance Appendix*, 3525. The usual subscription amount was $500 or $1,000 ($100 in 1910 is equivalent to about $2,800 in 2020 dollars). It is not clear how many organizations or companies contributed. In mid-1908, when the council had been semioperative for a year, NAM officials still complained that "most of these organizations are paying nothing toward the maintenance of the Association's funds" by making council contributions. Secretary to the President [Schwedtman] to J. M. McKinery, June 13, 1908, *Maintenance Appendix*, 1719–21; Williamson, "Seven Ways."

97. Secretary [George S. Boudinot] to Charles M. Jarvis, December 30, 1909, *Maintenance Appendix*, 3364.

98. See, for example, testimony of J. P. Bird and testimony of Martin M. Mulhall, and in particular testimony of James A. Emery, which is almost in its entirety taken up with the senators' efforts to get a handle on the various organizations and the relationships between them; after some fifty pages, Senator Reed bursts out: "Who was the dominating figure [at the council meetings]? Who really ran the thing? Whose was the final word?" All in *Maintenance Hearings*, 2736–43, 3265–66, 3707–69, Reed quoted on 3760.

99. Greene, *Pure and Simple Politics*, 107–16.

100. "Obituary: John Hopewell," *Bulletin of the National Association of Wool Manufacturers* 46 (April 1916): 150–52; Marquis, *Book of St. Louisans*, 309; "C. A. Schieren Dead, His Wife Is Dying," *New York Times*, March 11, 1914, 11; *Baltimore: Its History and Its People*, vol. 3, *Biography* (New York: Lewis Historical Publishing Company, 1912), 593–94.

101. Marshall Cushing to Dear Sir, March 28, 1906, *Maintenance Appendix*, 619–20.

102. H.R. Committee of Labor (table); H.R. Committee on the Judiciary (table); "Rough suggestions for candidates and campaign managers" (memo), n.d. (1906?), all in *Maintenance Appendix*, 563–65.

103. "Rough suggestions for candidates and campaign managers" (memo), n.d. (1906?), *Maintenance Appendix*, 563–65.

104. See Thomas R. Pegram, "McComas, Louis Emory," *American National Biography Online* (Oxford University Press, February 2000), http://www.anb.org/articles/05/05-00497.html; see also James Duncan to M. M. Mulhall, October 8, 1903, *Maintenance Appendix*, 107–8.

105. Testimony of Martin Michael Mulhall, *Maintenance Hearings*, 2450–68; an example of the letters written to McComas appears on 2455–56. On the prevalence of patronage jobs, see, for example, Ronald N. Johnson and Gary D. Libecap, "Patronage to Merit and Control of the Federal Government Labor Force," *Explorations in Economic History* 31, no. 1 (January 1994): 91–119; Olle Folke, Shigeo Hirano, and James M. Snyder, "Patronage and Elections in U.S. States," *American Political Science Review* 105, no. 3 (August 2011): 567–85.

106. Secretary [Cushing] to D. M. Parry, December 20, 1902; Secretary [Cushing] to Charles M. Jarvis, January 2, 1903; Secretary [Cushing] to D. M. Parry, March 14, 1903, Marshall Cushing to Dear Sir, March 29, 1904, Secretary [Cushing] to James A. Gary, May 28, 1904; James A. Gary to Marshall Cushing, May 31, 1904; Secretary [Cushing] to E. Stanley Gary, June 9, 1904, all in *Maintenance Appendix*, 50–56, 62–64, 88–92, 304, 350–52, 359–60. For the biography of James A. Gary, see *The National Cyclopaedia of American Biography* (New York: James T. White & Company, 1901), 11:16–17. Rumor had it that there was bad blood between Gary and McComas stemming from Gary's anger over McComas's effort to get a cabinet position at the time when Gary got his postmaster general appointment; see Frank Richardson Kent, *The Story of Maryland Politics: An Outline History of the Big Political Battles of the State from 1864 to 1910* (Baltimore, MD: Thomas and Evans Printing Company, 1911), 219. See also Secretary [Cushing] to Oscar Murray, June 13, 1904; unsigned to Marshall Cushing, February 5, 1905; and unsigned unaddressed letter [Cushing to Mulhall], March 26, 1906, all in *Maintenance Appendix*, 362, 474–75, 614–15.

107. State legislatures chose senators before the ratification of the Seventeenth Amendment in 1913. It may be that the NAM's campaign against prolabor Republicans in Mary-

land had contributed to delivering the state election to Democrats in 1903, but that was probably not the NAM's aim; it had apparently hoped to strengthen the opponents of the pro-McComas and prolabor factions of the Republican Party. The documentary record on the NAM involvement in the 1903 campaign is not as strong as it might be; overall, the documentation from the first couple of years of the NAM's campaigning is sparser than for later periods. The strongest evidence indicating NAM involvement in the primaries is an unsigned letter dated September 2, 1903, to "My Dear C" (probably Cushing) whose writer reports a conversation with "our friend D, the assistant to Senator McComas," in which "D" lamented that "a lot of the manufacturers in [McComas's] district are fighting him tooth and nail all on account of the 8-hour bill" and that "Parry, the president of the National Association of Manufacturers, is putting both time and money into the fight." *Maintenance Appendix*, 105. Also, Mulhall's testimony in Congress indicates that he supported the anti-McComas faction of the Maryland Republicans in the 1903 primaries, and he later boasted that his Workingmen's Protective Association had been involved in that fight; Cushing's close correspondent James A. Gary was instrumental in opposing the McComas organization in those elections. In addition, Daniel A. Tompkins, who sat on the NAM board of directors and was an active member, later stated that he thought "the association had some influence in electing McComas to stay at home." Tompkins to Van Cleave, February 19, 1908, *Maintenance Appendix*, 1378. However, there are also some holes and contradictions in the evidence: there are no letters between Cushing and Mulhall clearly verifying any activity by Mulhall in the primaries, for instance, while there is a letter by officials of the Workingmen's Protective Association dated in the summer of 1903 and supporting McComas. See testimony of Martin Michael Mulhall, *Maintenance Hearings*, 2451; *New York Times*, May 30, 1903, 1; Edwin T. Booth and Louis T. Parsano, Workingmen's Protective Association, to the officers and members of the Iron Molders' Union of North America, Local 409, July 12, 1903; and Martin M. Mulhall to Ferdinand C. Schwedtman, February 23, 1908, both in *Maintenance Appendix*, 102–3, 1384–86.

108. Greene, "Dinner-Pail Politics."

109. The NAM's campaign for Littlefield took most of the summer of 1906, beginning with a week-long visit from NAM secretary Marshall Cushing to ensure Littlefield's selection in the June primaries and concluding with Mulhall's efforts on location in August and September, which included recruiting a couple of dozen workingmen to organize political support in Rockland and in the countryside and sowing discord among union workers in Maine. Some of the details of the efforts are recounted in the testimony not only of Mulhall but also of Samuel Gompers, who was in the area campaigning against Littlefield (e.g., the distribution of free whiskey, though it is unclear in Gompers's testimony if the whiskey was supposed to be an enticement to vote for Littlefield or a hindrance to voting). The money for the pro-Littlefield efforts came, it seems, mainly from the NAM, which in turn raised it from New England manufacturers. How much was spent is impossible to ascertain; Mulhall later claimed that the manufacturers spent some $40,000 for Littlefield (nearly $1.2 million in 2020 dollars), but he was always prone to exaggeration. Still, even if the sum spent was only half that, it would have been impressive: for example, the AFL's political budget for the whole election season totaled less than $10,000 (even if its member unions carried some costs independently), and according to Samuel Gompers, the AFL spent a total of only $1,500 on the Littlefield campaign. Testimony of Martin Michael Mulhall,

Maintenance Hearings, 2586, 2590; Greene, *Pure and Simple Politics*, 115–17; testimony of Mr. Samuel Gompers, President of the American Federation of Labor, US Congress, House, Select Committee Appointed under H. Res. 98, *Hearings on the Charges against Members of the House and Lobby Activities of the National Association of Manufacturers of the United States and Others*, 63rd Cong., 1st sess., July 12–August 18, 1913, 2505, 2414; Williamson, "Seven Ways." Other electoral campaigns in these years in which the NAM was involved included supporting House Judiciary committee chairman John Jenkins, first supporting and then opposing House Labor Committee chairman John Gardner, and a failed bid to elect the longtime NAM ally James E. Watson as governor of Indiana; on the last especially, see Greene, *Pure and Simple Politics*, 202–10; and Greene, "Dinner-Pail Politics."

110. Unsigned to Herman S. Hastings, March 29, 1911; M. M. M. [Mulhall] to J. P. Bird, April 4, 1911; James Emery to John Kirby Jr., April 26, 1912, all in *Maintenance Appendix*, 3826–27, 3830–31, 4059–62. On the NAM's explicit recruiting in the South, see also the remarks of John Temple Graves urging the NAM to make Atlanta the location of its 1905 national convention: "The Association needs to enlarge its membership, to increase its influence throughout the Republic. . . . The North is already splendidly organized, and through the work of this Association northern Congressmen are brought into harmony with the wishes of the Association. The South is yet unorganized, or incomplete in its organization, and southern Congress men have been found standing sometimes as an obstacle to the industrial legislation which you desire." NAM, *Proceedings* (1904), 245–46. (The next year's annual meeting was indeed held in Atlanta.)

111. Chairman [Schwedtman] to J. P. Bird, April 7, 1913, *Maintenance Appendix*, 4150–51.

112. James A. Emery to John Kirby Jr., December 15, 1911, *Maintenance Appendix*, 3980.

113. James A. Emery to John Kirby Jr., April 26, 1912, *Maintenance Appendix*, 4059–62.

114. Greene, *Pure and Simple Politics*, 230, 247–48.

115. Philip Burch reports that the NAM "placed no representatives in high federal posts" during the administrations of Presidents McKinley, Roosevelt, and Taft. *Elites in American History*, 200n158. See also, for example, the NAM's plan to get James Watson, a close ally in Congress, appointed in Taft's cabinet and its abandoning of that effort as hopeless: Ferdinand C. Schwedtman to M. M. Mulhall, December 26, 1908; unsigned to Ferdinand C. Schwedtman, December 31, 1908; unsigned to Ferdinand C. Schwedtman, January 12, 1909; and Ferdinand C. Schwedtman to M. M. Mulhall, January 16, 1909, all in *Maintenance Appendix*, 2477, 2480–81, 2503–5, 2524–27.

116. Forbath, *Law and the Shaping*, 156–58, 193. Gompers quoted in Clyde W. Summers, "Industrial Democracy: America's Unfulfilled Promise," *Cleveland State Law Review* 28, no. 1 (1979): 31; underlining the hyperbole, Summers comments that Gompers was "apparently unaware that the feudal barons, not the serfs, won at Runnymede."

Chapter 7. The Battle over Public Opinion

1. *The Wageworker*, November 24, 1905, 1. On the epigraph: This quip is attributed to Yogi Berra (the famous baseball commentator Lawrence Peter Berra) in several online quote collections and newspaper articles discussing his famous quotes; I have not seen it attributed to anyone else, but neither does a reliable source for the quotation seem to

exist. One might keep in mind that according to *Bartlett's Familiar Quotations* (citing *Sports Illustrated*, March 17, 1986), Yogi Berra also said, "I really didn't say everything I said." John Bartlett, *Bartlett's Familiar Quotations*, 18th ed., ed. Geoffrey O'Brien (New York: Little, Brown and Company, 2012).

2. *The Wageworker*, October 20, 1905, 5. *The Wageworker*, whose tagline was "A Newspaper with a Mission and without a Muzzle that is published in the interests of Wageworkers Everywhere," was run by Will M. Maupin, a member of the International Typographical Union, the union of the striking printers. "About The Wageworker," Chronicling America, accessed December 7, 2020, https://chroniclingamerica.loc.gov/lccn/sn86063459/. Holdom was infamously antiunion, and in the elections of the previous year, the Chicago unions had tried to oust him from his position. See the *Chicago Daily Tribune*, May 16, 1904, 5. The printers' strike is discussed more extensively in chapter 5.

3. *Los Angeles Times*, October 30, 1905, II, 4.

4. *Los Angeles Times*, November 6, 1905, 1.

5. The quote is from Holdom's decision. As was common at the time, many newspapers did not identify the AP as the source of the story; one that did was the *Los Angeles Herald*, October 18, 1905, 1.

6. See, for example, Scott M. Cutlip, *The Unseen Power: Public Relations, a History* (Hillsdale, NJ: Lawrence Erlbaum Associates, 2013). On public opinion polling, see Philip E. Converse, "Changing Conceptions of Public Opinion in the Political Process," *Public Opinion Quarterly* 51 (1987): S12–S24.

7. This continued to be the case long into the twentieth century, as, for example, Jack Metzgar points out in his discussion of the 1959 steel strike and the ways in which steel industry towns rallied around the workers, who of course were the indispensable patrons of all the local businesses. *Striking Steel: Solidarity Remembered* (Philadelphia: Temple University Press, 2000).

8. The source for numbers of papers is metadata compiled from the OCLC (Online Computer Library Center) WorldCat database, accessed through the US Newspaper Directory at https://chroniclingamerica.loc.gov/search/titles/. For the early 2000s, see Penelope Muse Abernathy, "The Expanding News Desert," Center for Innovation and Sustainability in Local Media, University of North Carolina at Chapel Hill, 2018, https:// www.cislm.org/wp-content/uploads/2018/10/The-Expanding-News-Desert-10_14-Web .pdf. On capital requirements: in one issue of the *Western Publisher*, a trade paper serving country weeklies, the classified section contained advertisements ranging from a Minnesota paper and job office for $500, to a North Dakota paper and job plant for $1,200, and "one of the best equipped and best paying newspapers in central Texas" for $7,500. *Western Publisher* 3 (June 1904): 56. In 2020 dollars, $500 in 1904 would be about $15,000, and $7,500 would be about $225,000. Williamson, "Seven Ways."

9. On objectivity, see Richard L. Kaplan, *Politics and the American Press: The Rise of Objectivity, 1865–1920* (New York: Cambridge University Press, 2001); see also Leonard Ray Teel, *The Public Press, 1900–1945* (Westport, CT: Praeger Publishers, 2006).

10. The *Taney County Republican* and the *Ripley County Democrat* were both published in Missouri; more information about them is available at "About the Taney County Republican," Chronicling America, accessed August 15, 2020, https://chroniclingamerica .loc.gov/lccn/sn89067390/; "About the Ripley County Democrat," Chronicling America,

accessed August 15, 2020, https://chroniclingamerica.loc.gov/lccn/sn89067083/. For a cover of the *Forest City Press* with the motto, see, for example, the November 12, 1903 issue, https://chroniclingamerica.loc.gov/lccn/sn93057084/1903-11-12/ed-1/seq-1/.

11. See "Labor and Radical Press History and Geography," Mapping American Social Movements, accessed August 15, 2020, http://depts.washington.edu/moves/laborpress_intro.shtml for visualizations of data on socialist, anarchist, and different kinds of labor publications.

12. Jon Bekken, "The Working-Class Press at the Turn of the Century," in *Ruthless Criticism: New Perspectives in U.S. Communication History*, ed. William S. Solomon and Robert W. McChesney (Minneapolis: University of Minnesota Press, 1993), 151–75.

13. Labor temples and union halls were, of course, also in themselves public messages, conveying the "substance and solidarity" of unions. Stephen McFarland, "'With the Class-Conscious Workers under One Roof': Union Halls and Labor Temples in American Working-Class Formation, 1880–1970" (PhD diss., City University of New York, 2014), 49, 56.

14. Jon Bekken, "'This Paper Is Owned by Many Thousands of Workingmen and Women': Contradictions of a Socialist Daily," *American Journalism* 10, no. 1/2 (Winter–Spring 1993): 3–5.

15. Sometimes these were centrally distributed and appeared in identical form in multiple papers; at other times the paper itself gathered them from several sources for printing in its own paper. For some examples, see, for example, the *Indianapolis Journal*, November 29, 1903, part 3, 10; *San Francisco Call*, November 15, 1906, 9; *Palestine Daily Herald,* June 18, 1904, 3 (and the identical Labor and Industry column printed in the *Kansas Agitator*, June 10, 1903, 2—this was probably distributed through readyprint; see below).

16. See, for example, "Perverting and Suppressing Union News," editorial, *American Federationist* 18, no. 7 (July 1911): 538–40. See also Bekken, "The Working-Class Press."

17. For consistency, the mainstream papers were selected to represent the same states as the labor papers (unfortunately, limitations posed by what has been digitized made it impossible to select papers from the same towns).

18. This is a very bare-bones explanation, of course. For a more detailed examination of the methodology, see https://github.com/vhulden/bossesunion/, which contains all the data and scripts along with an extensive discussion of word embeddings and tables of the similarity measures and context and similar words for a set of key terms like "socialism," "strikers," and so on. The analysis here uses the SVD PPMI method, which draws on ideas first introduced in Hinrich Schütze, "Dimensions of Meaning," in *Proceedings of Supercomputing '92* (Los Alamitos, CA: IEEE Press, 1992), 787–96. See also Omer Levy, Yoav Goldberg, and Ido Dagan, "Improving Distributional Similarity with Lessons Learned from Word Embeddings," *Transactions of the Association for Computational Linguistics* 3 (2015): 211–25; and Omer Levy and Yoav Goldberg, "Neural Word Embedding as Implicit Matrix Factorization," in *Proceedings of the 27th International Conference on Neural Information Processing Systems—Volume 2*, NIPS'14 (Cambridge, MA: MIT Press, 2014), 2177–85.

19. *New York Times*, September 9, 1910, 9. Since the text is not preprocessed to join multiword expressions like "New York City," the context words do not contain "New York City" as such but rather the individual components; still, it seems clear enough that

"New York" and/or "New York City" appear frequently. The list of main context words is "banker, york, city, new, prominent, business, chicago, dead, man, died, estate, george, home, known, real, son, john, late."

20. On Hearst's 1905 mayoral campaign, see Irwin Yellowitz, *Labor and the Progressive Movement in New York State, 1897–1916* (Ithaca, NY: Cornell University Press, 1965), chapter 9.

21. That is, the basic idea is that words that occur in the same texts repeatedly (say, *ball* and *pitcher* and *bat* and *diamond*) are likely to end up forming a topic. A topic is then represented by a list of words particularly characteristic of that topic. Note that texts are not classified into topics; each text contains multiple topics of different weights. Topic modeling was here performed with MALLET: Andrew Kachites McCallum, "MALLET: A Machine Learning for Language Toolkit," 2002, http://mallet.cs.umass.edu. The topic model selected has 150 topics. For reader-friendly explanations of topic modeling, see, for example, Matthew Jockers, "The LDA Buffet Is Now Open; or, Latent Dirichlet Allocation for English Majors," September 29, 2011, http://www.matthewjockers.net/2011/09/29/the-lda-buffet-is-now-open-or-latent-dirichlet-allocation-for-english-majors/; Shawn Graham, Scott Weingart, and Ian Milligan, "Getting Started with Topic Modeling and MALLET," Programming Historian, September 2, 2012, https://programminghistorian.org/en/lessons/topic-modeling-and-mallet. For a fuller discussion of how the method was used here, see https://github.com/vhulden/bossesunion.

22. As is always the case in examining topics produced by a topic modeling algorithm, one needs to go back and forth between the stories in which the topic is prominent and the topic modeler's output to make sense of the meaning of the topic. The list of words most prominently associated with this analysis and principles topic is "people men man great country life good public law power world government american time true things fact human free political."

23. "About the Labor Argus," Chronicling America, accessed August 15, 2020, https://chroniclingamerica.loc.gov/lccn/sn85059855/.

24. On this, see also Cameron Blevins, "Space, Nation, and the Triumph of Region: A View of the World from Houston," *Journal of American History* 101, no. 1 (June 2014): 122–47.

25. The figure showing the least *prominent* topics is simply the reverse of the most prominent ones, that is, the topics whose average "weight" in the labor material was lowest. The figure showing the least *characteristic* topics shows the labor topics that get the lowest score when the average weight of a topic in the nonlabor material is subtracted from the labor material. Thus, topics that are prominent in labor material but not in mainstream material would have a significantly higher number than those that were prominent in both the labor material and the mainstream material. Technically, this could mean that a topic that does not form a very large volume of labor material would emerge as nevertheless fairly characteristic of that material if it almost never appears in the mainstream material. However, looking at only nonprominent topics may skew the analysis by showing only topics that overall happened to be very small in any kind of material, which may be due more to the algorithm than to the topic. I have calculated both versions for top topics as well, but the results of the characteristic-topics analysis are similar enough to the prominent-topics one that I have only included the simpler analysis.

26. Tobias Higbie, *Labor's Mind: A History of Working-Class Intellectual Life* (Urbana: University of Illinois Press, 2019).

27. Wilbur Schramm and Merritt Ludwig, "The Weekly Newspaper and Its Readers," *Journalism Bulletin* 28, no. 3 (September 1951): 301–14.

28. On labor's later publicity efforts, see Fones-Wolf, *Selling Free Enterprise*.

29. Secretary [Cushing] to F. C. Schwedtman, October 9, 1906, *Maintenance Appendix*, 828–29.

30. The campaign was to "cover the labor problem, tariff revision, merchant marine and such kindred subjects as may be made a part of the policy of the association." Atherton Brownell to J. W. Van Cleave, May 25, 1907, *Maintenance Appendix*, 957–60.

31. Readyprint also went by the name of "patent insides," though in fact it was apparently equally common for the outside of the printing paper to be reprinted as for the inside.

32. See, for example, the query from the *Glenville Progress* of Minnesota about content: "Would you print a goodly sprinkling of Minnesota news and of the Northwest . . . and will your insides be free of whisky ads. I want a clean sheet." A. G. Morgan to Publishers' Newspaper Union, June 12, 1906, reprinted in US Congress, House, Committee on the Judiciary, *Trust Legislation, Hearings, Parts 1–3, Western Newspaper Union*, 62nd Cong., 2nd sess., June 11, July 8, 10, 12, 1912, serial no. 8, 1912, 271.

33. Testimony of Courtland Smith, US Congress, House, Committee on the Judiciary, *Trust Legislation, Hearings, Western Newspaper Union*, 9.

34. Testimony of William L. Witmer and Testimony of Daniel Webster Witmer, US Congress, House, Committee on the Judiciary, *Trust Legislation, Hearings, Western Newspaper Union*, 44, 45.

35. Nathaniel C. Fowler Jr., *The Handbook of Journalism: All about Newspaper Work* (New York: Sully and Kleinteich, 1913), 121, 116. See also US Congress, Senate, Committee on Printing, *Final Report on News-Print Paper Industry in United States*, 65th Cong., 1st sess., 7263 S. Doc. 49, June 13, 1917, 22.

36. The price for reading notices in the 1900 Kellogg's list was about 1.7 times the price of display ads. *Kellogg's Lists: 1919 Family Newspapers of the Better Class* (Chicago: A. N. Kellogg Newspaper Company, 1900).

37. The Kellogg's list for 1900, for instance, was divided into nine different lists, mainly covering the Midwest and South. The price for display advertising in the full list of 1,919 papers was $12.50 per agate line (basically one line of ordinary type of the width of one column), or the advertiser could choose individual lists, ranging from the smallest at fifty cents per line to the largest at two dollars per line—though "liberal discounts graded according to amount of order" were available; see *Kellogg's Lists*. For reference, $1.00 in 1900 equals $31.80 in 2020 dollars using the consumer price index (Williamson, "Seven Ways"). Historians of journalism note that reading notices were "ubiquitous" in the late nineteenth century; see Linda Lawson, "Advertisements Masquerading as News in Turn-of-the-Century American Periodicals," *American Journalism* 5, no. 2 (April 1988): 81–96. In 1917, however, Courtland Smith of the American Press Association (a readyprint and boilerplate supplier) claimed that "there are not many reading notices run" (US Congress, House, Committee on the Judiciary, *Trust Legislation, Hearings, Western Newspaper Union*, 23).

38. Testimony of Courtland Smith, testimony of George A. Joslyn, and testimony of Alfred Washington, *Maintenance Hearings*, 4623 ff. See also Alfred McClung Lee, *The*

Daily Newspaper in America: The Evolution of a Social Instrument (New York: Macmillan Company, 1937), 141–42, 212, 385–86.

39. William Kittle, "The Making of Public Opinion," *The Arena* 41, no. 232 (July 1909): 433 ff. The quote, according to the article, is from a letter written by a Mr. Grant of the bureau to the president of the Oconee Telephone Company.

40. Atherton Brownell to J. W. Van Cleave, May 25, 1907, *Maintenance Appendix*, 957–60.

41. *American Industries*, March 16, 1903; *American Industries*, May 15, 1906; *American Industries*, October 15, 1903. The short items were often reprinted from regional newspapers; one wonders if the same strategy applied here as in the case of Hendrick's magazine article, below, that is, whether some of these news items had originally been placed in the newspapers by the NAM itself.

42. Atherton Brownell to Ferdinand C. Schwedtman, October 10, 1907, *Maintenance Appendix*, 1071; Williamson, "Seven Ways."

43. Henry Harrison Lewis, "The Peril of Anti-injunction Legislation," *North American Review* 188, no. 635 (October 1908): 577–83. Author searches using the names of the major Century Syndicate employees and partners were run through the *Readers' Guide Retrospective* database (EBSCOHost), which indexes a significant number of major magazines from the early twentieth century, as well as through the ProQuest databases *American Periodicals Series Online* and *American Periodicals from the Center of Research Libraries*; these index both general-interest periodicals and trade and labor publications. The names of the syndicate personnel are from Atherton Brownell to James W. Van Cleave, August 22, 1907; President [Van Cleave] to Charles A. Becker, November 29, 1907; H. H. Lewis to Ferdinand C. Schwedtman, August 19, 1908, all in *Maintenance Appendix*, 1034–35, 1169–72, 1909. Note that the original searches were done in about 2010; however, test searches in November 2021 show that results for *Readers' Guide Retrospective* remain the same. The two ProQuest databases have since been combined into a single *American Periodicals* database (see https://www.proquest.com/americanperiodicals/productful ldescdetail/advanced), but its contents do not appear to have changed, as indicated by test searches in 2021.

44. The article in question was Burton J. Hendrick, "Battle against the Sherman Law," *McClure's Magazine* 31 (October 1908): 665–80, for which the association's officers and allies had, according to the NAM's Ferdinand Schwedtman, supplied "much of the information." A similar article on the tariff question was considered though apparently not published. Secretary to the President [Ferdinand C. Schwedtman] to H. H. Lewis, October 7, 1908; and Secretary to the President [Schwedtman] to H. E. Miles, October 20, 1908, both in *Maintenance Appendix*, 2153–54, 2245–46.

45. The quote is from Secretary [George S. Boudinot] to Charles M. Harvey, September 30, 1909, *Maintenance Appendix*, 3177. According to Marshall Cushing, Sleicher was "a great friend" of David M. Parry, the association's president from 1903 to 1905, while Ferdinand Schwedtman noted that Sleicher "has always had a warm regard for Mr. Van Cleave," NAM president from 1906 to 1908. See Secretary [Cushing] to F. C. Nunemacher, September 21, 1905; Secretary to the President [Schwedtman] to James A. Emery, October 29, 1908, *Maintenance Appendix*, 511, 2303–5. On the probability of Van Cleave having written the NAM-praising editorial, see the same letter from Schwedtman to Emery; for the editorial itself, see "Editorial from Leslie's Weekly of October 29, [1908]," reprinted in

Maintenance Appendix, 2410. On a different editorial apparently being written or edited by the NAM, see John A. Sleicher to [Charles M.] Harvey, July 28, 1909, *Maintenance Appendix*, 3039–40. Regarding Van Cleave's article, see Leslie's Weekly to James W. Van Cleave, July 2, 1908, *Maintenance Appendix*, 1794. Other magazines that are mentioned in the NAM correspondence as favorably (though not necessarily uncritically) inclined toward the association included *Van Norden's* and *Success*; see Ferdinand C. Schwedtman to James W. Van Cleave, November 20, 1907; H. E. Miles to H. H. Lewis, April 3, 1908; Secretary to the President [Schwedtman] to Charles M. Harvey, August 18, 1908, all in *Maintenance Appendix*, 1151–53, 1506–7, 1904–5.

46. Jack R. Hart, "Horatio Alger in the Newsroom: Social Origins of American Editors," *Journalism Quarterly* 53 (March 1976): 16. Daniel A. Tompkins, a longtime member of the NAM's board of directors, was publisher of the *Daily Charlotte Observer*, the *Charlotte Evening Chronicle*, and the *Greenville News*. Stephen Goldfarb, "Tompkins, Daniel Augustus," American National Biography Online (Oxford University Press, February 2000), http://www.anb.org/articles/10/10-01655.html. In addition to Sleicher, Van Cleave was also friends with his hometown editor, Charles M. Harvey of the *St. Louis Globe-Democrat* (the largest daily in St. Louis and, despite its name, Republican in affiliation). Harvey routinely received payment from the NAM for writing speeches and articles for Van Cleave, as well as editorials for *American Industries*, but the NAM adamantly denied that it had ever paid Harvey for an article published in the general press over Harvey's name. See, for example, Secretary to the President [Schwedtman] to Charles M. Harvey, April 8, 1908, and June 14, 1909, *Maintenance Appendix*, 1530–31, 2920. For the denial of any stealth in Harvey's writings, see testimony of Ferdinand C. Schwedtman, *Maintenance Hearings*, 4426–29. Although the statements of Marshall Cushing and Atherton Brownell, cited above, clearly show that the NAM had few scruples in general about leaving the reader in ignorance of the source of news and magazine stories, there is no evidence that Harvey ever wrote anything in magazines on the NAM's behalf. Nor does a search of the *Readers' Guide Retrospective* database reveal any articles by Harvey on industrial topics; he published extensively, but mostly on topics related to westward expansion and the development of the American West. The data on the *Globe's* circulation and political affiliation are from Edward P. Remington, *Edward P. Remington's Annual Newspaper Directory: A List of All Newspapers and Other Periodical Publications in the United States and Canada*, 20th issue (Pittsburgh, PA: Edward P. Remington, Newspaper Advertising, 1907), 156.

47. *Los Angeles Times*, December 20, 1907.

48. Although the correspondence does not mention this incident, its timing during the fall of 1907 would imply that it was designed by the Century Syndicate. In any case, placing this story would not have been difficult: Harrison Gray Otis, the owner of the *Los Angeles Times*, was a vehement antiunion employer and an NAM ally. On Otis, see, for example, Grace H. Stimson, *Rise of the Labor Movement in Los Angeles* (Berkeley: University of California Press, 1955).

49. Testimony of Martin M. Mulhall, *Maintenance Hearings*, 2881–83; and Samuel Gompers's remarks in American Federation of Labor, *Report of Proceedings of the Twenty-Seventh Annual Convention*, Norfolk, Virginia, November 11–23 inclusive (Washington, DC: National Tribune Company, 1907), 249–67. Also see Secretary to the President [Ferdinand Schwedtman] to Mr. J. Philip Bird, August 17, 1908, *Maintenance Appendix*, 1896–97.

Schwedtman is nearly certainly referring to this incident when he writes, "If it had not been for Mr. Van Cleave's presence of mind we would have at one time last year given the American Federation of Labor and the sensational press opportunity for a full page headline which would have been anything but creditable to the National Association of Manufacturers."

50. On strikebreaking, see Pearson, *Reform or Repression*, 77; for similar organizations in Great Britain, see Saluppo, "Strikebreaking."

51. The quotes are from the *Warren Sheaf*, November 27, 1902, 2, reporting on circulars sent out by a James W. Bellinger of New York, identified as a clerk secretary of a proposed association called the National Association of Independent Workmen of America. The headline of the story is "An Anti-Union Union."

52. *New York Sun*, October 25, 1903, 15. Various organizations with similar names appeared in news reports: American League of Independent Workmen, National Association of Independent Workmen of America, Independent Labor League of America. For more, see Hulden and Pearson, "The Wild West."

53. The organization's practical handling was done by one Charles Harriman, a former unionist now in charge of the labor portion of the pro-Littlefield campaign. Testimony of Martin M. Mulhall, September 3, 1913, *Hearings on the Charges against Members of the House and Lobby Activities of the National Association of Manufacturers of the United States and Others*, 1856, 1860. The Labor League later sent Mulhall a letter of thanks for "your time and money that you have spent so lavishly on our behalf." C. A. Harriman, J. W. McDonald, and K. K. Ward to M. M. Mulhall, September 11, 1906, reprinted in *Hearings on the Charges*, 1953.

54. *Lewiston Evening Journal*, August 15, 1906.

55. See, for example, H. E. Miles to F. C. Schwedtman, December 31, 1907; J. P. Bird to F. C. Schwedtman, August 14, 1908; George S. Boudinot to F. C. Schwedtman, September 18, 1908, all in *Maintenance Appendix*, 1244, 1883–84, 2067–68.

56. James A. Emery to Ferdinand C. Schwedtman, March 22, 1909, *Maintenance Appendix*, 2730–31.

57. *American Industries*, June 15, 1903, 4.

58. *American Industries*, January 15, 1903, 8, emphasis in original. The NAM also made its wishes known to newspaper editors centrally on occasion, such as sending a circular that aimed to highlight the viewpoints of employing printers in the 1906 Typographical Union strike, in which it pointed out that the employing printers were supported by "the manufacturers of the country, many of them advertisers and friends of yours." Secretary [Marshall Cushing] to Dear Mr.—, September 23, 1905 (form letter noting that it was sent to 225 members of the American Newspaper Publishers' Association), reel 2, Tompkins Papers. The same letter was also sent to 2,500 daily newspapers, dated October 7.

59. Lee, *Daily Newspaper*, table 29, 748–49; Linda Lawson, *Truth in Publishing: Federal Regulation of the Press's Business Practices, 1880–1920* (Carbondale: Southern Illinois University Press, 1993), 9.

60. Bekken, "The Working-Class Press," 165; see also Jon Bekken, "'No Weapon So Powerful': Working-Class Newspapers in the United States," *Journal of Communication Inquiry* 12 (July 1988): 104–19; Gerald J. Baldasty, *E. W. Scripps and the Business of Newspapers* (Urbana: University of Illinois Press, 1999), chapter 6.

61. Gerald J. Baldasty, *The Commercialization of News in the Nineteenth Century* (Madison: University of Wisconsin Press, 1992), chapter 3; George Seldes, *Lords of the Press* (New York: J. Messner, 1938); Susan Lucarelli, "The Newspaper Industry's Campaign against Spacegrabbers, 1917–1921," *Journalism Quarterly* 70, no. 4 (Winter 1993): 883–92; Edwin Emery, *History of the American Newspaper Publishers Association* (Westport, CT: Greenwood Press, 1970), chapter 8.

62. Unsigned [F. G. R. Gordon] to C. C. Lula, April 22, 1915. For responses, see, for example, Lee Tire & Rubber Company to F. G. R. Gordon, April 29, 1915 (stating that the magazine was read by people who bought cars, and its circulation was growing) and Vice President of Chalmers Motor Company to F. G. R. Gordon, April 30, 1915 (stating that no "advertiser has the right to dictate to a magazine anything in connection with their editorial policy"—and the magazine's readers could afford cars). All in box 187, folder 5, NCF Records.

63. On responses more inclined to use advertising power, see, for example, Beech Nut Packing Company to F. G. R. Gordon, April 29, 1915, box 187, folder 5, NCF Records.

64. Ted Curtis Smythe, "The Reporter, 1880–1900: Working Conditions and Their Influence on the News," in *Media Voices, an Historical Perspective*, ed. Jean Folkerts (New York: Macmillan, 1992), 221, emphasis in original; see also Ted Curtis Smythe, *The Gilded Age Press, 1865–1900* (Westport, CT: Praeger, 2003), chapter 8. By the early twentieth century, journalism was becoming more professional, but this process had yet to touch most newspapers, and in any case, wages remained generally low; see Teel, *The Public Press*, 28–29, 41–42.

65. Secretary [Cushing] to Frederick E. Matson, February 6, 1904, *Maintenance Appendix*, 236–37; testimony of Martin Michael Mulhall, *Maintenance Hearings*, 2446. The Century Syndicate's employee Henry Harrison Lewis eventually became the editor of the NAM's periodical, *American Industries*.

66. A search for the names of presidents David M. Parry, James W. Van Cleave, and John Kirby, as well as the names of Marshall Cushing (NAM secretary 1903–6) and George S. Boudinot (NAM secretary after 1907) in the *Readers' Guide Retrospective* for 1900–1915 yields a total of only eight articles: seven were published in the *Annals of the American Academy of Political and Social Science* and one in the *Engineering Record*; none were published in the popular press proper. A search with the keyword "national association of manufacturers" yielded only eight hits, seven of which had to do with the rather inglorious topic of a major congressional investigation into whether the association had engaged in illicit lobbying practices.

67. The study notes that even in the NAM's own literature, positive themes began to outnumber direct antilabor propaganda after 1913. George D. Blackwood, "Techniques and Stereotypes in the Literature of the National Association of Manufacturers Concerning Industry and Labor" (master's thesis, University of Chicago, 1947), 11–12, 58.

68. James A. Emery to Ferdinand C. Schwedtman, March 22, 1909, *Maintenance Appendix*, 2730–31. On the publicity value of being "affirmative rather than denunciatory negative," see H. E. Miles to F. C. Schwedtman, June 1, 1908, *Maintenance Appendix*, 1679–80.

69. Professional ad men, in fact, used phrases very similar to Emery's: as one noted, "It is not by his own taste, but rather by the taste of the fish, that the angler determines his

choice of bait" (quoted in Pamela Walker Laird, *Advertising Progress: American Business and the Rise of Consumer Marketing* [Baltimore, MD: Johns Hopkins University Press, 1998], 258).

70. Ferdinand C. Schwedtman, "Nation Wide Movement for Industrial Safety," *The Survey*, April 19, 1913, 102–4; Ferdinand C. Schwedtman, "Ounce of Prevention," *Harper's Weekly*, September 2, 1911, 9–10.

71. Ralph Easley quoted in Jensen, "The National Civic Federation," 180.

72. For a few representative examples, see, for example, "Industrial Conciliation," *New York Times*, December 18, 1900, 9; "Lever for Labor Peace," *Chicago Daily Tribune*, May 3, 1903, 3; "Will Urge Fair Play for Private and U.S. Labor," *Washington Post*, January 15, 1912, 5; "Election Reform Conference," *The Outlook*, March 17, 1906, 580–81; "An Able Defense of the Labor Union," *The Outlook*, March 16, 1912, 572 ff. On the Carnegie and Harriman dinners, see "An Evening of Industrial Peace," *New York Observer and Chronicle*, April 11, 1907, 478; and "Banker's Wife Dines Labor Delegates," *New York Times*, August 19, 1909, 1. In contrast to the NAM's poor results with most major magazines, a search with the keyword phrase "national civic federation" produced twenty-five hits in the *Readers' Guide Retrospective* database between 1900 and 1915; eighteen of these were in general-interest magazines. See also Jensen, "The National Civic Federation," 178–81.

73. James A. Emery to Ferdinand C. Schwedtman, March 22, 1909, *Maintenance Appendix*, 2730–31.

74. Cyphers, *The National Civic Federation*, 20; Jensen, "The National Civic Federation," 45.

75. For example, between 1900 and 1915, Ralph Easley published five articles, all labor-related, in *The Independent*, *McClure's Magazine*, and *Harper's Weekly*. (The information comes from an author search in the *Readers' Guide Retrospective* database.) All the articles were published between 1902 and 1904, which was the peak period of interest in the NCF's arbitration work, though later articles by Roland Phillips, a journalist affiliated with and regularly employed by the NCF, continued the campaign: see, for example, Roland Phillips, "What the Civic Federation Is Doing," *Harper's Weekly*, April 20, 1907, 570–71.

76. On the structure of the NCF and the functions of its various departments, see Cyphers, *The National Civic Federation*, chapter 1; and Bonnett, *Employers' Associations*, chapter 11.

77. Lawrence Abbott to Ralph M. Easley, November 4 and December 23, 1904, box 184, folder 1; Hamilton Holt to Ralph M. Easley, October 19, 1904, box 184, folder 7; Bradford Merrill to Ralph Easley, October 19, 1904, box 185, folder 1; Sereno S. Pratt to Seth Low, February 13, 1908, box 26, folder 3; Herman Ridder to Seth Low, February 13, 1908, box 26, folder 4; [secretary, name illegible] to William R. Corwine, April 13, 1908, box 27, folder 1; unsigned to Charles H. Taylor, June 4, 1908, and Charles H. Taylor to R. M. Easley, November 5, 1908, box 27, folder 2, all in NCF Records.

78. For example, in 1908–10, Easley wrote a whole series of letters to Charles Miller of the *New York Times*, asking for his advice on how to handle particular cases of antisocialist publicity and sending him material he might wish to use; Miller was apparently fairly active in the NCF's antisocialist campaign. See, for example, unsigned [Easley] to Charles R. Miller, July 11, 1908, February 15, 1909, March 22, 1909, October 13, 1909, and April 28, 1910; C. R. Miller to Ralph M. Easley, November 23, 1908, all in box 185, folder 2, NCF Records.

79. See, for example, "Injunction Assailed: Mitchell and Gompers before Civic Federation," *Washington Post*, December 13, 1906, 2.

80. Jensen, "The National Civic Federation," 51, 211, 308–10.

81. See, for example, Ralph M. Easley, "The Two Irreconcilable Foes of the Civic Federation," *NCF Review* 3, no. 8 (November 1909): 7 ff., a long piece contrasting the reasoned and moderate position of the NCF with the extremism of both socialists and antiunion employers. For an example of NCF mockery of NAM's logical inconsistencies, see the piece "Some Anti-Boycotters' Boycotts," *NCF Review* 2, no. 1 (April 1905): 8.

82. John Kirby Jr., "A Disloyal and Unpatriotic Organization," *American Industries*, August 1911, 10; see also Kirby, "The Goal of the Labor Trust," *American Industries*, February 1910, 15–19 (an article responding to Easley, "Two Irreconcilable Foes," quoted above).

83. "The Trade Agreement in Five Great Industries." On Easley's private defenses of the closed shop, see the exchange between Marcus M. Marks and Easley discussed in the second section of chapter 3.

84. Easley, "What Organized Labor Has Learned"; see also Easley, "Work of the NCF"; Ralph M. Easley, "National Civic Federation," *The Independent*, August 28, 1902, 2065 ff.

85. Zerzan, "Understanding the Anti-radicalism of the National Civic Federation," 199.

86. See, for example, Easley, "Two Irreconcilable Foes."

87. There are different interpretations regarding the reasons behind this shift. Christopher Cyphers, for instance, attributes it mainly to the passing of the NCF's presidency from Mark Hanna to August Belmont and to a crystallization of or return to the federation's broader purpose, "social and public policy reform" (*The National Civic Federation*, 32–34). John Zerzan, on the other hand, contends that the shift resulted from the failure of most of the trade agreements promoted by the federation—a failure partly resulting from rank-and-file workers' dissatisfaction with the federation's actions, which tended to favor employers. See Zerzan, "Understanding the Anti-radicalism of the National Civic Federation."

88. The Department of Industrial Economics (memorandum), enclosure in unsigned to Jeremiah Jenks, May 11, 1906, box 255, folder 4, NCF Records.

89. On the need for antisocialist speakers not affiliated with major capitalists, see unsigned [Easley] to J. S. Crawford, June 6, 1910, box 184, folder 3; and unsigned [Easley] to Elisabeth Marbury, February 7, 1910, box 185, folder 1, NCF Records.

90. Unsigned [Easley] to Henry Holt, November 4, 10, 16, and 20, 1909; Henry Holt to R. M. Easley, November 6, 15, and 18, 1909, all in box 184, folder 7, NCF Records. On promotion of Gordon's articles in the press, see also Easley's (apparently successful) effort to get articles by Gordon and another antisocialist labor unionist, E. A. Moffett, published in the *New York Sun*: unsigned [Easley] to F. G. R. Gordon, April 22, 1909, box 184, folder 5; and unsigned to E. B. Mitchell, July 15, 1909, box 185, folder 2, NCF Records.

91. For example, when it seemed that Gordon's employment at the Bureau of Immigration and Naturalization might be in jeopardy, Easley wrote Supreme Court justice William Henry Moody, Vice President James S. Sherman, and Senator Henry Cabot Lodge to make sure Gordon would keep his job. Easley argued that Gordon's work was probably being badmouthed by socialists at the bureau and that as "Labor and other bureaus over there are giving jobs to Socialists" it "behooves us" not to fire prominent antisocialists. Moody and Lodge replied, reassuring Easley of the security of Gordon's position. Unsigned [Easley] to William Henry Moody, to James S. Sherman, and to Henry Cabot Lodge, all

dated March 9, 1909; W. H. Moody to R. M. Easley, March 10, 1909; H. C. Lodge to Ralph M. Easley, March 12, 1909, all in box 184, folder 5, NCF Records. For direct payments and references to salary, see, for example, unsigned [Easley] to E. A. Moffett, January 18, 1909, and E. A. Moffett to R. M. Easley, January 20, 1909, box 185, folder 2, NCF Records.

92. See the notes for the discussion of F. G. R. Gordon in the previous section, as well as E. A. Moffett to Easley, January 18, 1909; "To the Editor of New York Times" by Anti-Gorky (E. A. Moffett), March 26, 1909; unsigned [Easley] to E. A. Moffett, June 24, 1909 (about responding to a "Socialistic" article in the *New York Sun*); E. A. Moffett to R. M. Easley, January 19, 1909 (about a letter reacting to material in *The Outlook*), all in box 185, folder 2, NCF Records. On the *Outlook* matter, see also Easley's efforts to get Moffett's response published: unsigned [Easley] to William B. Howland, January 7, 1909; Harold J. Howland to R. M. Easley, January 8, 1909; Chairman Executive Council [Easley] to Harold J. Howland, January 11, 1909, all in box 184, folder 7, NCF Records; for the published response, see E. A. Moffett, "Public Opinion," *The Outlook*, March 6, 1909, 537 ff.

93. Unsigned [Easley] to F. G. R. Gordon, April 21, 1913, box 187, folder 4, NCF Records. In this letter, Easley is clear that even the newspapers did not know of the NCF's involvement in Gordon's supposed response: "Of course, there is nothing to indicate where it came from; only the Tribune people will know somebody was using your name."

94. Quote from "The Gorky 'Incident'" (unsigned draft), n.d., 2–3, box 255, folder 4, NCF Records (about the scandal surrounding the 1906 visit of the Russian writer Maxim Gorki to the United States, during which it was discovered that the woman accompanying him was not his wife). For exchanges where Easley praised and promised to promote conservative woman writers, see Easley's letters with southern writer Corra Harris (who had criticized Charlotte Perkins Gilman) and with the antisuffragist and promoter of women's higher education Annie Nathan Meyer. Unsigned [Easley] to Mrs. L. H. Harris, March 25, 1909; Corra (Mrs. L. H.) Harris to Ralph M. Easley, March 31, 1909; unsigned [Easley] to Mrs. L. H. Harris, April 7, 1909; Chairman Executive Council [Easley] to Walter P. McGuire, May 28, 1908; Chairman Executive Council [Easley] to Annie Nathan Meyer, March 15, 1909, all in box 184, folder 6, and box 185, folders 1 and 2, NCF Records.

95. For example, the *NCF Review* defended Gompers when he was being harshly criticized in the wake of the McNamara brothers confessing to bombing the *Los Angeles Times* in the context of a strike in structural steel (discussed in chapter 8). It also continued to promote the AFL in the wake of World War I, when the wave of antiradical repression known as the First Red Scare cast a pall on all labor and Left activity. See, for example, Easley's article defending Gompers from claims that he condoned the McNamara dynamiting in *NCF Review* 3, no. 12 (February 1912): 13 ff.

96. See, for example, unsigned [Easley] to William D. Foulke, September 3, 1912, box 187, folder 2; unsigned [Easley] to H. A. Garfield, May 12, 1913, box 187, folder 2, NCF Records.

97. Kaplan, *Politics and the American Press*, 142, 175, 193–94 (quote on 194).

Chapter 8. Defending the Status Quo Ante Bellum

1. Quoted in H. M. Gitelman, "Management's Crisis of Confidence and the Origin of the National Industrial Conference Board, 1914–1916," *Business History Review* 58, no. 2 (Summer 1984): 156. On the epigraph: The modern form of this saying is apparently

adapted from one or more 1960s sources, mostly military-related. The website Quote Investigator cites several close relations of the phrase from the 1960s; the earliest of these is a comic strip from a 1961 US Navy publication with the phrase "all liberty is canceled until morale improves," with other similar ones following, including a 1965 newspaper report of a junior officers' prank sign in Vietnam stating "no beer, card playing, mail call, idle time, movies, R & R, until morale improves." See "The Floggings Will Continue Until Morale Improves," Quote Investigator, accessed April 3, 2022, https://quoteinvestigator.com/2020/07/15/morale/.

2. Gitelman, "Management's Crisis," 163.

3. A full list of participants can be found in Gitelman, "Management's Crisis," 163n26. Participants included, among others, several representatives of the NAM, the presidents of the National Founders' Association and the National Metal Trades Association (both important open-shop advocates), and several business representatives who were also NAM members.

4. Unsigned [Walter Drew] to F. A. Vanderlip, January 27, 1917, series V, box 11, National Industrial Conference Board Records, accession number 1057, Hagley Museum and Library, Wilmington, DE. Hereafter cited as NICB Records.

5. Frank Duffy to John Mitchell, August 13, 1908, box 256, folder 2, NCF Records.

6. This official of the International Longshoremen, Marine and Transportworkers' Association, identified as MGI, referred specifically to Samuel Mather of Pickands, Mather and Co.; besides being incensed that Mather seemed to side with the dock managers in an ongoing dispute on the Great Lakes, MGI complains that Mather claimed he "favors trades unions" but failed to prevent Pickands, Mather and Co. from introducing individual rather than union contracts, though he "controls nearly three fourths of all the Pickands, Mather Company's stock." MGI to R. M. Easley, May 27, 1908, reel 13, John Mitchell Papers, accession number 1629, microform, Hagley Museum and Library, Wilmington, DE.

7. Strike data for these years is patchy at best—no federal agency collected statistics on strikes between 1906 and 1915. John Griffin has estimated the data for 1906–15 from the records of seven state labor bureaus (Connecticut, Kansas, Maryland, Massachusetts, New Jersey, New York, and Rhode Island); the federal Bureau of Labor Statistics estimated data for 1914 and 1915 when it resumed its collection of strike data in 1915, but according to Griffin, those compilations clearly underestimate strike activity. See John I. Griffin, *Strikes: A Study in Quantitative Economics* (New York: Columbia University Press, 1939), tables 1 and 2 (38–39 and 43–44) and chapter 7. See also Rosenbloom, "Work Stoppages."

8. Ingham, "A Strike." Information about the appearance of the McKees Rocks strike on the *New York Times* front pages is based on a search for the phrase "pressed steel" in the ProQuest Historical Newspapers database, limited to front-page articles from the *New York Times* between July 1, 1909, and September 30, 1909, with results checked manually.

9. Orleck, *Common Sense*, chapter 2; Meredith Tax, *The Rising of the Women: Feminist Solidarity and Class Conflict, 1880–1917* (New York: Monthly Review Press, 1980), chapter 8; Daniel Sidorick, "The 'Girl Army': The Philadelphia Shirtwaist Strike of 1909–1910," *Pennsylvania History: A Journal of Mid-Atlantic Studies* 71, no. 3 (Summer 2004): 323–69.

10. Lawrence Cappello, "In Harm's Way: The Lawrence Textile Strike Children's Affair," in *The Great Lawrence Textile Strike of 1912: New Scholarship on the Bread & Roses Strike* (New York: Routledge, 2014); *New York Times*, February 11, 1912, 1 (headlined "150 Strike Waifs Find Homes Here").

11. Thomas G. Andrews, *Killing for Coal: America's Deadliest Labor War* (Cambridge, MA: Harvard University Press, 2008), chapter 7; Scott Martelle, *Blood Passion: The Ludlow Massacre and Class War in the American West* (New Brunswick, NJ: Rutgers University Press, 2007).

12. Andrews, *Killing for Coal*, chapter 7; Martelle, *Blood Passion*.

13. Fine, *"Without Blare of Trumpets,"* 95–103.

14. *American Industries*, January 1912, 14.

15. Allen F. Burns, "For a Just Industrial Peace," *The Survey*, March 16, 1912, 1926.

16. Richard W. Judd, *Socialist Cities: Municipal Politics and the Grass Roots of American Socialism* (Albany: State University of New York Press, 1989); Laslett, *Labor and the Left*, 162–65.

17. Herbert Shapiro, "Lincoln Steffens and the McNamara Case: A Progressive Response to Class Conflict," *American Journal of Economics and Sociology* 39, no. 4 (October 1980): 397–412.

18. Weyl quoted in the *New York Times*, April 7, 1912, 6 (headlined "Sees Grim Warning in Lawrence Strike").

19. Heath W. Carter, *Union Made: Working People and the Rise of Social Christianity in Chicago* (New York: Oxford University Press, 2015); Elizabeth Fones-Wolf and Ken Fones-Wolf, "Lending a Hand to Labor: James Myers and the Federal Council of Churches, 1926–1947," *Church History* 68, no. 1 (March 1999): 62; *Courier-Journal*, December 10, 1909, 2; *Courier-Journal*, September 4, 1910, A3.

20. Fones-Wolf and Fones-Wolf, "Lending a Hand," 67; Ken Fones-Wolf, "Religion and Trade Union Politics in the United States, 1880–1920," *International Labor and Working-Class History*, no. 34 (Autumn 1988): 47–48; Christopher H. Evans, *The Social Gospel in American Religion: A History* (New York: New York University Press, 2017), 100–103.

21. Greene, *Pure and Simple Politics*, 230, 247–48; Melvyn Dubofsky, *The State and Labor in Modern America* (Chapel Hill: University of North Carolina Press, 1994), 52; *Christian Science Monitor*, June 1, 1912, 15.

22. For a comprehensive account of the election of 1912, see Lewis L. Gould, *Four Hats in the Ring: The 1912 Election and the Birth of Modern American Politics* (Lawrence: University Press of Kansas, 2008).

23. Weyl quoted in the *New York Times*, April 7, 1912, 6.

24. Allen F. Davis, "The Campaign for the Industrial Relations Commission, 1911–1913," *Mid-America: An Historical Review* 45, no. 4 (October 1963): 211–28.

25. Among the public members, the NAM was hoping for the appointment of someone like University of Chicago economist J. Laurence Laughlin or Columbia University president Nicholas Murray Butler; both made frequent appearances in the NAM's *American Industries*. As an example of an employer candidate that the NAM would like but that would likely be unpalatable to others, the letter-writer mentioned C. W. Post, the idiosyncratic and vehemently antiunion force behind the Citizens' Industrial Association of America. At one point the NAM had also considered suggesting men from one of its astroturf worker organizations as representatives of labor but came to the conclusion that this would be "as much out of place as it would be" for organized labor to suggest employer representatives from some "quasi-Employers' Associations." Unsigned to John Kirby Jr., August 27, 1912, *Maintenance Appendix*, 4106.

26. Unsigned to Ferdinand C. Schwedtman, August 29, 1912, *Maintenance Appendix*, 4108.

27. James A. Emery to John Kirby Jr., December 18, 1912, *Maintenance Appendix*, 4135. See also unsigned [Schwedtman] to F. A. Barker, December 27, 1912, in which Schwedtman speculates that the appointment "may add materially to our present activity and prestige." *Maintenance Appendix*, 4140–41.

28. Davis, "The Campaign," 224–25 (notes 44 and 59 contain the lists of Taft and Wilson appointees, respectively).

29. Walsh to George Creel, quoted in Stromquist, *Reinventing "the People,"* 175.

30. McCartin, *Labor's Great War*, 24–30.

31. Testimony of John D. Rockefeller Jr., US Commission on Industrial Relations, *Final Report and Testimony*, 7763–7895.

32. Status of the Open Shop, n.d., series VII, box 127, NAM Records.

33. US Commission on Industrial Relations, *Final Report and Testimony*, 17. The official final report was written by Basil Manly, director of research and investigation for the commission. It had the support of Walsh and the labor members but was condemned by the other members of the commission. See Stromquist, *Reinventing "the People,"* 184–85.

34. For more on n-grams and on how this n-gram was created, see https://github.com/vhulden/bossesunion. Google's Ngrams are described at https://books.google.com/ngrams/info and presented in Michel et al., "Quantitative Analysis."

35. McCartin, *Labor's Great War*, 8.

36. Walter Weyl, *The New Democracy: An Essay on Certain Political and Economic Tendencies in the United States* (New York: Macmillan Company, 1912), chapter 7, quote on 293n1.

37. Victor S. Yarros, "The Coming Industrial Democracy," *American Journal of Sociology* 24, no. 6 (May 1919): 672–80. For basic biographical information, see "Victor Yarros, 1865–1956," *Social Service Review* 31, no. 1 (March 1957): 94.

38. Stromquist, *Reinventing "the People,"* 166.

39. Commons, *Myself*, 171, 173.

40. "Industrial Relations Commission Reports," *American Industries*, September 1915, 12 ff.

41. *NCF Review* 4, no. 2 (December 1913): 13; *NCF Review* 4, no. 3 (March 1914): 9, quote from the latter source.

42. Unsigned [Easley] to Vincent Astor, May 21, 1915, box 186, folder 3, NCF Records.

43. It seems that Easley had prepared to testify at the USCIR hearings and had also expected that the USCIR would ask for the NCF's assistance in drafting a bill on industrial relations. Neither happened. Though two NCF officials (Gertrude Beeks and John Hays Hammond) did testify, Easley was never invited, which he suspected was because Walsh "had heard that I was unfriendly to their investigation"—which Easley rather was, being of the opinion that it gave too much attention to representatives of the Industrial Workers of the World and to the likes of the famous attorney Clarence Darrow, who had, among other things, defended the McNamaras. See Unsigned [Easley] to Vincent Astor, May 21, 1915, box 186, folder 3, NCF Records. See also R. M. Easley to James Couzens, April 22, 1915, box 186, folder 7, NCF Records. For the expectation that the NCF would be asked for bill-drafting help, see unsigned [Easley] to W. D. Baldwin, July 29, 1914, box 186, folder

4, NCF Records. For NCF testimony at USCIR, see testimony of Gertrude Beeks, US Commission on Industrial Relations, *Final Report and Testimony*, June 10, 1914, 2215–32; testimony of John Hays Hammond, US Commission on Industrial Relations, *Final Report and Testimony*, January 29, 1915, 7987–8003.

44. Unsigned [Easley] to Charles A. Eaton, December 30, 1912, box 187, folder 2, NCF Records.

45. Unsigned [Easley] to William D. Foulke, September 3, 1912, box 187, folder 2, NCF Records. In conjunction with letters about the survey, Easley often sent along a draft of an article that laid out his views of the extent and dangers of socialism in American institutions and noted that this explained the need for such a survey. The draft is in "Progress versus Social Chaos—Which Is the Tendency?," article draft, n.d. [ca. July 1912], box 188, folder 1, NCF Records. It is unclear if the article was ever published.

46. Quote from William D. Foulke to Ralph Easley, n.d. [marked September 1912], box 187, folder 2, NCF Records; see also John H. Gray to Seth Low, October 14, 1913, box 187, folder 6, NCF Records. NCF president Seth Low, too, had tried to at least head off the explicit anti-socialist goal of the progress survey, arguing that "a campaign of open antagonism" would be "just as fatal as if we were to enter into politics." Seth Low to Ralph M. Easley, July 22, 1912; unsigned [Easley] to Seth Low, July 23, 1912, both in box 188, folder 1, NCF Records. On Easley's belief that discontent was really an indication of progress (because progress had reduced people's acceptance of hardship), see the excerpts from the remarks Easley had planned to deliver at the USCIR hearings in 1914, first half published in *NCF Review* 4, no. 12 (April 1919): 12–14, and the second half in *NCF Review* 4, no. 13 (April 1919): 3–4. See also unsigned [Easley] to H. P. Davison, September 27, 1912, box 186, folder 8, NCF Records; and unsigned [Easley] to J. D. Beck, July 8, 1914, box 186, folder 4, NCF Records. Christopher Cyphers argues that as the NCF presidency moved from Seth Low to V. Everett Macy in 1916, the check that Low had put on Easley's antiradical activism was removed, and the NCF "tacked directly into the ultraconservative winds that blew across the nation's social and political landscape." *The National Civic Federation*, 173.

47. *Chicago Daily Tribune*, June 29, 1913, 1.

48. James A. Emery to Henry A. Towne, July 22, 1913, *Maintenance Appendix*, 4168.

49. See, for example, *Washington Post*, June 30, 1913, 1; *New York Times*, July 13, 1913, 1.

50. Report of J. P. Bird, minutes of the meeting of the board of directors, May 18, 1914, series XIII, box 199, NAM Records.

51. Greene, *Pure and Simple Politics*, 255. See also Delton, *The Industrialists*, 78–80.

52. McCartin, *Labor's Great War*, 40–45.

53. Jacob Kramer, *The New Freedom and the Radicals: Woodrow Wilson, Progressive Views of Radicalism, and the Origins of Repressive Tolerance* (Philadelphia: Temple University Press, 2015), 79–99; Elizabeth McKillen, *Making the World Safe for Workers: Labor, the Left, and Wilsonian Internationalism* (Urbana: University of Illinois Press, 2013), chapter 4.

54. McKillen, *Making the World Safe*, 116–22, 147–50; McCartin, *Labor's Great War*, 56–58.

55. McKillen, *Making the World Safe*, 121–22; Jennifer Luff, *Commonsense Anticommunism: Labor and Civil Liberties between the World Wars* (Chapel Hill: University of North Carolina Press, 2012), chapter 3.

56. H. M. Gitelman, "Being of Two Minds: American Employers Confront the Labor Problem, 1915–1919," *Labor History* 25, no. 2 (March 1984): 203.

57. Gitelman, "Being of Two Minds"; McCartin, *Labor's Great War*, 86.

58. Magnus Alexander to Walter Drew, A. W. Berresford, Frederick S. Clark, and Herbert H. Rice, January 29, 1918, series V, box 11, NICB Records.

59. McCartin, *Labor's Great War*, 86; quotes from Magnus Alexander to Walter Drew, A. W. Berresford, Frederick S. Clark, and Herbert H. Rice, January 29, 1918, series V, box 11, NICB Records.

60. Principles of the War Labor Board reprinted in the *Arizona Republican*, March 31, 1918, 1.

61. McCartin, *Labor's Great War*, 89.

62. Newcomb Carlton, president of Western Union, quoted in the *Atlanta Constitution*, June 3, 1918, 1. The union in question was the Commercial Telegraphers' Union of America.

63. Taft quoted in the *Atlanta Constitution*, June 3, 1918, 1. See also William Howard Taft, "The Western Union and the National War Board: A Plain Statement of the Plain Facts in the Case," *Courier-Journal*, July 21, 1918, A4.

64. *Christian Science Monitor*, July 1, 1918, 1; *Atlanta Constitution*, July 6, 1918, 1; *New York Tribune*, July 7, 1918, 1; *Atlanta Constitution*, July 14, 1918, 1.

65. Walter Drew to Magnus Alexander, July 9, 1918, series V, box 11, NICB Records. Drew does not mention the Western Union case explicitly, but he clearly means the report in that case, as he quotes directly from it: "The precedent [was] established in the report of Walsh and Taft to the effect that the employer 'need not recognize or deal with the union in any way'"; compare a quote from the report in the Western Union case that the company was "not [to] be required in any way to deal with the union or recognize it." *St. Louis Post-Dispatch*, June 3, 1918, 8. It is a little unclear why Drew felt that "Frankfurter and his crowd" were more of a threat than the NWLB. Frankfurter, arguably, was more inclined to emphasize expert leadership and less affiliated with labor than was Frank Walsh. Perhaps Drew was thinking of Frankfurter's support of Theodore Roosevelt's 1912 candidacy as the standard bearer of the new (and short-lived) Progressive Party or of Frankfurter's willingness to use his contacts to put pressure on the copper companies in his role on the Mediation Commission. However, the Mediation Commission did not force the companies to negotiate with unions, and it imposed a prohibition on strikes for the duration of the war. See Michael E. Parrish, *Felix Frankfurter and His Times* (New York: Free Press, 1982), 55–57, 87–94. On Walsh, see Stromquist, *Reinventing "the People,"* chapter 7.

66. Walter Drew, "Observations on Bridgeport and Smith & Wesson Cases," September 23, 1918, series V, box 11, NICB Records.

67. McCartin, *Labor's Great War*, 86–88.

68. McCartin, *Labor's Great War*, 86–93, 174–78.

69. Magnus Alexander to Walter Drew, March 31, 1919; Walter Drew to Magnus Alexander, April 1, 1919, both in series V, box 11, NICB Records.

70. Executive Draft of Principles of a Labor Policies Program, June 16, 1919, series V, box 11, NICB Records, emphasis added.

71. See Labor Policies Program as Revised by the Committee on a Labor Policies Program, December 29, 1919, series V, box 11, NICB Records.

72. In presenting the statement of principles, Harry A. Wheeler of the US Chamber of Commerce explained that it originally came from the NICB members, and it incorporates in slightly different form much of the NICB's labor policies draft. US Department of Labor, Office of the Secretary, *Proceedings of the First Industrial Conference (Called by the President)*, October 6–23, 1919 (Washington, DC: GPO, 1920), 79–83; Labor Policies Program as Agreed Upon Tentatively by the Committee on a Labor Policies Program, September 25, 1919, series V, box 11, NICB Records. In fact, James Emery had recommended that the NICB should complete and publicize its labor principles ahead of the conference so as to stake out a clear position that would provide a "rallying point for public opinion" and avoid a situation where employers were presented with a "program . . . sprung upon you to your embarrassment." James A. Emery to National Industrial Conference Board, September 12, 1919, series V, box 11, NICB Records. Magnus Alexander deemed the employer group's statement of principles "clear and strong and courageous." M. W. Alexander to Walter Drew, telegram, October 9, 1919, series V, box 11, NICB Records.

73. Quoted in McCartin, *Labor's Great War*, 189.

74. US Department of Labor, Office of the Secretary, *Proceedings of the First Industrial Conference*, 5–13; see also McCartin, *Labor's Great War*, 191–92. McCartin notes that among those *not* invited were Frank Walsh, William Howard Taft, and other men with wartime experience as public representatives on labor boards and that the composition of the public group "so offended . . . the UMW representative to the conference, John L. Lewis, that he resigned in protest prior to the first meeting."

75. National Industrial Conference Board, *The Vital Issues in the Industrial Conference at Washington, D.C.*, October 6–23, 1919 (Boston, MA, November 1919); US Department of Labor, Office of the Secretary, *Proceedings of the First Industrial Conference*, 22–23, 47–48.

76. US Department of Labor, Office of the Secretary, *Proceedings of the First Industrial Conference*, 155. As J. W. O'Leary explained in later discussion (p. 200), the form of the resolution (including the second clause guaranteeing the right not to join) came from two members of the public group, Charles Edward Russell (a journalist and former member of the Socialist Party) and H. B. Endicott (the head of the Endicott Johnson shoe company).

77. US Department of Labor, Office of the Secretary, *Proceedings of the First Industrial Conference*, 155; see also the explanation (on p. 188) of Matthew Woll (vice president of the AFL) to the effect that labor had agreed to this additional clause precisely so as to make clear that there was no *obligation* to join a union.

78. H. B. Endicott, the shoe manufacturer in the public group who was responsible for writing the second clause of the proposition, reported that he had been told that labor would never accept it and that he himself was insulted and angered by the employers' refusal to endorse the proposition when labor had made such a clear effort to meet them halfway. US Department of Labor, Office of the Secretary, *Proceedings of the First Industrial Conference*, 193–94, 233, 255–57.

79. National Industrial Conference Board, *The Vital Issues*; see also A. A. Landon of the American Radiator Co. (representing the public group), US Department of Labor, Office of the Secretary, *Proceedings of the First Industrial Conference*, 159.

80. US Department of Labor, Office of the Secretary, *Proceedings of the First Industrial Conference*, 175. The full employer resolution read: "That, without in any way limiting the right of a wage earner to refrain from joining any association or to deal directly

with his employer as he chooses, the right of wage earners in private as distinguished from Government employment to organize in trade and labor unions, in shop industrial councils, or other lawful form of association, to bargain collectively, to be represented by representatives of their own choosing in negotiations and adjustments with employers in respect to wages, hours of labor, and other conditions of employment, is recognized; and the right of the employer to deal or not to deal with men or groups of men who are not his employees and chosen by and from among them is recognized; and no denial is intended of the right of an employer and his workers voluntarily to agree upon the form of their representative relations." The wordiness did not escape the conferees; as the dry goods merchant George R. James from Tennessee (representing the public group) commented: "I am opposed to [the resolution] for the reason that, to my mind, it contains too many words" (182).

81. Only the public group voted in favor of the resolution amended with the words "and other organizations"; labor and employers voted against. In explaining employers' refusal to accept a similar modification of the resolution, the president of the US Chamber of Commerce, Harry Wheeler, noted that the modifications "do not meet the situation which was the only reason we had for declining to support the original Chadbourne resolution," that is, the resolution presented on the eighth day of the conference. While Wheeler did not elaborate, the main objections raised by employers at that point concerned the failure of the resolution to protect employers against having to allow their men to unionize through existing unions and then having to negotiate with the representatives of those unions. "Shop organization" quote is from Gompers late in the conference. US Department of Labor, Office of the Secretary, *Proceedings of the First Industrial Conference*, 155–62 (statement of Frederick Fish), 166–96 (statement of Ferguson), 231, 237, 270.

82. The full text of the final resolution was as follows: "The right of wage earners to organize without discrimination, to bargain collectively, to be represented by representatives of their own choosing in negotiations and adjustments with employers in respect to wages, hours of labor, and relations and conditions of employment is recognized." The employer quote is from Frederick P. Fish, president of the NICB and former president of AT&T. US Department of Labor, Office of the Secretary, *Proceedings of the First Industrial Conference*, 250–51, 275.

83. National Industrial Conference Board, *The Vital Issues*, quotes from 11, 15; employer resolution quoted from US Department of Labor, Office of the Secretary, *Proceedings of the First Industrial Conference*, 175. In drawing a distinction between collective bargaining and collective bargaining with a union, Alexander was in line with Walter Drew's views: Drew affirmed a "right to organize" but applied that right to workers rather than to unions and ruled outside acceptable bounds such things as an effort by a union to organize a shop where no active labor conflict was taking place. Fine, *"Without Blare of Trumpets,"* 164–65.

Chapter 9. *The Gift That Keeps on Giving*

1. NAM, *Proceedings* (1920), 204, 276. The next year's treasurer's report notes that the expenses of publicizing the platform ran to over $13,000 (nearly $170,000 in 2020 dollars). National Association of Manufacturers, *Proceedings of the Twenty-Sixth Annual Convention*, New York City, May 16–18, 1921 (New York: Issued from the Secretary's Office),

118–21; Williamson, "Seven Ways." About the epigraph: This phrase translates roughly as "If work were such a treat, surely the bosses would do it themselves." As a traditional folk saying, the phrase has no direct attribution; a version of the proverb ("Jos työ herkkua olisi, herrat sen olisivat aikoja tehneet") appears in, for example, Matti Sadeniemi, ed., *Nykysuomen sanakirja*, lyhentämätön kansanpainos, 13th ed. (Porvoo, Finland: WSOY, 1992), 1:438.

2. NAM, *Proceedings* (1920), 229–32.

3. NAM, *Proceedings* (1920), 232–35.

4. Allen M. Wakstein argues that rather than reasserting a policy it had been committed to all along, the NAM in the immediate postwar period was reacting to circumstances: that it had essentially suspended judgment and maintained a conciliatory policy until the President's Industrial Conference failed, at which point it decided that it needed "to reassess its position and to seek out the means by which the labor situation could be handled" and came to the decision to adopt, "based upon already established employer philosophy," the policy of the open shop. "The National Association of Manufacturers and Labor Relations in the 1920s," *Labor History* 10, no. 2 (March 1969): 163–76. However, the evidence that Wakstein cites contains nothing that would indicate a genuine commitment to conciliation, let alone to any rapprochement with labor unions, and as noted in the preceding chapter, the conference failed largely because of employers' stiffnecked resistance to independent (noncompany) labor unionism.

5. William Howard Taft, "The Open Shop Problem: The True Issue and the False as to the Rights of Labor and Employer in the Premises," typescript noting publication in the *Philadelphia Public Ledger*, January 22, 1921, in RG 98-002, 41/15, AFL-CIO Papers.

6. Unsigned [Walter Drew] to F. A. Vanderlip, January 27, 1917, series V, box 11, NICB Records. For more on the NICB, see chapter 8.

7. The first of the NICB's "research reports" was published in 1917; by early 1923, there were sixty research reports and twenty-two "special reports." See the lists on the back pages of National Industrial Conference Board, *Changes in the Cost of Living, July, 1914–March, 1923*, research report no. 60 (New York, 1923).

8. NAM, *Proceedings* (1921), 33; National Association of Manufacturers, *Proceedings of the Twenty-Seventh Annual Convention*, New York City, May 8–10, 1922 (New York: Issued from the Secretary's Office). The treasurer's reports in the NAM's annual conventions do not really follow a standard format from year to year, so budget comparisons are difficult to make with regard to specific items. However, the category specifically for the "Open Shop" (which probably only indicates the expenses of the *Open Shop Bulletin* and possibly includes the NAM's new *Open Shop Encyclopedia*, discussed below) reached over $7,000 in 1921 and well over $13,000 in 1922 (about $100,000 and $200,000, respectively, in 2020 dollars) and hovered on either side of $12,000 for 1924, 1925, and 1926. See Williamson, "Seven Ways"; National Association of Manufacturers, *Proceedings of the Twenty-Ninth Annual Convention*, New York City, May 19–21, 1924 (New York: Issued from the Secretary's Office); National Association of Manufacturers, *Proceedings of the Thirtieth Annual Convention*, St. Louis, Missouri, October 26–28, 1925, also the proceedings of a special meeting of members held in New York City, February 20, 1925 (New York: Issued from the Secretary's Office); National Association of Manufacturers, *Proceedings of the Thirty-First Annual Convention*, New York City, October 5–7, 1926 (New York: Issued from the Secretary's Office).

9. "Status of the Open Shop," memo, n.d., series VII, box 127, NAM Records. The Open Shop Conference called by the NAM in October 1922 and attended by many of the organizations that had since the opening of the twentieth century been key players in the open-shop campaign (e.g., Los Angeles Merchants and Manufacturers Association, Detroit Employers Association, National Erectors' Association) unanimously agreed to refrain from organizing a new national body. "Open Shop Conference," memo, October 9, 1922, series VII, box 127, NAM Records.

10. "Status of the Open Shop," memo, n.d., series VII, box 127, NAM Records; James Emery to Stephen C. Mason, February 12, 1920, both in series VII, box 127, NAM Records. See also Delton, *The Industrialists*, 94.

11. On the NAM's later publicity campaigns, see Fones-Wolf, *Selling Free Enterprise*.

12. On the 1920s in general, see, for example, Lynn Dumenil, *The Modern Temper: American Culture and Society in the 1920s* (New York: Hill and Wang, 1995).

13. Rosenbloom, "Union Membership"; Robert L. Friedheim, *The Seattle General Strike*, Centennial ed. (1964; repr., Seattle: University of Washington Press, 2018); David Brody, *Labor in Crisis: The Steel Strike of 1919*, Illini Books ed. (1965; repr., Urbana: University of Illinois Press, 1987), 113.

14. Robert K. Murray, *Red Scare: A Study in National Hysteria, 1919–1920* (Minneapolis: University of Minnesota Press, 1955), chapter 5.

15. Beverly Gage, "Why Violence Matters: Radicalism, Politics, and Class War in the Gilded Age and Progressive Era," *Journal for the Study of Radicalism* 1, no. 1 (2007): 106. See also Gage, *The Day Wall Street Exploded: A Story of America in Its First Age of Terror* (New York: Oxford University Press, 2010).

16. On vigilante, law enforcement, and army violence against the IWW, see Dubofsky, *We Shall Be All*, chapter 15; and White, *Under the Iron Heel*. The point about court injunctions is made in Forbath, *Law and the Shaping*, 109–10. On attacks on May Day 1919 Socialist parades, see Murray, *Red Scare*, chapter 5.

17. See, for example, the editorial praising the overwhelming anti-Bolshevism of the AFL and comparing the American labor movement favorably to its European counterparts, allegedly willing to contemplate the overthrow of their governments. "American vs. European Labor Policies," editorial, *NCF Review* 5, no. 5 (September 1920): 12. Although it became increasingly focused on hounding radicals in the 1920s, the NCF also continued to engage on matters like workmen's compensation and remained fairly prominently in the news, even if not to the extent of the early years. Cyphers, *The National Civic Federation*, 172–77.

18. Samuel Gompers in US Department of Labor, Office of the Secretary, *Proceedings of the First Industrial Conference*, 116.

19. Ole Hanson, "Bolshevism and Readjustment," National Association of Manufacturers, *Proceedings of the Twenty-Fourth Annual Convention*, New York City, May 19–21, 1919 (New York: Issued from the Secretary's Office), 382–99. On Hanson's hero status, see Friedheim, *The Seattle General Strike*, 154–56.

20. L. E. Sheppard (of the Order of Railway Conductors) paraphrasing "one of the employers' group" (US Department of Labor, Office of the Secretary, *Proceedings of the First Industrial Conference*, 277).

21. "Interlocking Lobby Dictatorship," memo, February 10, 1923, series VII, box 127, NAM Records. The memo notes that "nearly all the facts here cited are from the December 1, 1922 issue of the Woman Patriot." That issue of the *Woman Patriot* (whose tagline

was "Dedicated to the Defense of Family and the State, AGAINST Feminism and Social-ism") was mainly devoted to lambasting the passage of the Sheppard-Towner Act, though the idea of "interlocking directorates" of women's organizations seems to have been the NAM's own. *Woman Patriot*, December 1, 1921, Nineteenth Century Collections Online (Gale Cengage), link.gale.com/apps/doc/IMXCMC665386761/NCCO?xid=47819ca8. On antiradicalism and women's movements more generally, see Kirsten Delegard, *Battling Miss Bolsheviki: The Origins of Female Conservatism in the United States* (Philadelphia: University of Pennsylvania Press, 2011), which focuses on the role of conservative women in that battle.

22. "Interlocking Lobby Dictatorship," memo, February 10, 1923, series VII, box 127, NAM Records.

23. President Edgerton's speech at the banquet, NAM, *Proceedings* (1921), 373.

24. Delton, *The Industrialists*, 104–5. On women's clubs: for example, speeches at and other cooperation with women's clubs were suggested as important efforts by the respondents to the query about radical politics, "Memorandum in re radical activities," n.d. [late 1923?], series VII, box 127, NAM Records.

25. The process was rather drawn out; when elected, Berger had already been indicted for violating the Espionage Act by speaking against the war, for which he was convicted; his appeal on this conviction was pending when he tried to begin his term in Congress. A special committee was appointed in the House to investigate the matter, and the first exclusion vote came in November 1919. Berger was reelected in December 1919 and excluded again in January 1920. He lost his election bid in November 1920. Murray, *Red Scare*, 226–29 and chapter 13.

26. "Status of the Open Shop," memo, n.d., series VII, box 127, NAM Records.

27. Kramer, *The New Freedom*, chapter 6.

28. "Memorandum in re radical activities," n.d. [late 1923?], series VII, box 127, NAM Records.

29. "Principles and Recommendations Drawn by the Open Shop Committee," February 12, 1921, series VII, box 127, NAM Records. These recommendations are reproduced in the report of the Open Shop Committee in NAM, *Proceedings* (1921), 33, which also notes that the recommendations were approved by the board of directors on the above date.

30. "Status of the Open Shop," memo, n.d., series VII, box 127, NAM Records.

31. Montgomery, *Fall of the House of Labor*, 241–44; Lizabeth Cohen, *Making a New Deal: Industrial Workers in Chicago, 1919–1939* (New York: Cambridge University Press, 1990), 160–62.

32. Sanford Jacoby, *Employing Bureaucracy: Managers, Unions and the Transformation of Work in the 20th Century*, revised ed. (1985; repr., Mahwah, NJ: Lawrence Erlbaum Associates Publishers, 2004); Marchand, *Creating the Corporate Soul*.

33. Jacoby, *Employing Bureaucracy*, 99–103.

34. Summers, "Industrial Democracy," 32–33. See also chapter 8.

35. Charles Aubrey Eaton, "The Goodyear Way: How One Great Industrial Organization Is Banishing Unrest by Educating Its Employees to Be More Efficient Workers, Better Citizens and Happier Human Beings," *Frank Leslie's Weekly*, May 1, 1920, 550 ff.

36. Eaton, "The Goodyear Way."

37. "Goodyear Industrial Representation Plan," *National Association of Corporation Schools Bulletin* 6, no. 8 (August 1919): 361–65. Goodyear's plan was of the form designed by management consultant John Leitch; plans of this model existed at dozens of companies. Another model of employee representation plans was the one applied at the Colorado Fuel and Iron Company, the Rockefeller-owned company notoriously involved in the Ludlow Massacre in 1914. Instead of an elaborate assembly, the CF&I established a company committee consisting of both management representatives and workers. This model, too, was in use at several companies. Bruce E. Kaufman, "Accomplishments and Shortcomings of Nonunion Employee Representation in the Pre-Wagner Years: A Reassessment," in *Nonunion Employee Representation: History, Contemporary Practice, and Policy*, ed. Bruce E. Kaufman and Daphne Gottlieb Taras (New York: Routledge), 21–60, 27–28.

38. "Goodyear Industrial Representation Plan."

39. Paul W. Litchfield, *The Industrial Republic: A Study in Industrial Economics* (Akron, OH, 1919). As identified on the cover leaf, Litchfield was the vice president and factory manager of Goodyear Tire and Rubber.

40. Others included Eastman Kodak, General Electric, and the Colorado Fuel and Iron Company. National Association of Manufacturers, *American Trade Index: Descriptive and Classified Membership Directory of the National Association of Manufacturers of the United States, Arranged for the Convenience of Foreign Buyers*, 13th ed. (New York: Published for the National Association of Manufacturers, 1917).

41. The committee was originally chaired by Ferdinand Schwedtman, who had also been in charge of the NAM's accident prevention and workman's compensation work. Proceedings of the Board of Directors and Executive Committee; Industrial Betterment (remarks by Schwedtman), both in National Association of Manufacturers, *Proceedings of the Twentieth Annual Convention*, New York City, May 25 and 26, 1915 (New York: Issued from the Secretary's Office), 30–33, 93–100.

42. Report of the Committee on Industrial Betterment, Health, and Safety, NAM, *Proceedings* (1919), 10–29.

43. On representation leading to strikes, see Henry M. Leland in NAM, *Proceedings* (1919), 37–38. For other fears, see the reports of the NAM's Committee on Industrial Betterment, Health, and Safety in NAM, *Proceedings* (1920), 83; and NAM, *Proceedings* (1922), 9.

44. Remarks of Captain [William P.] White, NAM, *Proceedings* (1919), 29–36.

45. Jonathan Rees, "What If a Company Union Wasn't a 'Sham'? The Rockefeller Plan in Action," *Labor History* 48, no. 4 (November 2007): 457–75, cites as examples of such concessions the Colorado Fuel and Iron Company's creation of a mutual benefit association for health insurance and its building of a clubhouse for a YMCA.

46. Kaufman, "Accomplishments and Shortcomings," 30–31.

47. Bruce Nissen, "The Remarkable Rehabilitation of Company Unionism in Recent Industrial Relations Literature," review essay, *Critical Sociology* 25, no. 1 (April 1999): 59–79, 64.

48. Comments of Isaac W. Frank, NAM, *Proceedings* (1919), 41–42. Frank was specifically suggesting that White's antiunion remarks should not "go on record as being the public official statement of this Association."

49. Report of the Open Shop Committee in NAM, *Proceedings* (1921), 33.

50. Delton, *The Industrialists*, 93–95.

51. "Open Shop Conference," memo, October 10, 1922, series VII, box 127, NAM Records. See also Fine, *"Without Blare of Trumpets,"* 210–11.

52. Edgerton in August 1921, quoted in Wakstein, "NAM and Labor Relations," 167.

53. Edgerton's remarks in a discussion on the report of the Open Shop Department, NAM, *Proceedings* (1922), 25.

54. Edgerton's remarks, NAM, *Proceedings* (1922), 26–27.

55. The quotes are from comments by an official of the NAM on suggestions made by members on publicity. "Memorandum in re radical activities," n.d. [late 1923?], series VII, box 127, NAM Records.

56. Noel Sargent, "Open Shop Department April 1–December 31, 1921," n.d., series VII, box 127, NAM Records.

57. "Status of the Open Shop," memo, n.d., series VII, box 127, NAM Records.

58. Evans, *The Social Gospel*, 128–30; Charles E. Harvey, "John D. Rockefeller, Jr., and the Interchurch World Movement of 1919–1920: A Different Angle on the Ecumenical Movement," *Church History* 51, no. 2 (June 1982): 198; Commission of Inquiry, Interchurch World Movement, *Report on the Steel Strike of 1919* (New York: Harcourt, Brace and Howe, 1920), 246–49.

59. *Minnesota Daily Star*, December 27, 1920.

60. *Christian Science Monitor*, August 31, 1920, 9; *Courier-Journal*, December 27, 1920, 10; *American Israelite*, February 3, 1921, 4.

61. NAM, *Proceedings* (1922), 158; "Open Shop Department," memo, June 6, 1922, series VII, box 127, NAM Records.

62. Elizabeth Fones-Wolf and Ken Fones-Wolf note that the FCC made a concerted push in the mid-1920s to revitalize its industrial work, including hiring a proponent of industrial democracy to head its new Industrial Relations Division. See Fones-Wolf and Fones-Wolf, "Lending a Hand."

63. *Chicago Daily Tribune*, October 6, 1926, 1.

64. Eldon G. Ernst, "The Interchurch World Movement and the Great Steel Strike of 1919–1920," *Church History* 39, no. 2 (June 1970): 212. Charles Harvey argues that John D. Rockefeller had committed significant funds to the IWM in the hopes that it would secure harmony in industrial relations. "I know of no better insurance for a businessman for the safety of his investments, the prosperity of the country and the future stability of our government than this movement affords," Harvey quotes Rockefeller as writing to George Peabody. "John D. Rockefeller, Jr.," 202. Harvey also argues that Rockefeller's long-term advisor Raymond Fosdick convinced him to approve the steel strike report for publication to maintain his (rather precarious but expensively cultivated) reputation for industrial liberalism. The IWM's fundraising drive with other businessmen, however, had failed to produce as much as expected; most preferred to give to specific denominations, perhaps in part because the IWM seemed too committed to the social gospel and social involvement. See also manufacturers' admission that they were withdrawing funds from the IWM in *Christian Science Monitor*, August 31, 1920, 9.

65. "Status of the Open Shop," memo, n.d., series VII, box 127, NAM Records.

66. "Report on Open Shop Department," May 14, 1921, series VII, box 127, NAM Records.

67. National Association of Manufacturers, *Open Shop Encyclopedia for Debaters: A Reference Book for Use of Teachers, Students, and Public Speakers*, 3rd rev. ed. (New York: National Association of Manufacturers, 1922).

68. Carly S. Woods, *Debating Women: Gender, Education, and Spaces for Argument, 1835–1945* (East Lansing: Michigan State University Press, 2018); Egbert Ray Nichols, "A Historical Sketch of Intercollegiate Debating: I," *Quarterly Journal of Speech* 22, no. 2 (April 1936): 213–20; Nichols, "A Historical Sketch of Intercollegiate Debating: III," *Quarterly Journal of Speech* 22, no. 4 (December 1936): 259–78; Claudia J. Keenan, "Intercollegiate Debate: Reflecting American Culture, 1900–1930," *Argumentation and Advocacy* 46, no. 2 (September 2009): 79–97.

69. NAM, *Proceedings* (1921), 126; NAM, *Proceedings* (1922), 158; see also untitled report to Mr. Benton, December 16, 1930, series VII, box 127, NAM Records. The NAM noted that "in Texas alone last year [1921? 1922?] 1,000,000 persons attended debates on the open shop." "Status of the Open Shop," memo, n.d., series VII, box 127, NAM Records.

70. Edith M. Phelps, ed., *University Debaters' Annual: Constructive and Rebuttal Speeches Delivered in Debates of American Colleges and Universities during the College Year, 1919–1920* (New York: H. W. Wilson Company, 1920); Phelps, ed., *University Debaters' Annual: Constructive and Rebuttal Speeches Delivered in Debates of American Colleges and Universities during the College Year, 1920–21* (New York: H. W. Wilson Company, 1921); Phelps, ed., *University Debaters' Annual: Constructive and Rebuttal Speeches Delivered in Debates of American Colleges and Universities during the College Year, 1921–22* (New York: H. W. Wilson Company, 1922).

71. NAM, *Proceedings* (1922), 158.

72. "Report on Open Shop Department," May 14, 1921, series VII, box 127, NAM Records.

73. James Emery to Stephen C. Mason, February 12, 1920, series VII, box 127, NAM Records.

74. Secretary's Report, NAM, *Proceedings* (1922), 158.

75. Delton, *The Industrialists*, 94.

76. Wakstein, "NAM and Labor Relations."

77. Cohen, *Making a New Deal*, 184. A classic work on labor in the 1920s is Irving Bernstein, *The Lean Years: A History of the American Worker, 1920–1933* (Boston: Houghton Mifflin Company, 1960).

78. Membership declined dramatically after 1921, perhaps as it became clear that the labor threat was receding. After 1933 it rose again, from 1,491 in 1933 to 2,912 in 1937 and 7,500 in 1939, reaching a peak of 16,500 in 1948 before beginning another decline. See Gable, "A Political Analysis," 191. The NAM's income went from $177,000 in 1932 to $1,439,548 in 1937 ($3.3 million and $25.9 million, respectively, in 2020 dollars). See Richard W. Gable, "NAM: Influential Lobby or Kiss of Death?," *Journal of Politics* 15, no. 2 (May 1953): 254–73, 260; Williamson, "Seven Ways."

Coda

1. General Secretary [Easley] to John A. McMahon, April 25, 1903; see also John A. McMahon to Ralph M. Easley, April 14, 1903, both in box 6, folder 2, NCF Records.

2. A contemporary German picture album quoted in Nigel Rothfels, *Savages and Beasts: The Birth of the Modern Zoo* (Baltimore, MD: Johns Hopkins University Press, 2002), 155.

3. Rothfels, *Savages and Beasts*, 153.

4. Carl Hagenbeck, *Beasts and Men: Being Carl Hagenbeck's Experiences for Half a Century among Wild Animals*, trans. Hugh S. R. Elliot and A. G. Thacker (New York: Longmans, Green and Co., 1911), 134.

5. Clarence S. Darrow, "Chester Suspects Wacker," *Journal of the Switchmen's Union of North America* 10, no. 12 (October 1908): 775–83.

6. For example, in 1899, when the NCF's predecessor, the Chicago Civic Federation, was newly formed, Darrow had penned an acerbic open letter to Ralph Easley, refusing an appointment with the CCF. "I cannot recall," wrote Darrow, "where it ever undertook to interfere with an individual scheme or project that had either friends or money to sustain it." Further, Darrow complained, the CCF's good-government projects focused on the wrong level: "It does not seem to understand that the shyster lawyer who operates around justice courts is harmless beside the corporation lawyer and the promoter of trust organizations, and that the bucket shop dealer is a person of no consequence compared with the operator of the Board of Trade." C. S. Darrow to Ralph M. Easley, reprinted in the *Chicago Daily Tribune*, February 9, 1899, 7.

7. Darrow, "Chester Suspects Wacker."

8. Darrow, "Chester Suspects Wacker."

9. Metzgar, *Striking Steel*, 33–36.

10. There is, of course, a massive literature on the impact of the New Deal's legal regime on labor, on the role of labor in shaping the New Deal, and on labor's decline in recent decades. That literature and those discussions are well beyond the scope of this book. A good starting point for delving into them is Nelson Lichtenstein, *State of the Union: A Century of American Labor*, rev. and expanded ed. (Princeton, NJ: Princeton University Press, 2012).

11. Mark E. Warren, "What Can Democratic Participation Mean Today?," *Political Theory* 30, no. 5 (October 2002): 677–701; Warren, *Democracy and Association* (Princeton, NJ: Princeton University Press, 2000).

12. Theda Skocpol, *Diminished Democracy: From Membership to Management in American Civic Life* (Norman: University of Oklahoma Press, 2003).

13. Jane F. McAlevey, *No Shortcuts: Organizing for Power in the New Gilded Age* (New York: Oxford University Press, 2016).

14. Michael J. Sandel, *The Tyranny of Merit: What's Become of the Common Good?* (New York: Farrar, Straus and Giroux, 2020), especially chapters 4 and 7.

15. With the single exception of an August 2009 poll, majority opinion has approved of unions in every poll conducted by Gallup since 1936, and recently public opinion has turned clearly favorable toward unions. In an August 2021 poll more than two out of three respondents, or 68 percent, said they approved of unions—less than ten percentage points lower than the all-time high of 75 percent, reached most recently in January 1957. Gallup, "In Depth Topics: Labor Unions," accessed November 5, 2021, https://news.gallup.com/poll/12751/labor-unions.aspx. The historical average is 62.1 percent (from fifty polls conducted between 1936 and 2021).

16. Grace Clements, in Studs Terkel, *Working: People Talk about What They Do All Day and How They Feel about What They Do* (New York: New Press, 1972), 388.

17. James Pope, "Labor's Constitution of Freedom," *Yale Law Journal* 106, no. 941 (January 1997): 1026.

Index

employers' analysis, postwar political and societal landscape, 214–17; business of America, 217–21; business viewpoint, 226–30; personnel management and company unions, 221–25
Engels, Friedrich, 219
equity powers (courts), 147
E. W. Bliss Company, 157–58

family wage, 77
Farmer-Labor Party, 220
Farmer's Alliance, 55
Farwell, Nicholas, 52
Farwell v. Boston and Worcester R.R. Corp., 52
Faust, Edward, 128
Federal Council of Churches (FCC), 199, 226–27
Federal Society of Journeymen Cordwainers of Philadelphia, 50
female reformers, 59
Feminist Lobby, 219
Ferracute Machine Company, 103
Field, Marshall, 111
Filene, Edward A., 96
Fink, Leon, 54
Fish, Frederick P., 87
Fones-Wolf, Elizabeth, 16
Forbath, William, 16, 142, 151
Forest City Press, 173
foundry and metal manufacturing, 98–104; in Europe, 107–8
freedom of contract. *See* liberty of contract
Freegard, Edwin, 84
free labor, 38, 49, 58; ideology, 52
free rider problem, 20–21, 24, 37, 67, 73
Frick, Henry, 92
Friedman, Gerald, 24, 57
Friedman, Tami, 16

Gage, Beverly, 217
garment industry, 75–77, 104, 120, 196–97
Gary, E. Stanley, 166
General Trades' Union of New York, 47
German immigration, 120
glass industry, 64
Glen Echo Country Club, 123
Glessner, John J., 112
Glickman, Lawrence, 16
Gompers, Samuel, 6, 30, 36, 55–56, 60, 63, 65, 70–85, 185, 191, 206, 211, 233
Goodyear factory, 223

Goodyear Industrians (employee representation plan), 222
Gould's Blue Book, 121
governance, 6, 18, 37–38, 44; craft governance, 14, 44–45, 53–54, 62, 142; faculty governance, 258n36; local governance, 46, 116; municipal governance, 148; public governance, 45; self-governance, 45; union governance, 54, 68, 233; workers and, 18–19; workplace governance, 14
government contract work, 139, 157–58, 199
Government Printing Office, 33
Great Depression, 1930, 16, 230
Great Railroad Strike, 1877, 25, 73
Greene, Julie, 16, 159, 205

Hagenbeck, Carl, 231–32
Hagenbeck animal show, 231–32
Hale, David, 51
Hammond, John Hays, 95
Hanna, M. A., 83
Harper's Weekly, 189
Harriman, Florence Jaffray (Mrs. J. Borden), 93, 189
Harriman, J. Borden, 93
Harris, Howell, 4, 105–6
Hattam, Victoria, 16
Haydu, Jeffrey, 16, 107, 114
Haymarket Affair, 116
Hepburn, William P., 156
Hepburn bill, 156
H. H. Franklin Manufacturing Company, 102
Hillquit, Morris, 80–81
H. N. Strait Manufacturing Company, 149–50
Holdom, Jesse, 153, 170
Holt, Hamilton, 189
Hopewell, John, 165
Horne, Jeremiah, 51
Howe, Frederic C., 93
Hughitt, Marvin, 87
Hyman, Richard, 78

Illinois Manufacturing Company, 96
immigrants, 75; AFL attitudes toward, 72–76; anti-immigrant sentiment, 114, 205–6; Asian, 12–13, 72–75; in employer organizations, 97–98, 128; employer worries about radicals among, 115–16; Irish and German immigration, 120; in the labor movement, 196–97, 226–27; mine

VILJA HULDEN is an associate teaching professor at the University of Colorado Boulder.

The Working Class in American History

The University of Illinois Press
is a founding member of the
Association of University Presses.

University of Illinois Press
1325 South Oak Street
Champaign, IL 61820-6903
www.press.uillinois.edu